The Sexual Culture of the French R

D1765629

When the French invaded Italy in 1494, they were shocked by the frank sexuality expressed in Italian cities. By 1600, the French were widely considered to be the most highly sexualized nation in Christendom. What caused this transformation? This book examines how, as Renaissance textual practices and new forms of knowledge rippled outward from Italy, the sexual landscape and French notions of masculinity, sexual agency, and procreation were fundamentally changed. Exploring the use of astrology, the infusion of Neoplatonism, the critique of Petrarchan love poetry, and the monarchy's sexual reputation, the book reveals that the French encountered conflicting ideas from abroad and from antiquity about the meanings and implications of sexual behavior. Intensely interested in cultural self-definition, humanists, poets, and political figures all contributed to the rapid alteration of sexual ideas to suit French cultural needs. The result was the vibrant sexual reputation that marks French culture to this day.

KATHERINE CRAWFORD is Associate Professor of History at Vanderbilt University. She is the author of *Perilous Performances: Gender and Regency in Early Modern France* (2004) and *European Sexualities, 1400–1800* (2007).

University of Edinburgh

30150   025714012

Cambridge Social and Cultural Histories

Series editors:
Margot C. Finn, *University of Warwick*
Colin Jones, *Queen Mary, University of London*

New cultural histories have recently expanded the parameters (and enriched the methodologies) of social history. Cambridge Social and Cultural Histories recognises the plurality of current approaches to social and cultural history as distinctive points of entry into a common explanatory project. Open to innovative and interdisciplinary work, regardless of its chronological or geographical location, the series encompasses a broad range of histories of social relationships and of the cultures that inform them and lend them meaning. Historical anthropology, historical sociology, comparative history, gender history and historicist literary studies – among other subjects – all fall within the remit of Cambridge Social and Cultural Histories.

A list of titles in the series can be found at
www.cambridge.org/socialculturalhistories

The Sexual Culture of the French Renaissance

Katherine Crawford

Vanderbilt University

CAMBRIDGE
UNIVERSITY PRESS

CAMBRIDGE UNIVERSITY PRESS
Cambridge, New York, Melbourne, Madrid, Cape Town, Singapore,
São Paulo, Delhi, Dubai, Tokyo

Cambridge University Press
The Edinburgh Building, Cambridge CB2 8RU, UK

Published in the United States of America by Cambridge University Press, New York

www.cambridge.org
Information on this title: www.cambridge.org/9780521749503

First published 2010

Printed in the United Kingdom at the University Press, Cambridge

A catalogue record for this publication is available from the British Library

ISBN 978-0-521-76989-1 Hardback
ISBN 978-0-521-74950-3 Paperback

Contents

List of illustrations

Preface and acknowledgments

In his essay "On Some Verses of Virgil," Michel de Montaigne comments:

The gods, says Plato, have furnished us with a disobedient and tyrannical member, which, like a furious animal, undertakes by the violence of its appetite to subject everything to itself. To women likewise they have given a gluttonous and voracious animal which, if denied its food in due season, goes mad, impatient of delay, and, breathing its rage into their bodies, stops up the passages, arrests the breathing, causing a thousand kinds of ills, until it has sucked in the fruit of the common thirst and therewith plentifully irrigated and fertilized the depth of the womb.[1]

Montaigne's references to ancient conceptions of the body are familiar. Acknowledging male desire briefly, Montaigne zeroes in on women as voracious and out of control sexually. Their desire is physiological; their humoral balance and health depend on the physical necessity of irrigation. The ability to control desire rationally is implicitly absent in women, while some men – strong, rational, properly functional masculine men – will not allow themselves to be overcome by disobedient physicality. But Montaigne goes on to trouble this standard view: "The Indian women who see the men in the raw, have at least cooled their sense of sight . . . Moreover, Livia used to say that to a good woman a naked man is no more than a statue." As is his practice, Montaigne multiplies his examples, drawing on ancient and contemporary sources. There are strategies, he says, for women to modify their sexual nature. The problem, in the end, Montaigne insists, is the men: "In short, we allure and flesh them by every means; we incessantly heat and excite their imagination; and then we bellyache." Although not in so many words, Montaigne assures us that sex is about gender, and about the meanings we attach to both sex as biological difference and sex meaning sexual acts.

The loci of meaning for a French man in the Renaissance were his immediate world and the past he claimed as his own. Montaigne invokes antiquity repeatedly in laying out his comments about sex. France is perhaps less obvious, but the unsettled world in which Montaigne made his way had its peculiarities

---

[1] Michel de Montaigne, *The Complete Essays of Montaigne*, trans. Donald Frame (Stanford University Press, 1965), III, 5, p. 654.

which were foundational for Montaigne's skeptical, self-exploratory essay project. Cultural encounters, especially with "Italy" (that is, the area we now call Italy) had revitalized French aesthetics. "On Some Verses of Virgil" draws on such encounters with Pietro Aretino and Giovanni Boccaccio, as well as Catullus, Horace, Augustine, a brief account of Priapic rituals among Roman matrons and references to Egyptian practices at Bacchanals.[2]

In Montaigne's immediate historical moment, religious schism and political crisis combined to unsettle Renaissance France. Analysis of the Wars of Religion has been extensive. I invoke here only a few important aspects of the period from 1562 to 1598 – the beginning of sectarian strife to the Edict of Nantes.[3] Violence, usually small-scale as wars go, became endemic for several reasons. As James B. Wood has demonstrated, the inability of the monarchy to sustain a military position meant that armed encounters continued sporadically until exhaustion.[4] The quality of the violence steadily escalated over successive encounters, and the intensification of sectarian hatred led to fantasies of annihilation. The most notorious of these was St. Bartholomew's Day (August 24, 1572).[5] The "season" of killing that ensued did not eradicate the Protestants, but it did harden both Catholic and Protestant sentiments, and instantiate the hatred between them.[6] The failure of leadership by the monarchy was quite spectacular. Effectively fronting the government for Charles IX, Catherine de' Medici did not comprehend the sectarian commitments of ardent Catholics and Protestants. When the monarchy offered edicts of toleration, religious affiliations at court created intractable factional struggles. The Catholic Guise family against Admiral Coligny, the Princes of Condé against the Montmorency family, and the conflicts within the royal family between Henri III and his younger brother, the duc d'Alençon, were just the most prominent of these alignments.

[2] Montaigne, *Complete Essays*, III, 5, 652–3.
[3] Mack P. Holt, *The Wars of Religion* (Cambridge University Press, 1995) extends the period of conflict on the grounds that the monarchy did not control the situation reliably until it destroyed the independence of La Rochelle under Louis XIII and Cardinal Richelieu. For the intellectual context, see especially Denis Crouzet, *Les Guerriers de Dieu: la violence au temps des troubles de religion, vers 1525–vers 1610*, 2 vols. (Seyssel: Champ Vallon, 1990) and *La Genèse de la Réforme française, 1520–1562* (Paris: SEDES, 1996).
[4] James B. Wood, *The King's Army: Warfare, Soldiers, and Society during the Wars of Religion in France, 1562–1576* (Cambridge University Press, 1996).
[5] The literature is vast, but one of the recent controversies – about the responsibility of the monarchy in touching off the massacres – covers much of the ground. See Marc Venard, "Arrêtez le massacre," in *Revue d'histoire moderne et contemporaine*, 39 (1992): 645–61; Denis Crouzet, *La Nuit de la Saint-Barthélemy: un rêve perdu de la Renaissance* (Paris: Fayard, 1994); and Jean-Louis Bourgeon, *L'Assassinat de Coligny* (Geneva: Droz, 1992); *Charles IX devant la Saint-Barthélemy* (Geneva: Droz, 1995).
[6] On the expansion of violence and its extensions throughout France, see Janine Garrisson Estèbe, *Tocsin pour un massacre: la saison de Saint-Barthélemy* (Paris: Centurion, 1968) and Nicole Vray, *La Guerre des Religions dans la France de l'ouest. Poitou–Aunis–Saintonge, 1534–1610* (La Crèche: Geste, 1997).

Montaigne refracts the double threat of religious and civil strife in his recurrent engagements with sexual issues. The political connection to the sexual was both personal and inescapable for Montaigne: he served as Mayor of Bordeaux, holding the city on behalf of Henri III, the most sexually controversial king in French history (about whom, see Chapter 5 below). Montaigne's recounting the variety of customs and beliefs about sex around the world and through time defuses the claims for absolute correctness that fueled such violence. Discussing sex was not an escape so much as part of a larger strategy to think through the changing, unpredictable, and violent world in which Montaigne explored his beloved texts and himself.

Montaigne was less interested in pinning down meaning than allowing that its proliferations had to be recognized. Making meaning, especially skeptical meaning, was an arduous business. Not only were there all those ancient texts now available, but also the world was opening up. Montaigne's essay "Of Cannibals" offers one encounter with New World difference, but other essays are peppered with brief moments of cultural difference around the world. Indians pardon the sun when battle goes badly; in Peru, beauty is a matter of who has the largest ears; the king of Mexico makes war to collect prisoners for his sacrifices; where the ancient Romans accustomed their populace to cruelty through animal sacrifice, the Turks established hospitals for animals.[7] Examples could be multiplied.

But, you say, your book is supposed to be about sexual culture, not religious conflict or the opening up of knowledge of the world. Montaigne appears as my prologue because he embodied, articulated, and pondered so many of the currents, ideas, and changes of his day. He weighs in on all the areas I explore in this book. Ancient ideas about sex appear throughout, and even Orpheus, who figures centrally in Chapter 1, makes a fleeting appearance in the *Essays*.[8] Montaigne evinces skepticism about astrology and its predictive propensities with respect to reproduction.[9] "Of Friendship," his extended tribute to Etienne de La Boétie, includes a Neoplatonic parsing of desire between men, a vexed subject throughout the French Renaissance and no less so for Montaigne.[10] Contemporary poetry, both asexual and otherwise, makes its way

---

[7] Montaigne, *Complete Essays*, "We should meddle soberly with judging divine ordinances," I, 33, 160; "Apology for Raymond Sebond," II, 12, 355; "Of Moderation," I, 30, 149; "Of Cruelty," II, 11, 318.

[8] Montaigne, *Complete Essays*, "Apology for Raymond Sebond," II, 12, 324.

[9] Montaigne, *Complete Essays*, "Of Prognostications," I, 11, 27–30. See also "Of Vanity," III, 9, 734.

[10] Montaigne, *Complete Essays*, "Of Friendship," I, 28, 135–44. For discussions of Montaigne and friendship, see for instance Marc D. Schachter, "'That Friendship Which Possesses the Soul': Montaigne Loves La Boétie," in *Homosexuality in French History and Culture*, ed. Jeffrey Merrick and Michael Sibalis (New York and London: Haworth, 2001), 5–21; and Danielle Clark, "'The Sovereign's Vice Begets the Subject's Error': The Duke of Buckingham,

into several essays.[11] Montaigne's veiled criticism of Henri III for immoderate behavior in his religious devotions was part of the sexualized critique of the monarchy extending back to François I.[12] Montaigne's engagements are typical of his place and time. Sex was a space in which evoking different customs was (and is) easy to do. In some ways, sex itself was easy. Procreation and pleasure were the basic goals. But the apparatus of belief around how to achieve positive ends, particularly around pleasure, was more complicated. The ancients and other populations around the globe could only offer their astounding array of beliefs, justifications, rituals, assertions, certainties, and falsehoods. People like Montaigne had to sort them out for self and society.

With all due thanks to Montaigne for the essay form, for allowing and encouraging the trying of ideas in writing, the project which follows is an essay about making and changing meanings of sex and sexuality in Renaissance France. Elements of this story will be familiar. France was part of the larger culture of Europe and a vital player in the conversations of the Renaissance. Other aspects will be less so. This essay is about intersecting, overlapping priorities, meanings, and understandings that came together to make a specifically French sexual history. At the same time, it reveals that the cultural choices of French readers, writers, poets, thinkers, astrologers, politicians, religious figures, peasants, jurists, and artists (to name just the more textually obvious contributors) can be understood to share ideas, ideals, and mechanisms with other sexual cultures. It is a book about France, albeit France in the world. The short version of the story is that the French were widely regarded as prudish and unsophisticated in matters of sex and sexuality in the late fifteenth century. Comments about French reactions to Italian and ancient customs encountered actually or textually make this reputation for sexual squeamishness plain. By the reign of Henri IV (1589–1610), the French were the randy bastards of Europe, known for their sexual style in language, art, and comportment. This book is an account – by no means the only one possible – of how that transformation came about.

All projects we choose to undertake, including book-sized ones, are always essays in another sense. They reveal (to readers, but also to authors) bits of what the author thinks important enough to spend countless hours researching, ruminating upon, writing, rewriting, and subjecting to others for comment, criticism, and the occasional pat on the head. I suspect by the end, my self will be apparent in my choices and my arguments. As is always the case, finding that self is in fact the work of many people over many years. This project has

---

'Sodomy,' and Narratives of Edward II, 1622–28," in *Sodomy in Early Modern Europe*, ed. Tom Betteridge (Manchester University Press, 2002), 46–64.

[11] See for instance Montaigne, *Complete Essays*, "On Some Verses of Virgil," III, 5, 678 (Mellin de Saint-Gelais); "Apology for Raymond Sebond," II, 12, 381 (Pierre de Ronsard).

[12] Montaigne, *Complete Essays*, "Of Moderation," I, 30, 146.

been long in the making and my debts are myriad. Years ago, the University of Chicago was the first home of this project. Friends, now colleagues, from graduate school intervened at various points, making suggestions, offering encouragement, and allowing me to test ideas. I am particularly grateful to Greta Rensenbrink, John Shovlin, Kate Hammerton, and Stephane Gerson. Sir Colin Lucas pushed me to think in expansive terms and to branch out in my interests. Jan Goldstein encouraged me to frame the recent historiography around sexuality in Early Modern Europe, an exercise that was both illuminating and intellectually crucial. Lauren Berlant urged me to consider the structural workings of power and gender, and in so doing, changed utterly my view of the world – past and present. At Vanderbilt, intellectual guidance came in many forms. I particularly thank Barbara Bowen, William Caferro, Dyan Elliott, Lynn Enterline, James Epstein, Mona Frederick, Joel Harrington, Sarah Igo, Jane Landers, Leah Marcus, Catherine Molineux, Ruth Rogaski, Holly Tucker, and David Wasserstein for their generosity. Jeffrey Merrick has helped me since I was an undergraduate, and I cannot thank him enough. In many ways, this book never would have happened without him. Mack Holt has more than once reeled me in when I was about to seriously misstep. William Beik remains an inspiration both as a scholar and a gentleman. Kathryn Norberg taught me that it was a good thing to focus on human foibles like sex. Lynn Hunt pointed me in the direction of the dirty bits. Megan Armstrong reminded me to take the human side of sexuality seriously. Joyce Chaplin, Ron Schechter, Gregory Brown, Sara Chapman, Tip Reagan, Matthew Gerber, Lisa Jane Graham, Sarah Hanley, Orest Ranum, Edna Yahil, Judith Miller, Sharon Strocchia, and Carole Levin nudged me in fruitful directions and away from blind alleys. René Marion let me, on too many occasions to count, bend her ear about the strange things I was finding. Rachel Donaldson, Olivia Grenvicz, and Jane Crawford read the entire draft manuscript, for which I am deeply grateful. They were heroic in helping me correct errors and clarify the dusty bits. Any and all errors that remain are mine alone.

   Material and logistical support came from Marshall Eakin, Daniel Usner, Elizabeth Lunbeck, Richard McCarty, Carolyn Dever, Owen Williams, and my parents, George and Holly Crawford and Jane and Bernie Frischer. Fellowships at the Robert Penn Warren Center for the Humanities, the Folger Shakespeare Library, from Vanderbilt University, and the Western Society for French History have been materially and intellectually invaluable. Copious thanks to Cari Winterich at Art Resource. Michael Watson at Cambridge University Press has been unfailingly enthusiastic, and the editorial team at the Press, especially Helen Waterhouse, Rebecca du Plessis, and Thomas O'Reilly, has been nothing less than outstanding. Parts of Chapter 3 appeared in a very different form in "Marsilio Ficino, Neoplatonism, and the Problem of Sex," *Renaissance and Reformation; Renaissance et réforme* 28/2 (2004), 3–35. Different versions of aspects of Chapter 5 were published in "Love, Sodomy, and Scandal: Controlling the Sexual Reputation of Henry III," *Journal of the History of Sexuality* 12/4 (2003) 513–42, and "The Politics of Promiscuity: Masculinity and Heroic Representation at the Court of Henry IV," *French Historical Studies* 26/2 (2003), 225–52.

Last is never least in such a list. Zoey died while I was writing this book, and Kathryn Schwarz lived. Neither was a small thing, and this book is for them.

Note on citations

I have generally used the spelling conventions in the original texts, except that I have utilized "i" in place of "j" for French and "u" in place of "v" for Latin citations. Where a macron over a vowel indicated an absent "m" or "n," I have supplied the letter. Where "g" was utilized instead of "e" (as in "ung"), I have modernized the spelling. Translations of French and post-classical Latin are my own unless otherwise indicated. I have consulted the *Dictionnaire historique de la langue française*, ed. Alain Rey et al., 3 vols. (Paris: Dictionnaires Le Robert, 1998) in order to translate according to sixteenth century habits of vocabulary and syntax, although my translations are utterly utilitarian.

List of abbreviations

AN	Archives nationales de France
BL	British Library
BN	Bibliothèque nationale de France
FHS	*French History Studies*
HMES	Lynn Thorndike, *A History of Magic and Experimental Science*, 8 vols. (New York: Columbia University Press, 1923–1958).
JHS	*Journal of History of Sexuality*
JMEMS	*The Journal of Medieval and Early Modern Studies*
JMRS	*The Journal of Medieval and Renaissance Studies*
PMLA	*Proceedings of the Modern Language Association*
RQ	*Renaissance Quarterly*
SCJ	*Sixteenth-Century Journal*

Introduction: sexual culture? France? Renaissance?

The first premise of this book is that the French Renaissance understood sex and sexuality in ways that look strange to us. Neither a matter of identity nor restricted to individual acts, sexual expression occupied, saturated, and helped organize modes of thinking to which we, for the most part, have little access. Sex as it was understood in the French Renaissance was less a matter of modern origins and more a synecdoche that allowed for elasticity around the deployment of sexuality. This is not to argue that Renaissance sexuality was somehow more free than modern formulations of it. Rather, I contend that sexual knowledge and understanding organized and was utilized in ways that reflected Renaissance rather than modern sensibilities. Love, procreation, marriage, intimacy, friendship – all had sexual dimensions, the changing contours of which reveal much about sexuality and Renaissance society as it was, and is, constructed.

It seems that some questions ought to be immediately obvious. What were those sensibilities? How were they different from Medieval ones before or modern ones after? How might I offer to explain why the Renaissance mattered? Why France? Why sex? Let me begin with the nature of the thing by way of a rather dense little ditty. Pierre de Ronsard wrote a sonnet that ended:

Le Roi ne m'aime point pour estre trop barbu:	The king does not love me for being too much with beard
Il aime à semancer le champ qui n'est herbu,	He likes to seed the field which is not grassy
Et comme le castor chevaucher le derriere:	And like the beaver, rides the behind
Lors qu'il foute les culs qui sont cons estrecis	When he fucks the assholes that are tight cunts
Il tient du naturel de ceux de Medicis,	He takes after the nature of the Medici
Et prennent le devant il imite son pere.	And in taking the lead he imitates his father.[1]

---

[1] Pierre de Ronsard, *Œuvres complètes*, ed. Paul Laumonier, Isidore Silver, and René Lebègue, 20 vols. (Paris: Marcel Didier, 1914–1967), vol. XVIII, 417. The editors reject the claims of earlier editors and accept this and other sonnets as part of Ronsard's oeuvre. Laumonier, Silver, and Lebègue point out that the piece appears in multiple contemporary manuscripts and is noted by the journalist Pierre de L'Estoile as by Ronsard. See Ronsard, *Œuvres complètes*, vol. XVIII,

I expect this is not the Ronsard most people know. The court poet who challenged French writers to purify and exalt French language as exemplary of the heights of human achievement is using sexual slander to denigrate the king, Henri III. The simple back-story is that Ronsard was slipping out of favor. Younger poets such as Philippe Desportes were receiving more of the king's largesse. The standard supplement to that very pragmatic set of issues is that Ronsard disapproved of Henri III's management of the kingdom – Ronsard and seemingly almost everyone else. At this point, the Wars of Religion had left the country in tatters. The monarchy was in debt to the tune of 100 million livres by 1576 and enormously dependent on Italian financial expertise and banking resources.[2] The intersections with sex are not always as obvious, but it is impossible not to notice how it saturates Ronsard's poem. The reference to Henri's alleged preference for his young male favorites, or *mignons*, is immediately sexualized around the assumption that gender hierarchy within same-sex male relationships featured an older (bearded) man and his younger, not-yet-bearded, lover.[3] The poem attacks Henri for enjoying such a relationship, but Ronsard puts the king, as the sexual initiator, in the dominant role. Sort of. Henri is also effeminized because he desires men. By invoking Henri's Italian mother, Catherine de' Medici, Ronsard tapped into the xenophobia directed at Italians, and merged it with the widespread assumption that Italians were sexually corrupt. Henri was emasculated and corrupt by association. Henri's sexual traits are cast as "genetic," to use a deliberate anachronism, in that his gender and sexual miscues were inherited from his mother and father. More obliquely, Catherine was infamous for her devotion to astrology, and invoking her was to suggest that Henri was star-crossed progeny in the sense that generation – the Renaissance term for procreation – was marked by the configurations of the heavens. Henri's failure to generate reflected the will of the heavens and cast doubt on him as the representative of the fertile realm of France. Oblique too, but in a cumulative sense, was the critique of Henri as a failed ideal, too bound by earthly concerns and desires to achieve either the status of a Platonic philosopher-king or the transcendence of a Neoplatonic lover. The sensibilities in this brief example are expansive, diffuse, and allusive. Rather than defining the sexual as a thing with specificity, Ronsard comes at it from odd angles and includes topical cultural referents to pack his poem with multiple levels of scandal and critique that ultimately imply Henri is not entirely fit to be king.

415, n. 1. This poem is discussed in Guy Poirier, *L'Homosexualité dans l'imaginaire de la Renaissance* (Paris: Champion, 1996), 139, relative to the controversies around Henri III.
[2] Martin Wolfe, *The Fiscal System of Renaissance France* (New Haven: Yale University Press, 1972), 159; Henry Heller, *Anti-Italianism in Sixteenth-Century France* (University of Toronto Press, 2003), 164–70.
[3] There is no analysis for France, but for England, see Will Fisher, "The Renaissance Beard: Masculinity in Early Modern England," *RQ* 54 (2001): 155–87. The cultural origin of this sexual combination in the west is the Greek *erastoi*.

All of the domains that figure in the essay that follows are represented in Ronsard's lines. He includes the notion of the Renaissance, astrology, Neoplatonism, poetry, and politics as influences on sexuality. Through consideration of these categories, I will address the questions that opened this introduction. But first, my use of several terms requires some explanation. "Heterosexual," "homosexual," their other familiar forms ("heterosexuality" and "homosexuality"), and the less common "heteronormative" are anachronisms, but for these purposes, they abbreviate cumbersome, longer locutions that reflect much deeper historical patterns in French thought. In defense of their appearance in what follows, first, I use them always with an awareness of the anachronism. Second, I do not use the terms to refer to modern notions of foundational sexual identity. "Homosexual" refers to sex acts (actual or imagined) between persons of the same biological sex; "heterosexual" between persons of different biological sex. "Homosexuality" and "heterosexuality" are used when assumptions about persons and behaviors are attached to sexual expression without presuming that the person about whom the assumption is made felt any generalized identificatory attachment. "Heteronormative" reflects the tendency to assume value judgments that construct limited heterosexual behaviors as the norm and everything else (including a number of sexual practices involving men and women) as deviant.

I use these terms in order to move past them. Invoked most often to describe modern identity categories, their origins and configurations have been debated. Historians and theorists have spent much energy analyzing Michel Foucault's famous intervention: "As defined by the ancient civil or canonical codes, sodomy was a category of forbidden acts; their perpetrator was nothing more than the juridical subject of them. The nineteenth-century homosexual became a personage, a past, a case history, and a childhood, in addition to being a type of life".[4] In Foucault's wake, historians became absorbed in whether acts might accumulate to a functional, if unstable, notion of identity. Accordingly, some scholars maintain that early modern sodomy points toward nascent notions of homosexual orientation that began to coalesce in urban contexts in association with group or subculture behavior.[5] More broadly, Foucault's description

---

[4] Michel Foucault, *The History of Sexuality: An Introduction*, trans. Robert Hurley (New York: Pantheon, 1976), 43.

[5] The classic account here is Alan Bray, *Homosexuality in Renaissance England* (London: Gay Men's Press, 1982). On homosexual subculture in Renaissance France, see Maurice Lever, *Les Bûchers de Sodome* (Paris: Fayard, 1985), 67. See also Michael Rocke, *Forbidden Friendships: Homosexuality and Male Culture in Renaissance Florence* (Oxford University Press, 1996) and Guido Ruggiero, *The Boundaries of Eros: Sex, Crime and Sexuality in Renaissance Venice* (Oxford University Press, 1985) for early modern Italian examples. On emergent subcultures in eighteenth-century Europe, see Randolph Trumbach, *Sex and the Gender Revolution*, vol. I, *Heterosexuality and the Third Gender in Enlightenment London* (University of Chicago Press, 1998); Theo van der Meer, "Sodom's Seed in the Netherlands: The Emergence of Homosexuality

of sodomy as an "utterly confused category" prompted investigation into the meanings attached to sex in the past. On the one hand, historians confirmed sodomy's capaciousness: it meant masturbation, several forms of same-sex sexual behavior, bestiality, non-procreative sex (oral or anal most commonly) between a man and a woman, or any form of sex in which conception was impossible.[6]

On the other hand, the more historians filled in the missing pieces about sexual practices in the past, the more intractable the question of identity came to seem. When John Boswell argued that same-sex relationships between men, which he termed "gay," existed under relatively benign conditions until the late Middle Ages, he posited that innate behavior created identity.[7] Less radically, some historians, such as Joan Cadden and Joseph Cady for the Middle Ages and early modern France respectively, reconstructed contexts in which specific versions of sexual identity emerged long before the nineteenth century.[8] In whatever form, the underlying question has been about the relationship of sodomy to modern homosexuality. Trying to defuse tensions over Foucault's contention that there was no "homosexual" identity before the nineteenth century, David Halperin argued that the identity question was more strategic than most accounts would allow, seeing Foucault's intentions in describing the emergence

in the Early Modern Period," *Journal of Homosexuality* 24 (1997): 1–16. Trumbach's insistence on men distinguishing themselves by heterosexual coitus is problematic, but his research on the context of identity formation is highly suggestive.

[6] Foucault, *History of Sexuality*, 101. For the early modern meanings of sodomy, see Cynthia B. Herrup, *A House in Gross Disorder: Sex, Law, and the 2nd Earl of Castlehaven* (New York: Oxford University Press, 1999), 30–4 and Jeffrey Merrick and Bryant T. Ragan, Jr., eds., *Homosexuality in Early Modern France: A Documentary Collection* (New York: Oxford University Press, 2001). See also William Naphy, *Sex Crimes from Renaissance to Enlightenment* (Stroud: Tempus, 2002) for the changing sexual climate.

[7] This is often shorthanded as "essentialism," and the principle texts are John Boswell, *Christianity, Social Tolerance, and Homosexuality: Gay People in Western Europe from the Beginning of the Christian Era to the Fourteenth Century* (University of Chicago Press, 1980) and "Revolutions, Universals and Sexual Categories," in *Hidden from History: Reclaiming the Gay and Lesbian Past*, ed. Martin Duberman, Martha Vicinus, and George Chauncey (New York: NAL Books, 1989), 17–36. For a summary of the essentialism/construction debate, see Robert A. Nye, ed., *Sexuality* (Oxford University Press, 1999), 4–10. See also Jeffrey Weeks, *Sexuality*, 2nd edn. (London and New York: Routledge, 2003) and Rictor Norton, *The Myth of the Modern Homosexual: Queer History and the Search for Cultural Unity* (London: Cassell, 1997), esp. 11–33, 98–9, 132–5 for rupture and continuity models respectively.

[8] Joan Cadden, "Sciences/Silences: The Natures and Languages of 'Sodomy' in Peter of Albano's *Problemata* Commentary," in *Constructing Medieval Sexuality*, ed. Karma Lochrie (Minneapolis: University of Minnesota Press, 1997), 40–57; Joseph Cady, "The 'Masculine Love' of the 'Princes of Sodom' 'Practicing the Art of Ganymede' at Henri III's Court: The Homosexuality of Henri III and His Mignons in Pierre de L'Estoile's *Mémoires-Journaux*," in *Desire and Discipline: Sex and Sexuality in the Premodern West*, ed. Jacqueline Murray and Konrad Eisenbichler (University of Toronto Press, 1996), 123–54. See also discussions of later contexts, especially Jeffrey Merrick, "Commissioner Foucault, Inspector Noël, and the 'Pederasts' of Paris, 1780–3," *Journal of Social History* 32 (1998): 287–307 and Michael Rey, "Parisian Homosexuals Create a Lifestyle, 1700–1750: The Police Archives," *Eighteenth-Century Life* 9 (1985): 179–91.

of sexual identity as a product of discourse and a political strategy to challenge hegemonic narratives of sexuality.[9] But Halperin has also been taken to task for his tendency to consider antiquity alongside modernity while regarding all that lies between as unhelpful with respect to defining sexual identity.[10]

One aim here is to revisit the chronological span Halperin avoids in order to move beyond the debates over sexual acts vs. identities and essentialism vs. social construction that resulted from engagement with Foucault's assertions. I am guided in part by seemingly contradictory understandings of sexuality in early modernity. Jonathan Goldberg argues that sodomy was always a matter of "relational structures." Homoerotics within and across texts can be traced, analyzed, and deconstructed, but the "sodomite" was never a stable identity category. In that sodomy meant so many things depending on time and place, this was – and to a degree still is – utterly true.[11] Meanwhile, some historians have argued that early modern people used "sodomy" and "sodomite" quite specifically. They knew it when they saw it.[12] Both amorphous relationality and specificity of particular cases routinely operate at once. While we often know very little about how people generalized their behavior, we do know that they thought about sex in various domains, and that the persistence of old ideas was difficult to maintain when new ones clamored onto the scene. That I assert this to be the case would seem to indicate that I am not much of an essentialist, in that rupture is evidently much at work in moments of change. At the same time, continuities in sexual practice (there are only so many possibilities with respect to "doing it," although perhaps infinite variations on them) are undeniable and often reassuring to those who engage in them. Seeing this dual operation being formulated and deployed, I maintain, gets us closer to understanding the lineaments of sexual culture.[13]

By analyzing a specific place and time, what people made of sex when their cultural assumptions were under question or even threatened can become evident. Specificity helps to reveal sexuality as a fundamental ideological formation. As a social system, sexuality partakes of the general quality of ideology:

[9] David M. Halperin, "Forgetting Foucault: Acts, Identities, and the History of Sexuality," *Representations* 63 (1998): 93–120.
[10] Carla Freccero, *Queer/Early/Modern* (Durham, NC and London: Duke University Press, 2006), 31–50.
[11] Jonathan Goldberg, *Sodometries: Renaissance Texts, Modern Sexualities* (Stanford University Press, 1992), 20.
[12] See for instance Helmut Puff, *Sodomy in Reformation Germany and Switzerland, 1400–1600* (University of Chicago Press, 2003); Maria R. Boes, "On Trial for Sodomy in Early Modern Germany," in *Sodomy in Early Modern Europe*, ed. Tom Betteridge (Manchester University Press, 2002), 27–45.
[13] "Culture" can have many meanings. I am using it as an analytical term aimed at understanding the significations that French society deployed. My presumption is that the system of signifying meaning indicates what members of that society think about themselves and locates that culture relative to others outside it.

it is hard to see. For Louis Althusser, ideology is disguised by its own seeming inevitability:

> It is indeed a peculiarity of ideology that it imposes (without appearing to do so, since these are "obviousnesses") obviousnesses as obviousnesses, which we cannot *fail to recognize* and before which we have the inevitable and natural reaction of crying out (aloud or in the "still, small voice of conscience"): "That's obvious! That's right! That's true!"[14]

Recognizing the "obvious," however, blocks theoretical development. Recognition is taken as enough. Althusser imagines that scientific discourse could possibly obviate or circumvent ideological subjection, but he concedes that attempts to generate historical distance in order to recognize ideological formations are not entirely successful. Indeed, one of the foremost modern "ideological state apparatuses," to use his term, is education. In modern society, the school/family has replaced the church/family as a primary locus of ideology.[15] I am not going to refute Althusser in that I do not dispute the intractable omnipresence of ideology, but I do think, following Slavoj Žižek, that Althusserian ideology rests on a presumption of ignorance: "'[*I*]*deological' is a social reality whose very existence implies the non-knowledge of its participants as to its essence* – that is, the social effectivity, the very reproduction of which implies that the individuals 'do not know what they are doing.'"[16] This suggests that denaturalizing ideological formations might reveal them, at least in part.

The Renaissance created conditions of denaturalized knowledge – by provoking change, this period laid bare some of the ideological support for the "obvious" state of things. For that reason, I am drawn to problems of continuity and discontinuity and to questions of sexuality which help illuminate them. My project is not a queer reading of the French Renaissance, but I do draw on queer theory. Jonathan Goldberg and Madhavi Menon have argued for the notion of "homohistory."[17] This is not a history of homosexuality, but a willing suspension of the certainty of heterosexual norms in historical contexts. The idea is to refuse, consciously, acceptance of the simple equation of sexual difference and chronological change. Ancient sodomy in, say, classical Athens is not the same as Renaissance sodomy in Florence, which is not the same as sodomy in twenty-first-century Dallas, Texas. But the similarities in what people did and thought about it are at least as important as the changes.

[14] Louis Althusser, "Ideology and Ideological State Apparatuses (Notes towards an Investigation)," in *Lenin and Philosophy and Other Essays*, trans. Ben Brewster (London: New Left Books, 1971), 121–73; see esp. p. 161.
[15] Louis Althusser, "A Letter on Art in Reply to André Daspre," in *Lenin and Philosophy*, 203–8; see esp. pp. 206–7; Althusser, "Ideology and Ideological State Apparatuses," 136–7, 127.
[16] Slavoj Žižek, *The Sublime Object of Ideology* (London: Verso, 1989), 21. Emphasis in the original.
[17] Jonathan Goldberg and Madhavi Menon, "Queering History," *PMLA* (2005): 1608–17.

Conscious evocations or rejections of the past seem improbable to me, but the Texas queer might inadvertently or unknowingly recall the Athenian citizen or the Florentine merchant when he does his sexual business.

Of course the reality is that we all do live in our own times as heirs to historical moments past. Because the Renaissance was an especially revealing collision of cultural imperatives, it is an especially ripe area to explore what people thought about sex. Ironically, the idea of homohistory encourages seeing the range of languages of love, desire, sodomy, lust, inadequacy, and procreation, to name just a few of the recurrent issues that exercised French Renaissance writers and readers. Awareness of the persistence of sameness increases awareness of possibilities and borrowings. At the same time, the self-conscious reflections on the past by Renaissance humanists, poets, and artists help to highlight infusions of new or renewed sexual thinking. My aim is to underscore both the consistency of disruption as ancient myth encounters Renaissance problems and the differences in the qualities of those disruptions around French cultural priorities.

By looking at a place (France) in a specific time (the Renaissance), this essay aims to understand how sexualized categories took shape as they did. How might time and place matter for better understanding sexuality? Historians are still trained in chronological divisions we more or less accept as having meaning: antiquity, the Middle Ages, the Renaissance, modernity, and so on, with an extensive and growing list of subdivisions and specificities. We also recognize that, in lived experience, such periodizations were rarely evident to those who lived in them, and that the differences between, say, late antiquity and the early Middle Ages are not always clear. Yet, I want to hold out for the Renaissance as having distinct characteristics in matters of sex and sexuality, particularly compared to the periods before it.[18] This essay assumes that the European Middle Ages, with its constant references to the Catholic Church as the central maker of sexual meaning, had its own distinct responses to problems of sexuality and desire. The lineaments of these responses are explored in works as diverse as Pierre J. Payer's studies of confessional literature, James A. Brundage's work on canon law, and various explorations of female sexuality relative to Catholicism, all of which display the influence of the Catholic Church on sexual norms.[19] We know that marriage was a matter of doctrine drawn from

---

[18] For a refusal of the idea of periodizing sex, see Merry E. Wiesner, "Disembodied Theory? Discourses of Sex in Early Modern Germany," in *Gender in Early Modern German History*, ed. Ulinka Rublack (Cambridge University Press, 2002), 152–77.

[19] Pierre J. Payer, "Confession and the Study of Sex in the Middle Ages," in *Handbook of Medieval Sexuality*, ed. Vern L. Bullough and James A. Brundage (New York: Garland, 1996), 3–31; *Sex and the Penitentials: The Development of a Sexual Code 550–1150* (University of Toronto Press, 1984); *The Bridling of Desire: Views of Sex in the Later Middle Ages* (University of Toronto Press, 1993); James A. Brundage, *Law, Sex, and Christian Society* (University of

St. Paul and St. Augustine, neither of whom regarded sex in a positive light, and that the value of sexual desire was highly disputed through much of the Middle Ages.[20] We have to some extent inherited the great oxymoron that chastity and virginity are sexual virtues. Whatever one makes of John Boswell's claims for "gay" Christians in the early Middle Ages, his work makes clear that clerics routinely considered matters of sexual normativity. Mark D. Jordan has demonstrated how Catholic thought on sodomy was shaped by such Church luminaries as Albert the Great and Thomas Aquinas, and more polemically, by Peter Damian.[21] The definition of sexual misdeeds of heretics (with the Church defining the contours of heresy) and the fusion of doctrinal and sexual deviance were largely the work of clerics.[22]

The Church did not cease to matter in the Renaissance, and Christianity remained a force in shaping understandings and discipline around sex, but

Chicago, 1987); "Sex and Canon Law," in Bullough and Brundage, eds., *Handbook*, 33–50. On women, see for instance Uta Ranke-Heinemann, *Eunuchs for the Kingdom of Heaven: Women, Sexuality and the Catholic Church*, trans. Peter Heinegg (New York: Doubleday, 1990); Bernadette J. Brooten, *Love between Women: Early Christian Responses to Female Homoeroticism* (University of Chicago Press, 1996); Joyce E. Salisbury, ed., *Sex in the Middle Ages: A Book of Essays* (New York: Garland, 1991); and Joseph H. Lynch, *Godparents and Kinship in Early Medieval Europe* (Princeton University Press, 1986). More generally, see Joan Cadden, *Meanings of Sex Difference in the Middle Ages* (Cambridge University Press, 1993); the essays in Vern L. Bullough and James A. Brundage, eds., *Sexual Practices and the Medieval Church* (Buffalo, NY: Prometheus, 1982); Charles Trinkaus and Heiko Oberman, eds., *The Pursuit of Holiness in Late Medieval and Renaissance Religion. Papers from the University of Michigan Conference* (Leiden: Brill, 1974); and the special issue of *JHS*, ed. William N. Bonds and Barbara Loomis (2001), 10:3/4.

[20] See for instance Peter Brown, *The Body and Society: Men, Women and Sexual Renunciation in Early Christianity* (New York: Columbia University Press, 1988) and *Augustine of Hippo: A Biography*, 2nd edn. (Berkeley: University of California Press, 2000); John O'Meara, "St. Augustine's Attitude to Love," *Arethusa* 2 (1969): 46–60; James A. Brundage, *Sex, Law and Marriage in the Middle Ages* (Brookfield, VT: Variorum, 1993); Anne Barstow, *Married Priests and the Reforming Papacy* (New York and Toronto: Mellen, 1982); Charles A. Frazee, "The Origins of Clerical Celibacy in the Western Church," *Church History* 41 (1972): 149–67; Dyan Elliott, *Spiritual Marriage: Sexual Abstinence in Medieval Wedlock* (Princeton University Press, 1993), and for a different view, see Margaret McGlynn and Richard J. Moll, "Chaste Marriage in the Middle Ages: 'It Were to Hire a Greet Merite,'" in Bullough and Brundage, eds., *Handbook of Medieval Sexuality*, 103–22.

[21] Mark D. Jordan, *The Invention of Sodomy in Christian Theology* (University of Chicago Press, 1997). For context, see Walter Wakefield and Austin P. Evans, *Heresies of the High Middle Ages* (New York: Columbia University Press, 1969); Jeffrey Richards, *Sex, Dissidence and Damnation: Minority Groups in the Middle Ages* (London and New York: Routledge, 1991); and Allen J. Frantzen, "Between the Lines: Queer Theory, the History of Homosexuality, and Anglo-Saxon Penitentials," *JMEMS* 26 (1996): 245–96.

[22] For various perspectives, see Glenn Burger and Steven F. Kruger, eds., *Queering the Middle Ages* (Minneapolis: University of Minnesota Press, 2001); Karma Lochrie, ed., *Constructing Medieval Sexuality*; Phyllis A. Bird, "'Male and Female He Created Them': Gen. 1:27b in the Context of the Priestly Account of Creation," *Harvard Theological Review* 74:2 (1981): 129–59; Wayne Meeks, *The Origins of Christian Morality* (New Haven: Yale University Press, 1993).

gradually, the dominance of the Church diminished. Municipalities displaced the Church courts in Italy and later, in Germany.[23] The infusion of humanism and the study of ancient texts offered philosophical and moral paradigms besides Christianity that held great appeal for some.[24] All of this meant that Christianity's centrality as a way of organizing thought about sex waned. (Catholic) Christianity, however multi-vocal it could be, had a unity of purpose in defining sex in terms of sin. Secular and humanist interests offered instead contending loci of understanding and power around sex. The construction of normative sexuality in the Renaissance included adaptations of "new" (that is, old or long-discredited and then revived) texts, discoveries of new bodies (of land and peoples), and the pressure of competition for cultural priority between nations, institutions, and individuals.

The last on that list brings us especially to France, where the Renaissance was repeatedly marked by claims for French linguistic superiority and for France as the heir to the ancients through the mechanism of *translatio studii et imperii*. While always a part of the wider European Renaissance, French efforts to distinguish French culture were especially self-conscious and salient. Whether one argues – as Pierre Jodogne has done – that the French Renaissance began with the transfer of the papacy to Avignon[25] or one follows the more conventional claim that late fifteenth-century cultural communication, including the Italian Wars beginning in 1494, was the crucial contact between the French and the "Italians," French humanists developed an insistent nationalism as part of their

---

[23] Edward Muir and Guido Ruggiero, eds., *History from Crime*, trans. Corrada Biazzo Curry, Margaret A. Gallucci, and Mary M. Gallucci (Baltimore: Johns Hopkins University Press, 1994); H. Schilling, "History of Crime or History of Sin? Some Reflections on the Social History of Early Modern Church Discipline," in *Politics and Society in Reformation Europe*, ed. E. I. Kouri and Tom Scott (London: St. Martin's, 1987); Nicolas Davidson, "Theology, Nature and the Law: Sexual Sin and Sexual Crime in Italy from the Fourteenth to the Seventeenth Century," in *Crime, Society and the Law in Renaissance Italy*, ed. Trevor Dean and K. J. P. Lowe (Cambridge University Press, 1994), 74–98; Thomas V. Cohen and Elizabeth S. Cohen, *Words and Deeds in Renaissance Rome: Trials before the Papal Magistrates* (University of Toronto Press, 1993); Richard von Dülmen, *Theatre of Horror: Crime and Punishment in Early Modern Germany*, trans. Elisabeth Neu (Cambridge, MA: Polity Press, 1990); Patricia H. Labalme, "Sodomy and Venetian Justice in the Renaissance," *Tijdschrift voor Rechtsgeschiedenis* 52 (1984): 217–54; Richard J. Evans, *Rituals of Retribution: Capital Punishment in Germany, 1600–1987* (Oxford University Press, 1996); John Theibault, *German Villages in Crisis: Rural Life in Hesse-Kassel and the Thirty Years' War, 1580–1720* (Atlantic Highlands, NJ: Humanities Press, 1995).

[24] For the European context, see James Hankins, *Plato in the Italian Renaissance*, 2 vols. (Leiden: Brill, 1990) and Paul Oskar Kristeller, *Il pensiero filosofico di Marsilio Ficino* (Florence: Sansoni, 1953). Other disruptions of Christian hegemony came from Catullus. See Julia Haig Gaisser, *Catullus and His Renaissance Readers* (Oxford: Clarendon, 1993). The phenomenon of "civic humanism" contributed as well. The discussions are extensive; see James Hankins, ed., *Renaissance Civic Humanism: Reappraisals and Reflections* (Cambridge University Press, 2000) for a range of positions.

[25] Pierre Jodogne, *Jean Lemaire de Belges, écrivain franco-bourguignon* (Brussels: Palais des Académies, 1972), 51–67.

understanding of Renaissance values. Despite the novelty of much associated with humanistic study, French engagement with Renaissance humanism has been located in terms of its continuities with the past over time and by place.[26] Franco Simone's analysis of the absorption of Petrarch in France was crucial for understanding the dynamics of such cultural exchange in nationally specific terms.[27] Simone emphasized the cultural interplay between the Italians and the French and argued that the notion of the French taking over the Renaissance was overblown. But the question of specificity, as we shall see, was elaborated by French writers and artists, developed in the sixteenth century, and routinely cast in terms of the "new" learning.

In making a case for the Renaissance (singular) in Europe, the debates over large-scale cultural shifts have collectively suggested that France was an acute locus for self-conscious engagement with precepts emanating from Italy and antiquity. Many have documented the extensive anti-Italian rhetoric in France.[28] The political dimensions of anti-Italianism are several, but two beg special notice. First, the French monarchy relied on and then rejected Italian financial supports and the inclusion of Italians in royal patronage networks. Recently, Nicolas Le Roux and Xavier Le Person have demonstrated the complex workings of political change in terms of Italian connections and political patronage.[29] Second, historians and art historians have demonstrated that the artistic patronage of the monarchy drew heavily on Italian expertise.[30] The

---

[26] See for instance the essays in A. H. T. Levi, ed., *Humanism in France at the end of the Middle Ages and in the Early Renaissance* (Manchester University Press, 1970).

[27] See especially Franco Simone, *Il Rinascimento francese: studi e ricerche* (Turin: Società editrice internazionale, 1961). For the continuing influence of Simone, see Pierre Blanc, ed., *Dynamique d'une expansion culturelle: Pétrarque en Europe, XIVe–XXe siècle: actes du XXVIe congrès international du CEFI, Turin et Chambéry, 11–15 décembre 1995: à la mémoire de Franco Simone* (Paris: Champion, 2001). In addition to Simone, see Alberto Tenenti, *Il senso della morte e l'amore della vita nel Rinascimento: (Francia e Italia)* (Turin: Einaudi, 1989), which traces a different node of cultural contact.

[28] See discussions in Heller, *Anti-Italianism in Sixteenth-Century France*; Jean-François Dubost, *La France italienne: XVIe–XVIIe siècle*, preface Daniel Roche (Paris: Aubier Montaigne, 1997).

[29] Nicolas Le Roux, *La Faveur du roi: mignons et courtesans au temps des derniers Valois* (Seyssel: Champ Vallon, 2001); Xavier Le Person, *"Practiques" et "Practiqueurs": la vie politique à la fin du règne de Henri III, 1584–1589*, preface Denis Crouzet (Geneva: Droz, 2002). For institutional shifts in the monarchy, see J. Russell Major, *From Renaissance Monarchy to Absolute Monarchy: French Kings, Nobles, & Estates* (Baltimore: Johns Hopkins University Press, 1994). The question of the character of the French government is central to historical inquiry about the seventeenth century. For the center of the storm about "absolute monarchy," see William Beik, *Absolutism and Society in Seventeenth-Century France: State Power and Provincial Aristocracy in Languedoc* (Cambridge University Press, 1985).

[30] See for instance R. J. Knecht, *Renaissance Warrior and Patron: The Reign of Francis I* (Cambridge University Press, 1994) and *The French Renaissance Court* (New Haven and London: Yale University Press, 2008); Anne-Marie Lecoq, *François Ier imaginaire: symbolique et politique à l'aube de la Renaissance française* (Cahors: Tardy Quercy, 1987); Sylvie Béguin, *L'Ecole de Fontainebleau: le maniérisme à la cour de France* (Paris: Gonthier-Seghers, 1960); Eugene Caroll, "Rosso in France," and Sydney Freedberg, "Rosso's Style in France and

engagement with Italian influence was a kind of fort-da game in France, in which Italian money, political connections, and artistic knowledge formed an irresistible object that the French tried repeatedly to fling away knowing that it would always return.

French ambivalence about Italian influence fed the use of sex and sexuality as a mode of cultural differentiation in the context of Renaissance cultural competition. Michael Rocke has found significant policing and prosecution of sodomy in sixteenth-century Florence, and has argued that sodomy resulted from larger demographic patterns. Late marriage for men (only one in four could expect to marry before age 32) meant that many men were unable to obtain access to heterosexual coitus that marriage presumably provided.[31] That Renaissance Europeans did not know the statistical particulars is immaterial; they certainly knew the Florentine reputation for sodomy. As Helmut Puff points out, "to florence" was a verb for sodomy in sixteenth-century Germany.[32] The sexual polemics that circulated about the Papacy and the Catholic clergy, especially after the emergence of Lutheran dissent in 1517, only increased the prevalence of assumptions about Italian sexual deviance and the alleged propensity for sodomy. French sexual polemics made much of the association of "Italian" with sexual corruption. In 1561, *Le Tigre* accused the cardinal de Lorraine of learning to pimp while in Rome. His foreign habits supposedly undermined honest French households, while he enjoyed sex with prostitutes and boys.[33] *Le Reveille-matin des François*, published in 1574, attacked Catherine de' Medici as a sexually corrupting "putain" [whore] who was determined to control the king by introducing him to sexual debauchery, especially sodomy.[34] The list could be multiplied *ad nauseam*.

The larger point is that sex was implicated in the concatenation of Renaissance values with which the French wrestled mightily. Consider this poem by the Bishop of Angoulême, Octavien de Saint-Gelais (1468–1502):

Et celle gent qu'on appelle ytalicque	And this people who one calls Italian
Dont les peres par extreme vouloir	Whose fathers by extreme will
Leur acquirent louenge magnifique	Acquired magnificent praise for themselves
Pour à jamais en triumph valoir,	For ever in triumph to furnish,

its Italian Context," in *Actes du colloque international sur l'art de Fontainebleau*, ed. André Chastel (Paris: CNRS, 1975), 17–28 and 13–16 respectively.

[31] Rocke, *Forbidden Friendships*.

[32] Puff, *Sodomy in Reformation Germany and Switzerland*, 13.

[33] François Hotman, *Le Tigre de 1560 reproduit pour la première fois en fac-similé*, ed. Charles Read (Geneva: Slatkine, 1970), 3, 73–4, 82.

[34] [Nicolas Barnaud?], *Le Reveille-matin des François: et de leurs voisins, composé par Eusebe Philadelphe, cosmopolite, enforme de dialogues* (Paris: Editions d'histoire sociale, 1977), 112, 94. See also pp. 37 and 40 for efforts to corrupt the king. (Originally 1574; authorship remains disputed.)

Regenerant comme chascun peut veoir	Regenerating as each can see
A laissé perdre en vice irreparable	Left lost in irreparable vice
Le dyademe excellent et notable	The excellent and notable diadem
D'honneur parfaict et de grande prouesse,	Of perfect honor and great prowess,
Comme lasche, remplye de mollesse.	As wanton, and filled with indolence.[35]

Admiration gives way to disappointment as the poetic persona eyes contemporary Italians as compared with their Roman forbears.[36] The cause of Italian degeneration is sex: they are lascivious and soft. "Mollesse" is less obvious now, but it was associated in the Middle Ages with "mollities" (softness) as a derogatory term for masturbation and its sexual connotations.[37] Implicitly, the ability to recognize and judge decadence was a sign of moral and sexual superiority. The French critic was staking his cultural credit against Italy as the inferior heir of the glorious ancient past through intimate accusations of sexual discredit.

One poem does not an argument make, but it is part of the network of understandings that French humanists and poets, polemicists and politicians generated to define the sexual culture of the French Renaissance. In each of the areas analyzed in the chapters that follow, aspects of those processes are seen in operation and in conflict with other priorities of the moment or the age. In broad terms, some of what occurs involves eliding homosexual and homosocial behavior, formulating heterosexual productivity in positive terms, and organizing masculinity as a disciplinary structure. I have chosen five domains that were central to thought about these matters – the Renaissance inheritance of antiquity, astrology, Neoplatonism, poetry, and politics – in which to explore these processes. Two sizable caveats seem obvious at this juncture. First, I do not treat any of these issues exhaustively. Instead, I offer a reading of the evidence that attempts to be representative. For instance, I explore the sexual rewritings of Renaissance texts through the figure of Orpheus, a choice based on the rich history of the character, the range of his sexual adventures, and his popularity. The forces at work in shaping his story in the Renaissance are apparent in other texts and other characters, but I chose Orpheus because his story offered so much on so many levels. The second caveat is that I do not treat several obvious categories in and of themselves. Religion, art,

---

[35] Octavien de Saint-Gelais, *Le Séjour d'honneur*, ed. Frédéric Duval (Geneva: Droz, 2002), 302. (Originally 1503.)

[36] See Lionello Sozzi, *Rome n'est plus Rome: la polémique anti-italienne et autres essais sur la Renaissance* (Paris: Champion, 2002) for the extent of such feeling.

[37] See Jordan, *Invention of Sodomy*, 102–6, 145 on the uses of "mollities." Renaissance use sometimes referred to malleability, which was seen as a feminine trait. See for instance Simon de Vallambert, *Cinq Livres, de la maniere de nourrir et gouverner les enfans de leur naissance* (Poitiers: de Marnefs & Bouchetz, freres, 1565): "elles au contraire sont plus molles, & plus delicates" (p. 159). Women were believed to be more humid, which supposedly made them softer (p. 160).

law, medicine, exploration – all make appearances, but I have not addressed them directly in terms of their own narratives. There are reasons for each omission beyond the obvious desire of wanting to someday finish this book. I originally imagined religion as its own chapter, but I chose to weave it back into the other narratives in order to highlight the ways philosophers, astrologers, poets, and the like dealt with religious strictures around sex.[38] Although artistic representations do appear, I do not engage in full-scale artistic analysis because unraveling the layers of influence by patrons, artists, and presumed audiences would take me too far afield from what an image was saying about sex. I have drawn on Rebecca Zorach's analyses particularly with respect to French investment in notions of fertility and abundance,[39] but I have refrained from extensive art-historical interpretation of my own. When law and medicine dealt with sex, the gaps between the empirical data of cases and the discursive products of formal legal or medical practice were such that they required a whole different set of methodological tools than I was prepared to wield.[40] As for exploration, I reserve that for another day and for a more fulsome meditation on the intersections of gender, sexuality, and race.

What is left, then, is a project organized around a set of interconnected ideas and recurrent themes in five chapters. The first two chapters ask where one might go to find meaning about sex in the time and place that was Renaissance France. How did the French construct their knowledge of sex in the face of their expanding knowledge of antiquity and their encounters with Italian Renaissance humanism? This dimension analyzes the construction of discourses around sex by a group of men (mostly) who wanted to establish the specificity of their own linguistic tradition and did so through the recuperation, celebration, and disciplining of sexualized understandings of the ancient past.

The structuring claim throughout is that sex is created in language as well as in deed. Chapter 1, "The renaissance of sex: Orpheus, mythography, and making

---

[38] Studies of religion, gender, and sexuality have been crucial to my understanding. Among those I have relied on are James R. Farr, *Authority and Sexuality in Early Modern Burgundy* (New York: Oxford University Press, 1995); Barbara B. Diefendorf, *Beneath the Cross: Catholics and Huguenots in Sixteenth-Century Paris* (New York: Oxford University Press, 1991) and *From Penitence to Charity: Pious Women and the Catholic Reformation in Paris* (Oxford University Press, 2004); Lucien Paul Victor Febvre, *Le Problème de l'incroyance au XVIe siècle: la religion de Rabelais* (Paris: Michel, 1968); Philip T. Hoffman, *Church and Community in the Diocese of Lyon, 1500–1750* (New Haven: Yale University Press, 1984); Keith P. Luria, *Sacred Boundaries: Religious Coexistence and Conflict in Early Modern France* (Washington, DC: Catholic University Press of America, 2005); Thierry Wanegffelen, *Ni Rome ni Genève: des fidèles entre deux chaires en France au XVIe siècle* (Paris: Champion, 1997); and more generally, Ole Peter Grell and Bob Scribner, eds., *Tolerance and Intolerance in the European Reformation* (New York: Cambridge University Press, 1996).

[39] Rebecca Zorach, *Blood, Milk, Ink, Gold: Abundance and Excess in the French Renaissance* (University of Chicago Press, 2005).

[40] For the legal issues, see Farr, *Authority and Sexuality in Early Modern Burgundy*.

sexual meaning" takes up the figure of Orpheus as he appears over time. I argue that in the process of translation, reconstruction, and dissemination, figures such as Orpheus are simultaneously authorized by their classical origins and taken (in all senses of that term) to represent newly emergent notions of sex, gender, and sexuality. The received tale in either its Virgilian or Ovidian iterations is densely packed with problematic articulations of sexual intimacy. The appropriation of Orpheus as an ideal poet and the civilizing influence of his poetry seemed to enable commentators and French poets to graft Orpheus onto a project of linguistic patriotism. But the sexual history of Orpheus troubled that appropriation. Recall that Orpheus' devotion to his wife, Eurydice, leads him to seek to restore her to life after she has been relegated to Hades. However, his ambivalence about the prospect of marriage is such that his actions cause her permanent death. Orpheus' pederasty and violent death at the hands of the Baccantae proved even more susceptible to appropriative moves despite evident anxiety about the homosexual and homosocial dimensions of his tale.

The Renaissance treatments of Orpheus are the product of a long lineage of stories meeting new intellectual and critical imperatives and the gender stresses those imperatives produced. The Renaissance as a period of disruption and consolidation around gender norms under-girds much of this project. In *Tough Love*, Kathryn Schwarz takes up the questions of gender and sexualized embodiment in the English Renaissance, revealing presumptions both within and about Renaissance texts. The myth of the Amazons, Schwarz argues, confirmed and disrupted early modern notions of domesticity. Female warriors imagined by Renaissance authors presented challenging figurations of feminine desire and disrupted binary assumptions about sexual difference. Schwarz emphasizes the ways that gender organizes sexual understanding.[41] The uses and abuses of Orpheus, especially the attempts to straighten out his (queer) sexual responses, work in similar terms. Poets and pedagogues, annotators and appropriators tried to manipulate gender to claim Orpheus for sexual propriety. To some extent, Orpheus as the good husband emerged as an exemplar of corporeal self-control by the end of the Renaissance, but his failure to retrieve Eurydice from Hades and his homosexual turn tugged at the claims for Orpheus' status as an exemplary husband.

In effect the question of Chapter 1 is: what does it say of a culture that the hero of marriage is a figure who decided at the last minute that he did not want his wife back after all? In the Renaissance, many might have answered that question by reference to the stars. Chapter 2, "Heavens below: astrology, generation, and sexual (un)certainty," looks at how contemporaries understood astrology to reveal heavenly configurations that facilitated or impeded love and

---

[41] Kathryn Schwarz, *Tough Love: Amazon Encounters in the English Renaissance* (Durham, NC and London: Duke University Press, 2000).

"generation." Two disparate issues shaped astrology's relationship to generation. First, there is the question of continuity in a world in which, as Keith
Thomas eloquently put it, magic was on the decline.[42] Despite the Copernican reconfiguration of the universe, astrology practitioners initially continued
much as they had for centuries. Astrologers told people whether to marry,
when to do so, and with what sort of person. Astrological texts, both learned
and popular, warned against bad partners and recommended good ones – with
"good" and "bad" being suitably elastic as terms. Astrology enabled sexual
partnerships, could prevent bad (shameful, sinful, or unpleasant) relationships,
and offered the promise of continuity through generation. The instrumental-
ity demonstrated by the retention of astrology points to the second issue: the
place of gender in the understanding of sexed bodies. Prompted by Foucault's
neglect and the work of Thomas Laqueur, historians and literary scholars have
explored the status and nature of the sexualized body in the early modern past.[43]
While critics have taken issue with aspects of his argument, Laqueur presented
a powerful case for the significance of gender as organizing sexual thinking.[44]
Gendered perceptions of sex figure in how Renaissance people understood the
sexual content of astrology as it mediated the distance between the corporeal
and the heavenly. The stars sometimes operated in different ways on women,
and in uniform ways on both women and men at other times. This is the broad,
wide, and deep reliance on astrology relative to sex that requires recuperation.
For purposes of the debates over whether the body was seen as male by default,
astrology offers a mediating account: men and women are sexually distinct,
but influenced and defined by the same factors. Whatever post-Enlightenment
scoffing we may wish to throw at astrology, in everyday Renaissance life,
astrology provided crucial sexual guidance. In France, where generation was
linked insistently with images of nation, the health of the realm as facilitated by
the stars became a crucial aspect of sexualized identity in Renaissance France.

[42] Keith Thomas, *Religion and the Decline of Magic* (London: Weidenfeld & Nicholson and
New York: Scribner, 1971).
[43] Feminist critiques of Foucault include Dianna Taylor and Karen Vintges, eds., *Feminism and the
Final Foucault* (Urbana: University of Illinois Press, 2004); Margaret A. McLaren, *Feminism,
Foucault and Embodied Subjectivity* (Albany: State University of New York Press, 2002).
[44] Thomas Laqueur, *Making Sex: Body and Gender from the Greeks to Freud* (Cambridge, MA:
Harvard University Press, 1990). For related analyses, see Kathleen Coyne Kelly, *Performing
Virginity and Testing Chastity in the Middle Ages* (London and New York: Routledge, 2000),
especially the chapter "Hymenologies"; Kathleen Coyne Kelly and Marina Leslie, eds., *Menacing Virgins: Representing Virginity in the Middle Ages and Renaissance* (Newark, DE and
London: Associated University Presses, 1999); and Marie H. Loughlin, *Hymeneutics: Interpreting Virginity on the Early Modern Stage* (Lewisburg: Bucknell University Press, 1997). For
critiques, see Katharine Park and Robert A. Nye, "Destiny is Anatomy," Review of *Making
Sex: Body and Gender from the Greeks to Freud* by Thomas Laqueur, *New Republic* (February
18, 1991): 53–7. See also Lorraine Daston and Katharine Park, "The Hermaphrodite and the
Orders of Nature: Sexual Ambiguity in Early Modern France," *Gay and Lesbian Quarterly* 1
(1995): 419–38.

Astrology was a familiar framework doing new work but doing so under new stress generated by the intellectual innovations of the Renaissance. Some of these innovations are the subject of Chapters 3 and 4. In addition to the role that Christian sexual mores had long played in delineating sexual meaning, understandings of what constituted "good" or "bad" sex were defined in philosophical and poetic terms in the Renaissance. The absorption of Neoplatonism and the adoption of Italian and Neo-Latin poetic forms provide evidence for case studies about the effects of novel intellectual practices on sexual thought. In different ways, both were about love, but where Neoplatonism represented the (contested) codification of heterosexuality, poetry presented tremendous problems for the masculine subject within heterosexual love language.

This part of the story begins with Chapter 3, "Neoplatonism and the making of heterosexuality." I examine the French reaction to Neoplatonism (particularly of the Florentine variety) in terms of the propensity of the French to rewrite homosocial understandings of desire, beauty, and reciprocity in heterosexual terms. With their emphasis on love defined as a desire for beauty that worked toward salvation, Neoplatonists often found themselves hopelessly mired in problems of corporeality. In 1469, Marsilio Ficino wrote, "Femine profecto viros facile capiunt, facilius autem ille que masculam quandam indolem pre se ferunt. Et tanto facilius masculi quanto similores sunt viris quam femine" [Women truly easily capture men, and even more easily those women who bear a masculine character. So much more easily, men catch men, as they are more like men than are women].[45] One can imagine the confusion about what to do. From the first systematic French grappling with Ficino by Symphorien Champier, philosophical speculation recurred to the problem of "proper" desire.[46] French writers, including Louys Le Roy, Barthélemy Aneau, Giles Corrozet, Guillaume de La Perrière, Antoine Héroët, Thomas Sébillet, and Jean Serres found that sexual desire at once exceeded the description of abstract, intellectual gratification fostered by Ficino and was inextricably entangled in the processes that led to that goal.

Because desire was so disruptive, French Neoplatonists marshaled theoretical and philosophical support in favor of desire as articulating heterosexual normativity. Because the lineaments of both "heterosexual" and "normative" have changed a great deal over time, I read the French Renaissance with an awareness of resistance, evasion, and creative self-misreading around matters of love and desire. Analyses of "lesbian" desire, the meanings attached to sexual abstinence, and the perverse pleasures of virginity as a sexuality guide

---

[45] Marsilio Ficino, *Commentaire sur le banquet de Platon*, ed. and trans. [into French] Raymond Marcel (Paris: Société d'édition "Les belles lettres," 1956), 253. The English translation is mine.

[46] Symphorien Champier, *Nef des dames vertueuses composees par maistre Simphorien Champier Docteur en medicine* (Paris: Jehan de La Garde, 1515). First edition: 1503.

my thinking.[47] That is, many studies have demonstrated that non-normative, non-reproductive sexuality had a complex place in early modern culture. In part, that place was to define the "normal" through providing a span of suspect and laudable exceptional cases. As Valerie Traub has argued, the English in their Renaissance depicted and discussed lesbian desire articulated in terms of female–female eroticism frequently. Female homoeroticism in poetry, fiction, medical texts, travel narratives, art and on stage had specific purposes in a context in which protecting chastity from male seduction or aggression was important.[48] Neoplatonism represents a similar case in that its relationship to normativity changed because of issues of sexual security. Attracted to Ficino's aim of revitalizing Christianity through the infusion of Plato into Catholic theology, French interlocutors were troubled because the "truth" about a central concept in Ficino's theology, beauty, was that it was deceptive. French Neoplatonists gradually restructured Ficino's homosociality (drawn from Plato) as heterosexual compatibility and generative potentiality. Because of this reading of Neoplatonism, French theorists, poets, and fiction writers had to address what happened when women were inserted into Ficino's homosocial model. Gender issues, sometimes expressed in sexual terms, were central to the repudiation of homosociality in favor of procreative heterosexuality that became the "truth" about Platonic philosophy.

The question of "truth" in sex shapes the narrative of Chapter 4, "Cupid makes you stupid: 'bad' poetry in the French Renaissance," as well. This chapter explores a powerful rhetorical convergence, which might equally accurately be called a collision: the development of a new language that identifies love as a transcendent emotional state against the emergence of sexually explicit scurrilous verse. These poetic forms, apparently at odds, nonetheless rely on a common vocabulary base and set of syntactical assumptions, a fact which is, to say the least, productive of discord. I trace the absorption and rejection of Petrarchan love idioms around the sexual politics of Petrarch's allegedly chaste desire for Laura. The French, eager to assert their poetic prowess against the Italians, did so over Laura's fictive dead body by maintaining that Petrarch lied about the chaste quality of his love. French poets insisted instead that consummation was a marker of emotional and physical authenticity. Articulating sexual fulfillment was a form of masculine honesty, as in a sonnet that begins with "French" kissing: "S'entre-meslent les langues dans la bouche," moves to physical play ("Flanc dessus flanc, redoubler escarmouche / . . . On soit saisy

---

[47] Valerie Traub, "The Perversion of 'Lesbian' Desire," *History Workshop Journal* 41 (1996): 23–49; John Rogers, "The Enclosure of Virginity: The Poetics of Sexual Abstinence in the English Revolution," in *Enclosure Acts: Sexuality, Property, and Culture in Early Modern England*, ed. Richard Burt and John Michael Archer (Ithaca, NY and London: Cornell University Press, 1994), 229–50; and Kathryn Schwarz, "The Wrong Question: Thinking through Virginity," *differences* 13:2 (2002): 1–34.

[48] Valerie Traub, *The Renaissance of Lesbianism* (Cambridge University Press, 2002).

d'un doux ravissement"), and ends with penetration: "Dedans ton Con j'ay mis mon vit refait / Je suis relascher [sic] ne l'ay-je pas . . . tue?" [We intermingle our tongues in our mouths / Groin on groin, redoubling our skirmish . . . One is seized with a sweet ravishment / Within your cunt, I stick my dick again, / I am released, have I not fucked?][49] The admission of vulnerability combines strikingly with the aggression of the language in a pattern that was typical of French Renaissance poetic articulations. In the agonistic competition for patronage and the effort to assert poetic subjectivity, anxieties over masculinity – poems about impotence, sodomy, lesbianism, cuckoldry, and venereal disease abound – emerged from the strictures of the Petrarchan discourse of unrequited desire.

One of the key areas of encounter between competing ideas about sexuality took place around notions of masculinity. Here, I begin by radically de-naturalizing masculinity in order to see its structuration in the past. In *Female Masculinity*, Judith Halberstam says, "I want to argue for a perversely presentist model of historical analysis, a model, in other words, that avoids the traps of simply projecting contemporary understandings back in time, but one that can apply insights from the present to conundrums of the past."[50] Halberstam explores the modern iterations of female masculinity, arguing that the flat taxonomy of masculinity actually contains unrecognized multiplicity. Halberstam wants to challenge the distillation process that reduces a range of understandings of sexuality and sexual behavior to limited, monochromatic categories. While female masculinity is not an area of inquiry for this project, Halberstam's perverse presentism is useful for thinking about the relationship between categories and the compression of their contents to produce categorical coherence.

Halberstam's destabilizing of masculinity to include women can be turned on its head, in a sense, so that masculinity becomes the troubled category – as it often was in early modernity.[51] Throughout this project, the perils of masculinity produce enormous problems for the articulation of male subjectivity.[52]

[49] BN MS 884, fols. 234v–235r.
[50] Judith Halberstam, *Female Masculinity* (Durham, NC: Duke University Press, 1998), 52–3.
[51] Most studies of early modern masculinity have explored England, with some attention to other parts of Europe. Bruce R. Smith, *Shakespeare and Masculinity* (Oxford University Press, 2000); Laura Levine, *Men in Women's Clothing: Anti-Theatricality and Effeminization, 1579–1642* (Cambridge University Press, 1994); Katrina Bachinger, *Male Pretense: A Gender Study of Sir Philip Sydney's Life and Texts* (Lewiston: Mellen, 1994); David Kuchta, *The Three-Piece Suit and Modern Masculinity: England, 1550–1850* (Berkeley: University of California Press, 2002). For Italy, see Valeria Finucci, *The Manly Masquerade: Masculinity, Paternity, and Castration in the Italian Renaissance* (Durham, NC and London: Duke University Press, 2003). For earlier periods, see Claire A. Lees, ed., *Medieval Masculinities: Regarding Men in the Middle Ages* (Minneapolis: University of Minnesota Press, 1994); and Jeffrey Jerome Cohen and Bonnie Wheeler, eds., *Becoming Male in the Middle Ages* (New York and London: Garland, 1997).
[52] Mark Breitenberg, *Anxious Masculinity in Early Modern England* (Cambridge University Press, 1996); Kathleen P. Long, ed. *High Anxiety: Masculinity in Crisis in Early Modern France* (Kirksville, MO: Truman State University Press, 2002).

Whether the context is poetry or politics or philosophy, I take seriously the ways that negotiating masculinity made subject formation a difficult prospect. I am not the only one to notice this. Todd W. Reeser, for instance, has argued for the contingent, nearly impossible strictures of masculinity as it was understood in Aristotelian terms.[53] He reconstructs the discourse of "moderation" as an unstable third term between excess and lack. He demonstrates that Aristotelian definitions of manhood were formulated in largely negative terms – as not too much and not too little. This left little more than general guidance to achieve and maintain a moderate position. Although he addresses aspects of Neoplatonism in French culture, Reeser notes in his analysis that he is neither accounting for Platonic notions of masculinity nor for the changes the introduction of Neoplatonism might have caused to the Aristotelian model. I argue that Neoplatonism offers a model of masculinity in which homosocial bonds between men supplement and at times supplant the Aristotelian notion of masculinity as moderation defined by the individual. No matter where a Renaissance man turned, masculinity was never a stable source of identification. This is starkly apparent in the negotiations of subjectivity and masculinity created by the sexual politics that informed the emergence of distinctly French poetic practices.[54]

The ideological dimensions of Renaissance textual practices developed within a political frame that was itself marked by and productive of sexual discipline. The discourse of sex shaped possibility, disability, and the prospects for inclusion (or exclusion) from the polity. Chapter 5, "Politics, promiscuity, and potency: managing the king's sexual reputation," takes up these issues in light of the prolonged crisis over royal generation – a theme that appears in several guises throughout the narrative of this project. From François I implicating royal authority in the debates over Petrarch's chastity with the discovery of Laura's tomb in 1533, to royal celebrations that featured references to French fertility supported by the Zodiac, to Louys Le Roy writing a Neoplatonic commentary as a wedding present for François II in 1558, to the sustained (although not always successful) efforts to control Henri IV's reputation as a virile and sexually productive monarch, generation as the reproduction of authority was a constant, chronic issue.

With procreative fertility as a baseline for "good" monarchical sexuality, the monarchy often created problems around the sexual reputation of the king. In tune with Renaissance modes of monarchical representation, the Valois kings, beginning with François I, played with gender and sexual ambiguity. Niccolò Bellin da Modena painted François as the bisexual embodiment of several pagan gods at the same time that the king extended his patronage to artists who

---

[53] Todd W. Reeser, *Moderating Masculinity in Early Modern Culture* (Chapel Hill: University of North Carolina Press, 2006).

[54] For approaches to subjectivity, I have relied on Kaja Silverman, *Male Subjectivity at the Margins* (London: Routledge, 1992).

Figure 1. Niccolò Bellin da Modena (1490–1569), *Portrait of François I*, colored engraving, Bibliothèque nationale de France, Paris.

Sometimes referred to as the "bi-sexual portrait of François I," this image depicts the king with the attributes of Mars, Minerva, Diana, Mercury, and simultaneously as the embodiment of Love. The combination of masculine and feminine presentation around the king was in keeping with early Renaissance modes of sexual representation.

depicted him as virile and potent. As Raymond B. Waddington has pointed out, François favored artistic images that included the king in sexually complex circumstances.[55] François had Fontainebleau decorated with images of Venus conquering Mars, an iconography that effeminized the king while depicting him as a warrior.[56] Negative commentary elided descriptions of the king as virile for his numerous sexual escapades and effeminized by his attraction to women. Critics became more pointed when Henri II succeeded to the throne in 1547.[57] In honor of his mistress, Diane de Poitiers, Henri foregrounded the goddess Diana in artistic works that were produced under his patronage. The adulterous union combined with Diane's obvious power in political affairs increased concerns about the king's subjection to feminine influence.

Sovereignty became a particularly loaded locus of sexuality after Henri II's death, and the succession of his three sons, François II, Charles IX, and Henri III. As each brother in turn failed to reproduce (Charles did manage to have a son out of wedlock and a posthumous daughter; the other two did not muster anything in this regard), managing the royal sexual reputation became increasingly difficult. Henri III went to great lengths to assert his desire for children and to increase his chances of generating a son. But his efforts only drew attention to his failure. Critics implicated Henri III in charges of sexual excess, accusing him of everything from sexual intercourse with nuns to a range of carnal relationships with men.[58] One scabrous poem suggests the tone:

Les fruits qui croissent sur les eaux	The fruits that grow on the waters of the
De la mer de Sodome à l'oeil paraissent beaux.	sea of Sodom appear beautiful to the eye.
Mais au dedans sont pleins de cendre et pourriture.	But they are full of cinders and rot on the inside.[59]

---

[55] Raymond B. Waddington, "The Bisexual Portrait of Francis I: Fontainebleau, Castiglione, and the Tone of Courtly Mythology," in *Playing with Gender: A Renaissance Pursuit*, ed. Jean R. Brink, A. Champollion, E. Halphen, P. Lacroix, C. Read, T. de Loroque (Urbana: University of Illinois, 1991), 99–132.

[56] The effeminacy of François I was a widespread idea. See Paula Findlen, "Humanism, Politics and Pornography in Renaissance Italy," in *The Invention of Pornography: Obscenity and the Origins of Modernity*, ed. Lynn Hunt (New York: Zone, 1996), 49–108. See her discussion of Francesco Xanto Avelli's majolica, *The Christian King Fell Beneath Pavia* (1534), 103–6, which she reads convincingly as a reworking of one of "Aretino's Postures."

[57] As R. J. Knecht points out, Henri was baptized as "Henry" because he was named after Henry VIII of England. See Knecht, *French Renaissance Court*, 10. I am nonetheless utilizing common modern French practice in spelling his name Henri.

[58] The discussions of Henri III are extensive and will be addressed in Chapter 5, but for context around the question of sodomy, see especially Poirier, *L'Homosexualité dans l'imaginaire de la Renaissance*.

[59] Pierre de L'Estoile, *Mémoires-Journaux* de Pierre de L'Estoile, ed. G. Brunet, 11 vols. (Paris: Alphonse Lemerre, 1877), vol. IV, 6.

That the accusations were largely polemical points to the extent to which the language of sex took on political force. Henri IV understood this. Attempting to avoid the negative response that Henri III's actions had inspired, the first Bourbon monarch asserted an aggressively heterosexual masculinity.[60] As is the case with most reaction formations, his efforts backfired at times, resulting in images of the king as lascivious, excessive, and sexually subject to women and to his own desires. Efforts to discipline the monarch's possible acts included narratives about the sovereign body as embodying ungoverned sexuality. The king, in this sense, did not have two bodies: the political body was endlessly vulnerable to the corporeal one through a set of discourses in which intercourse had all its meanings, including our own contemporary sense.

In the end, sexual identity was created out of the definitional battles over where, how, and why sex mattered. The sexual and gender politics of Renaissance France *are* politics – both in the literal sense of participating in the formation of social subjects and in the larger sense that they enable and complicate relations to power. This project, then, is not just a story about what people long ago and far away thought about sex. It is about cultural processes through which subjects (in the monarchical and modern senses of the term) constituted themselves in relation to power, configured and understood as potency, sexual desire, and control over bodies.

We have known for some time that sexuality is endlessly complicated by the definitive efforts of its own narratives; what I suggest here is that the articulations of the French Renaissance provide a focused perspective on these processes. The sexual culture of this period was at once originary in some of its modern effects and exemplary of the sometimes strange habit of simultaneously believing in contradictory things. Recovering these dimensions, and examining the ways in which they illuminate one another, has important implications for the history of sexuality and for present-day sexual politics. To explore these implications, dear reader, please read on.

---

[60] Henri IV has attracted far less attention than did his predecessor with respect to sexuality, but see Katherine Crawford, "The Politics of Promiscuity: Masculinity and Heroic Representation at the Court of Henry IV," *FHS* 26:2 (2003): 225–52. See Robert A. Nye, *Masculinity and Male Codes of Honor in Modern France* (New York: Oxford University Press, 1993), esp. 15–30, for context.

1   The renaissance of sex: Orpheus, mythography, and making sexual meaning

Guy Le Fèvre de La Boderie devoted his epic, *La Galliade*, to declaring France the heir to the civilizations of Greece, Rome, and Egypt. In the course of linking the Gauls to ancient sources of wisdom, La Boderie invoked Orpheus:

Donq des Bardes Gaulois en ensuivant la trace	Thus the Gallic Bards in following the trace
Monta son instrument le grand Harpeur de Thrace	Mount by the instrument of the great Harper of Thrace.

Those traces were the "doux hymnes" [sweet hymns] that taught the Gauls the wisdom of the great civilizations past and encouraged them to new poetic feats. Invoked routinely as a poet, singer, philosopher, religious leader, psychopomp, and civilizing agent, Orpheus was linked to claims for the poetic brilliance of France. The complication was that Orpheus was also a sexual failure. He did not save his wife from Hades and instead, turned to the love of young men. La Boderie does not entirely ignore these aspects, but as many do, he rewrote them to imagine less problematic possibilities:

Je sois ton Euridice, et tu sois mon Orfee . . .	I am your Eurydice, and you are my Orpheus . . .
Ou ne retourne arriere, helas, si tu me prens	Where one does not return, alas, unless you take me.[1]

La Boderie's Orpheus allows that possibility, rather than perversion, makes Orpheus part of the French past and poetic future. The fusion of poetic mastery and sexual rehabilitation is not new to La Boderie. For Jean d'Auton a half-century earlier, Orpheus functioned similarly. The author expresses his admiration:

---

[1] Guy Le Fèvre de La Boderie, *La Galliade* (1582), ed. François Roudout; preface Robert Aulotte (Paris: Klincksieck, 1993), cercle 4, ll. 351–2; cercle 1, l. 476; cercle 1, ll. 1148, 1150. (First edition: 1578.)

23

| Vous, Orpheus, tant bien citharizant | You Orpheus play so well with your zither |
| Que les Enfers endormez par voz sons | That even Hell is lulled by your sounds.[2] |

Auton's glancing reference ignores Orpheus' failure to use his power over Hell to save his wife and the problems (pederasty, Orpheus' violent death at the hands of the Baccantae) that ensued in order to extol Orpheus as a positive model. Linking poetic mastery, French genius, and the wisdom of antiquity, appropriations of Orpheus also asserted sexual probity and prowess by straightening out Orphic perversities.

When writers and artists in the Renaissance confronted, embraced, and appropriated the complex traditions of antiquity, they found the sexual norms of ancient civilization as expressed in figures such as Orpheus variously fascinating, repellent, funny, blasphemous, titillating, threatening, and useful. For such artists as Michelangelo Buonarroti (1475–1564), sexualized male figures like Ganymede offered the opportunity to present idealized, Neoplatonically "perfect" love in human form.[3] "Ganymede" was also a sexual slur flung at "sodomites." It was used in this vein as a term of opprobrium against Henri III and his male favorites.[4] The discovery, dissemination, and translation of ancients such as Lucian, Xenophon, Plato, Catullus, and Plutarch introduced an astonishing range of sexual behavior as "normal." Lucian's smutty table talk, Plato's insistence on male–male love, Xenophon's unbridled passion for Clinias, Catullus' sexual (mis)adventures and homoerotic threats, and Plutarch's description of Greco-Roman elites enjoying anything and everything were understood as part of daily life in antiquity. The hegemony of Medieval Christian ethics cracked under the strain of knowing that the refined, sophisticated, powerful cultures of antiquity offered an expansive range of sexual possibility. Renaissance Europe retained, deepened, and extended the policing of sexual behavior while – and because – the further past threatened the Medieval consensus on most things sexual.[5]

---

[2] Jean d'Auton, "La Compaincte de Gennes sur la mort de dame Thomassine Espinolle," in *Chroniques de Louis XII*, ed. R. de Maulde La Clavière for the Société de l'histoire de France, 4 vols. (Paris: H. Laurens, 1889–1895), vol. IV, 20. Auton was the historiographer for Louis XII, and this poem dates from 1505.

[3] James M. Saslow, *Ganymede in the Renaissance: Homosexuality in Art and Society* (New Haven and London: Yale University Press, 1986).

[4] See below, Chapter 5.

[5] For policing efforts in Italy, see for instance Rocke, *Forbidden Friendships* and Ruggiero, *The Boundaries of Eros*. For England, see Bray, *Homosexuality in Renaissance England*, and Herrup, *A House in Gross Disorder*. For France, see Lever, *Les Bûchers de Sodome*, and Farr, *Authority and Sexuality in Early Modern Burgundy*. For Germany, see Puff, *Sodomy in Reformation Germany and Switzerland*, and E. William Monter, "Sodomy and Heresy in Early Modern Switzerland," *Journal of Homosexuality* 6 (1980/1981): 41–55. For Spain, see Rafael Carrasco, *Inquisición y represión sexual en Valencia: historia de los sodomitas (1565–1785)* (Barcelona: Laertes, 1985); E. William Monter, *Frontiers of Heresy: The Spanish Inquisition from the Basque Lands to Sicily* (Cambridge University Press, 1990).

In many ways, the impulses and implosions caused by the Renaissance encounter with ancient sexuality were most acute in France. Always a player in the intellectual and cultural developments in Europe, writers and artists in the area that we call France[6] used the new/old ideas of antiquity as part of a prolonged cultural mission. Articulated in linguistic, political, and artistic terms, this project aimed at moving France to the cultural forefront of Europe. This meant coming to terms with the central articulations of sexual ideology expressed in ancient texts and appropriating them to particularly French ends. Revisiting Medieval readings of Orpheus by means of the new methods of Italian humanism, French writers reworked the sexual story of Orpheus to satisfy French cultural imperatives. At the same time, transformation, misrecognition, and legitimation reveal the production of sexual ideology at the moment of transfiguration that is the Renaissance.

The argument – in this chapter and in this book – moves between the larger European context and France to flesh out my claims for locus and tempus. With respect to the story of Orpheus, the mythographic discourse over time and across Europe features the development of Orpheus as a marital figure who nonetheless retained the marks of his sodomitical, misogynous self. This story traces Orpheus briefly through the ages, during which meanings accumulated, and strategies of explanation, suppression, and denial developed. Drawing from the methods and meanings developed since antiquity, French Renaissance poets and writers made Orpheus serve the assertions about nation, language, and sexual prowess that were central to French self-definition at the beginnings of modernity.

The end of this story (in this chapter and, again, of this book) is the counterassertion and incorporation of earlier moves that marked seventeenth-century classicism. Formal conservatism in language and sexual propriety as gestural policy were in part reaction formations against Renaissance practices. But like all such cultural moves, crucial elements – no matter how carefully repudiated – remained forever within the national culture. My aim, then, is to offer a narrative in the traditional mode of change over time, while at the same time building a case for the depositing of the ghosts of sexualities past along the way. As theorist and literary critic Carla Freccero has argued, "queer time is haunted by the persistence of affect and ethical imperatives in and across time."[7] Part of

---

[6] The area that is now France was both different in its boundaries and more linguistically variable in the sixteenth century.

[7] Freccero, *Queer/Early/Modern*, 5. Freccero uses deliberate, and to my mind very productive, juxtapositions of early modern and "late" modern texts and moments to explore debates in queer theory. While some historians may balk, anachronism consciously deployed to expose the presumptions of past and present is often quite revealing. For other temporal interventions of this sort, see Carolyn Dinshaw, *Getting Medieval: Sexualities and Communities, Pre- and Postmodern* (Durham, NC and London: Duke University Press, 1999) and Judith Halberstam, *In a Queer Time & Place: Transgender Bodies, Subcultural Lives* (New York and London: New York University Press, 2005).

my aim is to suggest how Orpheus, and countless other, lesser-known figures from antiquity, haunt the ideological formations around sexual belief.

Antique Orpheus

Because his story never disappeared from view, Orpheus may not seem like a ghostly figure.[8] But aspects of the long tradition around him are less well known. Since the more obscure bits are often the blocks from which later treatments built their interpretations, a brief rendition of Orpheus' myth, including the parts that are often omitted, seems opportune.[9] Married to Eurydice despite inauspicious signs from the gods, Orpheus is distraught when she dies and ventures to the underworld to get her back. Charmed by the master poet's song, Pluto allows Orpheus to retrieve Eurydice on the condition that he not look back at her until the couple has exited Hades. Of course, Orpheus turns around and Eurydice recedes, dying again and permanently because of her husband's action. Despondent, Orpheus tries again, but he is denied access. He returns to the world of the living and retreats to the mountains of Thrace where he sings beautiful lamentations that attract animals and trees. In his mourning, Orpheus renounces the company of women and exhibits a sexual preference for young men. This angers the Baccantae, who kill and dismember him. Orpheus' severed head floats down the Hebrus river either still lamenting or calling out Eurydice's name depending on which version of the story one consults.

[8] Among the many references in antiquity are the works of Aeschylus, *Agamemnon*, 1629–30 in *Agamemnon, Libation-Bearers, Eumenides, Fragments*, ed. and trans. Herbert Weir Smith, appendix Hugh Lloyd-Jones (Cambridge, MA: Harvard University Press, 1996); Euripides, *Medea*, in which Jason says to Medea: "Neither gold in my house nor the power to sing songs sweeter than Orpheus is my prayer without fame to grace my lot!" See Euripides, *Cyclops, Alcestis, Medea*, ed. and trans. David Kovacs (Cambridge, MA: Harvard University Press, 1994); Euripides, *Bacchae*, 560–4 in *Bacchae, Iphigenia at Aulus*, Rhesus, ed. and trans. David Kovacs (Cambridge, MA: Harvard University Press, 2002); and Pausanias, *Description of Greece*, trans. W. H. S. Jones (Cambridge, MA: 1918–1935), 9.30.4–12 (Pausanias is skeptical about Orpheus' parentage and tells the tale of the women of Thrace attacking the poet "because he had persuaded their husbands to accompany him in his wanderings." See 9.30.4). Pausanias references Orpheus elsewhere, usually with much skepticism. See for instance 1.14.3, 2.30.2, 3.13.2, 3.14.5, 3.20.5, 5.26.3, 6.20.18, 9.17.7, 9.27.2, 10.7.2, 10.30.6–8.

[9] This chapter addresses Orpheus almost entirely outside his identification with the *prisca theologica*. Among the French discussions of Orpheus in this guise are Symphorien Champier, *Theologie orphice* and *Theologie trismegistice* in his *De Triplica Disciplina* (Lyon: no. pub., 1508) and *Contenta in hoc volumine Pimander Mercurii Trismegisti liber de sapientia & potestate dei* (Paris: H. Stephani, 1505) with some translation and commentaries by Lefèvre d'Etaples. Champier's role as a transmitter of Neoplatonic ideas will be analyzed in Chapter 3, but it is worth noting at this point that Champier relied heavily on Marsilio Ficino, who took up Orpheus as a theological figure several times. See for instance Marsilio Ficino, *Epistolae Marsilii Ficini Florentini* (Nuremberg: Antonio Koberger, 1497), "Orphica comparatio Solis ad Deum atque declaratio idearum," (bk. 6, letter no. cl) and "Orpheo versus de deo," (bk. 11, no. ccxxii), which draws on Eusebius. For the significance of the *prisca theologica* especially in France, see D. P. Walker, "The *Prisca Theologica* in France," *Journal of the Warburg and Courtauld Institutes*, 17:3/4 (1954): 204–59.

From the start, Orpheus was imbricated in a range of sexual discourses, but the other dimension that emerges from ancient retellings of his tale is his complicated gender locus. Orpheus had a peculiar relationship to traditional masculinity as it appears in Greek tradition. Like many mythological figures,[10] Orpheus owed his sustained place in the cultural imagination to the fact that his stories could be interpreted in various ways.[11] Thought to be the son of the muse Calliope and either the wine god Oeagrus or Apollo, in Greek tradition, the Thracian Orpheus was associated with two archetypal stories: Jason's quest to retrieve the Golden Fleece and the recovery of lost or kidnapped women. The *Orphica Argonautica* places the musician and poet Orpheus among the hyper-masculine, blood-soaked heroes of Greek legend. Orpheus' incongruous presence – his stories are of taming animals, rather than slaughtering; of using music to quell violence rather than indulging in bloodshed – is naturalized by his role in the Eurydice story. The attempt to retrieve Eurydice recalls the myth of Persephone.[12] In both the *Argonautica* and the Eurydice tale, Orpheus mediates: he assists Jason and he convinces the gods of the underworld to allow him to retrieve Eurydice from Hades.[13]

Orpheus' tendency toward the effeminate – he is Jason's helpmeet; he is overly uxorious – points to the ways that the image of Orpheus in antiquity revealed the illusion of masculine mastery and self-mastery. Retellings of Orpheus' story depict a counterproductive masculinity that is striking for its failure to generate. Orpheus' mediations were tied to sexual structures, which allowed for discussion around the social implications of object choice. Plato, for instance, denounced Orpheus as an effeminate musician in the *Symposium*

---

[10] Much effort has been spent arguing over whether Orpheus existed at some point. I am interested in the uses of his figure, rather than the question of his existence. For discussion of the question, see W. K. C. Guthrie, *Orpheus and the Greek Religion: A Study of the Orphic Movement* (London: Methuen, 1952) and *The Greeks and Their Gods* (Boston, MA: Beacon Press, 1955); on the skeptical side, see Ivan M. Linforth, *The Arts of Orpheus* (Berkeley and Los Angeles: University of California Press, 1941).

[11] More generally, scholars debate the meanings around "legend" and "myth," with the usual distinction being that myths involve gods and supernatural events, while legends refer to human time and actual people. Others dismiss such distinctions. For discussions of the issues, see for instance Robert A. Segal, *Myth: A Very Short Introduction* (Oxford University Press, 2004) and Andrew von Hendy, *The Modern Construction of Myth* (Bloomington: Indiana University Press, 2002). Orpheus seems to straddle the categories of myth and legend.

[12] Eurydice and Persephone were routinely conflated. See for instance Roger de Collerye, *Oeuvres de Roger de Collerye*, ed. Charles d'Héricault (Paris: P. Jannet, 1855), 133: "Proserpine et Orpheus / S'entreaymoient fort, ce dit Ovide." Collerye's poems were originally published in 1536. This is from his "Blazon des dames." The lost or abducted woman theme in Greek literature is epitomized by Helen of Troy.

[13] Anon., *Les Argonautiques orphiques*, ed. Francis Vian (Paris: Société d'édition, 1987). On the circulation of women, see for instance Herodotus, *The History*, trans. David Grene (University of Chicago Press, 1987), vol. I, 1–5. Plato, *The Republic*, ed. G. R. Ferrari, trans. Tom Griffith (Cambridge University Press, 2000), 586c, remarks that the passions surrounding Helen were foolish because she was not at Troy. She had been replaced by an image.

and a misogynist (for his rejection of women) in the *Republic*.[14] According to Phanocles, Orpheus loved the young Argonaut Calais.[15] This is not in itself problematic, since Orpheus is rendered as the active participant, but given Orpheus' pacific presence, his attentions do not sit entirely comfortably with Greek presumptions about sexual roles.[16] Orpheus' pederasty sometimes dropped from sight: stories, including Euripides' *Alcestis*, refer to Orpheus as successfully retrieving his wife from death.[17]

As Euripides suggests, Orpheus had to be rewritten to make him a good husband. To the modern, post-Freudian mind, the unvarnished version hardly seems positive. Myths are primordial formations of human emotions, offering cultural expressions of anxieties and norms. What does it say about a man who supposedly wants his wife back so badly that he braves Hell to retrieve her, but he gets cold feet at the last minute and dooms her eternally? Orpheus looking back ranks up there with Theseus "forgetting" to change the sails. Theseus kills his father by omission; Orpheus, when he is just about to have his wife back, kills her for good. As an expression of marital ambivalence, Orpheus' turning around speaks volumes. His second attempt to convince the powers of the underworld to let him try again speaks to his guilt – not only that he failed, but that he could not go through with the implications of success: marriage unto (permanent) death. Of the aspects of his response, his pederasty feels reactive, while his disembodied, postmortem longing for Eurydice puts him back in a marital structure of a peculiar, or rather, dead sort. Orpheus, in short, displays remarkable ineptitude as a man among men or for women.

With Virgil's rewriting of the story as tragic, the Roman versions of Orpheus magnify his gender dysphoria and enmesh him in sentiment within Roman gender norms. Published in the wake of the decisive battle of Actium (31 BC), Virgil's *Georgics* ends with the emotional tale of Orpheus losing his beloved wife. As William S. Anderson points out, despite its emergence from a rather different sort of text – the *Georgics* addresses realistic agricultural or pastoral situations – the Orpheus story features the recurrent Virgilian trope of thwarted love.[18] The setting is an explanation about what to do if a farmer's swarm of

---

[14] Plato, *Symposium*, trans. Christopher Gill (London: Penguin, 1999), 179d; *Republic*, 620a.

[15] See Neil Hopkinson, ed. *A Hellenistic Anthology* (Cambridge and New York: Cambridge University Press, 1988), 45–6, for the Phanocles fragment.

[16] On Greek sexual mores, see Kenneth J. Dover, *Greek Homosexuality* (Cambridge, MA: Harvard University Press, 1989); William Armstrong Percy, *Pederasty and Pedagogy in Archaic Greece* (Urbana: University of Illinois Press, 1996). For Roman practices, see especially Craig A. Williams, *Roman Homosexuality: Ideologies of Masculinity in Classical Antiquity* (New York: Oxford University Press, 1999).

[17] For a concise review of Greek Orpheus texts, see M. Owen Lee, *Virgil as Orpheus: A Study of the Georgics* (Albany: State University of New York, 1996), 1–17. For analysis of Euripides, see pp. 4–6.

[18] William S. Anderson, "The Orpheus of Virgil and Ovid: *flebile nescio quid*," in *Orpheus: The Metamorphoses of a Myth*, ed. John Warden (University of Toronto Press, 1982), 25–50.

bees dies. To attract a new swarm, the farmer must cultivate the putrefying corpse of a calf.[19] The practice is from Egypt, Virgil says, and the origins of it were in the failure of Aristaeus' swarm. Complaining to his mother, the nymph Cyrene, about the death of his bees, Aristaeus is sent to find Proteus in Egypt. Aristaeus captures Proteus and learns that his misfortune is the result of having caused Eurydice's death. Aristaeus had pursued Eurydice intending to rape her, but she died after being bitten by a poisonous snake while fleeing him. To placate Eurydice and Orpheus, Aristaeus must sacrifice four bulls and four calves. From the rotting sacrificial corpses, Aristaeus gets his new swarm of bees. Orpheus is introduced less as a vengeful presence than a mourning present absence. His decision to seek Eurydice in the underworld is about his love for her, and Virgil's Orpheus loses his wife because of his human failing:

cum subita incautum dementia cepit amantem,	when sudden madness possessed the unwary lover,
ignoscenda quidem, scirent si ignoscere Manes:	forgivable indeed, if the spirits of the dead understood how to pardon:
restitit, Eurydicenque suam iam luce sub ipsa	he stood still, and now by the light of day,
immemor heu! victusque animi respexit	unmindful alas! and his reason overcome, he looked back at his own Eurydice.

Eurydice excuses him, universalizing his action:

Illa "quis et me" inquit "miseram et te perdidit, Orpheu,	She said, "What is this, what great madness has destroyed
quis tantus furor?"	miserable me and you, Orpheus?"[20]

In Virgil's account, the mourning Orpheus refuses to get on with his life. He rejects remarriage but does not engage in pederasty, and is dismembered by the Thracian women. His head floats down the Hebrus river to the sea singing lamentations for his lost Eurydice. As Anderson argues, Orpheus is passive, futile in his pathos, and ineffectually effeminate in comparison to the dynamic Aristaeus.[21] Virgil's Orpheus is excessively attached to his wife, undermining his manly fortitude. The tragedy, it seems, is that Eurydice is married to an enthusiastic but inept husband.

Ovid's Orpheus is also weak, but his ineptitude lies elsewhere, as does the import of his story. Ovid structures his retelling around the song in Hades which was meant to convince Pluto to let Orpheus retrieve Eurydice. Virgil's set-up with Aristaeus is eliminated, and Eurydice's death is handled with brisk

---

[19] After a long introit, the question emerges at 4:67. See Virgil, *Eclogues, Georgics, Aeneid I–VI*, trans. H. Rushton Fairclough and G. P. Goold, rev. edn. (Cambridge, MA: Harvard University Press, 2006).

[20] Latin text from Virgil, *Georgics*, IV, ll. 488–91; 494–5. (My translation.)

[21] Anderson, "The Orpheus of Virgil," See esp. pp. 33–6.

efficiency. Although regarded by critics as parodic or satirical, Ovid insists that Orpheus' song has enough efficacy that he is allowed to lead Eurydice out of the underworld.[22] When Orpheus cannot help himself and turns around, Ovid provides the excuse: "quid enim nisi se quereretur amatam?" [what could she complain of if not that she was loved?] and Eurydice is reduced to saying only "vale" [farewell].[23] Repulsed in his efforts to gain another hearing, Orpheus mourns for seven days. He then gives up, returning to the world and retreating to the mountains of Thrace, where he disavows women:

seu quod male cesserat illi,	whether because of his poor success in
sive fidem dederat; multas tamen ardor habebat	love, or whether he had given his faith for all time once. Many women grieved,
iungere se vati, multae doluere repulsae	having been repulsed. For the people of
ille etiam Thracum populis fuit auctor amorem	Thrace, he was the author of giving love to young boys and enjoying the brief
in teneros transferre mares citraque iuventam	spring and first flower of youth.[24]
aetatis breve ver et primos carpere flores	

While on his mountain, Orpheus tells tales of problematic heterosexual love, such as the story of Myrrha's incestuous desire for her father.

Orpheus the sublime poet thus reveals himself as a misogynist, insisting on the negative reading of women when a positive view might equally apply. Myrrha is an easy target, but Atalanta's physical superiority over her suitors hardly seems an example of female inferiority. In the end, the women of Thrace become enraged by Orpheus' preference for men and his slandering of women. They tear him apart literally limb from limb, but the "happy ending" of the tale is that his death allows Orpheus to join Eurydice in Hades:

hic modo coniunctis spatiantur passibus ambo,	There, hand in hand, they stroll, the two together;
nunc praecedentem sequitur, nunc praevius anteit	Sometimes he follows as she walks in front,
Eurydicenque suam iam tuto respicit Orpheus	Sometimes he goes ahead and gazes back – No danger now – at his Eurydice.[25]

---

[22] See for instance Brooks Otis, *Ovid as an Epic Poet*, 2nd edn. (Cambridge University Press, 1970), 184–5. Patricia J. Johnson, *Ovid before Exile: Art and Punishment in the "Metamorphoses"* (Madison: University of Wisconsin Press, 2008), 96–116, argues that Ovid's Orpheus presents a poem that works in that it flatters Pluto and moves him to agree to Orpheus' request. Johnson locates this sort of efficacy in the politics of the Augustan principate.

[23] Ovid, *Metamorphoses*, trans. Frank Justus Miller, revised by G. P. Goold (Cambridge, MA and London: Harvard University Press, 1977, 1984), 10:61–2.

[24] Ovid, *Metamorphoses*, 10:80–5.

[25] Ovid, *Metamorphoses*, 11:64–6. Notably, the renowned poet has no more words. His interactions in Hades are entirely gestural.

The problems of marriage in life disappear in death. Ovid's "happily ever after" consists of Orpheus playfully reminding Eurydice of her death.

Virgil and Ovid taint Orpheus with multiple species of sexual ambivalence. Some of this reflects authorial preferences. Several commentators have noted Ovid's negative attitude toward pederasty on the grounds that it denies pleasure to the younger participant:

Odi concubitus, qui non utrumque resolvunt;	I hate copulation, which does not satisfy both [men]; that is why a boy's love
Hoc est, cur pueri tangar amore minus	has less appeal.[26]

For the *Metamorphoses*, John Makowski analyses Ovid's negative views of homosexuality and effeminacy. In Book IX, Ovid uses language with respect to Iphis to emphasize his negative feelings toward female homosexuality. Iphis refers to her love for Ianthe as a "cura prodigiosa," that is, a prodigious and monstrous care. Makowski points out that, as a prologue to the "gender play" that runs throughout Book X, Iphis is made to denigrate homosexual desire in comparison to bestiality. This sets up Ovid's parodic treatment in which Orpheus is pedantic and incompetent. Orpheus' efforts to denounce women and celebrate pederasty backfire: the man–boy love stories end badly, while the women fare reasonably well. As Makowski notes, things do not look good for Eurydice when she is reunited with her misogynous, bisexual husband.[27]

The parodic narrative suggests that Orpheus' desire is impotent. The centrality of the song convincing Pluto disguises this. Claims for Orpheus' musical mastery obscure the impossibility of generative union with Eurydice. Orpheus' desire is ineffectual – he causes Eurydice's second, final death by his failure to control himself – but the song as an artifact is effective enough to get his foot in the proverbial door by means of abject flattery. His song dislocates the generative heterosexual object choice into the abstraction of "art." His turn to misogynous pederasty marks another compensatory narrative that is also conspicuous for its failure: the trees that come at the behest of his song were once virile young men, but they have been transformed and so are no longer functional in human sexual terms. Orpheus' stories of sodomitical love collapse as illustrations of successful intimacy; those of female malfeasance suggest female autonomy and sexual agency. Even Myrrha takes care of herself after

---

[26] Latin from Ovid, *Ars Amatoria*, 2:683–4 in *The Art of Love and Other Poems*, trans. J. H. Mozley; revised by G. P. Goold, 2nd edn. (Cambridge, MA: Harvard University Press, 1979). My translation is above. Among those who have noted Ovid's outburst, see for instance William Keach, "Ovid and 'Ovidian' Poetry," in *Ovid: The Classical Heritage*, ed. William S. Anderson (New York and London: Garland, 1995), 179–217. See esp. p. 196.

[27] John F. Makowski, "Bisexual Orpheus: Pederasty and Parody in Ovid," *The Classical Journal* 92:1 (1996), 25–38.

committing incest with her father. Orpheus' own compensatory narrative of pederastic desire results in his dismemberment. His head floats to Lesbos, upon which Apollo bestows Orpheus' poetic gifts. Only in (non-generative) death is Orpheus reunited with his wife.

On these terms, Virgil's version takes on a different hue as well. Instead of a contrast between successful masculinity of Aristaeus and the failure of Orpheus, consider that Aristaeus fails in his rape attempt, is responsible for Eurydice's death, and kills his own precious swarm of bees.[28] The (feminized) Orpheus has the power to restore the bees. Conversely, Ovid recounts the failure of the masculine, patriarchal model of male efficacy in marriage. None of the compensations in Ovid's version – art, misogyny, homosexuality – produce generative marital sexuality. Ovid is circuitous and his tongue seems to be planted firmly in his cheek as he highlights the consequences of marital ineptitude.

Medieval Orpheus, or polymorphous unperversity

Without pretending to exhaustive coverage, Orpheus' post-classical Christian lives translated Orpheus into idioms the evolution of which involved flattening out Orpheus' masculine perversities and rendering Eurydice as prolifically problematic.[29] Despite Orpheus' apparent incompatibility with Christian sexual ethics, early Christian grappling with Orpheus tried to appropriate him. Orpheus' supposed *Testament* enabled apologists to take him up as a syncretistic figure. Eusebius of Caesarea (275–339) utilized expressions of monotheism in the *Testament* to support his attempts to integrate Greek philosophers into Christian orthodoxy.[30] Clement of Alexandria (c.150–211/216) deployed Orpheus as a pre-figuration of Christ, and as an ancient prophet who passed

---

[28] Lee, *Virgil as Orpheus*, 17, argues that Aristaeus is an heroic figure meant to contrast with the human, flawed Orpheus. Aristaeus is a stand-in for Octavian in this reading.

[29] Considerations of Ovid and Orpheus in the Middle Ages are many, but to start, consult John Block Friedman, *Orpheus in the Middle Ages* (Cambridge, MA: Harvard University Press, 1970); Giorgio Brugnoli, "Ovidio e gli esiliati carolingi," in *Atti del Convegno Internationale Ovidiano, Sulmona, maggio 1958*, 2 vols. (Rome: Istituto di Studi romani, 1959), vol. II, 209–16, which focuses on moral exempla from a range of Ovidian texts; Franco Munari, *Ovid im Mittelalter* (Zurich and Stuttgart: Artemis, 1960) for a variety of Ovidian influences on Medieval literature; Dorothy M. Robathan, "Ovid in the Middle Ages," in *Ovid*, ed. J. W. Binns (London: Routledge & Kegan Paul, 1973), 191–209; and Françoise Joukovsky, *Orphée et ses disciples dans la poésie française et néo-latine du XVIe siècle* (Geneva: Droz, 1970), 11–31. For a more specialized study, see Neil Wright, "Creation and Recreation: Medieval Responses to *Metamorphoses* 1.5–88," in *Ovidian Transformations: Essays of the "Metamorphoses" and its Reception*, ed. Philip Hardie, Alessandro Barchiesi, and Stephen Hinds (Cambridge Philological Society, 1999), 68–84.

[30] Eusebius of Caesarea, *Eusebium Pamphili De evangelica praep[ar]atione Latiunu[m] ex Graeco beatissime pater iussu tuo effeci* (Venice: Leonhardus Aurl, 1473), unpaginated.

on divine knowledge originally given to Moses to be fulfilled by Christian revelation.[31] Early Christian art often featured Orpheus as Christ.[32] Artists elided the musician who could tame animals with his lyre and Christ the good shepherd who tamed death. While their commentaries conflated Orpheus' journey to Hades with Christ's harrowing of Hell, both Clement and Eusebius compared Orpheus unfavorably to Jesus. For Clement, the ability to charm animals was inferior to the "new song" of Christ. For Eusebius, Orpheus could only tame animal spirits, but Christ (as the Word of God) healed souls through reason.[33]

The dual impulses – negative and positive – in Christian thought produced powerful obscurantism around Orpheus' sexuality. As a peaceful figure who calmed violent souls with his music, allowed himself to be dismembered, and journeyed to Hell to redeem his beloved, Orpheus was a plausible double for Christ. But the failed husband/sodomite made Orpheus sexual, ineffectual, and morally suspect. Christian interpreters responded by attempting to rewrite Orpheus as patriarchally successful, sexually chaste, or both. In the process, the layering of Orpheus' sexuality hid Ovid's subtler critique of illusory masculinity.

In finding Orpheus inferior compared to Christ, readings such as Clement's provided the idea of Orpheus-Christ with substantive points of contact, while the four levels of interpretation advocated by Medieval exegetes gave commentators tools to dampen the implications of Orpheus' sexual modes. Called levels of "sense," the modes of interpretation were termed allegorical, natural, historical, and tropological.[34] The levels are not always distinct, but some interpreters read the *Metamorphoses* as a spiritual allegory for the Christian life, with the life of Jesus and events of the New Testament understood to be present in Ovid's fables. The tropological is closely proximate to allegorical

---

[31] Clement of Alexandria, *Stromata*, in *Ante-Nicene Fathers. Fathers of the Second Century: Hermes, Tatian, Athenagoras, Theophilis and Clement of Alexandria*, ed. A. Cleveland Coxe (Grand Rapids: Eerdmans, 1986), I, xv, 315; V, iv, 449–50; V, xii, 463. In a similar vein, Lactantius considered Orpheus in sympathy with Christian understandings of the divine. See Lactantius [Lucius Caecilius Firmianus], *Lucii Coelii* [sic] *Lactantii Firmiani, Opera quae extant, Ad fidem MSS. Recognita et Commentariis illustrata* (Oxford: Theatro Sheldoniano, 1684), 15.

[32] Friedman, *Orpheus in the Middle Ages*, 38–85. See also Eleanor Irwin, "The Songs of Orpheus and the New Song of Christ," in *Orpheus: The Metamorphosis of a Myth*, ed. John Warden (University of Toronto Press, 1982), 51–62. For ancient images, see especially Ilona J. Jesnick, *The Image of Orpheus in Roman Mosaic* (Oxford: Archaeopress, 1997).

[33] Clement of Alexandria, *Exhortation to the Greeks*, trans. G. W. Butterworth (Cambridge, MA: Harvard University Press, 2003), 3–11; Eusebius, *Nicene and Post-Nicene Fathers of the Christian Church*, ed. Philip Schaff and Henry Wace (Grand Rapids: Eerdmans, 1952), 1:603 (Chapter 14 of "Oration of Eusebius"). Clement also regarded Orpheus' poems as morally dubious; see *Exhortation*, 43, 167.

[34] A. J. Minnis, *Medieval Theory of Authorship: Scholastic Literary Attitudes in the Later Middle Ages* (London: Scholar Press, 1984), 33–5.

interpretation in that commentators shaped the tales in terms of moral types and edifying moral lessons. "Natural" interpretation related events to physical phenomena. This level includes understanding characters and events in astrological terms, since many of the pagan gods were also planetary figures. The "natural" is closely related to the historical sense, which is largely euhemeristic interpretation and rests heavily on understanding stories and characters as having factual, if historically distant, referents.

The obvious expectation might be that different kinds of interpretation resulted in different versions of Orpheus. Instead, the interpretive move imagined Orphic gender and sexual imperatives in reductive terms around Orpheus' actions, but expanded the layering around Eurydice. This double move took some time to develop. Fabius Planciades Fulgentius (fl. late fifth century) called Orpheus "best voice" and Eurydice "profound judgment" based on etymological readings of their names. Others took Orpheus' name to mean "golden."[35] In the *Consolation of Philosophy*, Anicius Manlius Severinus Boethius (c.480–c.525) allegorized Orpheus as a warning against succumbing to earthly distractions. For Boethius, Orpheus' looking back was a failure of faith.[36] Boethius saw Orpheus and Eurydice together as the human soul moving toward God through love. As Jane Chance traces in detail, William of Conches (d. 1145) expanded on the overtones in the Boethius interpretation and drew on Fulgentius to render the Orpheus story within a series of Medieval Neoplatonic concepts. The Virgilian character, Aristaeus, paradoxically (given his back-story as a would-be rapist) described as "excellence," follows Eurydice because she is "desire," and she dies because she is "earthly pleasure." The descent into the underworld represents corporeality, worldliness, and Hell. When Orpheus succumbs to worldly temptation, dies, and is reborn into greater understanding, he achieves a kind of Neoplatonic ascent to the good.[37]

With Orpheus increasingly seen in salvific terms, open season on Eurydice began in earnest. When Nicolas Trevet (d. 1334), for instance, described

---

[35] Fabius Planciades Fulgentius, *C. Iulii Hygini Augusti Liberti Fabularum Liber, Ad Omnium poëtarum lectionem mire necessarius & ante hac nunquam excusus* (Basle: Joan Hervagium, 1535), 153. See also BN MS lat. 9323, fol. 95r.

[36] Anicius Manlius Severinus Boethius, *The Consolation of Philosophy*, trans., ed., and intro. William Anderson (Carbondale: Southern Illinois University Press, 1963), 82–3 (bk. 3, poem 12). For the influence of Boethius, see especially Pierre Paul Courcelle, *La Consolation de philosophie dans la tradition littéraire: antécédents et postérité de Boèce* (Paris: Etudes augustiniennes, 1967).

[37] Jane Chance, *Medieval Mythography from Roman North Africa to the School of Chartres, AD 433–1177* (Gainesville: University Press of Florida, 1994), 409–18. On different forms of Neoplatonism, including the influences of Plotinus and Avicenna, see Laura Westra, "Love and Beauty in Ficino and Plotinus," in *Ficino and Renaissance Neoplatonism*, ed. Konrad Eisenbichler and Olga Zorzi Pugliese (Toronto: Dovehouse, 1986), 175–87, and Giuseppe Saitta, *Il pensiero italiano nell'umanismo e nel Rinascimento*, vol. I, *L'Umanismo* (Bologna: Cesare Zuffi, 1949), 509–75, esp. 510 and 537.

Aristaeus as virtue and Orpheus as intellect, Eurydice became affection and folly.[38] The generosity of Fulgentius and the suggestive minimalism of Boethius gave way to disparaging assessments of Eurydice that magnified the incipient misogyny of the Ovidian set-up. John of Garland, an Englishman trained at Oxford who taught at Paris and Toulouse, called Orpheus a "vir ratio," but Eurydice is included as "wife" in a list that also includes "snake," "poison," and "flesh."[39] Variously lusty, flighty, or just difficult, Eurydice died (whether pursued by Aristaeus or as the victim of the snake without the implicit threat of rape) because, commentators insisted, her end was an appropriate allegorical lesson about what happens to a lusty woman.[40]

More systematic moralized reading in the *Allegoriae super Ovidii Metamorphosin* (c.1175) by Arnulf d'Orléans used Eurydice's supposed perfidy to obscure Orpheus' perversity. Drawing on Fulgentius' etymologies, Hades became Hell, and the fields in which Eurydice and the nymphs frolicked represented worldly enticement. Eurydice starts identified as good judgment, but becomes immersed in worldly pleasure and dies. Her death is her own fault, and because she is a woman. She falls back into Hell: "Mulieres siquidem proniores sunt in libidinem et vicia quam viri" [Women are indeed more prone to libidinous things and vices than men].[41] As Kathryn L. McKinley observes, "Arnulf (as with many other commentators) recasts the myth to obfuscate Orpheus' homosexual behavior after the loss of his wife." In Arnulf's version, Orpheus

---

[38] On Trevet, see Pierre Paul Courcelle, "Etude critique sur les commentaires de la 'Consolation' de Boèce (IX–XVe siècles)," *Archives d'histoire doctrinale et littéraire du Moyen Age* 12 (1939): 5–140.

[39] "Pratum delicie, coniunx caro, vipera virus, / Vir ratio, Stix est terra, loquela lira." [The field is delights, the wife is flesh, the viper is poison / The man is reason, Stix is earth, the lyre is eloquence.] John of Garland, *Integumenta Ovidii: poemetto inedito del secolo XIII*, ed. Fausto Ghisalberti (Milan: Principato, 1933), 67 (ll. 407–8). The *Integumenta* was composed before 1241, and probably in 1234. For dating and more on Garland's corpus, see Louis John Paetow, "*Morale Scolarium* of John of Garland (Johannes de Garlandia), A Professor in the Universities of Paris and Toulouse in the Thirteenth Century," in *Memoirs of the University of California* 4.2 (1927), 65–258. See pp. 109, 118 for dating. See also BN MSS lat. 8010 fol. 1ff. and 8008, fol. 153ff. (Guillelmus de Thiegiis prose commentary).

[40] Occasionally, Orpheus was the concupiscent one. See Colucio Salutati, *Colucii Salutati de laboribus Herculis*, ed. B. L. Ullman, 2 vols. (Zurich: Thesauri Mundi, 1951), 2: 503. (Book 4).

[41] BL MS Burney 224, fol. 188v. For a readily available version Arnulf of Orléans, *Allegoriae*, in *Arnolfo d'Orléans, un cultore di Ovidio nel secolo XII*, ed. Fausto Ghisalberti, *Memorie del Reale Istituto lombardo di scienze e lettere* 24 (Milan: Libraio del R. Istituto Lombardo di scienze e lettere, 1932), 157–234. On Eurydice's death, see p. 222. See Frank T. Coulson and Bruno Roy, *Incipitarium Ovidianum: A Finding Guide for Texts in Latin Related to the Study of Ovid in the Middle Ages and Renaissance* (Turnhout: Brepols, 2000), 83, n. 3 for types of glosses in Arnulf's corpus. Among the manuscripts that include Arnulf's commentary are BN MSS lat. 7996, 8001, 8010, 14135; Reims, Bibliothèque municipale MS 1262, fols. 2–25; Saint-Omer, Bibliothèque municipale MSS 670, 678, fols. 104r–111r. I consulted BL MS Burney 224, fols. 108r–130v for the commentary on Books 10 and 11; the gloss runs from 181v–191r. The integumenta are also partial and incomplete in BL MS Royal 12.E.XI, fols. 146r–179v. For Orpheus, see fols. 172r–178v.

transfers his affections to properly virile men instead of weak women: "sed amorem suum ad mares [sic] i. viriliter agentes transtulit" [but [he] transferred his love to men, to those acting manly, that is].[42] Arnulf is unusual in including the turn to men, an aspect that many of those who worked from Boethius avoided mentioning.[43] But Arnulf's denigration of women is the means of evasion. Misogyny here protects the Christianized text from pederasty.

The collective effect of demonizing Eurydice was that allegory increasingly excused Orpheus. Consider the *Ovide moralisé*, which warns against marriage through the allegorization around Eurydice. Probably the work of a Franciscan and produced originally in the early fourteenth century,[44] the *Ovide moralisé* was popular enough to survive in nineteen manuscripts before its first publication (with some alterations) in 1484.[45] For the author, Aristaeus is virtue, Orpheus is reason, and Eurydice is sensuality. The marriage is the union of reason and sensuality, but Eurydice falls into sin when she steps on the serpent, which is mortal vice. Eurydice's failure is disobedience to reason:

Par Orpheüs puis droitement   [By Orpheus then by right
Noter regnable entendement,   To note as ruling reason
Et par Euridice sa fame   And by Eurydice his wife
La sensualité de l'ame.   The sensuality of the soul.
Ces deux choses par mariage   These two things by marriage
Sont jointes en l'umain lignage.   Are joined in human lineage.
. . . Mes quant la sensualité   . . . But as for sensuality

[42] BL MS Burney 224, fol. 188v; Kathryn L. McKinley, *Reading the Ovidian Heroine: "Metamorphoses" Commentaries 1100–1618* (Leiden: Brill, 2001), 67. My reading of Arnulf is influenced by McKinley's analysis of his text. For the printed text, see Arnulf of Orleans, *Arnolfo*, 222. Giovanni del Virgilio solves the problem by making Orpheus a monk and the turning-away from women is his marriage to Christ. See BL MS Harley 1014, fols. 12r–57r, *Allegorie librorum ovidii* (Exposito moral fabulam extram ex methamorfoseo ovidii). Orpheus is discussed on fols. 43v–44v, 46v–47r. Giovanni del Virgilio is discussed in Friedman, *Orpheus in the Middle Ages*, 122–4.

[43] The so-called "Vulgate" commentary, a teaching text that dates back to about 1250 and was produced originally in central France, relies heavily on Arnulf. It also comments tersely on the sexual aspects of Orpheus' story, including one striking formulation describing the journey to the underworld as "contra naturam" – language usually associated with sodomy. On the "Vulgate," see Frank T. Coulson, *The "Vulgate" Commentary on Ovid's "Metamorphoses": The Creation Myth and the Story of Orpheus* (Toronto: Centre for Medieval Studies, 1991). See p. 121 for the "nature" language.

[44] See Renate Blumenfeld-Kosinki, *Reading Myth: Classical Mythology and Its Interpretations in Medieval French Literature* (Palo Alto: Stanford University Press, 1997), 90, on the Franciscan identification; A. J. Minnis and A. B. Scott, eds., with the assistance of David Wallace, *Medieval Literary Theory and Criticism, c. 1100–1375: The Commentary Tradition* (Oxford and New York: Clarendon, 1988), 318 dates it to 1316–1328. On the complicated manuscript history and relationship to Arnulf d'Orléans, John of Garland, and Pierre Bersuire, see Joseph Engels, *Etudes sur l'Ovide moralisé* (Groningen: Wolters, 1945), esp. 3–62.

[45] Anon., *Ovide moralisé, poème du commencement du quatorzième siècle, publié d'après tous les manuscrits connus*, ed. Cornelius de Boer, Martina G. de Boer, and Jeanette Th. M. van't Sant, 5 vols. (Amsterdam: J. Müller, 1915–1938), vol. I, 44–52.

Qui trop s'esloigne folement	Which too madly separates itself
De raisonable entendement,	From reasonable understanding,
. . . Et marche par consentement	. . . And walks by consent
Sor le serpent de mortel vice	On the serpent that is mortal vice
Qui gist souz la vaine delice.	Which lurks beneath the vain delights.[46]

Orpheus is once again excused for turning around and letting Eurydice die her second death. The author deflects in the mode of Ovid:

| Mes ne puet de lui blasmer | But do not blame him |
| Se ne se plaint de trop amer | One should not be blamed for loving too much.[47] |

The consequences for Eurydice are less important than the (initial) intentions of Orpheus.

But if poor Orpheus is not to blame for loving Eurydice too much, his subsequent behavior makes one wonder. He is ineffectual and despondent over Eurydice's fate, and, for three years, he goes without a wife or concubine and: "Si fuit toute amour femeline. / Toutes demes mist en refu." Until finally, "D'amour femeline et à faire / Des joennes malles lor deduit, / Dont or sont cil de Trace duit" [As if fleeing all feminine love / in refusing all women / to contradict all feminine love / and make young men by whom those of Thrace are now taught]. The descent of Orpheus into Hell is reason coming to understand vice. Turning around is leaving behind sensuality, and turning to men is fleeing the temptations of sexual pleasure with women:

C'est tous ceulz qui metent lor cure	It is all which gold can cure
En vaines cogitacions	In vain cogitations
Et aus vilz delectacions	And in vile delectation
Ou li mol femelin s'atendent.	Where soft feminine things await him.[48]

Orpheus seeks out boys because they are "pure" and "full of ignorance." Orpheus flees feminine love in favor of the masculine: "Foï toute amour femeline / Si se prist à la masculine." [Flee all feminine love / And take oneself to the masculine].[49] But in engaging with the pederastic aspect of the original, the allegorizing of the *Ovide moralisé* takes a surprising turn. The author expresses the Pauline anxiety that not wanting women can be a problem: "Primes à mortelment pechier / Contre nature et contre loi" [First to mortally sin / against nature and against the law]. Ovid's description of the turn to men is transformed into a warning against so doing:

---

[46] *Ovide moralisé*, book 10: ll. 220–5; 231–3; 241–3.
[47] *Ovide moralisé*, book 10: ll. 158–9. See 10: ll.148–53 for the turning-back moment.
[48] *Ovide moralisé*, book 10: ll. 179–80; 193–5, and 559–62 for the quotations; 401–3 on reason and vice and 412–15 on sensuality.
[49] *Ovide moralisé*, book 10: ll. 568, 590–1.

Les males amours que mouvoient	The bad loves that move
Cil que li fol pour dieus tenoient,	him who crazy for the gods becomes,
Qui les joennes malles amoient	who loves young men
Et l'amour de femes blasmoient,	and blames the love of women
Si tesmoignoit en sa doctrine	If he witnesses in his doctrine
Que miex vault l'amour masculine	that masculine love is better
Que cele aux femes ne faisoit.	than not making it to women.[50]

The solution to Orpheus' turnings – away from Eurydice and to men – would seem to support Orpheus as a lesson in marriage within the Christianized terms of the text. Orpheus gets dismembered because he not only returns to sin, but to worse sin after his wife dies. Once again, the author swerves in another direction entirely, connecting Orpheus with Christ ("Orpheüs denote à delivre / Jhesu Christ parole devine"; Orpheus denotes the delivery / of the divine word of Jesus Christ).[51] The author subsumes Orpheus' bad behavior – as a bad husband and a sodomitical subject – under the association of Orpheus with the son of God.

Heaping on meanings obscured failure by sheer proliferation. Pierre Bersuire (Petrus Berchorius, 1290?–1362) incorporated allegorical readings from Arnulf, the *Ovide moralisé*, and Fulgentius, among others.[52] Bersuire's allegories are often contradictory, but Ann Moss argues that Bersuire was unconcerned about inconsistency. A French Benedictine, Bersuire aimed to provide illustrative materials from which preachers might draw for their sermons.[53] Bersuire renders everything first in literal terms, and then offers multiple allegorical and tropological glosses.[54] The stretched allegories of the *Ovide moralisé* give way to unapologetically conflicting readings. At one point, Orpheus turning his back on Eurydice is renouncing marriage in favor of Scripture and religion; at another, Orpheus loses his soul like those who fall away from Christianity after being converted; at yet another, Orpheus (as Christ) is

---

[50] *Ovide moralisé*, book 10: ll. 2523–4; 2528–34. BL Additional MS 10324, fol. 214v uses the "sa doctrine" language in the same context, but the poem is otherwise considerably different. The reference is also in the explications of Book 11.

[51] *Ovide moralisé*, book 11: ll. 178–9.

[52] De Boer does not see the *Ovide moralisé* in Bersuire's corpus, but others do. See for instance Minnis and Scott, eds., *Medieval Literary Theory*, 318.

[53] Ann Moss, *Ovid in Renaissance France: A Survey of the Latin Editions of Ovid and Commentaries in France before 1600* (London: Warburg Institute / University of London, 1982), 25. See also Frank Coulson, "Hitherto Unedited Medieval and Renaissance Lives of Ovid (I)," *Mediaeval Studies* 49 (1987): 152–207. See p. 160. As Terence Cave, *The Cornucopian Text: Problems of Writing in the French Renaissance* (Oxford: Clarendon, 1979), 95, points out, the didactic practice remained a habit in French translation and commentary in other contexts as well. The translation of Erasmus's *Praise of Folly* in 1520 and the moralized version *Roman de la Rose* produced in the late 1520s worked similarly.

[54] For an introduction to Bersuire's text, see Fausto Ghisalberti, *L' "Ovidius Moralizatus" di Pierre Bersuire* (Rome: Ditta Topografia Cuggiani, 1933). For context more broadly, see Charles Samaran and Jacques Monfrin, "Pierre Bersuire, prieur de St-Eloi de Paris," *Histoire littéraire de la France* 39 (1962): 259–450. See pp. 336–45 on Ovid.

successful in his harrowing of Hell. Rather than tagging on the Orpheus/Christ reading, Bersuire embraces it and rewrites the story in a happy mode:

Quod videns Orpheus Christus in infernum personaliter voluit descendere & sic uxorem suam. i. humanam naturam rehabuit, ipsamque de regno tenebrarum ereptam ad superos secum duxit, dicens illud Canticorum. ii. "Surge, propera amica mea & veni."	Thus seeing Christ, Orpheus wished to descend to hell personally and in this way, he re-held his wife, that is human nature, snatching her away from the realm of darkness, and to the upper world with him he led her, saying this from Canticles 2: "Rise up, my fair love and come".[55]

While this is good for Orpheus, Eurydice is blamed for the events that befall her. Bersuire's Eurydice dies as the sinner returning to the sin like a "dog returning to his vomit." While Bersuire allows that Orpheus loved his wife too much, which led to concupiscence,[56] women are consistently dangerous for Bersuire. Because loving women too much was considered a sign of masculine weakness, Bersuire (following Arnulf) emphasized that Orpheus rejected effeminacy and embraced properly masculine pursuits.[57] The Thracian women who dismember Orpheus are variously tyrants who persecuted early Christians, the Jews who killed Christ, or simply lusty women of the sort that manly men ought to avoid.[58] Orpheus has not one, but many excuses, and women (Eurydice and the Baccantae) are the recipients of not occasional, but recurrent misogyny.

Underscoring this dynamic is the ellipsis around sodomy. Bersuire comments that Orpheus rejects women ("obhorrere copulam omnium mulierum" [abhorring copulation with all women]), but omits the sexual language about Orpheus' preference for young men.[59] Is it that Bersuire's angry women do not need the additional complication of Orpheus becoming a sodomite and pederast? Or that

---

[55] Pierre Bersuire, *Metamorphosis Ovidiana, moraliter explanata* (Paris: Ascensianis et sub Pelicano, 1509), fol. LXXIIIr. The subject is unclear, but because of the reflexive pronoun, Orpheus seems the logical choice. Among the manuscripts, see BN MSS lat. 8019, 8020, 8123, 8253a, 14136, 15145, 16787; BN MS nouv. acq. lat. 1830; Bibliothèque Mazarine, MS 3876 (591); Saint-Omer, Bibliothèque municipale MS 662; Troyes, Bibliothèque municipale MSS 1627, 1634. For the manuscript history, see Frank Coulson, "A Checklist of Newly Discovered Manuscripts of Pierre Bersuire's *Ovidius moralizatus*," *Scriptorium* 51 (1997): 164–86.

[56] "[T]anquam canis ad vomitum mentaliter revertuntur." Bersuire, *Metamorphosis Ovidiana*, fol. LXXIIIr. The imagery of the dog returning to its vomit appears recurrently, including in the *Ovide moralisé*, book 10: ll. 532–6.

[57] On the relationship between effeminacy and masculinity in the Middle Ages, see for instance R. Howard Bloch, *Medieval Misogyny and the Invention of Western Romantic Love* (University of Chicago Press, 1991), 113–42.

[58] Bersuire, *Metamorphosis Ovidiana*, fols. LXXIIIv–LXXIIIIv. The allegory of the Thracian women as the Jews who killed Christ is repeated by several commentators. It figures extensively in the Anon., *Ovide moralisé en prose* (Texte du quinzième siècle), ed. C. de Boer (Amsterdam: North-Holland Publishing, 1954), 268–9. Produced in 1466–1467, this version of Ovid had limited circulation, but the comment in the text indicates the persistence of the idea of Orpheus as a sodomite. On the textual history, see pp. 3–5.

[59] Bersuire, *Metamorphosis Ovidiana*, fol. LXXIIIv. Bersuire, departing from Ovid's scheme, includes Orpheus' death in Book 10 and begins Book 11 with Midas.

Bersuire is leery of hinting that male homosexuality could displace marriage? The evasion of homosexuality can be read as indifference, but even those who (following John Boswell) read the Middle Ages as tolerant of homosexuality allow that it became intolerant in the twelfth century.[60] Mathew Kuefler has argued that political and religious officials, particularly in France, demonized male intimacy as sodomitical in order to emphasize obedience to secular and ecclesiastical authority. This process included tainting noble military elites with effeminacy as a means of social control.[61] Bersuire's deflection of homosexuality involves the double violence of silencing and misogyny congruent with such an agenda.

To be sure, not all treatments disregarded the implications of sodomy in the Orpheus story. *The Romance of the Rose* reviled Orpheus:

those who will never keep to the straight track, but instead go overturning the plow, who confirm their evil rules by abnormal exceptions when they want to follow Orpheus (he did not know to plow or write or forge in the true forge – may he be hanged by the throat! – when he showed himself so evil toward Nature by contriving such rules for them).[62]

Death to the sodomite is unambiguous in its sentiments. But draconian language, like draconian enforcement of the law, was less common than milder condemnation.[63] In the *Ovide moralisé en prose*, the author, who abridged much from the earlier poetic text, retained the reference to Orpheus rejecting women and complained that he, "amuser follement à pecher par sodomye, contre nature" [amused himself foolishly by sinning through sodomy, against nature]. In case the author's disapproval was not plain enough, he added: "Dont il fist mal" [Thus he did evil].[64] That said, echoes of earlier interpretations undermine the condemnation to a degree. The exposition of the tale still describes Orpheus as "entendement raisonnable" [reasonable understanding], while Eurydice is "la sensualité humaine" [human sensuality]. She dies because she abandoned herself to mortal vice. Once Eurydice's guilt has been brought to the fore, Orpheus' pederasty slips away. The author refuses to comment on Orpheus'

[60] Boswell, *Christianity, Social Tolerance, and Homosexuality*, and for instance R. I. Moore, *The Formation of a Persecuting Society: Authority and Deviance in Western Europe, 950–1250* (Oxford: Blackwell, 1987).
[61] Mathew Kuefler, "Male Friendship and the Suspicion of Sodomy in Twelfth-Century France," in *The Boswell Thesis: Essays on Christianity, Social Tolerance and Homosexuality*, ed. Mathew Kuefler (University of Chicago Press, 2006), 179–212.
[62] Guillaume de Lorris and Jean de Meun, *The Romance of the Rose*, trans. Charles Dahlberg, 3rd edn. (Princeton University Press, 1995), 324. As Dahlberg notes, the language recalls Alain de Lille's *De planctu*, col. 449 C, which also condemns Orpheus for unnatural sexual proclivities. On *De planctu*, see Susan Schibanoff, "Sodom's Mark: Alan of Lille, Jean de Meun, and the Medieval Theory of Authorship," in *Queering the Middle Ages*, eds. Glen Burger and Steven F. Kruger (Minneapolis and London: University of Minnesota Press, 2001), 28–56.
[63] For negative attitudes in Medieval Europe, see for instance Louis Crompton, *Homosexuality and Civilization* (Cambridge, MA and London: Belknap Press, 2003), 178–212.
[64] *Ovide moralisé en prose*, 257.

return to the living, choosing instead to recount stories of Orpheus as an incomparable musician. In the interpretation of these episodes, the author expands on the insistence in the *Ovide moralisé* that Orpheus is the figure for Christ. His harp can release souls from Hell; the beautiful music he produces is the commandments of God and the articles of faith; his example of accepting death is a rebuke to worldly sinners.[65] Despite the revenge of the women of Thrace for his rejection of them and his preference for male company, Orpheus/Jesus is apparently an innocent lamb.

As with the twisty tales of Ovid, our story takes another turn before the French begin to engage earnestly with the implications of Renaissance textual practices in the late fifteenth century. At least one text indicates incipient signs that the Medieval Orpheus did not sit entirely well with sensitive readers. Initially printed in 1484 by Colard Mansion, *La Bible des poëtes* took Bersuire as its basis, but added to each episode. The effect was to suggest how to imagine significance in not entirely Christian terms. Many of the retellings are familiar. The author merges Virgil and Ovid so that Aristaeus chases the newlywed Eurydice, but she runs, "Car trop et de bon cueur aimoit son nouvel espoux orpheus" [Because she loved her new husband Orpheus too much and with a good heart].[66] Orpheus laments as usual, and then goes to Hell, where his song features the refrain, "Erudice [sic] demande seulement" [Eurydice only [I] request]. Again, we are not to blame Orpheus when he turns around because he loved her too much ["trop aymer"]. As in some earlier versions, Orpheus' rejection of women may be because he promised Eurydice fidelity or because he had soured on women:

Or ne scay la cause pourquoy, ou pour ce quil la voit promise a erudice, ou pour ce que tant fuy en estoit mesadvenu, mais toutes femmes avoit en hayne, refus et desdaign.

Now one does not know the reason why, or if it is because he promised Eurydice, or because enough had come to pass, but he held all women in hatred, refusal and disdain.

But the explication of the tale moves, albeit hesitantly, in new directions. In the "Sens historial" and without heavy allegorical embellishment, the commentary announces that Orpheus turned to young men seeking comfort in his mourning. The significance is a moral lesson; not an allegorical one, and the framing, while invoking God, uses the language of nature, rather than Christianity: "Trop est

---

[65] *Ovide moralisé en prose*, 254–69.
[66] *La Bible des poëtes, Métamorphose d'Ovide moralisé par Thomas Walleys et traduite par Colard Mansion* (Paris: A. Venard, 1484), fol. cviii(r). There were six editions between 1484 and 1531 under several titles. Thomas Walleys is a misattribution based on a conflation of John of Garland and Walleys. I have utilized a paginated edition and consulted P. Ovidius Naso, *Cy commence Ovide de Salmonen son livre intitule Methamorphose. Contenant xv livres particuliers moralisie par maistre Thomas Whaleys docteur en theologie de Tolose sainct dominique Translate & Compile par Colard mansion en la noble ville de Bruges* (Paris: Anthoine Verard, 1484).

oultre mesure cruel et contre nature ce vice" [This vice is too cruel a measure and against nature].[67] The *Bible des poëtes* does not allegorize at anything like the rate of earlier French versions, but it also lacks the historical apparatus or understanding of antiquity and offers only a basic moral message.

This simplification is apparent in the treatment of sin as a failure of reason – a theme that reached back to antiquity but which, in the Ovidian tradition of the Middle Ages, had been rendered in elaborate allegorical terms. Instead, the *Bible des poëtes* shapes the Orpheus story around marriage as producing social order through generation. In case the message that marriage is good and sodomy is bad was not clear enough, the account of the death of Orpheus emphasizes that the Thracian women were angered by "sa doctrine," identified as, "le mauvais traistre que les hommes & les jouvenceaulx attrait a lui" [the evil trait that he attracts men and young boys to himself].[68] Bonds between men, especially sexual ones, are repudiated. Collectively, the iterations for women and against men amount to the idealization of marriage through the occluding of other possibilities. Orpheus renounces women because he promised to be faithful to his wife, so he turns to homosociality. At the same time, marriage is a disappointment, and so he turns to men. The condemnations of sodomy indicate that "right" relations with men are not unproblematically a possibility. Marriage becomes the way to preserve the virtue of men. Not just the demonization of sodomy, marriage is the only state in which sex and virtue can be united, and they are linked against the bonds between and among men.

Something is afoot in the world of Orpheus mythography. To render Orpheus in Christian terms, early Medieval commentators of course bowdlerized the ancient texts, but even more, they did tremendous violence to Eurydice as part of a textual strategy to protect Orpheus' Christian significance. The interplay of Orphic incompetence around sexuality that saturated Ovid's tale disappeared in favor of the Orpheus/Christ whose sexual foibles could be laid at the feet of the wife he fails to save. Textually, the *Bible des poëtes* is a hybrid, emerging from the Medieval Christian multiplicities of Bersuire, but moving away from Bersuire's insistent allegories of Christian revelation. The logic of the *Bible des poëtes* is determined by notions of social order and not by Christian revelation. The commentary does not lack intense interest in context and historically proper understanding of Ovid, but the author does not yet have the vocabulary or skills to read Orpheus outside the Medieval Christian box.

Renaissance Orpheus: whither polymorphous possibility?

In many ways, Renaissance treatments of Orpheus look the same as Medieval ones. In addition to the intertextual appropriations, Renaissance humanists

---

[67] *La Bible des poëtes*, fol. cviii(v).   [68] *La Bible des poëtes*, fols. cxixr–cxixv.

reveled in the layered, often contradictory meanings in the text.[69] But the overriding interest in Medieval versions was to make Orpheus useful for Christian consumption. Christian allegorists were unconcerned, often uninformed, about anachronism or historical context. As Renaissance textual practices spread and the knowledge of antiquity grew, the insistence on Orpheus' identifications with Christian meanings gave way to readings that grappled with Orpheus as a man and a husband. Renaissance analysis rediscovered the emphasis on men and masculinity that had been central to the story in antiquity. Homosociality and pederasty accordingly ballooned as textual problematics. Renaissance attempts to render Orpheus in historically accurate terms facilitated both normative and subversive sexual appropriations.

Orpheus understood as the consummate poet and musician made these developments possible. With increased knowledge of antiquity but largely lacking the interest in the ironic and parodic elements in Virgilian and Ovidian accounts of Orpheus, early Renaissance humanists celebrated the Thracian bard as a figure of the civilizing artist and poet. Italian Neoplatonist Marsilio Ficino, who routinely cast himself as the new Orpheus, saw Orpheus as the prophet of divine order signaled in musical harmony.[70] Ficino and Giovanni Pico della Mirandola regarded Orpheus as the originator of much of Greek religious thought. For Angelo Poliziano, Orpheus was the presiding figure in an idyllic pastoral past.[71] These versions of Orpheus emerged from the gradual accumulation of knowledge about and understanding of antiquity, and were reflected in the attention humanists and educators paid to Ovid. Routinely used as teaching texts, Ovid's poetic works offered a wealth of information about ancient mores, customs, and material conditions. Because of this, Ovid was among the most popular of the ancient authors, and the *Metamorphoses* was his most republished and analyzed text. The work of prestigious commentators circulated across Europe with the influential commentary of the Italian Raphael Regius (c.1440–1520) setting the standard. Contributions by the likes of Georg Schuler or Sabinus (1508–1560), a German Protestant based in Königsburg, the Dutchman Gilbertus Longolius (1507–1543), and another German Protestant, Jacobus Micyllus (d. 1558; also called Jakob Moltzer or Molshem) developed the Regius commentary to its full extent. The *Metamorphoses* proved quite adaptable. It still provided material for preachers, but it was amenable to humanist

---

[69] The habit remained even after Bersuire's text was placed on the Index at the Council of Trent in 1559. See Moss, *Ovid in Renaissance France*, 27.

[70] See for instance John Warden, "Orpheus and Ficino," in *Orpheus: The Metamorphosis of a Myth*, ed. John Warden (University of Toronto Press, 1982) 85–110; D. P. Walker, "Orpheus the Theologian and the Renaissance Platonists," *Journal of the Warburg and Courtauld Institutes* 16 (1953): 100–20.

[71] See Angelo Poliziano, *La Favola di Orfeo composta da M. Angelo Poliziano, e ridotta ora la prima volta all sua vera e sincera lezione* (Padua: G. Comino, 1749). Originally published in 1472.

interpretation and methodology.[72] Humanists reduced the recourse to allegory in favor of an emphasis on rhetoric and context. This vein of new/old knowledge remapped Orpheus' sexual proclivities.

Ovid offered life lessons, but in the case of Orpheus, these entailed rereading the sexual aspects in ways that effaced Medieval, Catholic readings. Beginning with Regius, Renaissance commentators elided Medieval sexual solutions with a blend of historical interpretation, literary analysis, and moral suasion.[73] Humanistic critical methods produced an interest in understanding antiquity on its own terms. In Ovid, commentators recognized social values of ancient Rome that continued to apply in Christian society a millennium and a half later. The duty of the commentator was to bring out the rhetorical, grammatical, historical, artistic, and philosophical aspects of the text to make these values evident. Doing so reflected knowledge of the ancient context so as to avoid anachronism, reflected the commentator's scholarly erudition, and taught that morality had to be understood in historical context.

These priorities meant that Renaissance usage privileged historical and tropological interpretation at the expense of allegorical reading. The impetus behind historical interpretation came from humanist interest in the circumstances of antiquity, as well as an increasingly sophisticated ability to analyze historical change based on knowledge of language, material conditions, events, and chronology.[74] Tropological interpretation enabled the recuperation of pagan poetry for acceptable ends in Christian society. Conversely, humanists scoffed at the propensity toward anachronism that marked allegorical reading. Attacks on allegorists found an ally in the Catholic Church, which condemned allegorical Christianization of pagan texts in 1559.[75]

---

[72] Moss, *Ovid in Renaissance France*, 66–79. See also Henri Lamarque, "L'édition des œuvres d'Ovide dans la Renaissance française," in *Ovide en France dans la Renaissance* (Toulouse: Service des publications de l'Université de Toulouse–Le Mirail, 1981), 13–40.

[73] See for instance Ovid, *Fabularum Ovidii Interpretatio, Tradita in Academia Regiomonta, a Georgio Sabino* (Wittenberg: Clemens Schleich & Antonius Schöne, 1572). Compare this with the bare-bones summaries of Ovid, [*Metamorphoses*], ed. Bonus Accursius (Milan: Philip de Lavagnia, 1475). The edition is lavish in ornament, but without a title page, pagination, or signatures. The commentary is brief and blunt. Of Orpheus' rejection of women, Accursius says simply, "Postea dolore ac flaetu finito ne rursus coniugale desyderium experiretur: puerilem venerem instituit" [Once his pain and grief were over, he had no wish to try marriage again; he began the practice of boy-love] (unpag.; fabula i). This is not to say that all late Medieval commentators were comfortable with Orphic sexuality. See Ovid, [*Metamorphoses*] ed. Johannes Andreae (Leuven: Joannes de Westphalia, 1471), in which the Baccantae kill Orpheus for "spurning marriage." See sig. qiii(r). The text is without a title page, and while 1471 appears in the colophon, 1475 is sometimes given as the publication date.

[74] On these priorities for Renaissance scholars, see Anthony Grafton, *Joseph Scaliger: A Study in the History of Classical Scholarship*, 2 vols. (Oxford: Clarendon, 1983–1993).

[75] Moss, *Ovid in Renaissance France*, 27. Moss notes that commentaries omitted much of the allegory when reprinted after 1559.

Orpheus' Renaissance life began in earnest with the humanist commentary on the *Metamorphoses* by Regius initially published in Venice in 1493.[76] Regius's commentary found favor with humanists, pedagogues, and just plain readers.[77] Regius's frequently reprinted (and pirated) commentary situated Ovidian moral lessons along the lines of Renaissance values. His dedicatory eulogy of Francesco Gonzaga emphasizes liberality, justice, temperance, magnanimity, and military prowess as crucial characteristics of a well-rounded prince. Moral lessons grow from Ovid's vast erudition about his world, and Regius stresses that Ovid must be seen in context. The consequences of vice and virtue remain attached to Ovidian characters without remaking them into Christians before the spread of Christian revelation.

Regius uses his apparatus of knowledge to construct the Orpheus story so that it turns on an implicit model of the proper performance of marriage. Regius insists that the danger of men refusing marriage is the violence it provokes in women. Without male authority and guidance,

omnes aspernatus mulieres dicitur, primusque apud Thraces puerorum amoribus indulsisse. Id vero aegre ferentes Thraciae mulieres sacra Bacchi celebrantes illum cithara canentem ferasque mulcentem discerpserunt: cuius caput una cum cithara in Hebrum proiectum.	it is said he had contempt for all women and indulged his love for the boys of Thrace before them. Taking this badly, the women of Thrace, celebrating rites sacred to Bacchus, dismembered him who was singing and charming wild things with that zither: whose head with the zither were thrown into the Hebrus.[78]

---

[76] There were teaching texts that eliminated the Medieval accretions before Regius, but they were often spare in the extreme, offering little more than abbreviated summaries of the Ovidian tales. See in this vein Donatus, *Donati grammatici peritissimi fabularum breviatio Ovidii nasonis elegans et luccinta* (n. p.: no pub., n.d. [1480?]). Donatus mentions that Orpheus rejected women and instituted love between men. (Unpaginated; Liber X narrationes.)

[77] The first legal edition appeared as Ovid, *Metamorphoseos libri cum commento, Raph. Regii* (Venice: B. Locatellus for Oct. Scotus, 1493). Bartholomaeus Merula produced two pirated editions in 1492 and 1493. Regius sued Merula, and put out his authorized version instead. See Grundy Steiner, "Source-Editions of Ovid's *Metamorphoses* (1471–1500)," *Transactions of the American Philological Association* 82 (1951): 219–31, esp. 229–31. The first French edition was published in Paris in 1496, and some sixty editions followed by 1600, printed largely in France and Italy. In 1510, an enlarged edition with brief arguments drawn from Lactantius and tropological *enarratio* appeared under the title *P. Ovidii Nasonis Metamorphoseos libri moralizati*. For Lactantius, see *Lucii Coelii Lactantii Firmiani*. A translation of much of Lactantius, including *Of the False Worship of the Gods*, which provides much of the material for the Ovid argumenta, was also available. See Lactantius, *The Works of Lactantius*, trans. William Fletcher, ed. Alexander Roberts and James Donaldson, vol. XXI (Edinburgh: T. & T. Clark, 1871).

[78] Ovid, *P. Ovidii Nasonis Poetae Sulmonensis Opera Quae Vocantur Amatoria, cum Doctorum Virorum Commentariis partim huscusque etiam alibi editis, partim iam primum adiectis: quorum omnium Catalogum versa pagina reperies. His accesserunt Iacobi Micylli Annotationes* (Basle: Ioannem Hervagium, 1549), 227. Citations will be from this edition, which incorporates Regius's later additions and other addenda. Where there are discrepancies from earlier editions

Regius then explains the setting, such as ancient beliefs about the location of the door to Hell. In 1517, Regius added information about Hecate, Persephone, and the meanings of serpents that appear in ancient fables. We hear about Latona, Jupiter, and Cerberus; the geography of Thrace; and the opinions of Diodorus, Homer, and Horace on aspects of the tale. When they appear at all, the allegorical renderings of earlier commentaries are scaled back to a minimum. Sisyphus' stone is explained simply as "quo ambitiosi significantur" [indicating ambition].[79]

In the midst of establishing his claims for understanding Ovid's references, Regius pursues his interpretation of Orpheus' marriage. Regius opens the commentary on Book 11 recalling Orpheus' death using almost exactly the same language as Ovid used to describe it. Regius notes that Orpheus' head was about to be eaten by a serpent when Apollo transformed it into a rock.[80] The death of Orpheus is highlighted by repetition, and situated in the midst of ruminations about marriage customs such as the use of torches at weddings and the role of Hecate in ensuring a happy union. As for Orpheus' failure to accomplish his self-appointed mission, Regius allows that Orpheus failed himself and Eurydice in turning around, but leaves it at that. Eurydice gets almost no play, and Orpheus' resort to men is not mentioned. Regius builds up the deflection, padding his comment that "Orpheus never touched women at all" for three years after Eurydice's death with an explanation of elements of the Zodiac, a redirection that shifted attention to procreation that was presumptively under the purview of the stars.[81] The priority on information increases the semblance of veracity. For Regius and his readers, these are not interpretive flights of fancy,

of Regius, I will so indicate. In addition to the 1493 version cited above, I consulted Ovid, *Accipe Studiose Lector P. Ovidii Metamorphosin cum luculentissimis Raphaelis Regii ennarionibus: quibus plurima ascripta sunt: que in exemplaribus antea impressis non inveniuntur. Que sunt rogas. Inter legendum facile tibi occurrent* (London: Per claudiu Davost al's de troys, 1510) and *P. Ovidii Nasonis Metamorphosin castigissimam, cum Raphaelis Regii commentariis emendatissimis, & capitulis figuratis decenter appositis* (Parma: Francisci Mazalis, 1505).

[79] Ovid, *P. Ovidii Nasonis Poetae Sulmonensis*, 228–9.
[80] Ovid, *P. Ovidii Nasonis Poetae Sulmonensis*, 246. "Orpheus thracias mulieres aspernatus (ut diximus) in se earum odium traxit. Quare cum Bacchi sacra celebrarent, ipsum in ferarum coetu canentem aspexerunt, ac impetu facto dilacerarunt: caputque ac lyram in Hebrum fluvium coniecerunt, quae ad insulam Lesbon usque delata cum essent, serpens Orphei caput dilaniaturus ab Apolline in saxum fuit conversus" [Having rejected the women of Thrace (so we are told), Orpheus was inspired with a hatred of all other women. Therefore when they were celebrating the rites of Bacchus and caught sight of him singing to a gathering of wild animals, they tore him to pieces in a terrible assault: they tossed his head and Thracian lyre in the river, which were carried all the way to the isle of Lesbos and then Orpheus' head was turned to stone once the snake from Apollo had been torn to pieces]. The underlined was added in 1510.
[81] Ovid, *P. Ovidii Nasonis Poetae Sulmonensis*, 229: "Nam pisces Zodiaci ultimum obtinent locum annumque terminant. Significat igitur tres annos transiusse post Eurydices mortem, quibus Orpheus nullam tetigerat mulierem" [Now Pisces takes its final station and brings the year to a close. Therefore it marks three years have passed since the death of Eurydice during which Orpheus never touched a woman]. (Added in 1510.) On the associations of astrology and procreation, see below, Chapter 2.

Figure 2. This is a late Medieval / early Renaissance French rendering of Orpheus as he turns around to see devils retrieving his wife per the agreement with Pluto.
Anon. (French), *Orpheus and Eurydice*. From a French translation of Ovid's *Metamorphoses*, BL MS Royal 17 E Iv, fol. 155 (late fifteenth century). Photo: HIP/Art Resource, NY.

Figure 3. Orpheus singing to animals from Ovid, *Pub. Ovidii Nasonis Metamorphoseon Libri XV. In singulas quasque Fabulas Argumenta. Ex postrema Iacobi Micylli Recognitione* (Frankfurt: Moenum, 1582), 355. Folger Shakespeare Library.

By focusing on Orpheus charming animals rather than the trees (which, according to Ovid, were young men attracted to and transformed by the singer), Orpheus lost some of his association with pederasty.

but "facts" about the context of Ovid's poem. In the end, Orpheus needs to get over Eurydice and marry again. His failure to enter the matrimonial economy results in his destruction. For Regius, Orpheus' love for Eurydice makes him vulnerable to female violence. The Renaissance Orpheus fails out of masculine weakness rather than Ovidian or Virgilian effeminate uxoriousness.

That Ovid's critique of Orpheus' masculinity was not understood, or at least not worth mentioning, is apparent in that turning to men is not an option in Regius's version. This aspect of Orpheus' story is routinely played down in the commentary tradition that follows Regius. Willem Canter (Gulielmus Canterus, 1542–1575) notes in passing that the reason for Orpheus' death is his preference for men.[82] Longolius offers the standard account of Orpheus

---

[82] Ovid, *Pub. Ovidii Nasonis Metamorphoseon Lib. XV. Ex accuratiss. Andreae Naugerii castigatione. Reliqua proximè sequens pagella indicabit* (Antwerp: Christophe Plantin, 1566), 302.

Figure 4. Orpheus and the Baccantae from Ovid, *Pub. Ovidii Nasonis Meta-morphoseon Libri XV. In singulas quasque Fabulas Argumenta. Ex postrema Iacobi Micylli Recognitione* (Frankfurt: Moenum, 1582), 398–9. Folger Shakespeare Library.

Images of the death of Orpheus often feature threateningly phallic spears aimed at Orpheus' genitals, especially early on.

looking back because he cannot resist his "vehementem amorem" [vehement love] for Eurydice. Longolius suggests that shame caused Orpheus' change of preference. Once he got over the worst of his grief, Orpheus "puerilem Venerem instituit" [instituted love for boys].[83] Sabinus somewhat anomalously notes Orpheus' guilt for looking back at Eurydice. Nonetheless, he attributes Orpheus' death "de malis mulieribus" [to the evils of women], justifying the comment by using Euripides as his authority.[84] Jacobus Mycillus distills the causality:

---

[83] The edition consulted was Ovid, *Pub. Ovidii Nasonis Metamorphoseon, hoc est, Transformationum Libri quindecim. Com Donati clariss. Grammatici in potiores metamorphoseos Ovidii fabulas argumentis compendiarii, suis locis interiectis. His adiectae sunt ad dilucidam clamque lectionem adnotationes marginalis D. Gyberti Longolii. Henrici quoque Glareani adnotationes non vulgares res ad finem libri additae* (Cologne: Joannes Gymnicus, 1542), 311. See also the death of Orpheus, p. 343, which repeats the love for boys phrasing. The first edition printed in 1534, also in Cologne. Three editions were published in Paris. See Moss, *Ovid in Renaissance France*, 41.

[84] Ovid, *Fabularum Ovidii Interpretatio*, unpaginated (after sig. k5v).

puerilem amorem primus instituit, quam
ob caussam Thressae mulieres instinc-
tae in abditis locis solitudinem agentem
propter desiderium coniugis interfecerunt.

He determined on loving boys first, on
account of which the Thracian women,
inspired by desire for a spouse, they killed
him (who was in solitude) in a secret
place.[85]

In the hands of Mycillus, women become the moral arbiters: the Baccantae
directed their anger against the innovation of homosexuality, recalling both
older and later attributions of the "invention" of male homosexual sodomy to
Orpheus, but deflecting it onto the malevolent agency of women.

Renaissance commentaries emphasized contextual veracity as a cover for
the aspects of antiquity that commentators either did not understand or could
not embrace. In terms of sex, the effect was to foreground marriage to a degree
that produced tensions around textual effects. Two of these especially lurk
in the commentary tradition. First, marriage is problematic. No matter how
often Orpheus' fidelity to Eurydice is featured, the result is pederasty. Second,
removing the allegorical sheen means that women – either lascivious in the
case of Eurydice or violent in the case of the Baccantae – are no longer merely
metaphorically scary.

French Orpheus

Recurrences of disruptive Orphic sexuality might not seem promising ground
upon which to establish claims of linguistic superiority.[86] French claims in this
arena were often spurious, but as Wolfgang Kaschuba points out, that does
not matter. He notes, "foundation myths are tightly woven fabrics of dates and
ideologies, of semantics and aesthetics, of values and practices. They represent
extremely highly condensed cultural codifications that tell us 'quote me, use me,
believe me, but don't ask me!'"[87] For French humanists and poets, investment
in patriotic claims for French as a language emerged in part from thematic
and moral concerns about figures from antiquity such as Orpheus. Advocates
for French intellectual prowess linked sexual mastery and linguistic patriotism,

[85] Ovid, *P. Ovidii Nasonis Metamorphoseaon Libri XV. Raphaelis Regii Volterrano luculentissa explanatio, cum novis Iacobi Micylli, viri eruditissimi, additionibus. Lactantii Placiti in singulas fabulas argumenta. Eruditissimorum virorum coelii rhodigini, Ioan. Baptistae Egnatii, Henrici Glareani, Giberti Longolii, & Iacobi Fanensis, in pleraque omnia loca difficiliora annotationes* (Venice: apud Ioan Gryphium, 1565), 233.
[86] On the relationship of myth to national identity primarily in twentieth-century contexts, see for instance Bo Strath, ed., *Myth, Memory and History in the Construction of Community: Historical Patterns in Europe and Beyond* (Brussels: Peter Lang, 2000). See pp. 19–46 for issues in national myth-making, including the centrality of (faulty) historical memory.
[87] Wolfgang Kaschuba, "The Emergence and Transformation of Foundation Myths," in *Myth, Memory and History in the Construction of Community: Historical Patterns in Europe and Beyond*, ed. Bo Strath (Brussels: Peter Lang, 2000), 217–26. See p. 218.

and Orpheus was a key figure through whom they did this. Revisiting the sexual failures of the master poet proved to be a fertile ground for claiming linguistic authority through the sexual politics of repudiation and prescription.

The effort to present French language as superior to classical Latin and Greek was programmatic for French humanists. As Donald Kelley has argued, Guillaume Budé's *Annotations of the Pandects* (1508) began a lifelong series of comparisons between Roman and French legal entities in which Budé consistently upheld the superiority of French practices.[88] Like many French humanists, Budé celebrated the recovery of antiquity, but Budé insisted that French scholars at least match the level of the ancients. Kelley notes that Budé inspired a number of followers – Jacques Cujas and François Baudouin in law; Antoine Loisel and Louis Le Caron in legal history; Pierre Pithou and Etienne Pasquier with respect to French culture generally – to celebrate French traditions as superior to ancient ones.[89] Translators argued for the value and beauty of French, with Etienne Dolet theorizing translation and translators such as Jacques Amyot and Louys Le Roy offering more or less elegant vernacular versions of Plutarch and Plato respectively.[90] Poets joined the humanists to articulate a program of linguistic patriotism. Leading poetic theorist Joachim Du Bellay favored original creation in French inspired by knowledge of antiquity.[91] A range of advocates engaged with or invested in the poetic project of the Pléiade added to Du Bellay's insistence on the creative superiority of French vernacular poetry.[92]

[88] Among Budé's other works in this vein, see *De Asse et partibus eius libri quinque* (Paris: Ascensiania, 1516) [first edition 1514], *De Studio litterarum recte et commode instituendo, ad inuictissimum, & potentissimum principem Franciscum, regem Franciae* (Paris: I. Badius, 1532) [first edition 1527], and the posthumously printed vernacular work, *De l'Institution du Prince: Livre contenant plusieurs histoires, enseignements & saiges dicts des anciens tant grecs que latins* (Ivry: N. Paris, 1547).

[89] Donald R. Kelley, "France," in *The Renaissance in National Context*, ed. Roy Porter and Mikulás Teich (Cambridge University Press, 1992), 123–45, esp. 131–2. Another manifestation of the nationalist impulse is manifested by the debate over the origins of the Franks and the practice of distancing Frankish origins from Rome. See pp. 134–5.

[90] Etienne Dolet, *La manière de bien traduire d'une langue en aultre. D'advantage, de la punctuation de la langue francoyse. Plus, des accents d'ycelle* (Lyon: E. Dolet, 1540); Plutarch [Jacques Amyot], *Les Oeuvres morales et meslees de Plutarque, Translatees de Grec en François, reveuës & corrigees en ceste seconde Edition en plusieurs passages par le Translateur*, 3 vols. (Paris: Vasconsan, 1574), which includes a Platonic invocation of Orpheus (vol. III, fol. 674v); Louys Le Roy, *Le Sympose de Platon, ou de l'amour et de beauté, tradit de Grec en François* (Paris: Jehan Longis & Robert le Mangnyer, 1558); *Le Phédon de Platon, traittant de l'immortalité de l'âme* (Paris: S. Nyvelle, 1553). See also the critique by Charles Fontaine, *Le Quintil Horatian sur le premier livre de La Defense, et illustration de la langue françoise, et la suycte* (Lyon: Jean Temporal 1551). This is a very partial list.

[91] Joachim Du Bellay, *La Defense et illustration de la langue francoyse* (Paris: Arnoul L'Angelier, 1549).

[92] Jacques Peletier Du Mans, *L'Art Poëtique, departi an deus livres* (Lyon: J. de Tournes et G. Gazeau, 1555); Pontus de Tyard, *Le solitaire premier*, ed. Silvio F. Baridon (Lille: Giard, 1950) [first published in 1552]; and Pierre de Ronsard, *Abbregé de l'art poëtique françois. À Alphonse Delbene, abbé de Hautecombe en Savoye* (Paris: chez Gabriel Buon, 1565); and

The equipment to appropriate Orpheus for this project came in part out of the commentary tradition around Ovid. French contributions to the commentaries were not negligible, but neither were they outstanding. Publishers found a market in France. In addition to the circulation of the major commentaries throughout France, Ann Moss has identified 260 editions of Ovid published in France between 1487 and 1600; 71 of these were partial or complete versions of the *Metamorphoses*. This number does not include editions, especially Latin ones, that circulated freely across Europe. Some commentators had ties to France or French intellectuals: Sabinus was an admirer of Thomas Freigius, a follower of Petrus Ramus;[93] Willem Canter studied in Paris under Jean Dorat, who also taught several members of the Pléiade, including Ronsard and Jean-Antoine de Baïf.[94] French contributions to the commentary tradition were subdued compared to the success of Regius. Older French textual innovations played more of a role than new commentaries by French intellectuals. Bersuire's habit of reading Ovid for multiple meanings conditioned ways of thinking that allowed more than one understanding of a text. Likewise, the emphasis on the historical reading (the "sens historial") in the *Bible des poëtes* encouraged the development of humanistic interpretation in the direction of historical accuracy. A third French contribution came from Petrus Lavinius (Pierre Lavin, 1473–1524?), a French poet and Dominican preacher from Lyon who was friends with Jean Lemaire de Belges and Symphorien Champier. Drawing on Champier's Neoplatonism (see below, Chapter 3) and widely read in both pagan classical and early Christian authors, Lavinius offered humanists ways to read allegory in historically responsible ways. Lavinius drew moral lessons through allegory understood as part of the *prisca theologica*. Lavinius wrote commentary only for part of Book 1, but editions of Regius's commentary after 1510 picked up the methodology. Commentators found the Neoplatonic idea that poets veiled the truth for the sake of preserving it especially useful.[95]

Because the commentary tradition confirmed Orpheus as the consummate poet, he became a central link between antiquity and claims for French

Thomas Sébillet, *Art poétique françoys. Pour l'instruction dés jeunes studieus, & encor peu avancéz en la Pöesie Françoise* (Paris: Gilles Corrozet, 1548).

[93] On the significance of Peter Ramus, see George Huppert, *The Style of Paris: Renaissance Origins of the French Enlightenment* (Bloomington and Indianapolis: Indiana University Press, 1999), 37–49.

[94] Canter wrote summaries appended to the 1515 Aldine edition by Andrea Navagero (1483–1529). See Ovid, *Metamorphoseon . . . Naugerii castigatione*. On Dorat and allegorical interpretation, see Pierre de Nolhac, *Ronsard et l'humanisme: avec un portrait de Jean Dorat et d'un autographe de Ronsard* (Paris: Champion, 1921), 72–109.

[95] Preface addressed to Claude de Longwy in *P. Ovidii Nasonis metamorphoseos libri moralizati: cum pulcherrimis fabularum principalium figuris* (Lyon: Jacob Maillet, 1511). It was written in 1510, but published the following year. Lavinius is discussed in Moss, *Ovid in Renaissance France*, 31–6.

language and poetry. Concerns about language and the aggressive efforts to assert the value of French encouraged appropriations of Orpheus the poet. Thomas Sébillet merged the poetic, political and religious by including Orpheus among "monarchs and sovereign lords" who used their verses to teach men about the heavens.[96] Jacques Peletier was more modest, assigning to Orpheus the invention of the lyre, but leaving his larger role in the development of poetry implicit.[97] Invoking Orpheus' dismembered body in the episode of the frozen words from the *Quart Livre*, François Rabelais utilized Orpheus as a figure for fragmentation of language into national types.[98] For Pierre de Ronsard, Orpheus was the embodiment of the divine mission of poetry, which Ronsard cast in ethical terms and as a matter of social order.[99] Iterations of Orpheus the poet have been noted elsewhere: Françoise Joukovsky has traced the shift from Orpheus as a musician to Orpheus as the model poet in the sixteenth century.[100] Use of Orpheus involved the self-conscious assertion of French specificity with the result that the French interpretations and appropriations of Orpheus became a mode of cultural differentiation.

As with other aspects of claiming the superiority of humanist practice, the move to render Orpheus as emblematic of French values in poetic terms occurred first in the guise of translation. French translations fit Orpheus into a scheme of thematic appropriation that yielded an array of reinventions of Orpheus as a sexual signifier. A mix of linguistic assertion, patriotism, and grappling with the parameters of sexual normativity marked the translation of Ovid into French. Pointedly omitting the accretion of Medieval allegory began with Clément Marot's translation of Books 1 and 2. After Marot published the first book in 1534, Barthélemy Aneau translated Book 3 and published all three books in 1556.[101] Aneau abandoned further efforts when he heard that François Habert (c.1508–c.1561) was progressing rapidly on a version of the entire text. Dedicated to Henri II, Habert's dutiful and largely faithful version is not the height of elegance, but it is complete and with only occasional, albeit sometimes telling, additions. Habert addressed concerns about Ovid in his dedicatory poem by appropriating Ovidian themes in line with Renaissance secular and Christian principles. Habert maintained that the poem was consonant with the values of a prince in that it displayed "vos graces heroiques" [your heroic graces] back to Henri.[102] Magnanimity, prudence, courage, and honor

---

[96] Sébillet, *Art poétique françoys*, 2v.   [97] Peletier, *L'Art Poëtique*, 7.

[98] François Rabelais, *Le Quart Livre*, ed. Gérard Defaux (Paris: Livre de poche, 1994), 539 (Ch. LV). This edition is based on the 1548 and 1552 editions. See Cave, *Cornucopian Text*, 117 for comment.

[99] Ronsard, *Abbrégé de l'Art poétique*, 2v.   [100] Joukovsky, *Orphée et ses disciples*.

[101] See Clément Marot and Barthélemy Aneau, *Les Trois Premiers Livres de la "Métamorphose" d'Ovide*, ed. Jean-Claude Moisan with Marie-Claude Malenfant (Paris: Champion, 1997).

[102] François Habert, *Les quinze livres de la Metamorphose d'Ovide interpretez en rime françoise, selon la phrase latine* (Rouen: Thomas Mallard, 1590), 4. The colophon indicates that the

follow, and then Habert offers an interrogative defense of Ovid as proper for a Christian audience. Weren't Deucalion and Pyrrha rewarded for their piety? Doesn't Daphne defend her virginity? For Habert, Ovid provides basic Christian moral lessons:

Et quand Ovide escrit un Pallas	And when Ovid writes of Pallas
Aymer vertu, & y prendre soulas	Loving virtue, and taking solace there
Vierge tousjours, puis une Cytherée	Always a virgin, then a Cythrean
A folle amour sans cesser retirée,	Without ceasing retired to crazy love
Ne veut il pas monstrer le different	Can he not show the difference
De chasteté & du crime apparent	Between chastity and the evident crime
De paillardise au monde trop permise	of wantonness too permitted in the world
Pour verité en lumiere non mise?	For the truth not to come to light?[103]

Habert further defends Ovid as a teacher of rhetoric by appropriating the *Metamorphoses* in translation for the linguistic project advocated by the Pléiade. Habert echoes the assertions of Ovid's pedagogical value put forth by Regius, but where Regius posits pagan morality as congruent with Christian values, Habert's translation emphasizes the secular modeling the text can offer to French readers. Invoking Cicero and comparing Henri to Roman military greats, Habert says by putting Ovid in French ("en vostre langue"), the Valois name will be immortalized for the service Henri has done ("Au grand soulas, & profit des humains" [To the great solace and profit of mankind]).[104] Patriotic translation makes Ovid available for the regenerative project of making French a leading language.

As for Orpheus, Habert is almost entirely faithful to Ovid's poem, but not quite. A small but significant shaping of the reading of Orpheus provides distance between French poetics and its ancient, immoral forbears. Habert's Orpheus turns around, "Pour regarder d'un desire curieux" [out of a curious desire to see]. Eurydice turns into shadow and wind ("l'ombre & le vent"), and she makes no comment.[105] For three years, Orpheus avoids women on the grounds that he had promised fidelity to his wife. Habert inserts a telling addition:

printer was George l'Oyselet. The volume was originally published in Paris by M. Fezandat and E. Groulleau in 1557. Habert did not number lines in either the preface or the poem.

103 Habert, *Les quinze livres de la Metamorphose d'Ovide*, 7. Habert seems to have been inclined to an evangelical position, although he was careful to insist on his loyalty to the Catholic Church. See Gary Ferguson, *Mirroring Belief: Marguerite de Navarre's Devotional Poetry* (Edinburgh University Press, 1992), 77. Among Habert's religious works were *Les Epistres héroïdes, pour servir d'exemple aux chrestiens* (Paris: M. Fezandat, 1560), which invoked Ovid's *Heroides*.

104 Habert, *Les quinze livres de la Metamorphose d'Ovide*, 9, 12.

105 Habert, *Les quinze livres de la Metamorphose d'Ovide*, 598.

| On dict qu'en Thrace (ô faict d'ouyr indigne) | It is said that in Thrace (*a fact unworthy to hear*) |
| Il fut autheur de l'amour masculine. | He was the author of masculine love.[106] |

The parenthetical aside recalls the blunt comment of the *Ovide moralisé en prose*, and shapes Habert's translation of Orpheus' death. The Thracian women are "femmes furieuses," but their anger is explicable to Habert:

| Voicy, voicy celuy qui a pris | Here, here is he who took |
| De nous blasmer & nous mettre à mespris. | To blaming us and gave us over to scorn.[107] |

For Habert, male–male homosexuality makes everyone bad – Orpheus for betraying his promise to Eurydice; the Thracian women for their murderous rage; men for following Orpheus' lead in rejecting women. In Habert's self-conscious moral regeneration scheme, carefully adjusted poetry can warn of these dangers. At the same time, condemnation had to be circumscribed lest sexual immorality detract from the pedagogical value of the ancient text.

This was important because part of that pedagogical value was in directing readings of Orpheus to magnify French political values. In the program for Henri II's royal entrée into Paris in 1558, Etienne Jodelle fused the story of the Argonauts with masculinist efficacy for the edification of the king. Orpheus, Jodelle advised, moved rocks and trees with his music, which made him an appropriate model for "un grand Roy" [a great king].[108] Louis Des Masures (1515–1574) eulogized François I by comparing the sorrow of the French upon the king's death to Orpheus' at the loss of Eurydice:

Tel jadis le dolent Orphee	Once upon a time such was the doleful Orpheus.
. . .	. . .
Pleuroit d'Euridice la fee	Crying for the fact of Eurydice's
La seconde perte & la mort:	Second loss and death
Dont sur l'inexorable sort	Of which the inexorable fate
Sa harpe d'yvoire estoffee	His ivory harp stifled
Rendoit des notes nompareilles	Rendering unparalleled notes
Aux chesnes tendans les oreilles.	Stretching the ears of the oaks.[109]

Unlike translations constrained by knowledge of the whole text, poems could focus on aspects of the story. Des Masures avoids the homosocial problem by

---

[106] Habert, *Les quinze livres de la Metamorphose d'Ovide*, 600. Emphasis mine.

[107] Habert, *Les quinze livres de la Metamorphose d'Ovide*, 654.

[108] Etienne Jodelle, *Le Recueil des inscriptions, figures, devises, et masquarades, ordonnees en l'hostel de ville à Paris, le Ieudi 17 de Fevrier, 1558* (Paris: André Wechel, 1558), fol. 15v.

[109] Louis Des Masures, *Oeuvres poëtiques de Louis des Masures, Tournisien* (Lyon: Jean de Tournes, 1557), 18–19.

concentrating on the loss of Eurydice. Even allowing for selectivity, however, the emotional analogy between Orpheus the grieving husband and France the grieving people seems to be inverted: Des Masures puts the king in the part of Eurydice. This simultaneously effeminizes the king and marks the people of France as ineffectual in their love for him. The appropriation of Orpheus as a figure for patriotic reflection entails risky gendered entanglements.

That said, Des Masures pointed to ways that poets might adapt elements of Orpheus' story as they developed the corpus of French Renaissance poetry. Focusing on grieving and Orpheus' association with music to commemorate loss enabled poets to utilize Orpheus within acceptable sexual norms. Joachim Du Bellay, who invoked Orpheus repeatedly in his poetry, wrote *A Salmon Macrin* after Macrin's wife died in 1550. Du Bellay urges his friend to accept her death. For Du Bellay, Orpheus provides a warning: Orpheus fought Eurydice's death, but in the end, not only could he not retrieve her, he caused her second death. Du Bellay emphasizes the inevitability of separation:

La harpe Thracienne,	The Thracian harp
Qui commandoit aux bois,	That commands the woods,
Lamenta quelque fois.	Laments sometimes
Son pitoyable office	Its pitiful office
Aux enfers penetra,	To hell he penetrated
Ou sa chere Euridice	Where his dear Eurydice
En vain elle impetra.	In vain she impetrates.
Macrin, ta douce Lire,	Macrin, your sweet lyre,
La mignonne des Dieux,	The darling of the Gods,
Ne peult surmonter l'ire	Cannot overcome this ire
Du sort injurieux.	Of the injurious kind.
Il fault que chacun passé	One must allow each to pass
En l'eternelle nuit:	Into the eternal night:
La Mort, qui nous menasse,	Death which threatens us,
Comme l'ombre, nous suit.	Like a shadow, follows us.

Du Bellay counsels Macrin to accept his loss for now, but offers some consolation. Invoking the language of the Platonic androgyne, Du Bellay tells Macrin he will regain "ta douce moitié" [your sweet half] in heaven.[110] Du Bellay uses one ambiguous figure (the androgyne) to offset the difficulties of another (Orpheus). Du Bellay can do this because the idea that the androgyne signified marital completion was prominent in French Renaissance poetry.[111] Du

---

[110] Joachim Du Bellay, *Oeuvres poétiques*, ed. Henri Chamard, 8 vols. (Paris: Nizet, 1982–1984), vol. IV, 32, 29.

[111] See Robert V. Merrill, "The Pleiade and the Androgyne," *Comparative Literature* 1:2 (1949): 97–112. This article appears as chapter 4 of Robert V. Merrill with Robert J. Clements, *Platonism in French Renaissance Poetry* (New York University Press, 1957). On the other hand, the androgyne became distinctly more problematic by the 1570s. See Katherine Crawford, "The Impossibility of Indeterminacy: The Androgyne in Renaissance France." (In preparation.)

Bellay uses the Neoplatonic connotations of the androgyne to signal that marital love, however deferred, prevails. The completion of the androgyne displaces the other possibilities that Orpheus embodies. Polymorphous perversity falls by the wayside. The double invocation of ancient images provides the space for Du Bellay's construction of sympathetic advice.

Displacement could work more broadly in favor of French poetics. Revising Orpheus' tragic elements, Maurice Scève uses the association of Orpheus with poetic mastery to replace failure. Poetic prowess could defy death and define "good" sexuality:

Ainsi qu'Amour en la face au plus beau,	Thus love in the face of the most beautiful
Propice object à noz yeulx agreable,	Auspicious object, agreeable to our eyes
Hault colloqua le reluysant flambeau	Placed high the bright flame
Qui nous esclaire à tout bien desirable,	Which enlightens us to all desirable good
Affin qu'à tous son feu soit admirable,	So that his fire is admirable to all
Sans à l'honneur faire aulcun prejudice.	Without making any prejudice to honor
Ainsi veult il par plus louable indice,	Of my highly ennobled Orpheus
Que mon Orphée haultement anobly	Thus he wants by this praiseworthy index,
Maulgré la Mort, tire son Euridice	Despite Death, to pull his Eurydice
Hors des Enfers de l'eternel obly.	From the Hell of eternal oblivion.[112]

As Terence Cave remarks, Scève rewrites Orphic failure as success by truncating the story. The poet secures Eurydice's return to the world of the living.[113] For Scève, love conquers death through the medium of immortality in poetry. He sees no need to revisit failure that might require an excuse, and he vacates the pederastic turn by abbreviation. Eurydice is the object upon which the poet may act to demonstrate his poetic mastery. She is actually called an object, and the efficacy of love produces masculine bravado in saving her and in commemorating doing so. The muddy waters of failure and homoeroticism are overwhelmed by masculine efficacy as poetic brilliance.

Scève's was not the only chest-thumping retelling of Orpheus. When Pierre de Ronsard took up Orpheus, he did so as part of making programmatic claims for French poetry. Both theoretically and practically, this complicated matters around Orpheus' sexual story. The moving force of the Pléiade, Ronsard saw himself as the new Orpheus, the poet-prophet who would improve on the ancient past by making it French.[114] Ronsard invoked Orpheus and Eurydice twice in

---

[112] Maurice Scève, *Délie, object de plus haulte vertu*, ed. Gérard Defaux, 2 vols. (Geneva: Droz, 2004), vol. 1, 202. Dixaine CCCXLV. Originally 1544.

[113] Terence Cave, "Scève's *Délie*: Correcting Petrarch's Errors," in *Pre-Pléiade Poetry*, ed. Jerry C. Nash (Lexington: French Forum, 1985), 112–24. See esp. p. 120.

[114] For the context and development of Ronsard's ideas, see especially Pierre Mesnard, ed., *Lumières de la Pléiade* (Paris: Vrin, 1966); Henri Chamard, *Histoire de la Pléiade*, 4 vols. (Paris: Didier, 1939–1963).

Le Premier livre des amours (1553). The first poem places Ronsard above the abilities of ancient and Italian Renaissance forbears:

Amour, que n'ay-je en escrivant la grace	Love, have I not the divine grace
Divine autant que j'ay volonté?	As much as the volition?
Par mes escrits tu serois surmonté,	By my words you were overcome,
Vieil enchanteur des vieux rochers de Thrace.	Old enchanter of the ancient rocks of Thrace.
Plus haut encore que Pindare & qu'Horace,	Higher still than Pindar and Horace,
J'appenderois à ta divinité	I understand your divinity
Un livre faict de telle gravité	A book of such gravity
Que du Bellay luy quitteroit la place.	That Du Bellay quits him the place.
Si vive encore Laure par l'Univers	If Laura lives still in the universe
Ne fuit volant dessus les Thusques vers,	Do not fly under the Tuscan verses,
Que nostre siecle heureusement estime,	That our century happily admires,
Comme ton nom, honneur des vers François,	Like your name, honor French verses,
Victorieux des peuples & des Roys,	Victorious people and Kings,
S'en voleroit sus l'aile de ma ryme.	Would fly away the wing of my rhyme.[115]

Never modest about his poetic gifts, Ronsard asserts that his love poetry ranks with the best, and that it reflects French superiority in both letters and arms. Ronsard, who reworks Pindar and Horace throughout his corpus, nonetheless demotes them to a position below Orpheus, with whom Ronsard personally identifies and associates with his claims for primacy in poetry. Ronsard also has to displace Petrarch as the leading modern poetic voice and to assert the primacy of French over Italian (about which more below, in Chapter 4). Always combative, Ronsard asserts the association of poetry with the muscular virtues of agonistic combat. For Ronsard, masculinity can be both martial and literary. Françoise Joukovsky has found that Ronsard imposed his vision of Orpheus on other poets, and Orpheus as an outstanding poet remained in Ronsard's oeuvre throughout his career.[116]

But Ronsard's programmatic intentions are distinctly modified in Jean-Antoine de Muret's commentary. Ronsard's hyper-masculine skewing of the Orpheus story to omit other elements seems to invite Muret to recall Orphic sexual subversion. Rehearsing information about Orpheus, Muret alludes to pederasty by referring to Pindar's treatment of the Argonauts. Then Muret brings up Orpheus' end:

---

[115] Pierre de Ronsard and Marc-Antoine de Muret, *Commentaires au Premier Livre des Amours de Ronsard*, ed. Jacques Chomart, Marie-Madeleine Fragonard, and Gisèle Mathieu-Castellani (Geneva: Droz, 1985), 40 (Sonnet LXXII). The poems from this collection with Muret's commentary first appeared in 1553. The text above is reproduced in a facsimile of Ronsard's *Oeuvres* (1573).

[116] Joukovsky, *Orphée et ses disciples*, 61–103.

| Les femmes de Thrace, par ce que depuis la perte de sa femme Eurydice, il avoit tout le sexe feminin en haine & horreur, se mutinerent contre luy, & un jour ainsi qu'il chantoit . . . le dechirerent en pieces. | Because since the loss of his wife Eurydice, he had held the female sex in hatred and horror, the women of Thrace, themselves mutinied against him, and one day, while he was singing, they ripped him to pieces.[117] |

Muret leaves the pederasty unidentified but obvious. For Ronsard's poem, the discussion is also unnecessary. Muret went out of his way to bring up the circumstances of Orpheus' death. Muret's Orpheus is subject to violent repudiation for his sexual proclivities. The autobiographical association seems inescapable: Muret fled Paris in 1553 amidst charges of sodomy. He was burnt in effigy in Toulouse the same year, and he moved to Venice to evade prosecution in France. Negotiations to return to France were complicated by Muret's alleged involvement in another pederasty episode in Venice.[118] Muret's commentary, coming from his position as an erudite wunderkind, at once subverted Ronsard's appropriation of Orpheus for French poetry and situated poetic accomplishment in a masculinist ethic. The larger result was that neither Ronsard's Orpheus nor Muret escaped the implications of sexual impropriety that attended on that ethic.

Ronsard was not finished trying to overcome Orpheus' problematic past. Indeed, what could be more glorious than rescuing the father of poetry from his own sexual missteps? Ronsard displaces the pederastic subtext by truncating the narrative in the second of his sonnets on the subject of Orpheus in the *Premier livre*. Ronsard manipulates the deictics, imagining himself as Orpheus and revising the story of Eurydice's death so that he is present:

Le sang fut bien maudit de la Gorgonne face,	The blood of the Gorgon's face was greatly cursed,
Qui premier engendra les serpens venimeux!	which first engendered venomous snakes!
Ha! tu devois, Helene, en marchant dessus eux,	You must, Helene, in walking upon us
Non écrazer leurs reins, mais en perdre la race.	Not crush the reins, but lose the race.
Nous estions l'autre jour en une verte place,	The other day, we were in a green place,
Cueillans m'amie & moy des bouquets odoreux:	Gathering sweet-smelling bouquets, my love and I:

---

[117] Ronsard and Muret, *Commentaires*, 41.

[118] Charles Dejob, *Marc-Antoine Muret: un professeur français en Italie dans la seconde moitié du XVIe siècle* (Geneva: Slatkine, 1970 [1881]), 46–61, 131. Muret's scholarship in Italy included a commentary on Catullus, on which see Gaisser, *Catullus and His Renaissance Readers*, 146–68.

Un pot de cresme estoit au milieu de nous deux,	A pot-de-crème was in the middle of the two of us,
Et du laict sur du jonc cailloté comme glace:	And the milk pebbled on the bull-rush like ice:
Quand un serpent tortu de venin tout couvert,	When a winding snake all covered with venom,
Par ne sçay quel malheur sortit d'un buisson vert	By I cannot say what evil left the green shrub
Contre le pied de celle à qui je fay service.	Against the foot of her to whom I paid service.
Tout le coeur me gela, voyant ce Monstre infait:	All my heart froze, seeing this monster in fact:
Et lors je m'escriay, pensant qu'il nous eust fait	And this time I am writing, thinking what he has done to us
Moy, un second Orphée, & elle une Eurydice.	Me, a second Orpheus, and her my Eurydice.[119]

Ronsard's decision to end the poem with the physical separation of death allows him to suggest that his Eurydice has escaped death because he has made her immortal through poetry.[120]

Ronsard's studied invocation of antiquity throughout the poem obscures the human love dyad at the center. In this instance, Muret's erudition provides support through learned obfuscation. Muret's commentary makes much of the hatred of snakes, linking it back to the Medusa story in Ovid, in which Perseus took Medusa's head to Africa and populated it with snakes. ("Apres que Perseus eut tranché la teste de Meduse, il la prit par les cheveux, & l'emporta par les deserts d'Afrique" [After Perseus cut off the head of Medusa, he took it by the hair and carried it to the desert of Africa.]) Muret displays his knowledge, recounting an obscure tale in which Helen and Menelaus returned to Troy, where Menelaus was bitten by a snake and died. Helen then married the pilot who had been their guide. Ambivalence about women is plain enough in both Ronsard's poem and Muret's gloss, but Muret adds to it, recalling the serpent in the drama of original sin understood as the sexual fall of mankind. Women are associated with deprivation and death, but the male poet-actor can take over and provide redemption through poetic immortality. The patriotic poetic program championed by Ronsard and seconded by Muret appropriated sexual allusion, proclaiming mastery over it. A generous helping of mutual self-congratulation served to displace the homosocial space of poetic accomplishment with emphatic heterosexual eroticism.

[119] Ronsard and Muret, *Commentaires*, Sonnet LXXVII, 43.

[120] He does it again in *Sonets pour Hélène*. See Ronsard, *Œuvres complètes*, ed. Paul Laumonier, Isidore Silver, and René Lebègue, 20 vols. (Paris: Gallimard, 1993), vol. II, 400, Sonnet XLI: "Je seray ton Orphée, et toy mon Eurydice."

Theatrical representation carried out a similar move in visual terms, dropping homosociality and foregrounding Orpheus as a good husband. As a way to jettison the pederastic overlay of the story, this created a socially congenial Orpheus. For what his story says about marriage, Orpheus again proved subversive. Scholars believe that an interlude, *Descente d'Orphée aux enfers*, in the pastoral drama *L'Arimène* (1596) by Nicolas de Montreux was the first theatrical representation of the myth in France. The production was sponsored by the duc de Bretagne, presented first at his château in Nantes and published in two different editions in 1597. One of five interludes on mythical themes (the others were the giants against the gods, the abduction of Helen, the deliverance of Andromeda, and the death of Argus),[121] the story is highly truncated. Eurydice is already dead. Orpheus, desperately mournful, convinces Pluto to let him take her out of Hades, and Pluto agrees under the usual conditions. When Orpheus turns around, the interlude closes with him lamenting his rash action.[122] What is striking about this version of the story is the emphasis on Orpheus' devotion to his wife. All the other elements are stripped away so that Orpheus' failure is presented as proof positive of his devotion. Recycling one – but only one – of the possible readings, Montreux's narrative insists that Orpheus' love for his wife was so great that he could not help but turn around to look back at her. Honest to the story as far as it went, the *Descente* ends up suggesting that killing your wife out of love is heroic.[123]

Success and failure co-mingle in rewriting Orpheus as a faithful husband. The success lies in containing the figure's wayward sexuality so that he can be utilized on behalf of French artistic superiority. French authors straightened out Orpheus' kinks and made him "safe" for consumption. This involved not only removing the Medieval allegorical accretions, but taming Orpheus' polymorphous, unproductive sexual proclivities. French re-imaginings aimed

---

[121] Information about the piece may be found in François de Chapoton, *La Descente d'Orphée aux enfers. Tragédie (1640)*, ed. Hélène Visentin (Presses Universitaires de Rennes, 2004), 118–22.

[122] Nicolas de Montreux, *L'Arimène, ou Berger desespere, pastorale. Par Ollenix du Mont-Sacre Gentil-homme du Maine* (Paris: Abraham Saugrain, 1597).

[123] Operas about Orpheus skirted the question of his responsibility. Claudio Monteverdi's *L'Orfeo favola in musica* (1607) is the closest to the original story, with Orpheus doubting Pluto's promise and turning around. Monteverdi alludes to the homosexual turn in a limited way: His Orpheus, angry at all women, vows never to touch another. But rather than getting ripped apart for his rejection of women, Orpheus is spirited to heaven by Apollo. In Christoph Willibald Gluck's version, *Orfeo ed Euridice* (1762), Eurydice does not understand why Orpheus won't look at her, and he gives in to her entreaties, causing her death. Gluck alters the ending so that Love restores the couple. Jacques Offenbach's operetta *Orphée aux enfers* (1858; expanded to four acts in 1874) is a satirical retelling in which Orpheus is a terrible musician. His music annoys Eurydice so much that she has an affair with Pluto, and she leaves a note saying she is dead. The comedic reworking includes Jupiter throwing a lightning bolt that causes Orpheus to turn around and Eurydice joining the Baccantae.

to repudiate sodomy in favor of heterosexual desire. Sometimes these efforts to use the beauty and plasticity of French to forge a more effective normative tradition worked. French Orpheus loves women, not men or boys, and for French poets and artists, his violent end recedes under the force of his marital love. Even the failures are marked by the acknowledgment – repeated softly in translation, commentary, poetry, and theatrical production – that some of Orpheus' sexual story was beyond even the most forceful attempts to corral it. For the advocates of the French language, the failure was always Orphic, never French.

Coda: whither Orpheus

L'Arimène brought Orpheus into French theatrical consciousness. Orpheus' first appearance on stage masked his complicated sexual locus seemingly as a practical matter of the brevity of the interlude. More than time constraints, however, mattered when Orpheus was the issue. By the 1590s, the multiplicity of Orpheus' sexual adventures was starting to become a bit embarrassing. The story of tragic marriage, failed rescue, opportunistic (?) homosexuality, and sexual violence was too much for audiences – or at least, the royal, ecclesiastical and pedagogical officials who determined such things. Audiences were moving (or were moved) toward an understanding of sexual propriety as central to the ideological apparatus of bodily comportment. Public perversities (including cleric-poets such as Ronsard celebrating sex and love) were no longer welcome; private peccadillos were generally tolerated as long as the placid surface of social order remained intact.

The version of this change in language culminated in the celebration of classical representation in seventeenth-century France, which is evident in the commentary on Ovid's Orpheus. Consider the last of the great Renaissance commentators, Jacobus Pontanus (Jakob Spanmüller, 1542–1626), who specifically adapted his 1618 edition of the *Metamorphoses* for Jesuit educational purposes. In the teaching commentary that largely displaced Regius, Pontanus omitted the references to Orpheus' wayward sexual adventures entirely. In his summary of Orpheus' retreat to the mountains, Pontanus says that Orpheus, "à secundis nuptiis refugit" [flees from a second marriage].[124] Pontanus glosses Ovid's intentions:

---

[124] Ovid, *Ex P. Ovidii Nasonis Metamorphoseon Libris XV. Electorum Libri Totidem, Ultimo Integro. Ad eosdem novi Commentarii, sum Sectionibus & Argumentis: Studio & opera Iacobi Pontani de Societate Iesu* (Antwerp: Heredes Martini Nutii, 1618) [Facsimile, Garland, 1976], 394.

Quòd Orpheus à muliere tandem abhor-
ruerit, duplicem caussam profert, & lec-
tori iudicium relinquit. Vel quòd nup-
tiae primae secus cesserunt, veritus est
ne secundae quoque infaeliciter evenirent.
Vel quòd Eurydice celibatum post eius
mortem promiserat.

He left readers to judge the double reason
offered for the fact that Orpheus shrank
back from women. Either because his first
nuptials ended badly, he feared that second
unlucky ones to befall him, or because he
had promised Eurydice to be celibate after
her death.[125]

Without allegorizing, Pontanus attributes acceptable Catholic motivations to
Orpheus. One might have to marry, but having done it once, avoiding it a second
time was not only acceptable, but admirable. Orpheus' death is attributed to
the weakness of women (Pontanus cites Ecclesiastes, rather than Euripides, as
authoritative) and to the "insanity" of the Thracian women. Pontanus excises
Orpheus' homosexual phase. He is consistent about removing homosexuality
throughout: when he glosses the Ganymede story, Pontanus refers to Jupiter
taking the boy to the heavens but omits the pederastic motivations.[126] Jesuit
propriety prevails.

Cleaning up the messy sexuality of Orpheus is in keeping with the cultural
shift signaled by the Jesuits. As Sara Beam has demonstrated, Jesuit notions of
obedience, decorum, and cultural sophistication displaced the bawdy humor of
farce in early seventeenth-century French theatricals.[127] The Jesuits taught such
values in the hundreds of *collèges* they founded throughout France starting in
the late sixteenth century.[128] Despite a rocky relationship with the monarchy –
the order was expelled in 1594 but re-admitted in 1603[129] – the Jesuits gradually
made it clear that their teaching priorities matched those of a monarchy devoted
to maintaining order. The curriculum of the *collèges* reflected this. The *Ratio
studiorum* (Rules for Study) outlined the texts and expectations for students
throughout their education.[130] Pontanus's readings of Ovid and its occlusions
of Orpheus fit the program perfectly.

Propriety in education worked in concert with propriety in moral modeling. For centuries, Orpheus' sexual adventures had survived, albeit with
(mis)interpretations, (mis)readings, and obfuscations. Only with the triumph

[125] Ovid, *Ex P. Ovidii Nasonis Metamorphoseon . . . Iacobi Pontani*, 394–5.
[126] Ovid, *Ex P. Ovidii Nasonis Metamorphoseon . . . Iacobi Pontani*, 403 and 414.
[127] Sara Beam, *Laughing Matters: Farce and the Making of Absolutism in France* (Ithaca, NY and London: Cornell University Press, 2007), 210–40.
[128] Roger Chartier, Marie-Madeleine Compère, and Dominique Julia, *L'Education en France du XVIe au XVIIIe siècle* (Paris: Société d'édition d'enseignement supérieur, 1976), 159–68.
[129] Michel de Waele, "Pour la sauvegarde du roi et du royaume: l'expulsion des Jésuites à la fin des guerres de religion," *Canadian Journal of History* 29 (1994): 267–80.
[130] See *Ratio studiorum: Plan raisonné et institution des études dans la Companie de Jésus*, eds. Adrien Demoustier and Dominique Julia, trans. Léone Albrieux and Dolorès Pralon-Julia (Paris: Belin, 1997).

of classical self-control did the sexual Orpheus disappear. François de Chapoton's *La Descente d'Orphée aux enfers. Tragédie*, first performed in 1639, reworks Orpheus as a model of marriage and self-discipline. Tellingly, the dedication to Madame d'Oriac (probably Marguerite de La Croix, wife of Laurent Rabot d'Aurillac) praises the female patron for supporting the play by way of reparation for what women did to Orpheus. After all, Chapaton pronounces, "la France adore les escrits en protegeant le grand maistre de la Poësie" [France adores the writings that protect the grand master of Poetry].[131] The gender dynamics of the story remain; the sexual missteps do not. Orpheus is the loving husband who braves Pluto's realm because he is distraught, and even seeing his wife's shade inspires him:

Euridice mon coeur, quand vous m'estes renduë	Eurydice, my heart, when you were returned to me
Je crains en mesme temps de vous avoir perduë;	I feared at the same time to have lost you;
L'amour faict sur mes ses un combat furieux.	Love made a furious combat inside me.[132]

Orpheus turns around because he fears Pluto has lied to him and kept Eurydice for himself. In his retreat, Orpheus moves trees and enchants animals in strictly pastoral terms. The Baccantae kill Orpheus for ignoring them, but there is no suggestion that he turned to men for intimacy or sex. In fact, Orpheus' lament includes an emphasis on his own "chaste desires" ["mes chastes desirs"] for Eurydice. He is glad when the Baccantae attack him because he gets to die and be with his beloved.[133] Despite Orpheus' desire to die, the play closes with Bacchus punishing the Baccantae for murdering Orpheus on the grounds that his poetry was loved by the gods. The poet mattered; punishing his transgressions did not. Renaissance Orpheus lost his polymorphous perversity in favor of chaste marital rectitude, and his conformity enabled vengeance on his behalf. Orpheus ends up, then, entirely heterosexual and blameless. Aristaeus caused Eurydice's first death, untrustworthy Pluto was responsible for Orpheus looking back, and the Baccantae acted outside their scope in killing him. At least twenty versions of this story appeared in print or on stage over the course of the seventeenth century.[134] The success suggests that Orpheus could be translated into French culture best shorn of his wayward sexual bits.

---

[131] Chapoton, *La Descente d'Orphée aux enfers*, 17.
[132] Chapoton, *La Descente d'Orphée aux enfers*, IV, 7, ll. 1541–3.
[133] Chapoton, *La Descente d'Orphée aux enfers*, IV, 8, ll. 1589–96; V, 3, l. 1828; V, 4, ll. 1917–18, 1929–30. Eurydice leaves considerable carnage in her wake: Aristeus kills himself for his part in Eurydice's death.
[134] Chapoton, *La Descente d'Orphée aux enfers*, 115–17.

Figure 5. Orpheus and the Baccantae from Ovid, *P. Ovidii Nasonis Metamor-phoses, Argumentis Brevioribus ex Luctatio Grammatico collectis expositae: una cum vivis singularum Transformationum iconibus in aes incisis* (Antwerp: Plantiniana apud viduam, & Ioannem Moretum, 1591), 269. This later image features the Baccantae killing Orpheus with clubs and the focus on his offend-ing sexual organs is muted compared to earlier versions.

Orpheus is both a specific case and a general example of the deployment of sexual figurations as elements of Renaissance discourse in France. Orpheus is especially dense as a node of sexual knowledge and disinformation. His textual history is more continuous and his plentitude of perversities attracted a wider range of responses than other figures, but the processes of address-ing and utilizing the textual sexuality of a figure from antiquity were not at all unique. Sardanapalus was rediscovered in the Renaissance, and by the reign of Henri III, polemicists used him as shorthand to attack the king for his alleged sexual misdeeds.[135] Artemesia became emblematic of the overly

---

[135] On Sardanapalus, see for instance Antoine de Vias, *Le Sophologe d'Amour. Traictez plaisantz & delectables oultre l'utilité en iceulx contenue* (Paris: Gilles Corrozet, 1542), fol. 57r, which describes Pasiphaë and Sardanapalus, "& aultres incontinentz qui en amours commires cas nephandes je m'en delaisse, car pas ne vallent que pour iceulx cas descripre la plume soit

masculine, dominant woman whose actions caused effeminacy in her sons. Plato's androgyne was the object of extensive appropriation (good at first, but gradually more ambivalent) over the meanings of acceptable sexual love. Proponents of the Renaissance used such ancients and their proliferating meanings to reclaim the past, better it, recreate it, and eventually, make it safe for the French.

The irony is that Orphic possibilities engendered the contraction of embodied options. Pontanus points to the controlled classical body politics of Louis XIV's France,[136] and those politics have always had a sexual dimension. The multiplicity of readings of Orpheus' sexual adventures converged with and helped create the program of claiming the Renaissance for France. The pivot point was the poetic project of the Pléiade and Ronsard's imagining of French as a viable medium for revitalizing the classical literary heritage. The recovery of Ovid in the commentary tradition restored the elements of Orpheus' story obscured by Medieval allegorizing and provided the materials for appropriating Orpheus as a master poet, musician, husband, and lover. That the latter aspects of his story entangled poets and poetry in sexual ambiguity was fine for Ronsard, but sexual uncertainty did not remain a virtue to be celebrated.[137] The French Renaissance had made its bed and its heirs chose not to lie in it.

mise sur papier, ne les aureilles des honnestes gens entonnées du recit de leurs faictz" [and I refresh myself [recalling] the disastrous case of incontinent others in committed love, because it is neither worthy for the pen to describe it put on paper, nor for the ears of honest people, who are astonished by the recital of these facts]. On the political uses against Henri III, see for instance [Nicolas Barnaud], *Le Cabinet du Roy de France, dans lequel il y a trois Perles precieuses d'inestimable valeur* (n. p.: no pub., 1581), 305: "Ainsi, qui vous croiroit, la Cour est la Cabale / D'orgueil, d'ambition, de sombre lascheté. / D'un tas de fai-neants qui par oisiveté / Se veulent esgaler au mol Sardanapale."

[136] For the iterations and ambiguities of corporeal self-control under Louis XIV, see Sara E. Melzer and Kathryn Norberg, eds., *From the Royal to the Republican Body: Incorporating the Political in Seventeenth- and Eighteenth-Century France* (Berkeley: University of California Press, 1998), 1–130. For Ovid's fortunes continued, see Henri Bardon, "Sur l'influence d'Ovide en France au 17ème siècle," in *Atti del Convegno Internazionale Ovidiano di Sulmona del 1958*, 2 vols. (Rome: Istituto di Studi Romani, 1959), vol. II, 69–83. Bardon notes that Louis XIV was particularly interested in images (in paintings and ballets) from the *Metamorphoses*. Poets and fiction writers utilized Ovidian tropes and tales extensively as well.

[137] This was the case initially, but Ronsard developed more negative reactions to sexual ambiguity in other contexts. See below, Chapter 4.

2   Heavens below: astrology, generation, and sexual (un)certainty

In François Rabelais's (c.1484?–1553) satirical treatment of astrology in the *Tiers livre* of *Gargantua and Pantagruel*, Panurge is uncertain about whether he should marry. He goes back and forth, rehearsing the positives (lineage, intimacy, stability) and negatives (fear of cuckoldry, being beaten by his wife, impotence). Because Panurge is unable to decide, Pantagruel encourages recourse to various forms of divination. Initially, the two randomly pick and interpret passages from Virgil. Each time, Pantagruel offers a negative reading, and Panurge counters with a positive one. Pantagruel asserts that one passage means, "It signifies that your wife will be a whore, and consequently you'll be a cuckold." Panurge insists instead, "This augury denotes that my wife will be modest, chaste, and faithful, not up in arms, or rebellious, or headstrong and head-born like Pallas."[1] Frustrated by the lack of a clear answer, Panurge resorts to dream interpretation. Once again, he and Pantagruel disagree about the meaning of the dream, with Pantagruel warning that the wife in the dream who plants horns on Panurge means he will be cuckolded and Panurge insisting that the horns mean abundance and good fortune. Consultations with "experts" ranging from a sibyl to a philosopher and a physician provide no further clarity. Along the way, Herr Trippa, consulted in his guise as an astrologer, casts Panurge's horoscope and finds that it indicates cuckoldry: "For I find the seventh house malignant in all its aspects, and exposed to the assaults of the all the signs bearing horns, such as Aries, Taurus, Capricorn, and others."[2] Herr Trippa offers Panurge a panoply of other divinatory techniques, but this only vexes Panurge, who wants to be told unambiguously that he should marry and that it will all be fine when he does.

---

[1] François Rabelais, *The Histories of Gargantua and Pantagruel*, ed. and trans. J. M. Cohen (New York: Penguin, 1955), 317–18. The marriage question occupies much of the *Tiers livre* (pp. 289–432). As Todd W. Reeser notes, Panurge is attempting to moderate his excesses through marriage in order to inhabit an effective masculine position. See *Moderating Masculinity in Early Modern Culture*. Terence Cave discusses the fertility theme as related to cornucopian imagery and sexual potency throughout Rabelais' text. See *The Cornucopian Text*, 183–222.
[2] Rabelais, *Gargantua and Pantagruel*, 357.

Rabelais's skewering of divinatory practices gained traction because many readers in Renaissance France regarded the connection between marriage and the future as serious business.[3] Like Panurge, most Renaissance customers sought reassurance; unlike Panurge, most found that astrology offered certainties about love, marriage and sex. Consider the anonymous woman for whom an astrologer prepared an elaborate nativity.[4] The woman, born December 20, 1533, is told that Venus was in a favorable aspect, and that she will meet "d'une homme de noble plaisante, agreeable et elegante taille" [a noble man who is pleasant, agreeable, and of an elegant stature]. She will enjoy "diverses joyes & amours" [various joys and loves], the position of the moon will give her "plusieurs filles" [several daughters] and, "Le soleil en la segonde maison signifie proffict par bonne amour et dilection entre les gens" [The sun in the second house signifies profit through good love and delectation between people].[5] Because of the position of Pisces, she is at risk that her husband will love another woman, and she must be cautious because the Moon in the house of Venus inclines her to sensuality.[6] The certainties are cautious and organized with conventions much in mind. A handsome husband who might stray and the female inclination to lasciviousness are not terribly surprising, but the very conventionality of the predictions may have provided comfort. Tagged to the woman's particular nativity, general astrological "rules" gained personal specificity.

In some ways, it might seem that astrology is worlds away from the textual conundra of polymorphous Orpheus. Where Orpheus represents ancient culture for its perverse possibilities, astrology was resolutely normative. Where humanist textual techniques gained acceptance in the Renaissance, astrological practices came under increasing suspicion. The questions were on the rise even before the universe-altering effects of Nicolaus Copernicus took hold. How did a set of obviously problematic practices such as astrology survive? First, despite the apparent differences, both Orpheus and astrology occupied the same intellectual space. Astrology was grounded in the same ancient past and was the object of study for many of the same people who fretted about past perversions in Renaissance Christendom. Second – as the anonymous woman above discovered – astrology had much to say about sex (both biological difference

[3] Rabelais also took hack astrologers to task in *La Pantagrueline prognostication. Certaine, veritable & infaillable pour l'an perpetuel. Nouvellement composée au prouffit & advisement de gens estourdis & musars de nature, Par maistre Alcofribas, architriclin dudict Pantagruel* (Lyon: François Juste, 1542). This edition is regarded as the definitive text. See François Rabelais, *La Pantagrueline prognostication*, preface François Bon and Louis Dubost (Charente: le dé bleu, 1994), 10 for comment.
[4] In addition to presentation copies of horoscopes, royal decoration sometimes included horoscopes. Janet Cox-Rearick, *Dynasty and Destiny in Medici Art. Pontormo, Leo X and the two Cosimos* (Princeton University Press, 1984), 166–7, notes that the Medici family often festooned their residences with horoscopes.
[5] BN MS fr 2489, fols. 8v–9r, 17v, 20v.   [6] BN MS fr 2489, fols. 22r–23r.

and sexual acts), generation, and marriage. Astrology was, and is, about many things, but one central theme is sex. Astrologers understood heavenly config- urations that facilitated or impeded love. Astrologers told people whether to marry, when to do so, and with what sort of person. Astrologers warned against likely adulterous partners, fornicators, and poor performers, while indicating faithful spouses, chaste partners, and prolific unions. On levels both popular and intellectual, people believed that the sexual content of astrology mediated the distance between the corporeal and the heavenly. And it is people – not just men or women. The stars had effects – some different; some the same – on both genders. The mental world of French Renaissance sex included the negotiation of all these differences and similarities.

Stars, sex, and history

Recognizing that astrology was a sexual discourse is not how astrology is usu- ally viewed by historians.[7] Within the Renaissance, astrology helped to mark the contours of the "philosophy of man." The centrality of human endeavor, some historians claimed, defined the Renaissance as different from the Mid- dle Ages. In this reading, astrology was a throwback, properly repudiated by Renaissance thinkers. Jacob Burckhardt dismissed attempts by humanists to uti- lize astrology to understand the operations of the material world and regarded Giovanni Pico della Mirandola as the hero who destroyed the credibility of astrology. Burckhardt's thesis that the Renaissance was marked by the rise of the individual determined his understanding of astrology. As a practice, astrol- ogy followed rules that destined or fated human beings. In a way replicating early modern concerns over free will that recurred in Renaissance arguments over the validity of astrology,[8] Burckhardt viewed it as subjecting free will and human agency to impersonal forces, and until Renaissance culture broke free of such thinking, individual identity could not blossom.[9] Yet Burckhardt ignored the fact that Pico was the anomaly. Astrology reached new heights of popularity

---

[7] For a brief account of taking astrology seriously, see Günther Oestmann, H. Darrel Rutkin, and Kocku von Stuckrad, "Introduction: Horoscopes and History," in Günther Oestmann, H. Darrel Rutkin, and Kocku von Stuckrad, eds., *Horoscopes and Public Spheres: Essays on the History of Astrology* (Berlin and New York: Walter de Gruyter, 2005), 1–9.

[8] Much debate about astrology in the Christian west centered on the question of free will vs. astral determinism. Almost every extensive treatment of astrology included a statement acknowledging free will and denying, more or less strongly, that the stars dictated human destiny. See Pierre Freyburger, "Le problème du fatalisme astral dans la pensée protestante en pays Germaniques," in *Divination et controverse religieuse en France au XVIe siècle* (Paris: Ecole normale supérieure de jeunes filles, 1987), 35–55, and Y. Tzvi Langermann, "Some Astrological Themes in the Thought of Abraham ibn Ezra," in *The Jews and the Sciences in the Middle Ages* (Aldershot and Brookfield, VT: Ashgate, 1999), 28–85. For a Renaissance French critique of astrology centered on the free-will question, see David Finarensis, *L'Epitome de David Finarensis, medicin, de la vraye astrologie* (Paris: Estienne Groulleau, 1547).

[9] Jacob Burckhardt, *The Civilization of the Renaissance in Italy*, trans. S. G. C. Middlemore (New York: Modern Library, 2002).

in the Renaissance. Historian Eugenio Garin accepted Pico as a spokesman for individual initiative, but saw astrology in the Renaissance in more productive terms relative to debates over history, magic, and Neoplatonism. He emphasized that even Pico accepted much of astrology, and Garin took seriously how investigations into astrology and its shortcomings shaped notions of change and understandings of the place of humanity in the cosmos.[10]

While he turned Burckhardt's Pico to rather different purposes, Garin continued a tradition of focusing on the high intellectual side of Renaissance astrology. The focus is apparent going back to Lynn Thorndike, who regarded the thirteenth century as a high-water mark in scientific activity. He was contemptuous of Renaissance practices like astrology, which he felt contributed to the decline of scientific practice.[11] At the same time, Thorndike's *History of Magic and Experimental Science* provided a rich base of texts that revealed practices and habits of thought.[12] While his attention focused on printed debates, Thorndike gave a sense of how practitioners thought about the heavens. Studies of the conceptualization of the world through the astrological concepts of Pietro Pomponazzi or the medical astrology of Marsilio Ficino brought out the texture and complexity of Renaissance astrology.[13] Nonetheless, the tendency to dismiss astrology as at best a detour on the way to the rise of rational science remained.[14]

With the rise of attention to everyday life and social practice in the 1960s and 1970s, work like Thorndike's gave way to research into how common people and practicing astrologers regarded the heavens. Keith Thomas centered his analysis on the casebooks of Simon Forman, William Lilly, John Booker, and Richard Napier. From their consulting practices, Thomas reconstructed the daily business of astrology. On being asked a question, the astrologer drew up a horoscope and interpreted it. Thomas notes this usually took about 15 minutes, and astrologers often performed upwards of 1,000 consultations each year.

---

[10] Eugenio Garin, *Astrology in the Renaissance: The Zodiac of Life*, trans. Carolyn Jackson, June Allen, and Clare Robertson (London: Routledge & Kegan Paul, 1983). Originally published as *Lo zodiaco della vita* (Bari: Editori Laterza, 1976).

[11] See Lynn Thorndike, *Science and Thought in the Fifteenth Century: Studies in the History of Medicine and Surgery* (New York: Columbia University Press, 1929).

[12] Lynn Thorndike, *A History of Magic and Experimental Science*, 8 vols. (New York: Columbia University Press, 1923–1958). [Hereafter *HMES*.] Thorndike is disparaging about astrology here as well. See for instance vol. VI, 206, where Thorndike comments that there is finally "hope for the future" with the waning of astrological argument in the sixteenth century.

[13] Ernst Cassirer, *The Individual and the Cosmos in Renaissance Philosophy*, trans. and intro. Mario Domandi (New York and Evanston: Harper & Row, 1963), 73–122; D. P. Walker, *Spiritual and Demonic Magic from Ficino to Campanella* (London: University of London and Warburg Institute, 1958).

[14] This was true in the important reconsideration of astrology by Otto Neugebauer, "The Study of Wretched Subjects," *Isis* 42:2 (1951): 111. While opening up space for the study of astrology as a serious system of thought, Neugebauer still regarded it primarily in terms of the development of astronomy.

Astrology was readily available, and cheap enough for the impecunious (such as female servants) to utilize it. Thomas emphasized the precarious circumstances of early modern people in order to explain the recourse to divinatory or judicial astrology.[15] Within his magisterial study, Thomas situated astrology as part of a world view that collapsed by the end of the seventeenth century.[16] He maintained that astrology, despite its flexibility, finally failed to satisfy, although parts of it (medical astrology, meteorology) persisted in modified form. Thomas was certainly right that astrology receded as an explanatory framework, but its persistence requires further consideration. Not just a matter of mathematics or high-level interpretation of complex rules, astrology involved attention to the needs of the client or consumer. Horoscopes served as a means of self-expression, contributing to autobiographical analysis of the self.[17] Kocku von Stuckrad has argued that astrology maintained its credibility because its practices revealed and celebrated the personality of the customer.[18] The processes of astrology offered people more than just information.

Analysis of astrological practices represents one mode of fusing intellectual understanding of astrology with broader cultural readings of it as a social practice. Another mode has been to focus on a central figure. Textured reconstruction of the astrological beliefs of Pierre d'Ailly by Laura Ackerman Smoller offers a window into the intersecting concerns of a devout ecclesiastical politician and astrological theorist in the troubled period of the Great Schism.[19] Anthony Grafton has brilliantly located Girolamo Cardano as a Renaissance astrologer.[20]

---

[15] Predictive astrology (as opposed to medical or natural astrology) is often called "judicial" in the historical record and by historians. Richard Lemay argues that this is a mistranslation of the Greek for "prognostication" by Arab translators, who substituted "judgment" instead. See "The True Place of Astrology in Medieval Science and Philosophy: Towards a Definition," in *Astrology, Science, and Society: Historical Essays*, ed. Patrick Curry (Woodbridge, Suffolk: Boydell, 1987), 57–73. See esp. p. 67.

[16] Thomas, *Religion and the Decline of Magic*, 335–458. See also Samuel Jeake, *An Astrological Diary of the Seventeenth Century. Samuel Jeake of Rye 1652–1699*, ed. and intro. Michael Hunter and Annabel Gregory (Oxford: Clarendon, 1988). The diary is later, but reveals how one man located astrology in his life. I have been unable to locate any casebooks for France, but there is no reason to think French popular practices were significantly different than English ones.

[17] Kocku von Stuckrad, "The Function of Horoscopes in Biographical Narrative: Cardano and After," in *Horoscopes and Public Spheres: Essays on the History of Astrology* (Berlin and New York: de Gruyter, 2005), 225–40.

[18] Kocku von Stuckrad, *Geschicte der Astrologie. Von den Anfängen bis zur Genenwart* (Munich: Beck, 2003). See also Roy Willis and Patrick Curry, *Astrology, Science and Culture: Pulling Down the Moon* (Oxford: Berg, 2004), 97, 104–6 for the argument that preparing horoscopes was a source of meaning unto itself.

[19] Laura Ackerman Smoller, *History, Prophecy, and the Stars: The Christian Astrology of Pierre d'Ailly, 1350–1420* (Princeton University Press, 1994).

[20] Anthony Grafton, *Cardano's Cosmos: The World and Works of a Renaissance Astrologer* (Cambridge, MA and London: Harvard University Press, 1999). See also Nancy Siraisi, *The Clock and the Mirror: Girolamo Cardano and Renaissance Medicine* (Princeton University Press, 1997), which focuses on Cardano as a physician.

Correcting the image of Renaissance humanism as unfailingly devoted to the dignity of man, Grafton reveals how competition for patronage and utilization of print technology were aspects of an astrological career. Pierre Brind'Amour has situated Michel de Nostradamus in the same world, revealing that the "prophet of Sedan" was both an erudite and a con man. Nostradamus knew much of the theoretical and technical literature, but his methods were obscure, his calculations often faulty, and his justifications for his methods unsound.[21]

The careers of Cardano and Nostradamus point to related aspects of the historiography: analysis of controversies within astrology which were central to Renaissance life. Of its several contexts, one of the most important for astrology was as part of the religious crisis of the Reformation, and it is in this vein that it has been studied in France. For Denis Crouzet, the French Reformation produced and was the product of acute anxiety about impending doom. Crouzet's larger thesis addresses the cycle of religious violence produced by the climate of fear. Preaching sermons warning that the apocalypse was at hand, prophetic priests fed the panic over the future. Astrology provided some counterweight against such fears. Predictions of future events merged with incitements to violence in which God's wrath was supposed to be appeased by eradicating heretics.[22] While some critics have reacted with skepticism to the larger thesis, Crouzet's focus on anguish over religious belief relative to astrology is appropriate. Eschatological preoccupations and instability that erupted into sporadic but recurrent civil war made the need for reassurance about the future acute.[23]

Astrological configurations and portents signaled impending catastrophe, and contemporaries thought they did so in predictable ways. The work of Jean Céard located seemingly far more unpredictable happenings: monsters and prodigies. While mostly analyzing the culture around monstrous births and marvels, Céard traces patterns of thought related to astrology as well. Marvels were natural (according to Aristotle), signs from God (according to Cicero), or indications of the power of nature (according to Pliny).[24] The Augustinian reworking of the monstrous as miraculous allowed space for understanding

[21] Pierre Brind'Amour, *Nostradamus astrophile: les astres et l'astrologie dans la vie et l'œuvre de Nostradamus* (Ottawa and Paris: Presses de l'Université d'Ottawa and Klincksieck, 1993). While the most famous French Renaissance astrologer by far, Nostradamus was just one of many in this culture. He receives attention as appropriate to the issues.

[22] Crouzet, *Les Guerriers de Dieu.*

[23] On the idea of astrology as providing reassurance in troubled times, see for instance Don Cameron Allen, *The Star-Crossed Renaissance: The Quarrel about Astrology and Its Influence in England* (Durham, NC: Duke University Press, 1941), 47–8. Despite the title, Allen considers continental sources. Allen tends to excuse his favorite authors from "superstition," but he takes astrology seriously as a cultural formation.

[24] Jean Céard, *La Nature et les prodiges: l'insolite au XVIᵉ siècle, en France* (Geneva: Droz, 1977).

signs in the heavens within a religiously orthodox scheme. Some theorists and poets – Céard sees Pierre de Ronsard in this vein – accepted prophecy through astrological interpretation as a means of understanding God's presence in the world. Obviously, the world of religious war, sectarian violence, and monstrous births was a profoundly uncertain one. The texture of studies such as Crouzet's and Céard's brings out not just the uncertainty, but the desire to address it. Astrology provided a corrective within accepted understandings of the workings of the universe.

Theory and practice, erudite and popular, came together in the search for astrological answers. Astrologers featured sexual information not because it was titillating (although some critics feared that it was), but rather, because their clients wanted to tilt the odds in their favor with respect to securing a future for their descendants. Men and women wanted help choosing a good spouse, or at least, avoiding one compromised by the heavens. Some men wanted to know which women were likely to be chaste; others sought wives who would produce many children. A few wanted to know which women were likely to be adulterous or barren. Some people learned that their own geniture indicated a propensity toward lasciviousness or sterility; others, that they would marry more than once. Many parents discovered that they would have only girls or several of their children would die young. Even if the information was discouraging, astrology offered the prospect of a future. Astrology provided various kinds of assurances, but none so basic as those around sex and never with more urgency than when social order threatened to collapse.

How the heavens were understood came in for intense negotiation in Renaissance France. The backdrop against which developments in France took the shape they did was one of controversy within astrology itself. Long a part of the image and intellectual archive at all levels of society, astrology inspired vociferous attacks and spirited defenses recurrently from antiquity, through the Middle Ages, and into early modernity. I am neither going to rehearse all of the debates, nor address them in technical detail. I am going to pull through intersecting discussions as they addressed generation. Astrologers, theorists, and critics worried a great deal about timing – with respect to the moment of generation and in terms of specific queries. They also argued over the logic and accuracy of descriptions of the heavens. How the stars worked was as important as when certain effects could be expected to occur. Sex was not the only issue at stake in these debates, but sex enabled mediation between the heavens and the earth.

Where Chapter 1 was about claiming new meanings from ancient and Medieval materials, Chapter 2 is about retaining old meanings as they came under assault from new ideas. Rather than appealing to change and new assertions such as linguistic patriotism, advocates, enthusiasts, and consumers of astrology staked their claims on procreative utility. This solidified the normative tendency toward marital reproductive sex. Where humanists excised queer

Orphic bits, astrology enthusiasts (often humanists; often the same humanists who read and wrote about Ovid and Orpheus) provided a utilitarian logic for astrology in the face of routine and novel skepticism.[25] As an element in the sexual culture of Renaissance France, astrology's generative preoccupations made the universe, not just Earth, devoted to heterosexual normativity expressed through fertility and generation.

Shepherds and their calendars

Although direct access to individual beliefs about astrology is only occasionally available, articulations of the connections between the corporeal and the stars on a popular level are not hard to come by. Under several spellings and orderings of the title, the *Le Compost et Kalendrier des bergiers* was reprinted at least twenty-one times between 1493 and 1633.[26] Around the core text, various editions added information about health, physiognomy, and the Zodiac.[27] From its first edition, the *Kalendrier* included an outline of its contents that was repeated in all subsequent editions, regardless of additions and subtractions that often rendered the main sections indistinguishable from other topics. After two prologues, the five main parts (each with several subsections) were the calendar, the Tree of Vices, the Seven Deadly Sins, considerations of health, and basic astrology. Each section and the evolution of the editions over time tell a story of popular perceptions of the ways astrology was about sex. The *Kalendriers* aimed to teach consumers (readers, those who viewed the illustrations, listeners) how to negotiate a safer way through life on earth and toward salvation after it.

We do not know a great deal about those consumers, but the physical objects are suggestive. The core text was printed in Gothic letters with later additions sometimes in a hybrid of Roman and Gothic, and sometimes in Gothic – even long after Roman font was the preferred typeface of printers. Henri Zerner argues that Gothic letters persisted because they appealed to a less educated

---

[25] Nicolaus Copernicus died in 1543. His theoretical reconfiguration of the heavens, *De revolutionibus orbium coelestium*, was then published. This means that, smack in the middle of the story of this chapter, the heavens change order. It mattered not a whit to most of those who wrote about astrology.

[26] Heinrich O. Sommer, ed. *The Kalender of Shepherdes. The Edition of Paris 1503 in Photographic Facsimile, A Faithful Reprint of R. Pynson's Edition of London 1506. Edited with a Critical Introduction and Glossary* (London: Kegan Paul, 1892). The literature situating the *kalendriers* is limited, but see Auguste Denis, *Recherches bibliographiques et historiques sur les almanachs de la Champagne et de la Brie précédées d'un essai sur l'histoire de l'almanach en général* (Chalons-sur-Marne: Chez l'Auteur, 1880) and Geneviève Bollème, *Les Almanachs populaires aux XVIIe et XVIIIe siècles: essai d'histoire sociale* (Paris: Mouton, 1969).

[27] On the related genre of popular astrology pamphlets, see Dietrich Kurze, "Popular Astrology and Prophecy in the Fifteenth and Sixteenth Centuries: Johannes Lichtenberger," in *"Astrologi Hallucinati": Stars and the End of the World in Luther's Time*, ed. Paola Zambelli (Berlin and New York: Walter de Gruyter, 1986), 176–93.

public who had been taught to read Gothic letters. Learning a new font was work.[28] Gothic font also evoked the elongated forms of Gothic architecture, considered a French form. Typefaces reflected national identifications in the sixteenth century: the Italians switched rapidly to Italic or Roman; the French retained the Gothic with infusions of Roman and Italic.

This tradition-minded reading public looked to the *Kalendriers* for assistance with eschatological and agricultural concerns. The mediation of heaven and earth figures throughout the text. The prologues lay out the scheme of the *Kalendrier* in terms of teaching men (and they usually mean men) how to live a holy life. The author's prologue does this within a scheme in which degeneration marks human existence:

Autant de temps que l'homme est a venir en sa force, vigueur et beauté, autant en doit mectre par raison pour enviellir, affoiblir et tourner a neant.	As much time that a man has to come into his greatest strength, vigor and beauty, as much should be spent for the reason of aging, becoming feeble, and returning to nothing.[29]

The ages of man in which he is growing and developing are short compared to his decline. Men must prepare for the afterlife because life is short. The second prologue, by the wise shepherd who supposedly inspired the *Kalendrier*, traces the months of the year as representing the ages of man. Each month represents six years. In January, the child lacks strength and can do nothing to help the family "profit;" between the ages of 7 and 12 (February), the child grows just like the world gets warmer and greener; up to the age of 18 (March), the young man grows, sows, and plants. In April, he increases his abundance and learns to deal with setbacks like cold snaps. This covers ages 19–24, and then in May (up to age 30), he is strong and given to lusty pastimes. In June (years 31–36), the sun is at its peak, and so are his physical powers. The sun declines in July (37–42), bringing sadness, and in August (43–48), he learns to protect the goods he has gathered. Deterioration starts in earnest by September (49–56), with his powers receding. By October (57–63), he can do little that is productive, and is advised to turn to God and prepare for heaven. November (64–70) is marked by loss of heat and vitality, and in December, he grows cold like the earth to which he returns. The cycle of life as a yearly calendar tags the progression of human life to the agricultural pattern. The outline of the rest of the *Kalendrier* which closes the prologue announces that it will teach men how to proceed through the months and through life.[30]

---

[28] Henri Zerner, *Renaissance Art in France: The Invention of Classicism*, trans. Deke Dusinberre, Scott Wilson, and Rachel Zerner (Paris: Flammarion, 2003), 11–13.

[29] Anon., *Le grant kalendrier et compost des Bergiers* (Paris: Payot, 1525), unpaginated author's prologue.

[30] Anon., *Le Compost et kalendrier des bergiers* (Paris: Guiot Marchant, 1493), sig. aiiii(v).

As in the account of the life cycle, some aspects of the *Kalendrier* are more obviously concerned with generation than others, but in the miscellany of information, sex is always present. Consider the calendar proper – that is, the section that includes dates for feast days and eclipses. This segment opens with instructions about how to use dominical letters and golden numbers, along with a method for finding the holy days using the joints of the hand.[31] Tables of feast days with poems about the relevant activities for that part of the Zodiac follow. In more lavish editions, each month is illustrated with an appropriate woodcut; in cheaper ones, the images usually remained but scaled down in size and complexity. In the 1499 edition, January features a man seated before a fire while a servant brings in wood, March illustrates planting, June highlights sheep shearing, July and August show harvesting, September is for crushing grapes into wine, and November is for slaughtering animals. The images are predominantly agricultural, but April and May dwell on human desire. The April woodcut features a man taking flowers to a woman sitting with her legs outstretched on the grass. In May, matters have advanced: now the couple are together on horseback, looking at each other amorously. As G. R. Quaife found for early modern England, couples riding together on horseback raised questions about their chastity.[32] The poem accompanying the May picture fends off criticism in advance:

Je suis le may par qui paree   I am May, by which appears
Est mainte belle damoiselle   Many a beautiful girl
Et en mon temps fut approuve   And in my time it was approved
Des docteurs la saincte querelle.   By doctors in holy quarrel.[33]

Approval is presumably courtship followed by marriage, situating desire in the context of God's creation through procreation. As part of the cycle of life, sex is natural.

At the same time, as the May poem suggests, all things in the world of the *Kalendrier*, including sex, must be disciplined along Christian lines. The next section, the Tree of Vices, explains sins of all kinds.[34] In most editions, the Tree is literalized as an image of a tree, with the seven deadly sins forming the

---

[31] Dominical letters are A–G assigned to the days of the week to aid in calculating feast days, especially Easter. Golden numbers are assigned to each year in order in the nineteen-year Metonic cycle, which is the common multiple for the lunar month.

[32] G. R. Quaife, *Wanton Wenches and Wayward Wives: Peasants and Illicit Sex in Early Seventeenth-Century England* (London: Croom Helm, 1979).

[33] Anon., *Compost et Kalendrier des bergiers* (Paris: Maistre Guy Marchant, 1500), unpaginated (May).

[34] Except for the 1499 version, which is unique in featuring a dance macabre and several dialogues with female protagonists. See Anon., *Le Kalendrier des bergieres* (Paris: en l'ostel de beauregart en la rue Cloppin a lenseigne du roy Prestre jehan, 1499).

Figure 6. "May," in Anon., *Le Grant Kalendrier et compost des Bergiers avecq leur Astrologie. Et plusieurs aultres choses* (Troyes: Nicolas le Rouge, 1529), unpaginated. British Library.

In the yearly scheme of the astrological *Kalendriers*, May is the month for romance. The couple on horseback suggests a sexual relationship. The bull in the upper right is a reference to Taurus.

main branches and smaller branches (each of which is subdivided into three parts) varying by sin. The Tree includes 17 branches for pride, 13 for envy, 10 for wrath, 17 for sloth, 20 for covetousness, 5 for gluttony, and 5 for lechery. Lust is the last category and among its parts are:

Fornication, adulterie, exces, de pensee, de corps, du de tous deux ensemble, non rendre devoir, abuser de ses cinq sens, superfluitie.

Fornication, adultery, excess – of thought, of body, or of both together, not doing one's duty, abusing the five senses, superfluity.

Nor does the text shy away from the content of these sins, defining each in case the reader is unclear:

Fornication: Avec toutes femmes mariees ou veufves, avec fille qui encore estoit pucelle, avec les communes ou corrumpues. Adultery: Devant homme congnoist autre femme que la sienne, ou femme accompaignee dautre que de son mary.

Fornication: With all married women or widowed women, with a girl who was still a virgin, with common [women] or corrupt ones. Adultery: Given a man knows another woman than his own, or a woman accompanied by other than her own husband.[35]

The narrative tries to corral sin in its message and structure. Women are both more prone to vice (they can be prostitutes or just bad women) and more policed (merely accompanying a man is adultery for a woman). The Tree is followed by a ballad decrying the instability of worldly affairs, which serves as a prelude for graphic images of punishments for the seven deadly sins. Both the narrative mechanism and the punishments recall Dante's *Inferno*: the narrator announces that Lazarus, come back from the dead, has seen what is done to sinners. Vivid woodcuts depict the slothful being harried by hideous devils and the lusty impaled on unsubtle phallic pikes. The warning against sexual sin treats it like a contagious disease:

Luxure est la fosse du deable laquelle fait cheoir les pecheurs desquelz aucuns aident au deable . . .

Lechery is the cesspool of the devil, which makes sinners choose in which ways they aid the devil . . . .

The sins of "maquerelles, paillars, putains" [macks, lechers, and whores] are the worst, because they seduce others into the sins of lechery with their words, songs, and "atouchemens" [touches].[36] The text takes on a narrative quality, offering the "garden of virtue" to those who cleanse their consciences. To that end, the narrator encourages reciting and understanding the main prayers of the Church (the Lord's Prayer, Credo, Ave Maria, Ten Commandments, and the five

---

[35] Anon., *Cy est enseigne et demonstre le kalendrier et compost des bergiers* (Rouen: chez Raulin Gaultier, 1505), unpaginated (part 2).

[36] *Kalendrier* (1505), unpaginated (part 2).

articles of the Church). Knowing these will lead to the Tower of Wisdom, which is identified as the Love of God. In case it was not clear already, the section culminates with the thumbnail version: a woodcut of the Tree of Virtues (topped with chastity) facing a Tree of Vices (topped with lechery). Echoing erudite Neoplatonic formulations,[37] proper negotiation of the perils of sex determines salvation.

But what does all this have to do with astrology? First, calendars were the work of those who studied the movements of the heavens. Second, with the cycles described, the gendered and sexualized stars in various guises influenced or governed the body. Medical astrology, the *Kalendrier* allows, offers knowledge of which sign prevails over the health of which body part. Doctors and patients, for instance, must pay attention to Scorpio if the problem is genital. Readers are advised that if one suffers from "douleurs & enfleures des genitoires" [dolorous things and inflammation of the genitals], blood-letting is recommended.[38] The text features an image of a man to illustrate the celestial influences on phlebotomy.[39] The man in the image is always naked, and he gets more androgynous and prudish over time. By 1551, he has become voluptuous in the hips and his penis is covered by a large letter "X."

Third, the *Kalendrier* provides information about how the stars effect humankind by means of stellar or planetary gendering. The text explains how to calculate the equinoctial and the Zodiac, provides information about the influences of the fixed stars, and gives lessons on reading the night sky. The technical aspects serve as a prelude for the gender and sexual characteristics of the planets and the Zodiac. Depictions of the planets divide them into male and female, with images of Saturn, Jupiter, Mars, and the Sun as men on one page and Venus and the Moon as women on another. Mercury is with the girls, with long hair and posed like a woman.[40] Deliberately androgynous, Mercury has small breasts and stringier muscles than the female planets to indicate that Mercury is changeable in its qualities.[41] All the planets are covered so as to

---

[37] See Chapter 3 below.

[38] Anon., *Le grand calendier et compost des bergiers compose par le bergier de la grand montaigne* (Lyon: Jehan Canterel, 1551), unpaginated (before sig. Jii).

[39] Human figures with the medical influences of the signs of the Zodiac go back to antiquity. See Charles W. Clark, "The Zodiac Man in Medieval Medical Astrology," Ph.D. diss. (University of Colorado, 1979), esp. 1–60. Clark traces the development of the microcosm (man) to macrocosm (universe) as a guiding analogy in medical thinking as it developed out of a variety of traditions.

[40] *Kalendrier* (1500), sig. kii(v) for the personifications of the planets.

[41] Under the influence of masculine planets, Mercury took on male characteristics, but when in relation to Venus especially, Mercury deferred to the feminine. Ptolemy emphasized Mercury's changeable nature. See Claudius Ptolemy, *Tetrabiblos*, trans. F. E. Robbins (Cambridge, MA: Harvard University Press, 1940/1998), II, 8 (pp. 186–7).

Figure 7. Anon., *Le Compost et kalendrier des bergiers* (Paris: Guiot marchant, 1493), sig. Hi. British Library.

Depiction of the corporeal effects of the signs of the Zodiac. Images like this one indicate which parts of the Zodiac effect different parts of the human body. Note that the images are arranged to cover the figure's sexual organs.

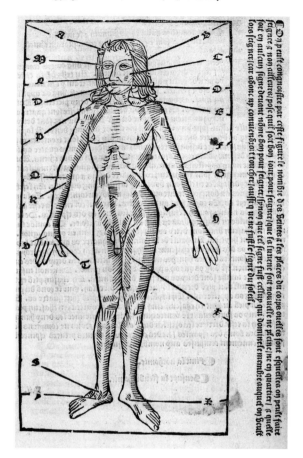

Figure 8. "S'ensuyt la fleubothomie des corps humains," in Anon., *Le Grant Kalendrier et compost des Bergiers avecq leur Astrologie. Et plusieurs aultres choses* (Troyes: Nicolas le Rouge, 1529), L lxxxiii. British Library.

In some contrast to the previous image, "Phlebotomy Man," another recurring image in astrology texts, is naked. In some versions the "x" that points to his genitals is actually positioned over them to cover them.

bring attention to their hidden genitals: stars or faces cover their privates. The gendering matters because each planet has areas of influence determined by gendered characteristics. Venus is beautiful and flirtatious, and so, dominant in love. A poem explains that "she" governs love and sex ("Venus planette suis nommee / Des amoureux forte & aymee" [I am named Venus / Planet of great lovers and the loved]).[42] Most versions of the *Kalendrier* include a woodcut featuring a man and a woman in a bath with a musician playing while a second couple canoodle in the background. The elemental characteristics of the planets thus link human physiology and behavior with sexual congress and the presumption of generation as a central mode of human efficacy within an astrological vision of the universe.

While some technical information disappears in later editions (for one, the chart of the phases of the Moon drops out), all of the sexual references above appear in almost every printing. Over time, the astrological connections between human generation and the influence of the stars increased, as indicated by the addition of information devoted to proper understanding of the effects of the stars on sex. By 1505, the compilers of the *Kalendrier* included a new section on the Zodiac that provided information about the dominant behaviors of those conceived under each sign. A man born in Aries, " . . . jusques a xxxiii ans il sera grant fornicateur & sera marie a xxv ans & sil ne se remarie il ne sera point chaste" [. . . up to 23 years old, he will be a great fornicator, and will be married at 25 years old, and if he does not marry again, he will not be chaste]. A girl born in Aries: " . . . perdra son mary & en recouvrera ung meilleur" [. . . will lose her husband but will get a better one]. Women born in Taurus could expect to have several husbands and many children, while those born in Aquarius would have many children but by one husband. Men born in Capricorn and Pisces would be fornicators, while a woman born in Libra, "ne sera pas chaste" [will not be chaste]. Both men and women born in Virgo, " . . . souffreront plusieurs temptacions tant que a grant peine y pourront resister: ilz delecteront de vivre en chastete, mais ilz soufferont beaucoup" [. . . will suffer many temptations, only with great effort will be able to resist: they will delight in living in chastity, but they will suffer much].[43] Every sign had something to say about marriage, sexual performance, or lascivious misconduct as a matter of personality.

Astrological advice about the body supports but also revises Thomas Laqueur's argument that early modern peoples saw the human body as having only one sex.[44] By 1529, another new section appeared, "Regime comment la femme se doit gouverner quant elle veult avoir enfans" [Regime on how a woman ought to govern herself when she wants to have children].[45] It explained how to recognize conception and if the child she was carrying was male.

---

[42] *Kalendrier* (1505), unpaginated (part 4).   [43] *Kalendrier* (1505), unpaginated (part 5).

[44] Laqueur, *Making Sex*; "Orgasm, Generation, and the Politics of Reproductive Biology," *Representations* 14 (1986): 1–41. A number of historians have been critical of Laqueur's thesis. See especially Katharine Park and Robert Nye, "Destiny Is Anatomy," *New Republic* (February 18, 1991): 53–7.

[45] Anon., *Le grant kalendrier et compost des Bergiers avecq leur Astrologie* (Troyes: Nicolas le Rouge, 1529), beginning sig. Oiiir.

Figure 9. Anon. (sixteenth century), *The Constellation Virgo*, engraving, Bibliothèque nationale de France, Paris.
    Female personifications of the Zodiac were often depicted in classical garb with traditional suggestions of fertility (the wide hips and abundant drapery, for instance) and in sexualized terms (the posture of Virgo presents her as sexually forward).

Readers were advised to give beer and fennel to nursing women to help them develop abundant milk. The section advises women on how to recover from delivery (including recipes), on preventing the midwife from forcing the baby out, on restoring menses, and on proper humoral balance to ensure pregnancy. Steeped in humoral theory, all of this is standard early modern medical advice.[46] Linking the astrological and medical one last time – the Moon, the reader is told, catalyzes changes during pregnancy because of its humidity. This information is about making sure that procreative sex works as it should under the protection of, and with the aid of, the heavens above. That the stars were thought to have effects regardless of gender confirms the notion that humans were seen as fundamentally the same. But in producing certain kinds of men and women and in influencing female bodies in distinctive ways, the heavens recognized sex difference.

The *Kalendriers* and their insistent focus on reproduction as governed by the stars simplified the complexities of astrological theory in the service of material ends and within Christian ethics. Over time, editors made the instructions, advice, and admonishments more elaborate, especially around sex. Editions featured more axioms geared toward procreative success. That there was a market for this, that consumers found it useful is signaled by not just the persistence of the genre, but the increasing density and complexity of procreative direction over time. Whether this content produced or resulted from the pragmatic need for generative success at the level of the *Kalendriers* and consumers of them is not recuperable. What is recuperable is that the more rarified learned conversations about astrology took up the cause of procreation to defend the science and art of reading the stars.

The degenerating universe

Throughout the debates over timing and interpretation, generation connected earthly existence to the machinations of the heavens. As one pamphlet describing the characteristics of the decans (the ten-degree subdivisions of each sign of the Zodiac) put it:

Car ainsi qu'escrit Aristote, telles conversions d'ans & de temps faictes par ce Zodiaque, ensuivent la generation & corruption des animaux & toutes choses.	Because thus it is written by Aristotle, that such changes in the years and of the weather made by the Zodiac follow the generation and corruption of animals and all things.[47]

---

[46] For the context of humoral medical advice, see for instance Nancy G. Siraisi, *Medieval and Early Renaissance Medicine: An Introduction to Knowledge and Practice* (University of Chicago Press, 1990); Jonathan Sawday, *The Body Emblazoned: Dissection and the Human Body in the Renaissance* (London and New York: Routledge, 1995); and Mary Lindemann, *Medicine and Society in Early Modern Europe* (Cambridge University Press, 1999). Roy Porter and Lesley Hall, "Medical Folklore in High and Low Culture: Aristotle's Master-Piece," in *The Facts of Life: The Creation of Sexual Knowledge in Britain, 1650–1950*, ed. Roy Porter and Lesley Hall (New Haven: Yale University Press, 1995), 33–64, includes the observation that advice could be put to subversive uses. How to get pregnant, for instance, could be inverted into how to avoid pregnancy.

[47] Anon., *Astrologie naturelle, Par lequelle un chacun pourra sçavoir par sa nativité ce qui luy doit arriver suivant le cours des Planettes* (Paris: Michel Daniel, 1619), 4.

The explanation was at once prosaic (as the Sun moved through the sky, it was "apte à generation & procreation des choses" [apt in the generation and procreation of things]) and mysterious (why and how aptitude for generation created by the Sun's heat produced different effects was unclear). The Aristotelian corpus addressed several of these problems. In the *De caelo*, Aristotle analyzed the qualities of the heavens, or as he insisted, *the* heaven – a bounded object that encompassed neither increase nor decrease. Logic determined Aristotle's depiction of the universe. In brief, circular motion is natural and involves no change ("If the body which moves with a circular motion cannot admit increase or diminution, it is reasonable to suppose that it is also unalterable," and so, heaven is perfect and immutable. Within heaven, change is possible. Movement is either straight or circular, and either natural or unnatural. These are the basic rules that govern the stars and planets. The complexities of stellar movement are created by multiple influences working through the medium of the ether within an ungenerated and indestructible heaven. In *De caelo* and the *Meteorologica*, Aristotle suggests that ether acts as a fifth element. Although it does not operate like the other four elements (fire, air, earth and water) in terms of constituting matter, ether has a natural circular motion and can be found in the outermost stratum of heaven.[48] Fire and air move up; earth and water move down.[49] Movement occurred because of contrary elements as they existed in the usual course of things and as occasional manifestations of larger imbalances, and "it is in the contraries that generation and decay subsist."[50] Other effects were less regular and predictable, but no less a part of the system. Comets were the result of hot, dry exhalations caused by the turning of the celestial sphere. Aristotle described comets as dispersing dry, hot matter, and evidence for this was the association of comets with droughts.[51] Motion was more complicated, and Aristotle revised his thoughts about it. The *Physics* represents the version of Aristotle's understanding celestial motion as it was accepted in the Renaissance, in which, "Everything that is in motion must be moved by something."[52] After explaining natural and unnatural motion, the primacy of locomotion among the types of motion, and that rotation can be

---

[48] Quotation from Aristotle, *De caelo*, I, 3, p. 402. See also Aristotle, *Meteorologica*, trans. H. D. P. Lee (Cambridge, MA: Harvard University Press, 1952), book I, chapter 3, 339b, p. 13.

[49] Aristotle, *De caelo* in *The Basic Works of Aristotle*, ed. Richard McKeon, intro. C. D. C. Reeve (New York: Modern Library, 1941/2001), book I, chapter 2–3, (pp. 399–403); chapters 8–10 (pp. 413–21). See also *On Generation and Corruption*, book II, chapters 1–8 (pp. 507–23) for the properties and effects of the elements, including contrary, reciprocal, and compound modes of generation.

[50] Aristotle, *De caelo*, book I, chapter 3 (p. 402). This text was widely diffused in the Medieval *studia* and universities according to Roger French, "Astrology in Practical Medicine," in *Practical Medicine from Salerno to the Black Death*, ed., Roger French, Jon Arrizabalaga, and Andrew Cunningham Luis Garcia-Ballester (Cambridge University Press, 1994), 30–59. See pp. 49–50.

[51] Aristotle, *Meteorologica*, book I, chapter 7, 344a5–345a10, pp. 49–57.

[52] Aristotle, *Physics* in *Basic Works*, book VII, 1 (p. 340).

eternal, Aristotle allowed that something must move the heavens. The so-called "unmoved mover" facilitated the absorption of Aristotelian astronomy within Christian thought.[53] For astrology, the unmoved mover, along with spherical rotation, locomotion, and the elemental economy, created predictable patterns that followed behavioral rules, all of which had relevance for the sexual interpretations of astrology.

One of the most basic rules was that destruction was the lot of the planet at the center of the universe. Routine movement occurred because of contrary elements as they existed in the usual course of things and as manifestations of imbalances. Descriptions of the heavens following Aristotle – and until well after Copernicus suggested otherwise – regarded the Earth as stationary with the heavens moving around it in concentric circles tending toward perfection as they got closer to God. The strong hierarchical principle was not unique to Aristotle, but his insistence on hierarchy as the marker of teleology helped sustain the notion that the perfect heavens circled around the imperfect earth.

Motion resultant from the operations of planetary hierarchy figured in Aristotelian causality, which was central to astrological understandings of procreation. Of Aristotle's four causes (efficient, formal, material, and final), astrology texts regarded the heavens in terms of final and material causes. The predictive qualities of judicial astrology signaled the final cause. Gervasius Marstellerus was typical in adapting Aristotle in order to attribute all things to God: "Cause finalis est intentio cupientis ex viribus syderum futuros eventus praedicere" [The final cause is the intention to desire to predict future events from the stars].[54] Since one of the recurrent objections to astrology was astral determinism – the idea that the stars, rather than willed action (for Catholics) or God (for Calvinists), determined human life trajectories and events on Earth – the recourse to Aristotelian final cause language offered a mediating proposition. Most astrology texts described final causes as likelihoods mediated by the will of God.[55] The material cause was the motion of the heavens acting on the elements. While material causes were always regarded as the least significant in philosophical terms – the matter or substratum of a thing was less important than its essence (the formal cause), the source of a thing (the efficient

53 Aristotle, *Physics* in *Basic Works*, book VIII. On the development of his thought on the question of celestial motion, see Lindsay Judson, "Heavenly Motion and the Unmoved Mover," in *Self-Motion: From Aristotle to Newton*, ed. Mary Louise Gill and James G. Lennox (Princeton University Press, 1994), 155–71.
54 Gervasius Marstellarus, *Theoremata Gervasii Marstelleri Brisgoici, quibus, iuxta methodum dialecticam ostenditt, quid sit de arte diuinatrice, quam Astrologiam seu iudicariam vocant, sentiendum*, in *Artis divinatricis*, ed. Gervasius Marstallerus (Paris: Christianus Wechelus, 1549), 13–45. See p. 26.
55 Freyburger, "Le problème du fatalisme astral," and John Lewis, "Les prognostications et la propagande évangelique," in *Divination et controverse religieuse en France au XVIᵉ siècle* (Paris: Ecole normale supérieure de jeunes filles, 1987), 35–55 and 73–83.

cause), and especially the purpose or good of the thing (the formal cause) – in terms of generation, material was crucial.[56] The planetary bodies were efficient causes, while the formal cause of change on Earth was the intellect that moved the planets. The daily and annual movement of the planets, and the Sun in particular, effected the distribution of the elements. Planetary motions changed the balance and configuration of these elements, and thus, the heavens were responsible for corruption and decay, generation and growth on earth.[57] As Gad Freudenthal has observed, the question of the formal cause provided the connection between earthly matter and metaphysics. Aristotle theorized that matter is passive and tends toward declension or dissolution. Matter requires an external agent to give it form and structure. Earthly beings and substances are produced by a combination of formal and efficient causes working through the mechanism of the universal elements.[58]

The world of human reproduction resulted from and reflected the universe. Aristotelian biology maintained that in human generation, men provided the formal cause and women provided the material cause. A woman had a uterus, but was incapable of generating seed from the *catamenia* (menstrual discharge). A man, with a penis and scrotum, in Aristotle's view, produced seed that could engender offspring in the proper, uterine environment. The white, milky appearance of semen indicated that male heat had concocted male seed, something women (regarded as constitutionally colder) could not do.[59] Hierarchy and gender determined the nature of astral influence on generation, with the macrocosm of the heavens acting on the microcosm of human bodies through the mechanisms of sympathy, attraction, and repulsion.

The Ptolemaic tradition drew on Aristotelian ideas about the heavens, transforming causality in terms of generation. Three Ptolemaic works dealt with astrological subjects: the *Almagest* was a technical account of astronomy; the *Centiloquium*, attributed to Ptolemy until the Renaissance, was renowned for its theory of conjunctions; and the *Tetrabiblos*, which was devoted to astrology.[60] In the *Tetrabiblos*, Ptolemy noted:

---

[56] Aristotle, *Metaphysics*, in *Basic Works*, book I, chapter 3 (pp. 693–6).
[57] Aristotle, *De generatione et corruptione*, book II, chapter 10 (pp. 525–8); *Generation of Animals*, trans. A. L. Peck (Cambridge, MA: Harvard University Press, 2000), book IV, chapter 10, 777d–778a (pp. 476–83).
[58] Gad Freudenthal, "Maimonides' Stance on Astrology in Context: Cosmology, Physics, Medicine, and Providence," in *Moses Maimonides: Physician, Scientist, and Philosopher*, ed. Fred Rosner and Samuel S. Kottek (Northvale, NJ and London: Jason Aronson, 1993), 77–90. See esp. 78–9.
[59] Aristotle, *Generation of Animals*, book I, chapters 17–23, pp. 666–80.
[60] For an accessible modern edition, see Ptolemy, *The Almagest*, trans. R. Catesby Taliaferro, in *Great Books of the Western World 15: Ptolemy, Copernicus, Kepler*, ed. Mortimer J. Adler, 2nd edn. (University of Chicago Press, 1990), 1–478. For the *Centiloquium*, see Mellon MS 25, Yale University Beinecke Rare Book and Manuscript Library, fols. 77r–99r. This is a Latin translation by Johannes Hispalensis and includes the commentary by Haly ibn Ridwan. See also

A very few considerations would make it apparent to all that a certain power emanating from the eternal ethereal substance is dispersed through and permeates the whole region about the earth, which throughout is subject to change, since, of the primary sublunar elements, fire and air are encompassed and changed by the motions in the ether, and in turn encompass and change all else, earth and water and the plants and animals therein.[61]

Ptolemy referred to planets "in alliance" with each other, but other formulations included "in familiarity with," and "joined with" other planets to produce elemental effects.[62] Sometimes astrologers derived "copulation" from this language, especially in reference to the elements of planets and stars combining.[63] In the Ptolemaic description of astrology, sexual language marked the stellar effects that counteracted the inclination to degeneration that marked earthly existence. Heavenly bodies influenced generation through the elements emitted in their light.[64] The organization of the universe rested on and resulted from the centrality of generation within its cosmology.

Adapted by the Latin West, Aristotelian and Ptolomaic theory allowed space for God as the divine mover while accounting for the regular, observable functions of the natural world. Change, in this scheme, meant degeneration for the most part. Earth was corruptible; the heavens were not. The one routine correction on earth for the tendency toward corruption was generation. Astrological information and advice about sex facilitated reproduction, but finding one's way through that information was not always easy.

i   *The universe of controversy: timing*

Astrology was not a simple panacea for a degenerating universe. In fact, problems around generation were central in learned debates about astrology in the Renaissance. Astrological practice involved knowing the exact configuration of the heavens at a particular moment from a given latitude.[65] Timing

---

Ptolemy, *Liber quadripartiti Ptholomei* (Venice: Bonetus Locatellus apud Octavianus Scotus, 1493), which includes both the *Quadripartitum* and the *Centiloquium* with Haly's commentary.

[61] Ptolemy, *Tetrabiblos*, I, 2 (pp. 5, 7). Ptolemy treats ether as a fifth element at times. Here, it seems to function more as a medium.

[62] Ptolemy, *Tetrabiblos*, III, 13 (pp. 333–63).

[63] See for instance *Praeferatio Ioachimi Helleri in Isagogen Astronomicam Io. Hispalensis* in Marstellarus, ed., *Artis divinatricis*, 88–122. See esp. p. 101: "Martialibus signis copulates habere inuentum est" and the subsequent discussion of types of people created by negative planetary copulations.

[64] Jacques Amyot rephrases: "Quant à nous, nous voions bien qu'il y a beaucoup de similitude entre l'Amour & le Soleil: car ny l'un ny l'autre n'est feu materiel, comme quelques uns pensent, mais la chaleur de l'un et de l'autre est doulce & generative." See Plutarch [Jacques Amyot], *Les Oeuvres morales et meslees de Plutarque*, vol. III, 678v–79r.

[65] For technical aspects of early modern astrology, see for instance J. C. Eade, *The Forgotten Sky: A Guide to Astrology in English Literature* (Oxford: Clarendon, 1984).

mattered for casting horoscopes, nativities, elections, interrogations, and for making general predictions about the weather, disease, crop cycles, and worldly affairs. Astrologers interpreted the impact of the planets on the future depending on the relative positions of the planets, the Zodiac, and the fixed stars at an exact moment. The astrologer had to plot the positions of the seven planets (Saturn, Jupiter, Mars, Venus, Mercury, the Sun, and the Moon) in relation to the Zodiac. The time also determined the angular relationships among and between the Zodiac and the planets. The most important were the "aspects," which were the relationships between the planets. Opposition (180 degrees) and trine (120 degrees) were negative, while quadrature (90 degrees) and sextile (60 degrees) were beneficent. Although some considered it a separate category, conjunction was especially important because it meant that two or more planets were operating together. In astrological theory, the elements in the rays of planets acted together and reinforced each other in conjunctions. Quadrature and sextile offered some interaction of the elements, but opposition and trine usually caused the elements to hinder each other, resulting in damage on Earth. Each planet had characteristics, as did each sign of the Zodiac. A sixteenth-century French treatise described the planets in terms of their characteristics, the kinds of people they were likely to affect, qualities, "moeurs" or habits associated with them. Characteristics were elemental. The cold, humid Moon, for instance, influenced people toward travel and navigation, and things having to do with the sea. People dominated by the Moon were inclined toward being phlegmatic, prone to diseases of the cold and to stomach problems. The fixed stars could meliorate some characteristics, as could the "head and tail of the dragon," which were the points along the sun's path where the Moon's orbit, extended out into space, intersected it. The head reinforced whatever characteristic was in play; the tail opposed it.[66] The qualities of the planets, such as the heat of Mercury or Venus, had to be taken into account as shaping the sympathy or antipathy of the planets for each other. Similar relationships characterized the houses of the Zodiac, along with several further factors. The decans, sometimes thought to be demons influencing subsections of the Zodiac, and the paranatellonta, the stars that rose alongside the Zodiac, also influenced stellar relationships. Each house had areas of heightened influence: the second house was the locus of love and amorous delectation, the sixth focused on family, the eighth supported the accumulation of wealth. Despite specialization, all had some effects on just about everything. In astrological practice, timing was determinant because interpretation depended on the relationships created by exact configurations at a precise moment.

---

[66] Claude Dariot, *L'Introduction au iugement des astres, Avec un Traité des elections propres pour le commencement des choses* (Lyon: Maurice Roy et Loys Pesnot, 1558), 12.

Perhaps the most important moment was birth, as the marketplace for genitures or nativities indicates. Several historians have described astrology business practices in Renaissance Europe. Anthony Grafton emphasizes that publishers sought astrology texts that explained methodology to attract readers. The powerful, famous, and infamous were of particular interest. Among the controversial figures for whom astrologers published nativities were Jesus Christ and Martin Luther. Rivalries in the production and interpretation of genitures – Girolamo Cardano and Luca Gaurico quarreled over the nativity of Luther and vied for the patronage of François I – were common.[67] The standard was set by Gaurico, who published a collection of aphorisms to which he attached six books of horoscopes organized by subject: cities; ecclesiastics; princes; artists and humanists; those who died violently; monsters.[68] A generation later, Cyprian von Leowitz published his analysis of horoscopes.[69] In addition to the printed instruction manuals and commentaries, French customers sought out experts like Nostradamus.[70] Manuscripts of genitures reflect the enthusiasm for collecting original horoscopes.[71]

Despite their popularity, nativities were singularly vulnerable because of the importance of proper timing. Ptolemy preferred to cast a nativity based on the moment of conception, but recognizing that was impractical, he allowed that the exact moment of birth was acceptable. Even this was problematic before accurate clocks became widely available. To a critic like Pico, the technical problem of time-keeping made a mockery of the principles of precision upon which astrologers insisted.[72] John Calvin, drawing on Augustine, agreed:

---

[67] Anthony Grafton, "Geniture Collections, Origins and Uses of a Genre," in *Books and the Sciences in History*, ed. Marina Frasca-Spada and Nick Jardine (Cambridge University Press, 2000), 49–68.

[68] Luca Gaurico, *Tractatus astrologicae judiciariae de nativitatibus virorum et mulierum* (Nuremberg: Johannes Petreium, 1540). He published it first in Italian in 1539.

[69] Cyprianus von Leowitz, *Brevis et perspicua ratio judicandi genituras, ex physicis causis & vera experientia extructu* (London: H. Suttonus, 1558).

[70] Michel de Nostradame, *Nostradamus: lettres inédites* (Geneva: Droz, 1983).

[71] See for instance BN MSS fr 12293, 14763, and 14772 for geniture collections.

[72] Giovanni Pico della Mirandola, *Disputationes adversus astrologium divinatricem*, ed. and intro. Eugenio Garin, 2 vols. (Florence: Vallecchi: 1946–1952). The *Disputationes* was first published in Bologna in 1495. On the question of timing, see especially vol. II, 298–311, 332–39. On errors related to casting horoscopes, see vol. I, 458–63 and vol. II, 154–73. For discussion of Pico's polemical context, see especially Garin, *Astrology in the Renaissance*, 83–112. Pico was a follower of Girolamo Savonarola, who wrote his own condemnation of astrology. See Girolamo Savonarolae, *Opus eximium adversus divinatricem astronomiam, in confirmationem confutationis eiusdem astronomicae praedictionis, Ioan. Pici Mirandulae Comitis, ex Italico in Latinum translatum. Interprete F. Thoma Boninsignio* (Florence: Apud Georgium Marescotum, 1581). For the context of their astrological attitudes, see C. Vasoli, "Le débat sur l'astrologie à Florence: Ficin, Pic de la Mirandole, Savonarole," in *Divination et controverse religieuse en France au XVIe siècle* (Paris: Ecole normale supérieure de jeunes filles, 1987), 19–33.

| que l'heure de la generation est plus à considerer, laquelle le plus souvent est incogneue, car la mere n'a pas tousjours terme... pour enfanter selon qu'elle a conceu. | that the hour of generation is more to be considered, which most often is unknown, because the mother did not always know the term... in which she had conceived.[73] |

Critics fulminated; most astrologers acknowledged such concerns only to dismiss them.[74] The anonymous astrologer who cast the horoscope of François I announced the veracity of his predictions because of the precision of the moment of consultation.[75] Oger Ferrier acknowledged the Ptolemaic idea of trying to determine the moment of conception, but waxed poetic about the reliability of horoscopes based on the moment of birth.[76] Others advocated attempting conception under configurations that would likely lead to healthy pregnancy, delivery, and male children.[77] Timing and generation went hand in hand.

Productivity was not all that was at stake. The configuration of the heavens at a given moment shaped the sexual proclivities and characters of future generations. Popularized in part by Johannes de Indagine's widely circulating treatise, astrologers explained the sexual implications of being born under each decan of the Zodiac. The second decan in Taurus resulted in, "l'enfant est paillard, sujet à son plaisir desordonné" [the child is wanton, subject to his own disordered pleasures].[78] Gemini in the first decan caused girls to be sterile, and in the second, caused boys to suffer from maladies of the genitals. Much of Indagine's attention is on male children: those born in the second decan of Leo suffered from "thin" genitals, while boys born in the first decan of Virgo were of decent stature, but "sterile à engendrer enfans" [sterile for engendering children]. Both the third decan of Capricorn and the third decan of Aquarius produced men who loved women, although the latter were short ("de courte stature").[79] Circumventing Pico's complaint, astrologers insisted on the

---

[73] John Calvin, *Advertissement contre l'astrologie judiciaire*, ed. Olivier Millet (Geneva: Droz, 1985), 58. [Original: 1549.]

[74] Although critics did return to the problem. See for instance Claude Pithoys, *Traitté curieux de l'Astrologie Judiciaire, ou préservatif contre l'astronmantie des généthaliques* (Montbelliard: Jacques Foylet, 1641), 107–8.

[75] BN MS fr 5106, fols. 1r–31r. See esp. fols. 2v–3r. François I's mother, Louise de Savoie, employed Cornelius Agrippa for a time as an astrologer. Louise may also have kept an astrological diary. Historians have debated authorship. See Myra Dickman Orth, "Francis Du Moulin and the *Journal* of Louise of Savoy," in *SCJ* 13:1 (1982), 55–66.

[76] Oger Ferrier, *Des jugemens astronomiques sur les nativités* (Lyon: Jean de Tournes, 1550), 1, 4.

[77] BN MS fr 12290, fols. 79v–81v.

[78] Johannes de Indagine, *Chiromance & Physiognomie par le regard des membres de Lhomme faite par Jan de Indagine*, trans. Antoine du Moulin (Lyon: Jean de Tournes, 1556), 153. The first French edition was 1549; the first Latin edition was 1543. A knock-off pamphlet version of Indagine's typology was published as late as 1619. See Anon., *Astrologie naturelle*.

[79] Indagine, *Chiromance*, 153–7.

multiple effects of the stars. The timing of nativity, astrologers maintained, determined much.

The problem with nativities was timing the originary moment; the problem with elections and interrogations was whether they were valid at all. Elections involved the astrologer determining the right time to perform an action and interrogations required the astrologer to consult the heavens at the moment the question was asked to determine the course of action. For philosophical reasons that will be discussed below and because he found the lack of consensus about how to do them, Pico rejected elections and interrogations.[80] Claude Rapine agreed, rejecting interrogations as a form of astral determinism: "Ainsi la disposition de l'annee future ne peut estre presceuë, par figure du ciel" [Thus the disposition of future years can not be foreknown by the shape of heaven].[81] Rapine emphasized that events were influenced by many developments, and insisted that human efficacy was central to all outcomes. A man who fights, Rapine commented, wins because he is a stronger fighter, not because of the positions of the stars.[82] Michel de Montaigne regarded interrogatory prognostication as, "a notable example of the frenzied curiosity of our nature, which wastes its time anticipating future things, as if it did not have enough to do digesting the present."[83]

Elections and interrogations raised the hackles of some defenders of astrology. The Medieval Arab commentator Haly ibn Rodoan believed Ptolemy to be the author of the *Centiloquium*, which explained elections and interrogations. Bolstered by Abraham ibn Ezra's influential commentary, assumptions about their efficacy took hold.[84] While some commentators voiced skepticism about claims for Ptolemy's authorship, Grafton and Siraisi have argued that Girolamo Cardano was the first to apply philological analysis to the text of the *Centiloquium* to establish that it was spurious. Cardano then attacked

---

[80] Regarding elections, see Pico, *Disputationes*, vol. I, 106–13, vol. I, 466–73; on interrogations, vol. I, 500–7. Ficino, *Epistolae Marsilii Ficini Florentini*, book 9, no. 200, Ficino to Giovanni Pico della Mirandola argued to the contrary. Ficino's letters include extensive discussions about technical and interpretive aspects of astrology.

[81] Claude Rapine, *Des choses merveilleuses en la nature, où est traicté des erreurs des sens, des puissances de l'ame, et des influences des cieux*, trans. Jacques Girard de Tournus (Lyon: Macé Bonhomme, 1557), 136–7.

[82] Rapine, *Des choses merveilleuses*, 143, 188.

[83] Montaigne, *The Complete Essays of Montaigne*, I, 11 (Of prognostications), 27.

[84] Abraham ibn Ezra, *Abrahe Auenaris Judei, astrologi pertissimi in re iudicali opera* (Venice: Petrus Liechtenstein, 1507). Medieval French translations appeared as early as the thirteenth century. See also BN MS fr 1351, fols. 102–9 for a manuscript copy of the *Livre des elections*. For interrogations, see BL MS Sloane 2030, fols. 88r–94v, "Tractatus astrologicus de iudiciis sive de interrogationibus." On Medieval patterns of transmission of Arab astrological knowledge, see for instance Roger French, "Foretelling the Future: Arabic Astrology and English Medicine in the Late Twelfth Century," *Isis* 87 (1996): 453–80.

interrogations as magic and elections as fraud for pecuniary gain by unscrupulous astrologers.[85]

Despite such misgivings, most practitioners did a great deal of custom in elections. Medical elections – determining which days were fortuitous or otherwise for treatment – were big business. In 1555, Thomas Bodier published his *De ratione et usu dierum criticorum*, which featured fifty-five medical horoscopes from which Bodier derived aphorisms about proper treatment. Bodier insisted that the predictive power of horoscopes enabled physicians and patients alike to avoid terrible mishaps.[86] Oronce Finé also endorsed elections for determining when to perform phlebotomies and other medical procedures.[87] As late as 1614, Jean Taxil defended elections for a range of situations:

L'Astrologie, nous apprend à choisir, & eslire le temps, pour l'heureux succez de l'entreprinse d'un voyage. Pour planter, semer, bastir, & donner medecines aux malades.	Astrology teaches us to choose and to elect the time for the happy success of the enterprise of a voyage. For planting, seeding, building, and giving medicine to the sick.[88]

Politically, elections had their uses as well. Catherine de' Medici asked one of her favorite astrologers, Gabriele Simeoni, whether a specific day was propitious for the coronation of Charles IX. Simeoni answered at length.[89] Claude

[85] Anthony Grafton and Nancy Siraisi, "Between Election and My Hopes: Girolamo Gardano and Medical Astrology," in *Secrets of Nature: Astrology and Alchemy in Early Modern Europe*, ed. William R. Newman and Anthony Grafton (Cambridge, MA and London: MIT Press, 2001), 69–131. See p. 106.

[86] Thomas Bodier, *De ratione et usu dierum criticorum opus recens natum* (Paris: Audoënus Parvus, 1555), fol. 5r. See also fols. 28r and 36v for cases that Bodier believes would not have been fatal if the stars had been consulted.

[87] Oronce Finé, *Les canons & documens très amples, touchant l'usage et pratique des communs Almanachz, que lon nomme Ephemerides* (Paris: Guillaume Cavellat, 1556), 28–9. See also the discussion of elections for agricultural purposes (p. 30). The first, briefer edition was 1543. The section on elections was borrowed almost word for word by Antoine Mizauld. See his *L'Explication, usage et practique de l'Ephemeride celeste d'Antoine Mizauld* (Paris: Jacques Keruer, 1556), fols. 60v–65v.

[88] Jean Taxil, *L'Astrologie et physiognomie en leur splendeur* (Tournon: R. Reynaud, 1614), 154.

[89] BN MS Dupuy 588, fol. 174r: "In questo mezzo venutomo desiderio (il quale sempre studierà nel far il servitto) di – cognoscere qual giorno fosse migliore per la coronatione del Re, et per fortificare La radice della sua Natività trovo che del XVIe di guigno non se ne potria trovare un piu felicissimo per le ragioni ch un perfetto astrologo congosceranella una figura, chio Ie mando insieme con l'hora, che sara circa al mezzogiorno quando gli sara posta la Corona in capo. In altree havendo dato un'occhiata alla rivolutione di questo Anno, trovo che la Luna venuta al luogo di Saturno. Saturno occupando qullo del Sole di Giove & di Mercurio, Marte conguinto con la Luna et capo di Dragone et Giove nell'aspetto quadrato della Luna, dinotato questo anno grandissimi fastidii per conto della Relligione, che diverranno tanto maggiori, quanto pui Saturno diverrà dal di primo di Juglio possessore del Cancro. Et se bene a Jeuni huomini terrestri si ridono delle cose del Ciclo, gl'accidenti non dimeno apparecchiati chiariranno na hoggi e due anni La Ioro de se redenza." [In this way, you came desiring (one must always study in the

Dariot appended a treatise on elections to his brief introduction to astrology, announcing:

on en avant pour reprover ou rabaisser l'estude des sciences denontiatives, ou significatives des choses à advenir.	one has to reprove or to lower in advance the study of denunciative sciences or signifying things in the future.[90]

Elections could provide any sort of information, but for many astrology customers, they provided guidance about love and sex. Women seeking to get pregnant or fearing that they already were; pregnant women who wanted to know the sex of the child and what kind of person he or she would be; how many pregnancies a woman could expect – elections purported to answer these questions. Elections told people when to marry and have children, or conversely, when to avoid doing so. The *Instruction fort utile et necessaire pour l'astrologie judiciare* advocated elections for determining the timing of marriage as one of its central points.[91] Eberhard Schleufingeri insisted on them for procreation:

Ad procreandam prolem sanam & proceram, non sufficit astrorum aptatio, sed & medicorum regulae praecipientium coitum à desiderio sano, non super repletionem, nec vacuitate nimia &c. fieri debere, & à turpibus, difformibus, imaginationibusque alienis cavere.	To procreate tall and healthy offspring, it is not sufficient to adjust to the stars, but take account of the teachings of the doctors pertaining to coitus by means of healthy desire, not above satisfaction or excessive freedom, etc. One can be on guard against ugliness, deformities and other fantasms.[92]

doing this service) to know which day will be best for the coronation of the King, and to fortify further the roots of his nativity, I find that nothing can be found more felicitous than the 16th of June by reason of a perfect astrologer understanding a figure, which I send together with the hour, which will be about mid-morning, when the crown will be put on his head. Having an alternate date with an eye on the revolution of this year, I find that the Moon comes to the place of Saturn. Saturn occupies that of the Sun and Jupiter and Mercury, Mars conjoins with the Moon and the head of the Dragon and Jupiter in a quadratic aspect with the Moon, denoting that this year the growth of great troubles on account of Religion, which become most significant when Saturn departs from the first of July [as] the possessor of Cancer. And good for young men on earth if they give back again the things of Heaven, so that accidents do not toss the apparatuses that clarify from today and in two years, then will be his redemption.] The horoscope plotting the crucial positions is on fol. 175r. All that remains of Catherine's Hôtel de la Reine in Paris is the Colonne de l'Horoscope, another suggestion of her dedication to consulting the stars.

[90] Dariot, *L'Introduction au iugement des astres*, sig. a ii (r). Dariot wrote a Latin edition, but aimed the vernacular version at a wider audience to teach "les inclinations des Astres" to the public (sig. a ii (v)). The book was accessible enough to be translated into English in several editions. *A Breef and most easie Introduction to the Astrologicall iudgement of the Starres* (London: Thomas Purfoote, 1583[?]) is the first of these.

[91] BN MS fr 12290, fols. 74v–75r.

[92] *Assertio contra calumniators Astrologiae, doctroris Eberhardi Schleufingeri* in Marstallerus, ed., *Artis divinatricis*, 125.

Leowitz included love and marriage on his list of proper subjects for elections, and defended them as mechanisms developed by Arab astrologers that were consistent with Aristotelian physics.[93] Richard Roussat provided instructions for producing elections and interrogations on whether to enter a city, when to commence a voyage, if a position taken up for battle was likely to yield victory, and why to buy a particular kind of horse.[94] Recurring repeatedly to romance, marriage, and sex throughout his two-part treatise on astrology, Rossat offered brief, technical advice under the heading "For love:"

Quand on te demandera pour deux, s'ilz s'entr'ayment ou non, regarde le seigneur de la 11 ou 7, & l'ascendent de trois, ou de six, ilz s'ayment l'un l'autre: si c'est quatre, ou d'opposition: non mesmement si l'un estoit sire de douze, & si les deux autres se regardoient, l'amour seroit plus fort & plus ferme, & si tous deux y regardoient, l'amour est plus ferme & plus fort, mesmement si ce regard estoit de signes fixes.

When one asks two if they love each other or not, watch the lord of the eleventh or seventh [house], and the ascendant of the third or the sixth, if they love one another: if it is in quartile or in opposition, not only if this the lord of the twelve signs but if the other two regard it, love will be very strong and firm, and if the two gaze on each other, the love is most firm and most strong even if this gaze is from the fixed stars.[95]

While each instruction was brief, the ones about sex covered numerous sexual circumstances. He offered advice, "Pour scavoir si aucun aura filz en ligne, ou non" [For knowing if one will have a son in one's lineage or not]; "Pour scavoir si femme encente viendra au terme, & a son profit ou non" [For knowing if a pregnant woman will come to term, and if it will prosper or not]; "Pour scavoir si une femme enfantera un enfant ou deux" [For knowing if a woman is pregnant with one child or two]; "Pour scavoir en quel temps la femme enfantera" [For knowing the time when a woman will become pregnant]; "Pour scavoir si elle enfantera de nuict, ou de jour" [For knowing if she will give birth at night or during the day]; "Pour scavoir si une femme est enceinte, ou non" [For knowing if a woman is pregnant or not]; and "Pour scavoir si une femme à eu enfant ou non" [For knowing if a woman has had a child or not].[96] While the seventh house was the place of marriage and pregnancy, he warned to look out for the effects of the fifth house (because it was the locus of "conception des femmes") and the sixth house because it was sexually perilous, spawning suspicion of women, sexual envy, and fornication.[97] The seventh house could cause problems as

---

[93] Leowitz, *Brevis et perspicua ratio judicandi genituras*, unpaginated (after sig. pii).

[94] Richard Roussat, *Des elements et principes d'Astronomie, avec les universelz iugements d'icelle* (Paris: Nicolas Crestien, 1552), 13r–47v (first part).

[95] Roussat, *Des elements*, 12v (first part). He offers another formula that focuses on Venus and the Moon in part two. See fol. 37v (new pagination).

[96] Roussat, *Des elements*, fols. 67r–74r (first part).

[97] Roussat, *Des elements*, fols. 58r–v (first part).

well: "Icelle de la partie de la fornication des hommes se prend de jour" [Here is where men who fornicate take the day].[98] He suggested elections to avoid concupiscence, encourage fertility, and engender male children.[99] Whether or not Ptolemy endorsed elections and interrogations, in the Ptolemaic universe, astrologers offered knowledge of the conditions of sex by means of them.

Alternately condemned as non-Ptolemaic accretions and celebrated for their value in astrological practice, elections and interrogations were central to concerns about generation and sex. The attention to specific instances of timing demonstrates acute awareness about the need to get the momentary map of the heavens right. Skeptics scoffed, but defenders offered theoretical statements supported by horoscopes serving as illustrations. The sheer number of horoscopes suggests that people consulted regularly and often. Astrology enabled belief that one could hedge the bets in favor of good marriage, love, and children.

ii   *The universe of controversy, or how to . . .*

The theoretical emanations of interpretive schema based on particular moments stirred up critics and defenders; the next layer – knowing where the stars were in relation to each other and what those relationships meant – created additional controversies. The issues were at turns technical (having to do with calculating the ecliptic in order to locate the Zodiac, which was called domification) and interpretive (whether aspects created significant effects and what they might be). While disagreements over domification and aspects threatened astrology generally, sex was again particularly at issue. Since astrologers maintained that the houses and certain aspects shaped sexual personality and development, correct calculations and accurate interpretations around generation both shaped and confirmed astrological practice.

Domification seems like it should be straightforward. The astrologer divides the Zodiac into the twelve houses, starting with Aries at the point where the Sun's path crossed the horizon of the observer, which is the ecliptic.[100] The houses of the Zodiac are 30 degrees each, for a total of 360 degrees. The ecliptic, however, messes with this neat scheme, as it crosses the celestial equator at an approximately 23.5 degree angle. The Sun was supposed to cross the equator in the beginning of Aries, at the spring equinox. Because of precession, by

[98] Roussat, *Des elements*, fol. 43v (second part).
[99] Roussat, *Des elements*, fols. 43v–48v (second part).
[100] The choice of twelve houses seems to have been popularized by the work of John of Lignères in 1322. Other systems had six houses of 60 degrees, or eight of 45 degrees. John North, *The Norton History of Astronomy and Cosmology* (New York and London: W. W. Norton, 1995), 217–22.

the sixteenth century, the point where the Sun crosses the equator was no longer in Aries. Ptolemy had noticed the precession issue, and adjusted for it, but later observations revealed that his calculations had been incorrect. By the Renaissance, the choice was to continue to call the spring equinox Aries (regardless of the constellation in which it actually occurred) or to maintain the standard 30 degree divisions and allow that the Zodiac moved around the heavens. Because each sign had different sexual effects, the choice was potentially anxiety-producing.

Many astrologers countered the fear of uncertainty by using tables which listed positions by date (ephemeredes). Some tables were more accurate than others. The standard for centuries were the so-called Alphonsine Tables (1252), which were prepared on the orders of Alfonso X of Castile. Because they did not take into account the movement of the solar apogee and fixed the precession of the equinoxes at 49,000 years, they had some limitations. Georg von Peurbach (1423–1461) and his student, Regiomontanus (Johann Müller, 1436–1476) produced improved tables that remained the standard until Copernicus.[101] Erasmus Reinhold then published the first Copernican tables, further correcting the precession problem.[102] Given that there were several well-known, and many lesser-known, versions of the heavens, critics could reasonably argue that astrology was unreliable at best. Indeed, in his usual polemical way, Pico scoffed at astrologers for failing to solve the precession problem and for errors in calculation.[103] The mathematical complexities enabled rival astrologers to attack each other for the use of particular tables and for faulty understanding of the mathematics involved.

Defenders of astrology responded by asserting the accuracy, the fundamental logic of their calculations, and the underlying utility for understanding earthly matters. As J. D. North has argued, the six main systems for domification can be divided into fixed boundary and moving boundary methods.[104] Pierre Brind'Amour has traced the methods in terms of their proponents in the

[101] A new set of tables touched off a vogue for horoscopes in the sixteenth century. While only marginally more accurate than older ones, the new tables calculated positions for various latitudes, making it possible for astrologers all over Europe to use them. Attributed to Regiomontanus, the tables were actually begun by Peurbach and they gained renown with the advent of printing. See North, *Norton*, 253–9.

[102] On the problems with the Alphonsine Tables, see for instance Pierre Maurice Marie Duhem, *Le Système du monde*, 10 vols. (Paris: A. Hermann et fils, 1913–1959), vol. II, chapter 10. Georg von Peurbach's most important work was perhaps *Theorice nove planetarum cum commento* (n. p.: Vespuccius, 1508). [First edition: 1482.] On Regiomontanus and his influence, see *HMES*, vol. V, 332–77. Erasmus Reinholt's *Prutenicae Tabulae Coelestium Motuum* (Tübingen: Morhardus, 1551) offered improved method and more precision in calculating for precession.

[103] Pico, *Disputationes*, vol. II, 236–43; vol. II, 314–21; vol. II, 400–15. For concerns about the tables, see vol. I, 158–61.

[104] J. D. North, *Horoscopes and History* (London: Warburg Institute, 1986).

sixteenth century, four of which figured centrally in the debates about astrology.[105] Because of the preference for Ptolemy as an originary source, astrologers tended to divide the houses into equal parts following the method ascribed to him and developed by Firmicus Maternus in the fourth century. Cardano often used it, as did Jacques Peletier du Mans and Claude Dariot.[106] The second method, long the staple of university education, involved the division of quadrants into equal parts by longitude, as developed by Porphyry in the third century. This was the method taught in John of Sacrobosco's thirteenth-century textbook, which was republished in the sixteenth century.[107] Third was the "Arab method," so called because it was popularized by Alcabitius in the *Liber introductorius*, which involved dividing the quadrants equally using the right ascendant. Cardano considered this valid, although it had been supplanted by a fourth method developed by Regiomontanus, which used an astrolabe to divide the sky into circles that cut the ecliptic. Gaurico used this method in his *Tractatus*, and by the mid-sixteenth century, Antoine Mizauld defended it as the preferred practice of astrologers.[108]

Locating the proper house was critical for knowing what would, or at least might, result from a sexual encounter under its influence. For the translator of

[105] The description of the methods follows Brind'Amour, *Nostradamus astrophile*, 305–13. He in turn draws on North, *Horoscopes and History*. I have omitted two methods that were more marginal, although Finé advocated one of them (the "method of Campanus" or in North's terms, the "prime vertical (fixed boundaries) method." See Brind'Amour, *Nostradamus astrophile*, 313–16 for details.

[106] Jacques Peletier du Mans, *Commentarium de constitutione horoscopi in Iacopi Peletarii Cenomani Commentarii tres* (Basle: Joannem Oporinum, 1563), 49–66; Dariot, *L'Introduction au iugement des astres*, 7.

[107] John of Sacrobosco's was the primary teaching text at the University of Paris in the Middle Ages, and it remained a standard introduction to astrology well into the Renaissance. See for instance the French edition of his most famous text, *La sphere de Jean de Sacrobosco, augmentee de nouveaux Commentaires, & figures servant grandement pour l'intelligence d'icelle* (Paris: Chez Hierosme de Marnef, & la veufve Guillaume Cavellet, 1584).

[108] Mizauld, *L'Explication*, fol. 66v. Astrologers quarreled over the choice of method as part of their larger positioning with respect to astrology. In 1518, the Flemish mathematician Albertus Pighius accepted the Ptolemaic division of the Zodiac, denounced Arab methods as fatally flawed, and excoriated "ignorant and error-prone" practitioners who deviated from it as purveyors of superstition. See *Adversus prognosticatorum vulgus, qui annuas predictions edunt et se astrologos mentiuntur, Astrologiae defensio* (Paris: Henri Estienne, 1518), 7r(bis)–8v(bis); 11r. Pighius, who would later oppose Calvin on matters of theology, voiced his approval of astrology by claiming Ptolemy as the scientific founder of astrology. Gaurico and Cardano, who used different methods, attacked each other for their choices. In 1549, Gervasius Marstallerus's compendium of astrological texts by German humanists discussed the merits of various methods of domification. The penultimate treatise provided criteria for accepting or rejecting claims for dividing the Zodiac. See *Trapezontii libellus. Cur Astrologorum iudicia ut plurimum sint falsa*, in Marstallerus, ed., *Artis divinatricis*, 148–65, esp. 152ff. Leowitz, *Brevis et perspicua ratio judicandi genituras*, sig. d ii(v) acknowledged the controversy, but insisted that Regiomontanus's method was correct. Peletier du Mans, *Commentarium de constitutione horoscopi*, 60, 66, cast aspersions on the *Centiloquium* about domification by way of prefacing his mathematical basis for reconciling Regiomontanus and Ptolemy.

the *Livre d'Arcandam*, general rules describe dominant characteristics for either five or six situations under each sign of the Zodiac.[109] Despite the disclaimer about God's dominant role, the text assumes personality traits and family lineage are destined by the stars. Among the many claims, a man born under the belly of the dragon in Taurus, "il aimera singulierement deux femmes en sa vie, & couchera avec elles. Il sera luxurieux" [he will love two women singularly in his life and sleep with them. He will be lecherous]. If born at other times in Taurus, a man will be happy with women, and marry but remain childless for a long time, or have a mark on either his testicles or his penis, or, if he is born at night, he will be lusty and loved by women even though he is cold by nature.[110] In every sign under almost every configuration, sexual performance looms large. Men who will marry several times (Gemini, Cancer, Leo, Virgo, Scorpio, Capricorn, Pisces); women who remarry (Cancer, Leo, Libra, Scorpio, Sagittarius, Aquarius); men who are overly lusty (Taurus, Gemini, Leo, Scorpio, Sagittarius, Capricorn, Aquarius, Pisces); women who suffer damaged sexual reputations (Aries, Taurus – these women will suffer shame because they spend time in brothels in their youth – Leo, Aquarius); women renowned for the children they produce (Aries, Gemini, Capricorn, Pisces). Cancer makes adulterous men; Libra, Sagittarius, and Aquarius produce fornicators. Men under Virgo are sexually circumspect; women under Aries become prudes. Configurations of all twelve signs described conditions in which men and women could marry and produce children. Sometimes marriage does not work the first or second time, or the couple has daughters instead of sons, or they must wait for children, but eventually, the text reassures its readers, children will come.

The argument put forth by Copernicus that the Sun, not the Earth, was at the center of the heavens renewed concerns about domification. But rather than evince disappointment in astrology, enthusiasts proliferated the production of ephemeredes and discussion of them. Some astrologers continued to use and defend older tables. Paschasius Hamellius (Pascasio or Pasquier Duhamel), for instance, attempted to correct errors in the Alphonsine tables.[111] Others, like Oronce Finé, asserted their good practice by citing more recent tables and explaining their methods of calculating.[112] In *Mantice*, Pontus de Tyard

[109] For some signs, the parts are the head of the dragon, the tail of the dragon, virtues for men, virtues for women, and the fortune of the sign as a whole. For some signs, the author adds a sixth point, which is the belly ("ventre") of the dragon.
[110] Abraham Ben Meir ibn Ezra, *Livre d'Arcandam docteur et astrologue, Traictant de Predictions d'Astrologie* (Lyon: Benoist Rigaud, 1587), 32, 41–4.
[111] Paschasius Hamellius, *Divi Alphonsi romanorum et Hispaniarum regis, astronomicae tabulae in propriam integritatem restitutae* (Paris: Chrestien Wechel, 1545).
[112] Finé, *Les canons*, 9, 18. The first edition was in Latin in 1538 with a French translation in 1543. *HMES*, vol. V, 292–3 notes that Finé was castigated for his errors by Pedro Nunes, a professor of mathematics at Coimbra.

voiced a preference for tables adjusted for the revised image of the Copernican cosmos:

Et s'il plaist à quelqu'un d'experimenter combien sont insupportables les fautes des Tables vulgaires, soit d'Alphonse, ou de Regiomontan, ou de Blanchin, ou des autres semblables... et il trouvera les Pruteniques trop plus approchantes la verité.	And if it pleases someone to test how unbearable the mistakes of the vulgar Tables are, whether the Alphonsine, or by Regiomantus, or by Blanchin, or other similar ones... and he will find the Prutenic tables closest to the truth.[113]

Tyard went on to comment favorably on the tables of Johann Stadius and to castigate Petrus Pitatis for following Alphonsine calculations.[114] Tyard's unease about extant tables was great enough that he published his own in 1562.[115] Mizauld called for recognition of the sound principles and asserted the pedagogical value behind his tables.[116] Manuscripts without the same obvious pedagogical intention nonetheless aimed to demonstrate good practice by showing all their work, so to speak.[117]

The debates over stellar positions were especially fierce around the theory of conjunctions and other intensifying configurations. Pico criticized

[113] Pontus de Tyard, *Mantice: Discours de la verité de Divination par Astrologie*, ed. Sylviane Bokdam (Geneva: Droz, 1990), 186 (variant reading "g" includes Regiomontanus on the list). Originally published in Lyon in 1558, with an expanded edition published in Paris in 1575. Giovanni Bianchini, *Tabulae astronomicae et canones in eas Joannis Blanchini* (Venice: Simon Bivilaqua, 1495) is less well known, although Bianchini gets a number of nods in Renaissance astrology manuals. The structure of *Mantice* is akin to an *utramque partem* argument: Le Curieux is critical of astrology; Mantice defends it; the persona of the author comments at the end favoring Curieux for the most part. For this type of argument as part of Renaissance humanist intellectual training in France, see Zachary Sayre Schiffman, *On the Threshold of Modernity: Relativism in the French Renaissance* (Baltimore and London: Johns Hopkins University Press, 1991), 11–18.

[114] For Stadius, see for instance Johann Stadius, *Ephemerides novae et auctae Ioannis Stadii Leonnovthesii* (Cologne: Haeredes Arnoldi Birckmanni, 1560). For Pitatis, see Petrus Pitatis, *Almanach Novum Petri Pitati Veronensis mathematici* (Tübingen: Morhardum, 1544). Pitatis was committed to understanding the problem of calculating the stars because of his interest in calendar reform. See his *Compendium Petri Pitati veronensis in academia philarmonica mathesim profitentis* (Verona: Apud Paulum Ravagnanum, 1560).

[115] Pontus de Tyard, *Ephemerides Octavae Sphaerae seu Tabullae diariae ortus* (Lyon: Jean de Tournes, 1562).

[116] Mizauld, *L'Explication*, fol. 111v: "Ami lecteur, voila ce que pour le present je te puis communiquer sur l'explication des parties & practique de nostre Ephemeride celeste... je t'asseure que cy apres je te donnerai le present opuscule enrichy & illustré de toutes sortes d'exemples & demonstrations, en semblable volume, si Dieu me preste la vie. Comme aussi j'ay vouloir faire d'autres choses Astronomiques & celestes en semblable langue, pour ton usage & proffict." The tables may be found on fols. 78r–111r.

[117] See for instance BN MSS fr 2047, fol. 154v (Zodiac positions); 19934, pp. 273–76, (calculating positions for 1589); 667, fol. 8 (table of conjunctions); 1355, fols. 187v–197v (Zodiac positions); 9531 fols. 2r–31v (eclipses, conjunctions); 12287, fols. 21r–22v (foldout calendar with the rising and setting of the stars); 12290, fols. 9r–11r (planetary positions); and 14773, fols. 33v–34r (defends prognostications for 1570–72 with calculations).

conjunctions, arguing against them that the rays of the planetary bodies could not affect each other, and thus, could not cause effects on lesser beings.[118] Despite long acceptance of planetary qualities – many of which were observable phenomena (the Sun is hot; humidity or moisture does accompany the Moon, and so forth) – Pico took aim at the assignment of specific qualities to planets or constellations, dismissing them as utterly arbitrary.[119] Pico accused astrologers of being "absurd" and using "imagination" to elaborate stellar qualities when they did not even know the number of bodies in the sky.[120]

Against such critiques, defenders maintained that conjunctions and planetary relationships governed sex.[121] Philip Melancthon's widely known defense of astrology included claims that conjunctions figured centrally in generation:

Crases humanorum corporum & si multum sumunt à material seu à semine, tamen certum est eas valde temperari potestate siderum, ut nati paulò ante coniunctione cum Luna iam radiis Solis tegitur, longe sunt imbecillores aliis.	Thickness of human bodies, if they take much from material or from seed, these are certainly tempered by the power of the stars, so that those born a little before the conjunction when the moon is already covered by the rays of the sun are far weaker than others.[122]

Both Oger Ferrier and Orone Finé catalogued the positive and negative outcomes caused by conjunctions on generation.[123] A manuscript entitled, *Instruction fort utile et necessaire pour l'astrologie judiciare* allowed that the rays of

---

[118] Conjunctions had become part of western astrology largely through the influence of the pseudo-Ptolemaic *Centiloquium* and were widely regarded in Arabic literature as having great importance. See Al-Qabisi, *Al-Qabisi (Alcabitius): The Introduction to Astrology*, ed. Charles Burnett, Keiji Yamamoto, and Michio Yano (London and Turin: Warburg Institute / Nino Aragno Editore, 2004), 375–85, for texts attributed to Alcabitius on conjunctions and their fortunes in the Renaissance. For Pico on conjunctions, see *Disputationes*, vol. I, 520–623 (a mix of arguments about method and interpretation).

[119] Pico, *Disputationes*, vol. I, 274–95 on the alleged qualities of heavenly bodies.

[120] See *Disputationes*, vol. II, 8–151 and vol. II, 136–43. See vol. II, 348–53 regarding the count of stars. See also vol. I, 144–57 for further attacks on astrologers for their ignorance; vol. II, 326–33 for inconsistencies regarding the movements of the planets; and vol. II, 358–61 for astrology as "inanes et ridiculas." Book 6 includes extensive criticism along the same lines.

[121] Apologists cited historical examples of important events signaled by conjunctions. There had been a great deal of ink devoted to a conjunction in Pisces in 1524 that was supposed to result in massive flooding, but the floods never materialized and defenders retreated into retrospective quality of their proofs with respect to conjunctions. See for instance Taxil, *L'Astrologie*, 11–19. The great defender of conjunctions retrospectively was Cyprian von Leowitz. His *De coniunctionibus magnis insignioribus superiorum planetarum, solis defectionibus, et cometis, in quarta monarchia, cum eorundem effectuum historica expositione* (London: Langingae ad Danubium, 1564) attempted to demonstrate that conjunctions, along with comets and eclipses, had marked major historical events. He maintained that the disturbance marked by the 1524 conjunction was not floods, but the capture of François I and peasant revolts in Germany. See sig. g ii (v). (There was an edition in 1554 as well.)

[122] *Praefatio D. Philippi Melanthonis, in Iohannis Schoneri libros de iudiciis nativitatum*, in Marstallerus, ed., *Artis divinatricis*, 46–59. See p. 51.

[123] Ferrier, *Des jugemens astronomiques*, 132–48; Finé, *Canons*, 30 and unpaginated end matter.

Venus, "signifie en un bon signe en mariage et naissance d'une noble et belle lignée a cause d'une femme" [in a good sign, signifies marriage and birth of a noble and beautiful lineage because of a woman].[124] Elsewhere, Venus causes maladies of the genitals, and when in conjunction with Saturn, inspires women to have affaires with their valets. The opposition of Saturn and Venus, "signifie un homme paillart" [signifies a lecherous man], and if Mars is in opposition, readers are advised to avoid marriage. Cancer or Capricorn in quadrature with Venus will cause the births of bastards or whores. Saturn in conjunction with Venus can indicate marriage between partners of very different ages. The Moon in conjunction with Venus will cause a happy marriage, and if Jupiter is in the seventh house, a marriage between two virgins will be successful. Descriptions of planetary configurations that encourage childbirth and especially lead to male births follow.[125] The monarchy understood conjunctions to support royal fertility. At a banquet on December 22, 1518 hosted by François I to celebrate the Treaty of London, the courtyard was decorated with stars, images of the Zodiac, and images of profuse plenty. Quotations from the classics and scripture supported a reading of the peace as the result of a favorable conjunction that would encourage abundance through a return to the Age of Gold.[126]

Examples and formulae could be multiplied nearly endlessly, but over and over, Venus was the key. The opposition of Mars and Venus inspires sexual desire:

Aussi certainement que les Planetes Mars & Venus jointes ensemble engendrent des naturels lascifs & lubriques, aussi certainement Venus donne efficace aux medicamens qui acroissent au provoquent le sperme.

As certain as the Planets, Mars and Venus, joined together engender natural lasciviousness and lubricity, also certainly Venus gives efficacy to medicines that increase the provoking of sperm.[127]

The manuscript, *Traicté sommaire des Planettes et de leurs effects selon l'opinion des anciens Autheurs, qui en on Escript*, voices concerns about Venus, but is typical in asserting that Venus inspires copulation in marriage and turns

---

[124] BN MS fr 12290, fol. 3v.
[125] BN MS fr 12290, fols. 73v. See also 22v, 50v, 75v–77r, 80r–81v. On Venus in similar terms see also BN MS fr 1355, fol. 4r. Aspects and influences of all the planets are discussed on fols. 6r–27v.
[126] François danced in a gown festooned with astrological symbols, and the arrangement of the Zodiac referred to recent political and military events at Marignano. This example is drawn from Anne-Marie Lecoq, "Une fête italienne à la Bastille en 1518," in *"Il se rendit en Italie": études offertes à André Chastel* (Rome and Paris: Edizioni dell'Elefante and Flammarion, 1987), 149–68. Discussed in Knecht, *French Renaissance*, 72–4. Knecht notes that astrological themes figured centrally in several royal events. Lecoq notes the use of the same astrological symbolism on a lesser scale at other royal events. See pp. 158–9.
[127] Kaspar Peucer, *Le Devins, ou Commentaire des principales sortes de devinations* (Antwerp: Henrick Connix, 1584), 590.

beauty into love (through rays that enter the eyes and pleasing odors that captivate the sense of smell).[128] Without the planets, and Venus above all, human generation would be in doubt.

The advice and the myriad iterations of sexual possibility and disability were not unique to France, but the almost obsessive focus on generation is striking. Every discussion of astrology features generation and fertility. Partly, this was a function of the unsettled times. The intermittent wars between the Valois and the Hapsburgs, religious schism, and especially civil war from 1562, made the perils of early modern life more pronounced. The future was uncertain; generation assured the future. Partly, generation was an especially French concern. Ideas about the fertility of France were central to royal ideology and frequently linked to the poetic projects of the Pléiade (see Chapter 5 below). Astrology provided consumers with a locus to assure fertility and abundance. Astrologers needed to plot the houses of the Zodiac correctly and calculate the positions of the stars accurately to assure their patrons, customers, and readers. The insistence throughout the literature on the veracity of the relationships, on the efficacy of configurations that guaranteed a good marriage, a healthy partner, and children indicated that the critics were only going be paid so much heed. Sex mattered too much for the critics to be right or for the astrologers to be wrong.

iii   *The universe of controversy: generation redux*

Astrologers limited the possibility of being wrong by locating procreative relationships within the larger frame of Aristotelian and Ptolemaic cosmology. Simplified versions presented Ptolemy's cosmos in terms of the elements and humors of each major planetary body. Aries, Leo, and Sagittarius were hot, dry, and fiery. Taurus, Virgo, and Capricorn were cold, dry, and earthy. Cancer, Scorpio, and Pisces were cold, humid, and watery, while Gemini, Libra, and Aquarius were warm, humid and airy.[129] As for the planets, according to Oronce Finé (others varied the list somewhat), the Sun is hot and dry, the Moon is cold and humid, Saturn is cold and dry, Jupiter is hot and humid, Mars is hot and dry, and Venus is cold and humid.[130] From these basic "facts," sexual cosmology, the purpose of which was to guarantee French fecundity, took shape.

---

[128] BN MS fr 2083, fol. 7v, 20v, 30v–32r. See also Rabelais, *La Pantagrueline prognostication*, preface, Bon and Dubost, 27.

[129] This is from Indagine, *Chiromance*, 198, but such lists were common in astrological treatises. A similar version with the addition of some body parts especially affected appears in Jean Saulnier, *Cosmologie du monde, tant celeste que terrestre* (Paris: Michel Daniel, 1618), 114–15.

[130] Finé, *Les canons*, 25. Much of this was drawn directly from Ptolemy, *Tetrabiblos*, I, 4 (pp. 35–9). For variants, see Leowitz, for instance, who differentiated occidental and oriental characteristics, and left the Moon and the Sun off his list in *Brevis et perspicua ratio judicandi genituras*, unpaginated (after sig. fii). Dariot, *L'Introduction*, 11–12 modified the degree of some qualities. Mars is immoderately hot; the Sun is moderately dry, and so forth.

Fundamental physics determined the rules governing all bodies. Sympathy was the most basic force. For Kaspar Peucer, the "qualitez, temperatures & inclinations es estoilles" [qualities, temperatures, and inclinations of the stars] cause changes in relevant parts of the human body. Hot, cold, dry, or moist elements were added to bodies, causing them to develop and grow through "sympathie, convenance & conjonction" [sympathy, seemliness, and conjunction]. Citing Aristotle and Hippocrates, Peucer argues that the stars work by "troublant les humeurs, ou nettoyant & esclaircissant les esprits, ou rescueillant & fortifiant les facultez des principaux members" [troubling the humors, or cleansing and clarifying the spirits, or wrangling and fortifying the faculties of the principal members].[131] The process was not merely one of addition; much change was the result of antipathy. For Jacques Fontaine,

ces corps sont composez en premier lieu des elements: car les corps naturels sont affectez des qualitez contraires.	these bodies are composed in the first place of the elements, because natural bodies are affected by contrary qualities.[132]

Guillaume de La Perrière described the cosmos in terms of the elemental qualities and functions of the stars:

Dissouz [sic], le Ciel, Nature composée	Below Heaven, Nature composed
Des Elements en accordz discordantz,	Of the Elements in discordant accord
A se corrompre est tousjours disposée,	Disposed always to corrupt themselves,
Comme lon voit par effets evidents.	As one sees by evident effects.
Tout ce que veoit Diane claire & belle	All that clear and beautiful
Dessouz ses piedz, souffre corruption:	Diane sees below her feet, suffers corruption:
A ce defaut, nature renouvelle	By this default, nature renews
Les corps nouveaux aux par generation.	New bodies by new generation.[133]

In his introduction, La Perrière emphasized that the elements in circulation made the system immune to complete decay by facilitating generation.[134]

---

[131] Peucer, *Les Devins*, 605, 609–10. Sympathy is also central in Ptolemy, *Tetrabiblos*, I, 1–3 (pp. 3–35).

[132] Jacques Fontaine, *Discours de la puissance du ciel, sur les corps inférieurs, & principalement de l'influence contre les Astrologues judiciaries* (Paris: Gilles Gorbin, 1581), sig. bii (v).

[133] Guillaume de La Perrière, *Les considerations des quatre mondes, à savoir est: divin, angelique, celeste, & sensible* (Lyon: Macé Bonhomme, 1552), sig. kiir–v. *Considerations* III, V. See also *Considerations* II and IIII.

[134] La Perrière, *Les considerations des quatre mondes*, sig. a iv (v). Antoine Mizauld discussed the claim that the unchanging heavens produced change in other bodies, but he offered no resolution. See *Paradoxa rerum coeli, ad Epiponum Philuranum, & socios* (Paris: Federici Morelli, 1577). See fols. 14r–18v, paradox no. 4: "Quòd coelum corruptibilium omnium qualitatum sit expers. Et quoniam modo stellae sint dicendae calidae, frigidae, humidae, vel siccae." See also Mellin de Saint-Gelais, *Advertissement sur les Jugemens d'Astrologie à une studieuse damoyselle* (Lyon: Jean de Tournes, 1546) in *Le Trésor des pièces Angoumoisines*

Philippe Desportes slips in the occasional, tempered reference emphasizing the grandeur of cosmic fertility:

De la terre pesante, immobile et féconde, Semer d'astres le Ciel, d'un mot créer le monde.	Of the heavy earth, immobile and fecund, Are seeded the stars in Heaven, which in a word, created the world.[135]

Fertility reflected human beings in harmony with the universe, and facilitating that was the aim of French astrologers. Citing Aristotle's *On the Generation of Animals*, Jacques Fontaine insisted that movement of the stars distributed the elements to make generation possible:

le ciel qui perpetuellement tourne en rond, & sa vertu & puissance est semee sur les corps inferieurs . . . les effects principaux du ciel selon les philosophes, sont le mouvement de lieu, l'alteration & l'engendrement.	Heaven perpetually turns round, and its virtue and power are sown among inferior bodies . . . the principal effects of heaven according to the philosophers are movement from place, alteration, and engendering.[136]

In 1571, Antoine Mizauld wrote a treatise reiterating that the Moon, in combination with the Sun, had important elemental repercussions for procreation. They came together, "pour la generation, multiplication, continuation, & conservation des choses du monde inferieur & elementaire" [for the generation, multiplication, continuation, and conservation of things in the inferior and elementary world]. In addition to effects on animals, birds, stones, herbs, and maladies, the Moon prepared the female genitalia for generation, brought on menses, made children grow large in the womb, and lunar humidity inclined some men toward womanly characteristics.[137] In 1577, Mizauld reasserted the importance of the Moon, adding that the stars created variety in propagation and noting the importance of constellations for fertility.[138]

---

inédites ou rares publié sous les auspices et par les soins de la Société archélogique et historique de la Charente, vol. 2 (Angoulême: F. Goumard, 1867), 291.

[135] Philippe Desportes, "Sur les abysmes creux des fondements poser," in *Œuvres de Philippe Desportes*, ed. Alfred Michiels (Paris: Adolphe Delahays, 1858), 504–5 (*Oeuvres chrestiennes*, VII). See also Jean-Antoine de Baïf, *Euvres en rime de Ian Antoine de Baïf, Secretaire de la Chambre du Roy*, 4 vols. (Paris: Pour Lucas Breyer, 1572). See esp. vol. I, which explains the heavens in elemental terms.

[136] Fontaine, *Discours*, unpaginated. See bii(r) for Aristotle.

[137] Antoine Mizauld, *Secrets de la lune* (Paris: Federic Morel, 1571), esp. fol. 3r.

[138] Antoine Mizauld, *Harmonia superioris naturae mundi et inferioris* (Paris: Federici Morelli, 1577), 2v–3r: "Noverunt omnes, animalium pilos oculos, carnes, ungues, cornua, arborum ramos & herbarum folia, crescente Luna suum accelerare exortum, inspissari, multiplicari, & si caedantur, celeries renasci . . . Unde in mulierum mammis & animalium uberibus lac humidius evadit ac foecundius (uti etiam ventris excrementa) in augmento lunaris luminis, quàm decremento." [All new hair, eyes, flesh, claws, horns of animals, branches of trees and leaves of herbs, is made by the crescent Moon itself, by entreaty hastening, examining, multiplying, and if cut down, swift rebirth . . . Whence goes out humid and fecund milk from

Fecundity was the goal, and even skeptics conceded that astrology had valuable effects on generation. John Calvin, a significant critic of astral determinism, rejected astrology as contrary to the honor of God because it involved arrogating to human beings the knowledge of the future that properly belonged to God. Nonetheless, Calvin maintained that comets were part of the economy of matter in the universe relative to generation, which revealed God's pleasure:

Tant y a que ce sont inflammations qui se procreant, non point à terme prefix, ains selon qu'il plaist a Dieu	As much as there are inflammations which procreate themselves not at all at a predetermined time, thus according that it is pleasing to God.[139]

Pontus de Tyard, wearing his critical hat in the guise of Le Curieux's attack on astrology, conceded that elements from the planets infused human bodies:

Ainsi les Estoilles ne seroient cause en nous, que des effects corporels.	Thus the Stars would only be the cause in us of corporeal effects.[140]

The facts as understood in Renaissance France were that the elemental qualities of the stars, the planets, and human physiology operating through sympathy, antipathy, and attraction, made generation happen. Sex, properly done – with favorable configurations of the Zodiac and under benevolent planets – was supposed to work. The prospect that the astrologers held out was that, in a world marked by declension and death, positive results from sex were at least partly within an individual's control – not a small claim in a world rent by civil and sectarian strife.

Renaissance France, astrological uncertainty, and sex

Denis Crouzet has situated astrology in the French Renaissance with a different emphasis in terms of the eschatological concerns brought to the fore by the Reformation. He sees astrology as, "foncièrement pessimiste, accablante et oppressante . . . savoir le devenir est savoir le Mal s'approcher" [fundamentally pessimistic, overwhelming and oppressive . . . to know the future is to know that Evil approaches].[141] I have suggested that the crescendos of religious strife made astrology a potential source of reassurance. In fact, astrology was the resort of the pessimist and the optimist because of the especial pressures in France. As early as 1540, Giovanni Ferrerio reworked Pico's arguments against astrology in Latin with a French publisher in part to address religious

the breasts of women and fertile animals (as still venting excrement) in the rising light of the moon, in that way decreased.] See fols. 9r–11r for constellations and propagation.
[139] Calvin, *Advertissement contre l'astrologie*, 90.   [140] Tyard, *Mantice*, 117.
[141] Crouzet, *Les Guerriers de Dieu*, 114.

conditions in France.[142] In 1555, Esprit Rotier attacked astrology for replacing faith in the minds of those who wanted to blame the stars instead of flawed human nature for moral failings.[143] Nor was this merely textual posturing. Under pressure to assert its orthodoxy, the monarchy proved susceptible to concerns about astrology (despite Catherine de' Medici's routine recourse to it). In 1560 at Orléans, Charles IX issued a condemnation of astrology and related forms of divination.[144] As Pierre Brind'Amour has demonstrated, the attacks on Michel de Nostradamus were embedded in religious polemics.[145] But by the 1570s, astrological explanations with respect to religious civil war were increasingly common. François Junctin interpreted a comet as a sign of singular danger.[146] An anonymous pamphlet in 1587 warned France that the heavens were signaling the dangers of religious discord.[147] One of the early powerful apologists for Nostradamus linked his prophecies resolutely to events in the Wars of Religion.[148]

Sexual astrology allowed the co-existence of certainty about declension and the desire to escape it to make some sense. At the very least, figures such as Tyard's Le Curieux could imagine hope and despair around astrological possibility at the same time. Few moments in French history have been marked by such vivid simultaneity of contradictory expectations as the Renaissance. Neither religious war, nor internecine philosophical debate, nor Copernican astronomy could displace astrology.[149] The faithful fought over astrology's

---

[142] Giovanni Ferrerio, *De vera cometae significatione contra Astrologorum omnium vanitatem* (Paris: M. de Vascosan, 1540). The text was originally composed in 1531, but the preface was written with the tumultuous events of the 1534 in mind. See *HMES*, vol. V, 293–5.

[143] Esprit Rotier, *In praefatores Prognostiquósque futurorum eventuum, divinatricémque Astrologiam Libro duo* (Toulouse: Iacobi Colomerii, 1555), sigs. B4v–C1r.

[144] "Et parce que ceux qui se meslent de prognostiquer les choses advenuës, publians leurs almanachs et prognostications, passent les termes d'astrologie, contre l'expres commandement de Dieu, chose qui ne doit estre tolleree par princes chrestiens: Nous defendons à tous imprimeurs et libraires, à peine de prison et d'amende arbitraire, d'imprimer ou exposer en vente aucuns almanachs et prognostications…." in *Recueil général des anciennes lois françaises*, 29 vols. ed. François-André Isambert, Athanase-Jan-Léger Jourdan, Decrusy, and Alphonse-Honoré Taillandier (Paris: Librairie Belin-Leprieur, 1822–1829), vol. XIV, 71. See also vol. XVI, 215 ("Déclaration qui defend d'insérer dans les almanachs des predictions illicites").

[145] Brind'Amour, *Nostradamus astrophile*, esp. 63–101.

[146] François Junctin, *Discours sur ce qui menace devoir advenir la comete apparue a Lyon le 12 de ce mois de Novembre 1577 laquelle se voit encore a present par Maistre Francois Junctin* (Paris: Gervais Mallot, 1577).

[147] Anon., *Les quinze signes addressez es parties d'Occident vers les Royaumes d'Escosse, & Angleterre, significatifz de la ruine, fin, & consommation du monde* (Paris: Michel Buffet, 1587).

[148] Chavigny, *Commentaires de Sr de Chavigny Beaunois sur les centuries et prognostications de feu M. Michel de Nostradamus* (Paris: Anthoine du Breuil, 1596).

[149] It still came under attack. Pope Sixtus V condemned judicial astrology in his 1586 bull, *Coeli et terrae*. See Walker, *Spiritual and Demonic Magic*, 205–6, for discussion. In 1620, Jacques Ferrand ran afoul of the Inquisition for his *Traicté de l'essence et guerison de l'amour ou de la melancolie erotique* (Toulouse: Veuve J. et R. Colomiez, 1610) in part because his work

ability to offer some reassurance, especially about the intimacies of sex during a prolonged period of insecurity. Humanists interested in the heavens adapted them to Renaissance modes of thinking, reveling in the concatenation of doubt and desire for certainty. Astrologers retained and asserted the efficacy of heavenly influence by providing guidance for making a fruitful marriage, avoiding a sexually problematic partner, and recognizing one's own (bad) inclinations. Sex was one of the only ways to counteract the declension that marked life on earth. The forces emanating from the stars caused destruction and calamity, but also provided elements for generation. Sexual reproduction mediated between heaven and earth. Sex allowed mortal men a form of immortality and created new beings within the realm of corruption. Generation depended on sex as organized elementally by the heavens. Manuals that clumped people by sign or decan or horoscope were general in many of the ways that astrological predictions in general media are today. Broad assertions of heavenly influence provided illustrations of larger forces at work and invited consumers to seek out more personal, specific advice. Controversy may have been bad for business in some ways, but it was also a tease for the many who remained unconvinced that the criticisms of astrologers amounted to obviating the system. Astrology effectively claimed procreative heterosexuality as a sign of stellar efficacy and the French focused on generation as confirmation of national fecundity and abundance despite confessional war. Doubters and critics could not argue with the desired outcome. In the sexual culture of the French Renaissance, eschatology and generation made uncertain but productive bedfellows through the debates over astrology.

discussed astrology and love magic in the vernacular. For analysis, see D. A. Beecher, "Erotic Love and the Inquisition: Jacques Ferrand and the Tribunal of Toulouse, 1620," *SCJ* 20:1 (1989): 41–53.

3   Neoplatonism and the making
of heterosexuality

In an essay published in 1968, Paul O. Kristeller grumbled that had he lectured on Renaissance Platonism fifty years before, he could have assumed that it was an important aspect of western intellectual history. Instead, he found himself having to argue that Neoplatonism, especially the Florentine variety developed by Marsilio Ficino (1433–1499), had significance throughout Europe.[1] Kristeller allowed that Neoplatonism was less influential through universities and schools, but insisted that its tenets moved broadly and deeply through personal contacts, letters, and editions published all over Europe.[2]

Taking Kristeller's point in more detail with respect to France, Florentine Neoplatonism was thick on the proverbial ground. By the 1490s, Italian Neoplatonic thought was moving into France. Ficino's philosophy first appeared in relatively accessible form in his letters, an edition of which prompted much discussion in Paris.[3] Although unsystematic, the letters explained crucial concepts, clearly intriguing budding humanists, especially in Lyon. Among the works referred to by sixteenth-century French readers, Ficino's letters, the *De*

---

[1] Paul O. Kristeller, "The European Significance of Florentine Platonism," in *Medieval and Renaissance Studies: Proceedings of the Southeastern Institute of Medieval and Renaissance Studies, Summer, 1967*, ed. John M. Headley (Chapel Hill: University of North Carolina Press, 1968), 206–29.

[2] For convenience, I use the term Neoplatonism, although Kristeller reminds us that it was not a unified philosophy. See Kristeller's "The Scholastic Background of Marsilio Ficino: With an Edition of Unpublished Texts," in *Studies in Renaissance Thought and Letters* (Rome: Edizioni di storia e letteratura, 1956), 35–97.

[3] The letters were more like miniature treatises on various subjects. In the edition *Epistolae Marsilii Ficini Florentini*, Ficino includes a proemium setting the terms of the collection as a whole, which is divided into twelve books. Topics range from discussions of astrology (book 1, letter no. 6; book 3, no. 83; book 4, no. 113; book 5, no. 134; book 6, no. 146, no. 154; book 9, no. 200; book 10, no. 213; book 12, no. 231, no. 233, no. 234, no. 236), to a condemnation of Averroes (book 1, no. 14), to a meditation on the immortality of the soul (book 2, no. 50), to a rewriting of Cicero's *De officiis* (book 3, no. 94). Numerous letters throughout merge astrology and Neoplatonism around the concept of divine light working through the bodies of men. The collection as a whole is a riff on Petrarch's familiar letters, which in turn was a revival of sorts of Cicero's letters. See Jodogne, *Lemaire de Belges*, 249–50 on early reception of Ficino in France – first as a physician and later for his work on Plato.

triplica vita, and his commentary on Plato's *Symposium*, the *De amore*, received particular attention.[4] Records of individual readers are scarce, although Guillaume Postel marked up his copy of *De religione christiana* and works by Ficino and his followers figured in several book inventories.[5] Among the early detailed references to Plato's works are comments on *The Laws* by Symphorien Champier and Lefèvre d'Etaples's translation of and commentary on Ficino's *Pimander*.[6] The later commentaries by Pietro Bembo (in Italian in 1505 and in French in 1530), Léon Hébreu (published in Italian in 1535 and in French twice in 1551),[7] and Baldassare Castiglione (Italian in 1528 and French in 1537)[8] recurrently bolstered and renewed French interest in Neoplatonism. While the learned language of intellectual elites was still Latin, that many editions were in

---

4   For Ficino's letters in accessible form, Marsilio Ficino, *The Letters of Marsilio Ficino*, trans. London School of Economics and Political Science, 6 vols. (New York: Schocken Books, 1981, 1985). *De triplici vita* (Paris: Georges Wolf, c. 1496) was utilized by Symphorien Champier as the basis for his *De quadruplici vita* (Lyon: Stephani Gueynardi & Jacobi Huguentanni, 1507). Champier added other Neoplatonic texts and a section on the dignity of Lyon. His aim, like Ficino's, was primarily to render Plato within Christian paradigms. While it is not clear how extensive Champier's knowledge of Greek classics was, he did quote Plato's *Symposium*, probably known from Ficino's Latin translation, in *Nef des Princes* (Lyon: G. Balsarin, 1502), fol. 48v. Champier's work suggests that he did not know Greek. Other French editions of Ficino include *Platonis opera a Marsilio Ficino traducta* (Paris: Impressa in aedibus Ascensianis, 1518) with another edition in 1522; *Timaeus: vel De natura. Marsilio Ficino interprete* (Paris: P. Calvarin, 1536); *Theologica Platonica de immortalitate animorum duo de viginti libris* (Paris: Apud Aegidium Gorbinum, 1559).

5   Marsilio Ficino, *De religione christiana et fidei pietate opusculim* (Paris: Bertholdi Rembolt et Joannis Waterloes, 1510). The copy is shelfmark BN Rés. D. 80186. For the landscape of vernacular texts in personal collections, see Alexander H. Schutz, *Vernacular Books in Parisian Private Libraries of the Sixteenth Century According to the Notarial Inventories* (Chapel Hill: University of North Carolina, 1955).

6   Symphorien Champier, *Nef des dames vertueuses* (Paris: Jehan de La Garde, 1515), sig. j iv (r). Originally published in 1503. For the *Pimander* commentary, see Marsilio Ficino, *Mercurii Trismegisti Liber de Potestate et Sapienta Dei per Marsillium Ficinum traductus: ad Cosmum Medicem* (Paris: Wolffgango Hopyl, 1493).

7   Pietro Bembo, *Gli Asolani di messer Pietro Bembo* (Venice: Aldo Romano, 1505); editions consulted in Italian: Leone Hebreo [Léon Hébreu; Judah Abrabanel], *Dialoghi di amore* (Venice: Aldo, 1545) and in French: Léon Hébreu, *Philosophie d'amour de M. Leon Hebreu* (Lyon: Guillaume Roville et Thibauld Payen, 1551). Perhaps begun as early as 1502, the Pontus de Tyard translation, *Dialogues d'Amour* (Lyon: Jean de Tournes, 1551) has been reprinted in a modern edition: *Dialogues d'amour [par] Leon Hebreu. The French translation attributed to Pontus de Tyard and Published in Lyon, 1551, by Jean de Tournes*, trans. T. Anthony Perry (Chapel Hill: University of North Carolina Press, 1974). Further page citations are from this edition. For the debate about when exactly and in what language Hébreu originally wrote the *Dialoghi*, see Riccardo Scrivano, "Platonic and Cabalistic Elements in the Hebrew Culture of Renaissance Italy: Leone Ebreo and his *Dialoghi d'amore*," in *Ficino and Renaissance Neoplatonism*, ed. Konrad Eisenbichler and Olga Zorzi Pugliese (Ottawa: Dovehouse, 1986), 123–39.

8   The original French: Baldassare Castiglione, *Le Courtisan, nouvellement traduict de ytalicque en françoys par Jacques Colin d'Auxerre* (Paris: Jehan Longis et Vincent Sertenas, 1537). On the reception of Castiglione in France, see Peter Burke, *The Fortunes of "The Courtier": The European Reception of Castiglione's "Cortegiano"* (Cambridge: Polity, 1995).

the vernacular suggests some popularity of Neoplatonic texts.[9] Inspired by the attention to Plato that Ficino engendered, French translators prepared editions of several Platonic dialogues. Richard Le Blanc translated the *Ion* into French, and Etienne Dolet translated the *Axiochus*. Pierre du Val adapted the *Crito*, while Bonaventure des Périers drew explicitly on the *Lysis*.[10] Most French translators worked from Latin sources because education in Greek was comparatively limited.[11] Nonetheless, by 1558, Louys Le Roy had translated the *Symposium* directly from the Greek, although he relied on Ficino's interpretation for his extensive gloss. Le Roy also translated the *Timaeus* and part of the *Republic*.[12] By 1578, Jean de Serres had translated all of the dialogues into Latin, this time with comparatively little commentary.[13] Frances Yates has noted the cultural importance of Neoplatonism in the *Académie de Poésie et de Musique* established by Jean-Antoine de Baïf in 1570.[14] Even allowing for limitations around vernacular literacy, Plato and Neoplatonism as articulated by Ficino and his interlocutors were circulating extensively in France, as they were throughout Europe.

---

[9] Marsilio Ficino, *Commentaire de Marsile Ficin, Florentin: sur le Banquet d'Amour de Platon* (Poitiers: A l'enseigne du Pelican, 1546); *Discours de l'honneste amour sur le Banquet de Platon* (Paris: Chez Jean Macé, 1578) and another edition published as *Discours de l'honneste amour, sur le Banquet de Platon: Par Marsile Ficin*, trans. Guy le Fevre de la Boderie (Paris: Abel L'Angelier, 1588). See also Mario Equicola, *Les Six livres de Mario Equicola d'Alveto*, trans. Gabriel Chappuys Tourangeay (Paris: Jean Housé, 1584) with subsequent editions in 1589 and 1598; Giovanni Pico della Mirandola, *Le Commentaire du tres-illustre seigneur Comte Jean Picus Mirandulanus, sur une Chanson d'Amour, composé par Hierosme Benivieni* (Paris: Abel L'Angelier, 1588); Pietro Bembo, *Les Azolains de Monseigneur Bembo* (Paris: M. de Vascosan, pour luy et G. Corrozet, 1545) with reprintings in 1552, 1555, and 1572; and Hébreu, *Philosophie d'amour*. There were further editions in 1577 and 1595.

[10] Plato, *Le dialogue de Plato intitulé Io* (Paris: Chrestien Wechel, 1546); Plato, *Deux dialogues de Platon. Scavoir est: l'ung intitulé Axiochu*, in *Le Second enfer d'Estienne Dolet* (Paris: I. Tastu, n. d.), 85–120. [Originally Lyon, 1544.] For Pierre du Val, see Plato, *Dialogue de Platon intitulé Criton* (Paris: Michel Vascozan, 1547); for Bonaventure des Périers, see Plato, *Le discours de la Queste d'amytie dict Lysis de Platon*, in *Recueil des oeuvres de feu Bonaventure des Periers* (Lyon: Ican de Tournes, 1544), 1–41.

[11] Giuseppe Di Stephano, "L'Hellenisme en France à l'orée de la renaissance," in *Humanism in France at the end of the Middle Ages and in the Early Renaissance*, ed. A. H. T. Levi (Manchester University Press, 1970), 29–42. On the spread of Greek through the study of epigrams, see James Hutton, *The Greek Anthology in France and the Latin Writers of the Netherlands to the Year 1800* (Ithaca, NY: Cornell University Press, 1946). The first royal lecturers in Greek at the Collège de France (1530) were Pierre Danès and Jacques Toussain.

[12] Louys Le Roy, *Le Sympose de Platon*.

[13] Plato, *Opera quae extant omnia. Ex nova Ioannis Serrani interpretatione*, 3 vols. (Paris: Henr. Stephanus, 1578).

[14] Frances A. Yates, *The French Academies of the Sixteenth Century* (London: The Warburg Institute/University of London, 1947). The French also engaged extensively in the debates over the relative merits of Plato and Aristotle. Champier was among the early combatants. See Symphorien Champier, *Symphonia Platonis cum Aristotele: & Galeni cum Hippocrate D. Symphorani Champerii* (Paris: I. Badio, 1516).

Importance is not merely volume, of course.[15] This chapter argues that a central aspect of Neoplatonism was its role in articulating heterosexual normativity. In support of the French commitment to a sexual politics of fertility and generation, French intervention was crucial in transforming homoerotic Florentine Neoplatonism into a fundamentally heterosexual philosophical support for male–female desire. Attracted to Florentine Neoplatonism and several of its early emanations, French interlocutors gradually displaced the homoerotic core of Ficino's interpretation of Plato. In opting to emphasize women as objects of desire and signifiers of beauty, French Neoplatonists brought out the ambiguity inherent in Neoplatonism with respect to physicality and sex. The cautions articulated about the relationship of sex to salvation in a Neoplatonic mode helped advocates use heterosexual love to displace homoerotic rational desire. The emphasis on questions around desire used to undermine Neoplatonic homoerotics seeped intractably into presumptive heterosexuality. At the same time, the collapse of the attempt to use Neoplatonism to frame an expansive affective range did not remove the queer presumptions that went into making it default to the heteronormal.

Displacing homoerotics

To understand the transformation in Neoplatonism and its queer remainders, this story begins with three intertwined aspects of Ficino's understanding of beauty and desire as crucial to rational, salvific love. First, Ficino posits that love of beauty leads to contemplation of and union with God, which is often described as "participation" in the divine.[16] Ficino echoes and alters Dante's vision of ascending to the comprehension of love through his attachment to Beatrice as articulated in *La Vita Nuova*.[17] Where Dante implies an inevitable good in idealized love, as Ficino describes it, salvation is only one possible outcome of the love of beauty, and its achievement restores the human subject to God's love. As Ficino admits and his interlocutors abundantly demonstrate, love can be misguided, resulting not in participation, but rather, in damnation. Second,

---

[15] For a rather different focus on the transformation of Neoplatonism, see Edouard F. Meylan, "L'Evolution de la notion de l'amour platonique," *Humanisme et Renaissance* 5 (1938): 418–42.

[16] William R. Bowen, "Love, the Master of all the Arts: Marsilio Ficino on Love and Music," in *Love and Death in the Renaissance*, ed. Kenneth R. Bartlett, Konrad Eisenbichler, and Janice Liedl (Ottawa: Dovehouse, 1991), 51–60. Bowen argues that the concept of *harmonia* defined as "the proper arrangement of consecutive sounds, or, more abstractly, to the scale structure underlying true melody" is crucial to understanding Ficino's notion of love in his cosmology. Seeking beauty is disruptive of universal hierarchy, but *harmonia* provides unity. See esp. pp. 51–2.

[17] Dante Alighieri, *Vita Nuova. Italian Text with Facing English Translation*, trans. Dino S. Cervigni and Edward Vasta (Notre Dame, IN and London: University of Notre Dame Press, 1995). [Original: c. 1295.]

desire in Ficino's philosophy complicates his analysis at several points. Ficino imagines desire in homosocial terms, formulated around prevailing notions of male perfection relative to women. Ficino dismisses women as intellectually and morally inferior.[18] Third and least developed in Ficino's thought is the idea of reciprocity. Ficino construed reciprocity (particularly sexual reciprocity) as the result of mutual desire for beauty and therefore of limited scope; later Neoplatonists did not.

The contested issue throughout was the relationship of "love" to sex. By Ficino's time, the Christian distinction between sacred (non-corporeal) and profane (sexual, corporeal) love seemed to correspond to the Platonic notion of love as either philosophical or sensual. Ficino's project of translating and interpreting the Platonic corpus did not, however, fit so neatly. Christians had long regarded sensual love with suspicion. Sexual love was, in most senses, bad. Although necessary for the propagation of the species, sex distracted from salvation. The complex of prohibitions on timing, position, and intention during sex, built up beginning with the Church Fathers, enforced a disciplinary structure to prevent sex from leading the faithful astray.[19] In contrast, Plato required physical aspects of sensual love in order to produce the move toward philosophical understanding. Part of the idea in Christianity is to overcome corporeal desire on the path to God, which is similar to the Platonic journey from physical attraction to intellectual comprehension of the Idea of Beauty. But physical attraction is positively required in Plato's thought, rather than functioning as a negative cipher for Christians. When Neoplatonic thinkers sought to bring Plato back into the Catholic tradition in the Renaissance, one of the problems they faced was reconciling Plato's utilization of physical desire as an element in his philosophy with the Christian rejection of corporeal pleasure.

The problems associated with sex in the Platonic tradition stem from Ficino's construction of love and desire as salvific elements.[20] Recurrently in his

---

[18] On the homosocial aspect elsewhere in Ficino's work, see Marsilio Ficino, *Three Books on Life*, ed. and trans. Carol V. Kaske and John R. Clark (Binghamton: Renaissance Society of America, 1989), 29–30.

[19] On this structure, see for instance Payer, *Sex and the Penitentials*.

[20] On Ficino and love, see for instance Jean Festugière, *La Philosophie de l'amour de Marsile Ficin et son influence sur la littérature française au XVIe siècle* (Paris: Vrin, 1941). A few commentators have drawn out the sexual aspects. See especially Armando Maggi, "On Kissing and Sighing: Renaissance Homoerotic Love from Ficino's *De Amore* and *Sopre Lo Amore* to Cesare Trevisani's *L'impresa* (1569)," *Journal of Homosexuality* 49:3/4 (2005): 315–39, and Hiroshi Hirai, "Concepts of Seeds and Nature in the Work of Marsilio Ficino," in *Marsilio Ficino: His Thought, His Philosophy, His Legacy*, ed. Michael J. B. Allen and Valery Rees (Leiden: Brill, 2002), 257–84. Maggi traces the homoerotic structure of the *De amore* and iterations of homoeroticism in later texts; Hirai discusses Ficino's concept of "seminal" and related ideas in his corpus. For readings of Neoplatonism's sexual issues in different early modern contexts, see Katherine Crawford, "Marsilio Ficino, Neoplatonism, and the Problem of Sex," *Renaissance and Reformation; Renaissance et réforme* 28:2 (2004): 3–35.

commentaries on Plato's dialogues but particularly in his *Commentary on the Symposium*, or *De amore* (1469), Ficino argues that love and beauty, often in sexualized terms, provide the means to ascend to heaven.[21] At the same time, corporeal desire pulls body and soul downward, and inappropriate desire (variously defined) is difficult to distinguish from the salvific form.

Ficino maintains that finding spiritual – not physical – beauty in the male body is a marker of salvific attraction. Within a cultural context in which unrequited heterosexual love received tremendous play,[22] Ficino emphasized homoerotic elements:

Magice opus est attractio rei unius ab alia ex quadam cognatione nature... Ex communi cognatione communis innascitur amor, ex amore, communis attractio... Quin etiam formosus quisque teneris nos fascinat oculis. Viri eos eloquentie viribus et carminum modulis, quasi quibusdam, incantantionibus, deliniunt sibique conciliant.

The role of magic is the attraction of one thing to another because of a certain natural affinity... From their common kinship is born a love in common, and from love a common attraction... Even more, someone who is beautiful fascinates us with his eyes. Men delineate and unite with other men by their powers of eloquence and the charms of their songs, as if by incantations.[23]

Ficino again stressed the homoerotic interpretation when commenting on Plato's other significant rumination on love, the *Phaedrus*, in which Socrates discusses beauty in terms of his reaction to the physical beauty of the young man, Phaedrus.[24] Drawing at once on Plato's gender politics in his dialogues

---

[21] The project of rejuvenating Christianity is articulated most fully in Marsilio Ficino, *Theologia Platonica de immortalite animorum* (1469–74). For a brief discussion of the textual history, see *Platonic Theology*, trans. Michael J. B. Allen and ed. James Hankins and William Bowen, 6 vols. (Cambridge, MA: Harvard University Press, 2001–2006), vol. I, pp. vii–xvii and 315. On Ficino's efforts to produce a theological system, see Jörg Lauster, "Marsilio Ficino as a Christian Thinker: Theological Aspects of his Platonism," in *Marsilio Ficino: His Theology, His Philosophy, His Legacy*, ed. Michael J. B. Allen and Valery Rees (Leiden: Brill, 2002), 45–69.

[22] The literature on Petrarchan love with unrequited love as its central trope is vast, but for the cultural effects of Petrarchan poetry, see Roland Greene, *Unrequited Conquests: Love and Empire in the Colonial Americas* (University of Chicago, 1999) and François Lecercle, *La Chimère de Zeuxis: portrait poétique et portrait peint en France et en Italie à la Renaissance* (Tübingen: Narr, 1987). See also Chapter 4 infra, which focuses on sexual issues raised by Petrarch's corpus.

[23] Marsilio Ficino, *Commentaire sur le banquet de Platon*, ed. and trans. Marcel [hereafter *De amore*], 220–1. Marcel reproduced the Latin text from Ficino's autograph manuscript (Vatican MS Latin 7.705). The original date is 1469, although it was not published until 1484. All translations into English are mine unless otherwise indicated. I have consulted both Marcel's French translation and Sears Jayne's English translation, *Commentary on Plato's Symposium*, trans. Sears Jayne (Dallas: Spring Publications, 1978). See also Ficino, *Letters*, vol. IV, 66–7 (Ficino to Friends), in which Ficino slides from a female to a male object of beauty, and then to the seduction of the beautiful male body.

[24] Plato, *Phaedrus*, trans. John H. Nichols, Jr. (Ithaca, NY: Cornell University Press, 1998), 234d and 250d–251c. Armando Maggi discusses Ficino's modifications of the text that emphasize

and on the Aristotelian notion that men are inherently more perfect than women, Ficino saw beauty as first and foremost between men.[25] This is not surprising, given Plato's homosocial and homoerotic context, especially as articulated in the *Symposium*. Greek gender politics around sexuality focused on dyadic age hierarchies between men. Common wisdom regarded women as necessary for procreation but inferior in terms of pleasure, as well as politically irrelevant and philosophically uninteresting.[26]

Plato is not the only context, and Ficino takes Christian concerns about physical desire seriously. Ficino identifies physical attraction as earthly love, admonishing that it can prevent achieving participation in the divine. Ficino interprets Plato as saying that God, who is unity, extends hierarchically to the multiplicity of physical existence. Within the hierarchy, lesser forms always desire to return to God as the source of existence, and this desire is called love.[27] The mechanism through which souls seek God is beauty,[28] but bodily yearnings can follow the paths of beauty as well:

Tanta permutatio senioris hominis vergens ad iunioris similitudinem facit ut iste totum sui corpus in illum transferre et totum illius in se transfundere studeat, ut vel recens humor vasa recentia, vel vasa teneriora teneriorem consequantur humorem. Hinc multa inter se turpissime facere compelluntur. Cum enim genitale	So great is the complete change that occurs in an older man who is inclined toward the likeness of youth that it makes him to want to transfer the whole of his body to him [the young man] and to draw the whole of the youth into himself, so that either the vigorous humor may obtain young vessels, or the younger vessels may get younger

---

the homoeroticism. See "On Kissing and Sighing," 319–20. Michael J. B. Allen, "Cosmogony and Love: The Role of Phaedrus in Ficino's *Symposium* Commentary," *JMRS* 10:2 (1980): 131–53, demonstrates that Ficino's character, Giovanni Cavalcanti, is the stand-in for Phaedrus, and operates in relation to love for Ficino as Phaedrus did for Socrates.

[25] On the Aristotelian aspect, consult Ian Maclean, *The Renaissance Notion of Woman: A Study in the Fortunes of Scholasticism and Medical Science in European Intellectual Life* (Cambridge University Press, 1980), 9–15.

[26] See for example Dover, *Greek Homosexuality*; Daniel H. Garrison, *Sexual Culture in Ancient Greece* (Norman: University of Oklahoma Press, 2000), esp. 153–75. For the persistence and evolution of male homosexual relations in Roman antiquity, see Williams, *Roman Homosexuality*. Williams lucidly delineates differences between Greek and Roman sexual mores regarding male homosexual behavior. A free-standing comment in a letter to Cherubino about women suggests Ficino's engagement with them was, well, limited. After an extensive discussion about acceptable engagement with worldly matters for men, Ficino says: "Mulier: studeat ut quodammodo sit virilis maxime vero pudica" [Woman: She takes pains so that, in a certain way, she is seen by the greatest men to be truly modest]. See Ficino, *Epistolae*, book 3, no. 94.

[27] Ficino, *De amore*, 146–52. On love as desire for unity with God, see also Ficino, *Letters*, vol. I, 37 (Ficino to Michele Mercati) and Ficino, *Epistolae*, book 6, no. 141, to Raphael Riario: "Deus homo natus est hominibus: ut homines deo divini renascerent" [God was born a man to man: so that men are inspired by God to be reborn].

[28] On beauty in Ficino's corpus, see especially Michael J. B. Allen, *The Platonism of Marsilio Ficino: A Study of the Phaedrus Commentary, Its Sources and Genesis* (Berkeley: University of California Press, 1984), 185–203, esp. 188.

semen a toto corpore defluat, solo huius
iactu vel tractu totum corpus tradere se
posse confidunt et totum accipere.

fluids. Hence they are driven together to
do many disgraceful things. For when
the genital semen flows down the whole
body, they trust that only by ejaculating
or receiving this, they can surrender or
receive the whole body.[29]

Ficino the physician warns that sodomitical desire is shameful and sex between
men is not true love. Ficino assumes that standard Christian revulsion over
allowing the body too much power is self-evidently true.

What if it is not either self-evident or true, even on Ficino's own terms? The
development of the notion called "Platonic love," first in Ficino and then in
analysis of his work, indicates that the exclusion of the physical was not simply
achieved. Because it was seen as barely controlled at best, ejaculation could be
regarded negatively. Men who surrender are culturally suspect, but in Ficino's
philosophy, acceptance of love and participation in the divine that goes with it
necessarily involve some surrender. The solution of sorts was to describe the
desire to rise to God by means of seeking beauty through non-corporeal, non-
sexual love. To Kristeller (but not defined by Ficino), "Platonic love" meant
affection, friendship, and non-sexual love with another person.[30] While Ficino
emphasized non-sexual love, his discussions strained to distinguish sexual from
"pure" attraction.

The contradictory attraction and repulsion around homoerotic desire shaped
the absorption of Neoplatonism in different linguistic traditions. Historians
have noted that friendship was never entirely safe because of its homoerotic
slippages.[31] Armando Maggi points out that Italian Neoplatonism faded over
the course of the sixteenth century in part because of its attachment to fixed
and abstract principles.[32] While some Neoplatonic texts rejected homoeroticism by equating it with sodomy, it was more common for homoeroticism
to persist obliquely in Italian texts that undermined the official Neoplatonic
rules.[33] French interlocutors approached homoeroticism directly, but struggled

[29] Ficino, *De amore*, 251.
[30] Ficino, *Epistolae*, book 2, no. 76. Paul O. Kristeller, *The Philosophy of Marsilio Ficino*, trans.
Virginia Conant (New York: Columbia University Press, 1943), 285–8, identifies the Donati
letter as the source of the notion of Platonic love: "we began meanwhile to love each other,
so that apparently we have realized and perfected in ourselves that Idea of true love which
Plato formulates in that work. From this Platonic love therefore a Platonic friendship arises"
(286).
[31] See for instance the discussions in Katherine O'Donnell and Michael O'Rourke, eds., *Love,
Sex, Intimacy and Friendship between Men, 1500–1800* (London: Palgrave, 2003) and Alan
Bray, *The Friend* (University of Chicago Press, 2003).
[32] Maggi, "On Kissing and Sighing," 335.
[33] By 1525, Mario Equicola excoriates homoeroticism entirely. The mechanism is a denunciation
of sodomy. In the original Italian, Equicola calls sexual love between men "execrabile" and
against the laws of God and man. Engaging in sodomy makes men effeminate, which is against

to fix male–male desire as a reliable support of Neoplatonic transcendent love. Consider Symphorien Champier (1472?–1539), a physician from Lyon, who addressed homosocial love, bracketing it in safe social settings in his *Nef des dames*. Champier does not resolve the problems, but he provides a foundation upon which – sometimes against which – the French tradition is constructed. In a mix of genres within his text, Champier negotiates Ficino's homoerotic imperative. Champier appends a letter to the presentation copy of the first book of *Le Livre de vraye amour* addressed to his friend and fellow physician, André Briau.[34] Champier says he was contemplating Ficino's interpretation of Plato's *Symposium* and "in animi trutina in quem potissimum amorem meum converterem" [in the scales of my soul, [weighing] to whom especially I might direct my love],[35] when Cupid appeared and shot him. Cupid boastfully recounts his triumphs over even the king of the gods, and offers Champier a mischievous version of Ficino's typology of love.[36] When Cupid shoots Briau as well, Champier waxes poetic about the bonds of love between men in the medical profession. The intensity with which Champier describes his relationship and the phallic imagery supplied by Cupid's arrows delivered to both men indicate that Champier understood the implications of Ficino's rendering of transcendent love through male–male desire. In keeping with the preoccupation on fertility evident in French astrology, Champier dampens the homoerotics by retreating into the language of procreation, maintaining that generation creates beauty and the desire to contemplate

nature, and encourages feminine *cupiditas*. See Mario Equicola, *Libro di natura d'amore di M. Equicola* (Venice: Pietro di Nicolini da Sabbio, 1536), fol. 114r. The first Italian edition was 1525. When Equicola was translated into French, the passage on sodomy condemned male–male sexual desire unequivocally and at even greater length. See Equicola, *Les Six livres de Mario Equicola*, fol. 186v.

34   For an accessible version of the letter, see Symphorien Champier, *Le Livre de vraye amour*, intro. and ed. James B. Wadsworth (The Hague: Mouton, 1962), 43–50. Wadsworth reproduces the dedicatory letter in his edition, and I cite it from his text, as the 1503 first edition is exceedingly rare. The text of *Nef des dames* otherwise utilized is the 1515 edition, which was more widely circulated. The 1515 edition is available as a digitized text from the Bibliothèque nationale de France. A printed edition can also be consulted. See Symphorien Champier, *La Nef des dames vertueuses*, ed. Judy Kem (Paris: Champion, 2007). Champier is frequently dismissed for his derivative (albeit prodigious) output, but in terms of patterns of engagement with Neoplatonism, I maintain he was far more central than is usually recognized.

35   Champier, *Vraye amour*, 43.

36   Champier, *Vraye amour*, 45: "Etenim telis trifariam utor; nam in divinum modo amorem moveo, modo ad humanum, que duo honesta sunt amoris genera omnique petulantia denudata, demum in eum quem ferinum philosophi vocant qui et petulans est et lascivus concutio" [Indeed in three ways, I make use of my missiles: for I move toward divine love at one time; toward human at another, and these two are virtuous types of love, denuded of all lasciviousness; and I drive men to that love called bestial, which is wanton and lascivious by the philosophers]. Cupid was confused at times in the Renaissance with Ganymede, the young Trojan boy with whom Jupiter became enamoured. See Saslow, *Ganymede in the Renaissance*, 129–37. Images of Ganymede in France began appearing prominently in the 1540s. See pp. 179–85.

Figure 10. Antoine Caron (1521–1599), *Allegory of Funeral of Amor*, (1560–1570), oil on canvas, Louvre, Paris, France.

This image is sometimes thought to refer Pierre de Ronsard's renunciation of love poetry and sometimes described as an allegory on the death of Henri II's mistress, Diane de Poitiers. These possible identifications link the image to several recurrent themes about poetry and politics, but the image also deliberately idealizes and abstracts Love in a Neoplatonic vein.

it.[37] But Champier's language about Briau resonates with intense physical desire. The line between friendship and homosexual love was rather fine.

In his main text, Champier imagines homoeroticism contained by heterosexual mediation. Drawing on a tale from Giovanni Boccaccio's *The Decameron*, Champier takes the friendship between the Greek Gisippus and the Roman Titus as an exemplar of male–male love. Educated together at Athens, the men become close companions. Gisippus is betrothed to Sophronia, but Titus falls in love with her. Torn between his devotion to Gisippus and his desire for Sophronia, Titus wastes away. After Titus confesses his love, Gisippus convinces him

[37] Champier, *Vraye amour*, 47: "Vis quidam generandi genderande pulchritudinis, intelligendi vero potentia contemplande illius habet desiderium" [In fact, the power of generating has the desire to generate beauty; the power of understanding has the desire to contemplate beauty].

to take his place in the marriage bed because, "il aimoit mieulx perdre sa femme que son amy, car facillement on peult trouver une aultre femme mais non point une amy" [he would rather lose his wife than his friend, because it is easier to find another wife, but not a friend].[38] When Titus is called back to Rome, he takes Sophronia, who is shocked to discover she has been sleeping with Titus. Gisippus remains in Athens, but he is disgraced and exiled. He goes to Rome and takes refuge in a cave, where he is joined by a pair of robbers using the cave as a hideout. The bandits quarrel, one is killed, and the Praetorian Guard comes to investigate. Gisippus, having resolved to die, confesses to the murder knowing he will be put to death. Titus happens to be in the court for the sentencing, and recognizes his old friend. Titus tells the magistrate he was the murderer in order to save Gisippus. The power of friendship is such that the actual killer feels remorse and confesses as well. All three are sent to Octavian, who exonerates Titus and Gisippus and pardons the actual killer for good measure. Our heroes are fully reunited when Gisippus marries Titus's sister, and the two couples form a joint household. The connection between the men is mediated through Sophronia and Titus's sister. The sexual link through the wives is a result of the intimacy between the men.

Champier does not occlude the ambivalence created by male homoerotic desire. Male intimacy is constructed by deceiving Sophronia, and by regarding her is as interchangeable and expendable. Moreover, while the joint household was not uncommon in early modern Europe, it was uncomfortably close to incest by contemporary legal standards. Among the sexual unions prohibited under incest statutes were those with collateral relatives.[39] Champier's male–male love casts wives as placeholders and creates illicit, carnal, corporeal connections between men at the expense of society.

Like Champier, Charles de Sainte-Marthe articulates intimacy with his male friends, and allows that homoeroticism may supersede heterosexual intimacy. Sainte-Marthe wrote several Neoplatonic love poems to men, including "A P. de Marillac:"

---

[38] Champier, *Nef des dames*, sig. r iii (v). Giovanni Boccaccio, *The Decameron*, trans. and intro. G. H. McWilliam, 2nd edn. (London and New York: Penguin, 1995), for Titus and Gisippus (Day X, Story 8), see 745–64. Champier's ancient sources, in addition to Plato and Aristotle, included Herodotus, Aulus Gellius, and Ovid. See *Nef des dames*, sig. q ii (v) – sig. q iii (r) for some of these references. Champier invokes Eurydice as an example of a wife.

[39] Laurens Bouchel, *La Bibliothèque ou thresor du droict françois*, 3 vols. (Paris: Jean Girin et Barthelemy Riviere, 1671), vol. III, 368–9: "Inceste est, avoir compagnie charnelle avec son lignage, parenté, ou son affinité . . . Qui a affaire avec sa mere, niece, ou fille, il est à punir plus que l'adultere, par mort publique, scandaleuse et exemplaire: pour estre exemple aux autres de se garder de semblable offense" [Incest is to have carnal company with one's lineage, kin, or one's affinities . . . [He] who has an affair with his mother, niece, or daughter, he is to be punished more than for adultery, by a scandalous and public death, in order to be an example to others to guard against similar offense]. The first volume appeared in 1639, but the collection codifies case law and earlier definitions.

Que amour ne pourroit estre deshonneste	That such love could not be dishonest
Amour n'est rien que bonne volunté,	Love that is nothing but good will
Signifiante entiere affection,	Signifying total affection,
Amour à Bien est tousiours apresté,	Love for the Good is always harsh,
Amour aussi à ses fins arresté,	Love is also arrested at its end,
De pervenir à la perfection.	As it proceeds to perfection.
Amour pretend une coniunction	Love pretends to a conjunction
Individue, & par ainsi honneste,	Individual, and thus honest.
Or ne peut donq'estre Amour deshonneste.[40]	Now Love can not help but be dishonest.[40]

Sainte-Marthe struggles to separate *honnête* desire within a relationship articulated in terms of Neoplatonic notions of the uplifting and transformative power of love through connection to another man. Given the connotations of *honnêteté* in the Renaissance,[41] Sainte-Marthe vacillates between regarding his desire as pure and fearing its profane dimension. The very next poem in the collection describes the relationship between P[ierre] Tolet and Etienne Dolet as a chaste conjunction of hearts.[42] With these poems, Sainte-Marthe indicates that men find transcendent love with other men. His return to Tolet later in the collection – now described as his own friend – echoes Champier's evasions of homoeroticism in the Gisippus–Titus story. In a poem addressed to Tolet's lady, Sainte-Marthe praises her as virtuous and inspiring, but only to set her up:

Quiconques fois, mon cueur as excité,	At whatever time, my heart was excited,
Ma muse aussi à t'escrire incité . . .	My muse and friendship by private acquaintance
	Incited me to write to you.
Et amytié par privée accointance:	This notwithstanding, I know you enough
Ce non obstant, ie te cognois assés	By your writings that I read in days past.
Par tes escrits, qu'ay leu ces iours passés,	Writings, which are a sort of maker,
Escripts, qui sont d'une telle facture,	By which one knows your nature.
Que par iceulx on cognoist ta nature.	Writings, exhalations of an all-divine spirit,
Escripts, spirants un esprit tout divin,	
Et excedants le sexe feminin . . .	And exceeding the feminine sex . . .
Ie suis inclin iusques au Ciel haulser	I am inclined to raise as far as Heaven
Ceulx, que lon doibt par raison exaulcer . . .	Those to whom one can hearken by reason . . .
D'un mien Amy, qui t'a donné le cueur,	Of my friend, who has given you his heart.

[40] "A P. de Marillac," in Charles de Sainte-Marthe, *La poésie françoise de Charles de Saincte-Marthe . . . Plus un Livre de ses Amys* (Lyon: chez le Prince, 1540), 10.
[41] *Honnêteté* meant morally upright and chaste secondarily, while its opposite (*deshonnête*) referred more primarily to lascivious behavior. The asymmetry is apparent in the fact that, as Bette Talvacchia points out, even prostitutes (generally courtesans) could be *honnête* in their business dealings with their clients. See *Taking Positions: On the Erotic in Renaissance Culture* (Princeton University Press, 1999), 104–24.
[42] "A P. Tolet, Medicin du grand Hospital de Lyon, Sur l'amitie de luy, & de Dolet," in Sainte-Marthe, *La poésie françoise*, 11.

D'un mien Amy, lequel (non pas sans cause)	Of my friend, of whom (not without cause)
Sur ton Amour du sien entier fait pause...	On your Love his whole self awaits.[43]

Sainte-Marthe describes his love for Tolet as divine and not about pleasure. Insisting that his love is entirely spiritual, Sainte-Marthe exults his position – he is, after all, revealing true love – as superior. He in effect tells Tolet's girlfriend that he loves Tolet more than she does, that as a woman, she is incapable of loving Tolet as well. At the same time, Sainte-Marthe distances himself from the homosocial implications by addressing a woman in order to talk about a man. The homosocial intrudes on and precludes heterosexual connection.

Two decades later, anxiety about homoeroticism prompted articulations of a hierarchy of incorrect object choices. Men were still better, but French Neoplatonists struggled to circumscribe good and bad forms of homosocial connection. Etienne Pasquier (1529–1615) announces that when comparing men and women as possible lovers, loving women is inferior: "Voire que nous voyons par cest Amour feminin, avoir esté violée & rompue la loy de vraye amitié, qui estoit de l'homme à l'homme" [We see indeed that we have, by this feminine love, been violated and broken the law of true friendship, which was from man to man].[44] His example of male–male love is Champier's favorite, Titus and Gisippus with added emphasis on women as sexual objects to signal their inferiority. Louys Le Roy acknowledges Platonic love in the sense that Kristeller defined it, but offers a selective reading of its meanings. In his analysis, Le Roy uses the Phaedrus speech in Plato's *Symposium* to introduce examples of possible object choice: Alcestis for Admetus (a woman who loves a man); Orpheus for Eurydice (a man who loves a woman), and Achilles for Patroclus (a man who loves a man). Putting Orpheus in the heterosexual column is not surprising (see above, Chapter 1), but doing so indicates Le Roy's commitment to denying the homosexual turn at the center of Orpheus' story.

The parsing of possibility continues when Le Roy acknowledges male–male love. This is no small thing given that he denies the possibility of female–female love. But Le Roy is careful, defining male–male love as instrumental generosity. Rather than beauty or desire, Achilles is motivated by, "un acte franc & libre & de pure liberalité, au moyen dequoy il doibt estre plus remuneré par les Dieux" [a frank and free act of pure liberality, by means of which he should be more remunerated by the Gods].[45] Like Sainte-Marthe, Le Roy insists that men rely

---

[43] "A la Dame & bien aymée de M. P. Tolet, Medicin du grand Hospital de Lyon, son singulier Amy," in Sainte-Marthe, *La poésie françoise*, 172–5, esp. 173.

[44] Etienne Pasquier, *Le Monophile par Estienne Pasquier* (Paris: Jean Longis, 1555), fol. 60r.

[45] Le Roy, *Sympose*, fol. 16r. By way of emphasis, Le Roy appends a poem by Antoine Héroët on loving without being loved in return to close his commentary. Later, Le Roy takes Ficino to

on other men because women are deficient.[46] By way of illustration, he recounts the story of Harmodius and Aristogeton as opponents of tyranny, omitting their relationship as lovers. To underscore the inferiority of women as stemming from their carnality, Le Roy recalls that Venus committed adultery with Mars. Heterosexual malfeasance because of female sexuality displaces homosexual desire. As a faithful translator,[47] Le Roy admits the Platonic homoerotics, but erases sexual desire in the homosexual pairings.

However, Le Roy's insistent readings of love between men as noble self-sacrifice do not add up to rational transcendence. Sex kept creeping into Plato's text. Where explication combined with de-eroticizing could not work, Le Roy retreated into pronounced silence. Throughout, Le Roy's commentary is replete with fulsome explications, but when he is confronted with the attempted seduction of Socrates by Alcibiades, he announces that his disgust has led to omission:

Les propos ensuyvant d'Alcibiade & de Socrates sont pleins de grande liberté, qui lors regnoit par toute la Grece, mesmement en Athenes: & me semblent ne pouvoir aujourd'huy estre honnestement recitez . . . j'ay esté conseillé par mes amis d'omettre le reste que Platon a adjousté seulement pour plaisir, servant au temps & à la licencieuse vie de son pays: sans proposer aux François parolles non convenantes à leurs meurs, ny convenantes à la religion Chrestienne.	The following exchanges of Alcibiades and Socrates are full of great liberties, which used to reign throughout Greece, even in Athens: and it seems to me they can not today be honestly recounted [and] I have been counseled by my friends to omit the rest that Plato added only for pleasure, appropriate to his time and to the licentiousness of his country: without proposing to French people words inconsistent with their moral habits and the Christian religion.[48]

Le Roy's copious citations of Ficino indicate that he had the *De amore* and its Christianized reading of the episode available to him. Ficino emphasized that Socrates was never accused of "filthy" love, even by his detractors. Despite his ugly appearance, Socrates is described as love incarnate, and Alcibiades as admiring love itself in praising him.[49] Le Roy chose to remove the passage

---

task for allowing homoerotics into his commentary, sniffing that the Florentine did not know much about antiquity or nature (fols. 50v–52v).

[46] Le Roy, *Sympose*, fol. 19r.

[47] Jean-Claude Margolin, "Le Roy, traducteur de Platon et la Pléiade," in *Lumières de la Pléiade*, ed. Pierre Mesnard (Paris: Vrin, 1966), 49–62, argues that Le Roy was a superior translator, but a mediocre commentator. He developed new vocabulary terms to convey complex ideas more precisely, and he untangled difficult syntax with some facility.

[48] Le Roy, *Sympose*, fol. 180v. As James Hankins notes, omitting the sticky bits was a common occurrence with respect to Plato's homoerotics. See Hankins, *Plato in the Italian Renaissance*, vol. I, 70, 80, 137–8.

[49] Ficino, *De amore*, 242–5, 260–2. Of course Ficino undercuts this reading by then describing in some detail physical attraction between men. Ficino insists that Socrates serves humanity by being an example of non-lascivious love.

sympathetic to male–male love and its intimations of sodomy rather than attempt to recuperate it, and he was not the only one who did this sort of thing. Henri Estienne, in his influential volume of poems attributed to Anacreon, suppressed the homoerotic opening poem in the first edition and later relegated it to the section on "suspect" poems.[50] But Le Roy went further. Where Estienne was content with silent suppression and rearrangement, Le Roy constructed willful misreadings to make Neoplatonism safe for heterosexuality.

By 1578, Jean de Serres translated the passage, albeit from Greek into Latin, rather than French. Serres included Alcibiades' drunken entrance at the end of the *Symposium* and his attempts to seduce Socrates with lewd references to nude exercising at the public gymnasium. Serres offers little appended commentary, apparently allowing Alcibiades to condemn himself and homoerotic desire from his own mouth.[51] So we must suppose. Serres does not say so directly, but it seems highly improbable that he did not understand Alcibiades' meaning, and he was quite opinionated about sodomy elsewhere. Referring to Plato's androgyne:

Quod autem de Παιδεραστίας portento hîc ait, praeterquam quòd pudet pigétque mouere has sordes, hactenus est etiam refutatum.	But whatever one says here about the monstrosity of pederasty, except that it is shameful and disgusting to consider such sordid things, has at this point already been refuted.[52]

The silence around homosexual seduction is telling. As Marc Schachter observes, Serres's choice of the androgyne as the figure of (reviled) pederastic desire is odd unless Serres wanted to emphasize procreation and jettison the homoerotic elements celebrated by Plato.[53] Where Plato praised the male–male descendents of the androgyne and warned that the male–female version often turned out to be adulterous, Serres inverts the moral hierarchy to ensure that homosexual desire is on the bottom.

From diversion and diffusion to suppression and denunciation, the ways that Neoplatonists in France treated homoeroticism indicate the conflict engendered by a philosophy that imagined having to corral desire in the service of higher intellectual understanding without providing reliable markers for how to do that. Never entirely accepting of the notion that the connections

[50] Anacreon, *Anacreonis Teii Odae. Ab Henrico Stephano luce et Latinitate nunc primum donatae* (Paris: Henri Estienne, 1554). Further editions of the Estienne volume appeared in 1560, 1566, 1567, 1568, 1600, 1612, and 1626. On Anacreon and the influence of the poems attributed to him, see Patricia Rosenmeyer, "The Greek Anacreontics," in *The Classical Heritage in France*, ed. Gerald Sandy (London: Brill, 2002), 393–424. See p. 397 especially.

[51] Plato, *Opera quae extant omnia*, vol. III, 212–23.

[52] Plato, *Opera quae extant omnia*, vol. III, 189b.

[53] Marc Schachter, "Louis le Roy's *Sympose de Platon* and Three Other Renaissance Adaptations of Platonic Eros," *RQ* 59 (2006): 406–39. See esp. 421–4.

between men could provide the space for transcendent love, French Neoplatonists gradually stratified love objects, with homoerotic attachments designated as purely carnal and thus inhibiting transcendence. Rejecting homosociability was insufficient, however. Because of all the aporia around women as rational, intellectual lovers, French Neoplatonists had to reconstruct women as suitable objects of appropriate desire.

Add women and stir

Homosociality did not work; heterosociality would seem to provide the obvious solution. But Medieval courtly love tradition, the *querelle des femmes*, and Ficino himself all indicated that beauty – and female beauty especially – complicated that solution.[54] French Neoplatonists were especially troubled because the "truth" about beauty was that it was often deceptive. Ficino's Neoplatonism posited beauty's primacy in facilitating love that moved toward the divine; French Neoplatonism inherited strong suspicion of women as agents of carnal desire who masked their intentions by means of deceptive beauty. Rather than dismiss women, some French interlocutors engaged in efforts to categorize beauty and sexual desire as positive markers of physical transcendence. Against them, skeptics, cynics, and misogynists undercut the claims for women, but always in ways that added women to the mix.

Such moves were not obvious when Ficino first presented Neoplatonism in extended form. Following Plato, Ficino found women philosophically uninspiring. Likeness was between men or at least a matter of masculinity:

Femine profecto viros facile capiunt, facilius autem ille que masculam quandam indolem pre se ferunt. Et tanto facilius masculi quanto similores sunt viris quam femine.	Women truly easily capture men, and even more easily those women who bear a masculine character. So much more easily, men catch men, as they are more like men than are women.[55]

While men can be attracted to women (despite the fact that they are lesser beings), beauty is between men. Women were uninteresting; beauty was not. As Ficino's homosocial presumptions indicate, beauty was narcissistic. Loving another man was a form of self-loving. Beauty in this sense opened up space

---

[54] The *querelle des femmes* is usually traced back to Jean de Meung's *Roman de la Rose* (1398–1402), which insisted on the inferiority of women. The relationship between men and women continued to be a staple of French literature, enjoying a resurgence in popularity in the 1530s. Among the more prominent texts in this round were Henry Cornelius Agrippa, *Declaration de la Noblesse et Preexcellence du sexe feminin*, trans. Martin Le Pin (Lyon: François Juste, 1537), which attacked inequality by gender; and Jean de Marconville, *De l'heur et malheur de mariage* (Paris: J. Dallier, 1564) focused on women as sexually insatiable and generally inferior.

[55] Ficino, *De amore*, 253. On the importance of likeness to love, see also Ficino, *Letters*, vol. I, 197 (Ficino to Amerigo Corsini).

Figure 11. Léonard Limosin (c.1505–c.1577), *Venus and Cupid* (1555), enamel, originally Limoges; currently Louvre, Paris, France.

The move in French Neoplatonic thought toward a resolutely heterosexual articulation of love imagery is reflected in the popularity of sensual images of Venus, including ones that suggest the association of love and generation. That said, Venus and her son are also somewhat uncomfortably intimate, as in Limosin's enamel.

to admit women into Neoplatonism because they could reflect and reproduce one's self-love.

Beauty for Ficino was both crucial and exceedingly perilous. It provided the means to move toward God, but if mistaken – and because of desire, it was often mistaken – it could easily lead to damning corporeal entanglements. Ficino's analysis of the speech of Agathon in the *De amore* brings out the positive version in which external beauty is a reflection of internal perfection.[56]

---

[56] See Ficino, *De amore*, 178: "Interiorem bonitatem, exteriorem pulchritudinem dicimus" [We call interior beauty goodness and exterior, beauty]. See also pp. 188–90 for the same concept. Ficino vacillated on the question of correspondence between physical and spiritual beauty. See for instance Ficino, *Letters*, vol. II, 74 (Ficino to Giovanni Cavalcanti) and vol. IV, 67 (Ficino to Friends), which assert beauty of the body reflects beauty of the soul, while *Letters*, vol. I, 44–5 (Ficino to Peregrino Agli) warns that beauty of the body is a source of lust. The coherence between internal and external beauty was much disputed in art theory. See for instance the

God saturated creation with beauty as an expression of divine love. Physical attraction is the result of beauty drawn toward its like within beings created by God's love. Ficino asserts that beauty is not merely external symmetry or proportion; rather, it is timeless, unaffected by age or change, and emphatically not embodied:

Amor nullo impletur aspectu corporis vel amplexu. Nullam igitur naturam corporis ardet, pulchritudinem certe sectatur. Quo fit ut ea corporeum aliquid esse non posit.	Love is satisfied by no appearance or embrace. Therefore, it burns for no nature of the body; at any rate it does not have a passion for bodily nature, but pursues beauty. For this reason it cannot be corporeal.[57]

From this general description, Ficino goes on to contend that real beauty is attracted to the "Angelic Mind," one of the five ontological hypostases. Michael J. B. Allen has described the origins of the hypostases in Plotinus' work:

the whole philosophy of Plotinus... is a consequence of his dividing reality into a hierarchical series of ontological states where the higher subsumes the lower and the lower emanates from the higher and ultimately from the absolutely prime hypostasis, the transcendent One.[58]

While Ficino took his time deciding on his five (eventually settling on Mind, One, Soul, Quality, and Body), Mind is central to the understanding of beauty in the *De amore*. The process described by Allen is shorthanded by Ficino in sexual terms: "Sed enim animus noster, ea conditione genitus ut terreno corpore circumdetur, ad officium generandi declinat" [Our soul is engendered in such a condition that, contained in an earthly body, it is inclined to procreate].[59]

---

concerns in Gian Paolo Lomazzo, *Trattato dell'arte della pittura, scoltura et architettura* [1584], in *Scritti sulle arti*, ed. Roberto Paolo Ciardi, 2 vols. (Florence: Marchi and Bertolli, 1974), vol. II, 113–53, and in his *Idea del Tempio della Pittura* [1590], in *Scritti sulle arti*, vol. I, 292–8, 308–10. See also Lodovico Dolce, *Dialogo della pittura intitolato l'Aretino* [1557], in *Scritti d'arte del Cinquecento*, ed. Paola Barocchi, 3 vols. (Milan and Naples: Riccardo Ricciardi, 1973), vol. I, 792–4. On Neoplatonic notions in Renaissance art, see especially André Chastel, *Marsile Ficin et l'art* (Geneva: Droz, 1975); Francis Ames-Lewis, "Neoplatonism and the Visual Arts at the Time of Marsilio Ficino," in *Marsilio Ficino: His Theology, His Philosophy, His Legacy*, ed. Michael J. B. Allen and Valery Rees (Leiden: Brill, 2002), 327–38; Erwin Panofsky, *Studies in Iconology: Humanistic Themes In the Art of the Renaissance* (New York: Icon, 1972); Edgar Wind, *Pagan Mysteries in the Renaissance* (London: Faber & Faber, 1958); and Wind, "Platonic Justice, Designed by Raphael," *Journal of the Warburg Institute* (1937): 69–70.

[57] Ficino, *De amore*, 184.

[58] Michael J. B. Allen, "Ficino's Theory of the Five Substances and the Neoplatonists' *Parmenides*," *JMRS* 12 (1982): 19–44. See p. 19. Allen corrects Kristeller's reading of the hypostases in Ficino's thought.

[59] Ficino, *De amore*, 185. On the Angelic Mind and its relationship to Venus in Ficino's thought, see Clement Salaman, "Echoes of Egypt in Hermes and Ficino," in *Marsilio Ficino: His Theology, His Philosophy, His Legacy*, ed. Michael J. B. Allen and Valery Rees (Leiden: Brill, 2002), 115–35, esp. 123–25.

Allowing for sexual procreation, Ficino follows Christianized Aristotelian ideas in emphasizing that the material body is insignificant compared to the immortal soul. Ficino sums this up by asserting that, "ut ostenderet sola divinitatis inspiratione quid vera pulchritudo sit" [only by divine inspiration can men understand true beauty].[60] Understanding beauty is necessary for the ascent of the soul to the Angelic Mind, and thence to God. The Platonic source for this notion of ascent is often referred to as the "ladder of love," which appears in the *Symposium* when Diotima speaks of the love for a beautiful body inspiring love for all bodies. From this abstraction the lover discovers, in hierarchical order, love for souls, laws and customs, all branches of knowledge, the science of beauty, and absolute beauty itself.[61] For Ficino, the ascent is marked by degrees of agency: the body, which cannot move itself, rises to the soul, which can move itself, but which has an intelligence inferior to that of the Angelic Mind. As the highest good, God has the potency of cognition and is whole, rather than composite. Only through contemplating the beautiful body is comprehension of God possible.[62] Beauty is infused by God in all beings, and the quest for beauty as determined by sympathetic attraction is the mechanism for salvation of the soul.

So much for the easy part. Beauty was powerful stuff, and Ficino struggled to articulate desire in reliable terms with respect to it. Desire and beauty are inextricably linked in Ficino's formulation, and desire could disrupt the movement toward God around beauty. Ficino allows that desire for embodied beauty can overwhelm the senses and the intellect. Human will becomes unreliable at this point.[63] The pleasures of taste and touch can be so violent that they dislodge the

---

[60] Ficino, *De amore*, 199. See p. 188 on the pre-eminence of the soul.

[61] Plato, *Symposium*, trans. Gill, 210a–212a. There is a different version of the ladder of love in Giovanni Pico della Mirandola, *Commento a una canzone del Benivieni*, which was first published in 1519, but probably composed around 1486. On the context of its genesis and for an accessible modern edition, see Giovanni Pico della Mirandola, *De hominis dignitate, Heptaplus, De ente et uno*, ed. Eugenio Garin (Florence: Vallecchi, 1942), 10–11, 443–581. After the love for one beautiful body, Pico's next step involves the lover making the image of love more perfect and spiritual. Then the soul distinguishes universal beauty from sensory images of love. Awareness of the power of abstraction, and of ideal beauty follow. From there, the soul rises to approach ideal beauty intellectually, and then merges with the Angelic Mind to achieve complete awareness. Finally, and only with God's help, the lover attains union with God. This culminating step is not available to mortal beings, according to Pico, a difference from Ficino's understanding of love as offering the ability to achieve salvation.

[62] Ficino, *De amore*, 230–9.

[63] Ficino's account of the Aristophanes myth includes both the idea that the will is operative and that it is not. See *De amore*, 167–8. For more on Ficino's conception of the will, see Tamara Albertini, "Intellect and Will in Marsilio Ficino: Two Correlatives of a Renaissance Concept of mind," in *Marsilio Ficino: His Theology, His Philosophy, His Legacy*, ed. Michael J. B. Allen and Valery Rees (Leiden: Brill, 2002), 203–25, which argues for Ficino's innovative solution to the will/intellect problem. See also Kristeller, *Philosophy*, 256–88. Merrill, "The Pléiade and the Androgyne." See p. 109 for the argument that free will is impossible in Plato's philosophy because love is determined by God, but this is a bit reductive.

intellect from its proper state. Ficino describes this as corporeal love. Spiritual love, he insists, not only does not desire, but hates and shuns intemperance as contrary to beauty. Venereal desire can be recognized as corporeal if it leads to ugliness, which Ficino equates with disharmony. Following prevailing medical wisdom that saw the male body threatened by the expulsion of semen, Ficino assumes sex produces disharmony:

Quapropter libido conitus, id est, coeundi, et amor, non modo non iidem [idem?] motus sed et contrarii esse monstrantur.	Whereby on account of desire for coitus (that is, copulation) and love are shown not only as not the same, but to be contrary.[64]

Despite reassurances that love only seeks proper objects – "qui odit deformia, necessario turpia obscenaque fugit" [as it hates the ugly, it necessarily flees from foul and indecent things] – the attempt to occlude carnal desire from love is incomplete at best.[65] One answer to the desire problem for Ficino was to retreat into ungendered language. In Ficino's understanding of the immortality of the soul, identified by Charles Trinkaus as crucial to Ficino's positive evaluation of humanity, Ficino is adamant that the soul strives for God out of a "natural appetite" for truth. Ficino removes the gender distinctions when he asserts that the soul's desire for the good is contrasted with bodily appetites, including sexual ones. Ficino distinguishes between soul and body in *The Platonic Theology* by contending that the soul desires the good at all times, but desires corporeal pleasures only occasionally. Corporeal desires can be curbed; desire for truth cannot. But Ficino also admits that desire for God is "much more natural" than the desire for food or sex. Like the humoral body gendered masculine or feminine by virtue of its mix of humors, the difference is of scale or degree, rather than kind.[66] Another of Ficino's models for controlling desire, the Phaedrean charioteer, removes gender entirely, utilizing animal exemplars instead. In this interpretation, opposition between corporeal and physical love is the difference between rationality and appetite or concupiscence.[67] The repetitious efforts

---

[64] Ficino, *De amore*, 143. Marcel identified the manuscript variant iidem/idem. I have added punctuation for clarity. See Ficino, *Letters*, vol. I, 43 on the body depressed by corporeal desire. This notion appears elsewhere in Ficino's thought. In *Della religione christiana* (Florence: Giunti, 1563), 16, Ficino emphasizes that ejaculation was dangerous for the (male) mind or intellect.

[65] Ficino, *De amore*, 143. Ficino found himself defending his position long after the fact. See for instance his letter to Giovanni Calvacanti in *Epistolae*, book 1, no. 17, which defends the *De amore* and its arguments about physical beauty.

[66] Marsilio Ficino, *Théologie platonicienne*, ed. and trans. Raymond Marcel, 3 vols. (Paris: Les Belles Lettres, 1964–1970), vol. II, 253: "Quanto igitur naturalior est veri bonique quam cibi coitusque cupiditas." See Charles Trinkaus, *In Our Image and Likeness: Humanity and Divinity in Italian Humanist Thought*, 2 vols. (University of Chicago Press, 1970), vol. II, 461–505, esp. 488–9, for discussion of Ficino. Trinkaus notes that Ficino identifies human beings in a similar scale of difference relative to animals. See p. 497.

[67] Michael J. B. Allen, *Marsilio Ficino and the Phaedran Charioteer* (Berkeley: University of California Press, 1981), 78. The Latin: "Hinc revertitur iterum ad vires anime dividendas, et

to contain desire rhetorically indicate that the differences between acceptable and unacceptable forms were difficult to articulate; the repetition is a sign that Ficino suspected that readers needed special reinforcement on the subject.

French Neoplatonists picked up the cue that the desire problem was tricky, but rather than disengage from the gender dynamics as Ficino tried to do, they took on beauty and desire as gender issues.[68] The analytical frame for the French was the twin inheritance of the chivalric love tradition and the *querelle des femmes*. French Neoplatonists injected Ficino's ideas into the debates over male and especially female character. Of course, positive enthusiasm about women and misogyny often mixed, but for optimists, Neoplatonism served as a guide through the morass of "problems" presented by loving women. For pessimists, Neoplatonic ideas confirmed their worst beliefs about the dangers of women. These debates were not simply ludic play for the marketplace, as Floyd Gray has said of the *querelle des femmes*.[69] Rather the infusion of Neoplatonism puts the construction of sexual ideology on display.

Here again, Champier prepares the ground. He utilizes the Medieval love tradition and the *querelle des femmes* to work toward his culminating Neoplatonic intervention. Champier denounces misogynous attacks on women, calling those who attack women "gens pervers" [perverted men]. In the tradition of Giovanni Boccaccio's *De mulieribus claris* (1362) and Christine de Pizan's *Le Livre de la Cité des dames* (1405), Champier catalogues bad and good women. Women are often chaste and pure, he insists, despite famous problem cases such as Bathsheba and Delilah. Men forget "La chasteté du Susanne, la puritee de Lucresse . . . la vaillance de la royne Semiramie" [the chastity of Suzanne, the purity of Lucretia . . . and the valiant acts of the queen Semiramus].[70] The faults of men are greater, Champier argues, although he is confounded by the question of balance. His thumbnail biographies of chaste, brave, and pious women recuperate feminine virtue, but he is flummoxed by female inferiority prescribed in Genesis.[71] He announces that carnality must be controlled by men and women for the good of body and soul. To this point, both Champier's method and materials recall Medieval priorities and preoccupations.

---

rationem quidem aurigam vocat, geminos vero appetitus equos geminos: appetitum rationalem equum bonum, appetitum irrationalem equum malum; sed in hoc genere appetitum vergentem ad iracundiam minus malum, declinantem vero ad concupiscentiam magis malum" [Thence Socrates returns to dividing the soul's powers again: he calls reason the charioteer, the twin appetites, the paired horses; and the rational appetite he calls the good horse, the irrational appetite, the bad. The irrational appetite is less bad when it inclines to wrath; worse when it declines to concupiscence]. (79). Ficino returns to this contrast later to emphasize it. See p. 99.

[68] The French knew other Italian texts that dealt with the gender issues more forcefully, such as Bembo, *Les Asolains*, Hébreu, *Dialogues d'amour*, and Baldassare Castiglione, *Le Courtisan*.

[69] Floyd Gray, *Gender, Rhetoric and Print Culture in French Renaissance Writing* (Cambridge University Press, 2000).

[70] Champier, *Nef des dames*, sigs. bi (v) – ci (r).

[71] Champier, *Nef des dames*, sigs. I ii (r) – I iiii (r).

Instead of standing pat on religious pieties, Champier invokes Neoplatonic ideas as he attempts to sort out the good and bad in women. On the meaning of beauty, Champier invokes the *De amore*:

Amour n'est aultre chose que desir de chose belle et honneste . . . Et psource que amour n'est que desir de beaulté.	Love is nothing other than the desire for beautiful and honest things . . . And so love is only the desire for beauty.[72]

Beauty comes in three forms: of body, soul, and voice. The corporeal forms are dangerous:

L'enraigement et folie de concupiscence charnelle et venerée conduit à prodigalité, intemperance, infameté, et à choses villes.	The rage and folly of carnal and venereal concupiscence produces prodigality, intemperance, infamy, and vile things.[73]

With Ficino's understanding of beauty in mind, Champier asserts that infamy and ugliness are contrary to beauty, which means that, "Cest appetit charnel et venerée ne se peult dire amour" [This carnal and venereal appetite can not be called love].[74] But Champier has trouble making these ideas work in practice. Utilizing familiar stories, Champier attempts to describe proper versions of love between a woman and a man, between a man and a woman, and between two men. Each time, he labors to present strong examples of "good" desire, but his choices are rather strange. His marker of marital desire of wife for husband is Artemisia, who proves her love for her husband by drinking his ashes and building him a spectacular funerary monument. Her larger governing role, which many Renaissance commentators found unsettlingly masculine, Champier omits. Heterosexual love is demonstrated by "grand angoisse" [great anguish] and a modified form of postmortem cannibalism.[75] This is hardly a ringing endorsement for salvific desire.

The reverse situation, of the man who loves a woman, is stranger still. Champier folds an attempt to illustrate the difference between beauty of soul and body into the story of the love of Cymon for Iphigenie, drawn from another Boccaccio tale.[76] Cymon is "insensé et fol de nature et avoit la voix rude et laide" [foolish and wild by nature and has rough and ugly speech]. He has, "les meurs de beste plus que d'homme" [the manners more of a beast than of a man]. While in the forest, he sees "une belle fille et jeune, plaine de beaulté" [a

---

[72] Champier, *Nef des dames*, sig. q ii (r). Champier draws heavily on three of Ficino's chapters from the *De amore*: Oration 1: 4 (De utilitate amoris, pp. 141–4); 2: 3 (Pulchritudo est splendor divine bonitatis, 147–9); and 2: 8 (Exhortatio ad amorem, De amore simplici ac mutuo, 155–8).

[73] Champier, *Nef des dames*, sig. q ii (r).   [74] Champier, *Nef des dames*, sig. q ii (v).

[75] Champier, *Nef des dames*, sig. q iii (r). For the discomfort caused by Artemisia, see Sheila ffolliott, "Catherine de' Medici as Artemisia: Figuring the Powerful Widow," in *Rewriting the Renaissance: The Discourses of Sexual Difference in Early Modern Europe*, ed. Margaret W. Ferguson, Maureen Quilligan, and Nancy J. Vickers (University of Chicago Press, 1986), 227–41.

[76] Boccaccio, *The Decameron*, 367–78 (Day V, Story 1).

beautiful young girl, full of beauty]. Cymon is inspired to become an "homme civil" [civil man] in order to win her.[77] Champier wants the story to provide ways to read physical beauty as reflecting interior virtues. Cymon is beautiful despite his rude manners and moral defects because he is capable of responding to beauty. But the narrative occludes such a straightforward reading. Although Cymon corrects his faults, he is denied Iphigenie's hand in marriage because she is already promised to Passimonde of Rhodes. After Cymon ambushes the ship transporting Iphigenie, a storm traps his ship at Rhodes and he is taken prisoner. He is liberated by a Rhodian magistrate, Lysimacus, who enlists Cymon to prevent the double wedding involving Passimonde and Iphigenie and Lysimacus' beloved, Cassandra, to Passimonde's brother. The complex plot echoes the complications of desire, while a sort of repetition compulsion is played out when Cymon kidnaps Iphigenie again. This time, violent abduction is coupled with murder: Cymon kills Passimonde. How transcendent is the beast's love after all? Champier insists on four occasions that Cymon's love for Iphigenie's beauty is transformative, asserting that Cymon's love was not carnal or venereal. Perhaps, but martial prowess in the form of homicidal violence marks the contours of Cymon's desire.

Champier's recurrent concern is the misrecognition of desire. Since he imagines feminine beauty as part of the Neoplatonic project, he is anxious that women hold up their end. Not surprisingly, given his reliance on the *querelle des femmes* model, he sees women as more prone to the error of "faulse amour" [false love], and warns that "concupiscence charnelle est une espece de anragement et fureur" [carnal concupiscence is a kind of derangement and fury].[78] Women left to their own devices "devint lascive" [become lascivious]. Men must save women from "volupté mondaine" [worldly voluptuousness]. The retreat into denigration of women enables Champier to exhort his audience to fulfill gendered expectations:

O Dames, veillez estre amoureuses de vraye amour et nayant peur de ce que dit Platon quant il dit que celluy qui ayme est mort en soy mesmes et a vit en aultruy, car il vit en lachose quil ayme . . . O hommes soyes viriles. O dames soyes vertueuses prudentes et pudiques.

Oh Ladies, you should be in love with true love and not fear what Plato said when he said that those who love are dead in themselves, and live in another, because he lives in the thing he loves . . . Oh, men, be virile. Oh ladies, be virtuous, prudent, and chaste.[79]

---

[77] Champier, *Nef des dames*, sig. q iii (v) – sig. q iv (r).

[78] Champier, *Nef des dames*, after sig. r iv (v). The notion of divine fury, Philip Ford notes, enabled Renaissance Christians to assimilate Plato. Divine inspiration was used to explain Plato's understanding of Christian theological concepts long before Christ. See Philip Ford, "Classical Myth and Its Interpretation in Sixteenth-Century France," in *Classical Heritage in France*, ed. Gerald Sandy (Leiden and Boston: Brill, 2002), 331–49.

[79] Champier, *Nef des dames*. This concluding section is unpaginated. In Kem's edition of Champier, *Nef des dames*, it appears on pp. 250–1.

Female modesty and male virility determine the contours of proper desire. Champier makes women a part of the program, albeit an ambivalent part. He imagines women as (limited) agents in the search for true love.

Several Neoplatonically inflected interventions follow on Champier's attempt to delineate beauty and desire within the referential frame of the *querelle des femmes*. Antoine Vias offers a method of measuring beauty in women to hedge against their destructive propensities. The key for Vias is chastity: "jamais Beaulté n'eust paix avec Chasteté, mais tousjours sont en continuelle guerre" [Beauty can never live in peace with Chastity, but they are always in continual war].[80] Only rational assessment of a woman's chastity by men, only vigilant maintenance of chastity by women, can correct for feminine dissimulation.[81] Where beauty was supposed to point the way to transcendence, French texts emphasized its dangers. Warnings about the deceptive beauty of women abound. Typical of these is Gilles Corrozet's emblem, *Dessoubz beaulté gist deception*, which warns:

Que soubz claire beaulté,	That under pristine beauty,
Estre ne peult telle desloyaulté:	There can only be such disloyalty:
Et qu'elle avoit l'apparence & la face,	And she has the appearance and the face,
D'honnesteté & vertueuse grace.	Of honesty and grace.

Echoing some interpretations of Eurydice's death (see above, Chapter 1), the illustrating image compares the lusty woman to the snake lying hidden in the grass.[82]

Negotiating Neoplatonic language about desire and misogynous anxiety about women, some French humanists tried to develop a heuristic to recognize good and bad desire reliably. Guillaume de La Perrière's 1536 *Cent considerations d'amour* provides a catalogue of markers of bad desire. In his preface, La Perrière twice explains that he waited until he was 40 to feel mature enough to educate others on the ways that desire can turn men into idiots, or worse, lead

---

[80] Vias, *Le Sophologe d'Amour*, fol. 60r. Vias draws on the misogynous Medieval tradition, mentioning the notoriously anti-woman *Roman de la Rose*. On the cultural prominence of this text, see Pierre-Yves Badel, *"Le Roman de la Rose" au XIVe siècle: étude de la réception de l'œuvre* (Geneva: Droz, 1980) and Kevin Brownlee and Sylvia Huot, eds., *Rethinking the Romance of the Rose: Text, Image, Reception* (Philadelphia: University of Pennsylvania, 1992). The printing date of the edition of the *Sophologe* consulted is 1542, but the text dedicates the work to the princes returned from captivity, which would date the text presumably to some time close to 1525. According to Henri Baudrier, *Bibliographie lyonnaise* (Lyon: Société des amis de la Bibliothèque municipale de Lyon, 1895), 98, there was an edition published in Lyon by Claude Nourry in 1515 as well. I have not been able to find the earlier edition, but events mentioned suggest changes had been made to the text.

[81] Vias, *Sophologe*, fols. 45r, 43v, 48v. Vias included generative sex in marriage as chaste. See references to such on fols. 36r, 39r, and 47v.

[82] Gilles Corrozet, *L'Hecatongraphie (1544) & Les Emblemes du Tableau de Cebes (1543)*, ed. and intro. Alison Adams (Geneva: Droz, 1997), H26. The emblems are numbered in this edition, which is a facsimile. [First edition: 1540.]

them to damnation. He renounces Jean de Meung, maintaining the importance of understanding bad desire without blaming women. La Perrière notes that the body leaves physical traces of desire that can help separate good or "virtuous" love from lasciviousness. Desire is particularly dangerous because it ravishes the soul (no. 31), can make the lover forget God (no. 65), and

Maintz amoureux craignent par leur foiblesse,	Many lovers fear, by their weakness,
Destre damnez, pour amour, en enfer.	being damned because of love to hell.[83]

Physical desire is

rien que vivre sans vie,	only to live without life.
Mourir sans mort, repos plein de travaux.	To die without death, repose full of travails.
C'est volupté de douleur assouvie.	It is the voluptuousness of glutted anguish.[84]

La Perrière warns that bad love torments and distresses (no. 6, 17, 18, 29, 60, 82), makes men succumb to contradictory ideas (no. 16), and brings suffering and discomfort (no. 18, 24, 43). Signs include sudden fury, excessive grief, and crying (no. 3, 7, 91). Desire makes the body tremble with cold even when it is hot (no. 19), but more common is the feeling of burning. Desire causes a burning heart, a pale face, physical agitation, and mental exhaustion (no. 38, 43, 52). La Perrière's catalogue of negatives makes it difficult to imagine healthy desire, but it does offer legible markers of desire's physicality.

Gilles Corrozet attempts a similar move with respect to beauty. *La Diffinition et Perfection d'Amour* follows Ficino to a degree: "Amour est une desir de jouyssance de beaulté" [Love is a desire for the jouissance of beauty].[85] Beauty is not physical, but instead comes in the three forms (of soul, body, and voice) specified in the *De amore*:

Beaulté est une reluisante splendeur, tirant et ravissant à soy l'esprit humain. Beaulté de l'ame est ung luysant accord de bonnes moeurs, accompagné d'acquise doctrine. Beaulté de corps n'est aultre chose que	Beauty is a shining splendor; drawing and ravishing to itself the human spirit. Beauty of the soul is a glistening accord of good manners, accompanied by the established doctrine. Beauty of body is nothing other

---

[83] Guillaume de La Perrière, *Les Cents considerations d'amour, composées par Guillaume de la Perriere Tholosain. Avec une Satire contre fol Amour* (Lyon: Jaques [sic] Berion, 1536), no. 40. (The quatrains are numbered, but unpaginated.)

[84] La Perrière, *Les Cents considerations d'amour*, no. 73.

[85] Gilles Corrozet[?], *La Diffinition et Perfection d'Amour. Le Sophologe d'Amour. Traictez plaisantz & delectables oultre l'utilité en iceulx contenue* (Paris: Gilles Corrozet, 1542), fol. 8r. See fols. 3v and 7v for appeals to women to learn to understand love. Festugière, *Philosophie de l'amour*, 78–9 attributes *La Diffinition* to Corrozet largely on the grounds of similarity to other works. Less convincingly, Festugière describes *Le Diffinition* as a translation of Ficino, but its departures make it more of an interpretation.

une concorde ordonnée de membres avec decente couleur ou ligneature plaisante. Beaulté de voix... n'est autre chose que concorde de parolle suffisante.	than the ordered harmony of the members with decent color or pleasant order. Beauty of voice... is nothing but the harmony of sufficient words.[86]

Altering Ficino's terms toward a more performative notion of beauty in which the moral and sexual terms are supposed to be easily legible, Corrozet warns that being attracted to a person's spirit or voice or body is acceptable, but touching or sleeping with someone is not. Beauty of spirit is revealed by being virtuous and well mannered. Mere physical desire is the result of disorderly will,

qui se cognoist au toucher et coucher, se doibt nommer parturbation bestialle ou servile, et non beaulté, et moins Amour.	which knows itself by touching and laying down and ought to be named a bestial or servile perturbation, rather than beauty, and even less, Love.[87]

Those who fail to conform to these exteriorized notions of beauty are overly sexual. Disruptive sex (*volupté*), the kind that is steeped in sensuality, is the result of failing to make oneself beautiful.

Corrozet recognizes that the performative standard he articulates runs the risk of devolving into false love. He denounces those who insist that

Amour n'estre aultre chose que ceste volunté desordonnée d'homme à femme, sans permission de loy de mariage.	Love is nothing other than the disordered will of a man with respect to a woman, without the permission of the law of marriage.[88]

He insists that using reason to understand love is available to both men and women. Women, he says several times, must contemplate the nature of love if they are to avoid grievous error. He tells them: "si vous m'aymez non par coutume, non par avarice, non par gloire, mais par instinct de nature et similitude de complexion." [if you love me not by habit, nor from avarice, nor for glory, but by the instinct of nature and by the similarity in complexion], it is true

---

[86] *La Diffinition*, fols. 9v–10v.

[87] *La Diffinition*, fol. 11v. Pontus de Tyard, *Les Erreurs amoureuses*, ed. John A. McClelland (Geneva: Droz, 1967) [originally 1549–1555] closes with a dialogue between himself and "ma dame" in which desire leads to chaste love. He begins by admiring her: "Qu'en corps si beau, beau en perfection, / Il n'y entrat un peu d'affection, / De desir volontaire." When he expresses the fear that his desire will be inappropriately physical, she responds that contemplating her will save him: "A mon honneur affecté et constant, / Tu me trouveras tienne." See "Chant de chaste amour" in *Les Erreurs amoureuses*, vol. I, 179–85. See ll. 70–2, 113–14. Pléiade poets of course often invoked Neoplatonic concepts, but few offered sustained discussions. I have gestured toward a few obvious intertextualities. For sustained discussion of the Pléiade and Neoplatonism, see for instance Henri Weber, "Platonisme et sensualité dans la poésie amoureuse de la Pléiade," in *Lumières de la Pléiade*, ed. R. Antoniolli, R. Aulotte, M.-E. Balmas, A. Cioranesou (Paris: Vrin, 1966), 157–94; Merrill and Clements, *Platonism in French Renaissance Poetry*; and Robert M. Burgess, *Platonism in Desportes* (Chapel Hill: University of North Carolina Press, 1954).

[88] *La Diffinition*, fol. 10v.

love.[89] He scoffs at men who think that love is acquired by marriage and without effort, emphasizing that love entails mastery of the will and self-denial of seductive pleasures. The negative frame for the performative parameters of love may seem unstable, but he is optimistic that people, women especially, can learn how to achieve transcendent love.

The pedagogy of love takes on further dimensions with Antoine Héroët's *La Parfaicte amye* (1542). Héroët adopts the voice of a woman struggling to make sense of the philosophy relative to her life. As Lynn Enterline demonstrates, Jacques Lacan's insistence that the self is created in embodied form in language can be revealed through the Renaissance practice of "cross-voicing." Ovid is the exemplary ancient (male) author who articulates feminine subjectivity by adopting the female voice, and the practice appears routinely in Italian (especially Petrarchan) and English Renaissance poetry.[90] While part of a display of his skill at adopting a female persona, Héroët inhabits the contradictory and fungible qualities of the speaking subject when he articulates the complications of Neoplatonism as he sees them. Rhetoric this may be, but it also expresses the gender and power in play in Neoplatonic sexual ideology.

In part, Héroët offers the story of a woman accepting Neoplatonism as she has been taught it by her lover. The distinction between carnal, worldly love and transcendent, rational love is set up through the protagonist, Amye, who is an unhappily married woman. She wants to be faithful to her husband, but she is consumed by the more compelling love she has for her lover ("Amy"). Amye is torn between the spiritual love Amy has described in Neoplatonic terms and anxiety about her sexual reputation as a married women. Struggling to transcend, Amye reflects on the idea that beauty is the key to love and she sifts through her experience of it. She acknowledges that women are usually content to desire a man based on appearance, but this love is different, in part because: "Plus il vieillist, plus je le trouve aymable" [The more he grows old, the more I find him lovable]. Echoing the misogynous side of the *querelle des femmes*, Amye allows that female beauty is usually deceptive.[91] It lies and, "Beaulté de femme estre indigne d'aymer" [Beauty in woman is unworthy of love]. Nor are these the only issues. She understands that, "A estre aymé qu'à veoir aultre attiré/ De la beaulté que a tant desiré" [To be loved is to see others seduced / with the beauty that was so much desired], but she knows that beauty is in the eye of the beholder: "S'il veut beaulté, belle luy sembleray" [If he wants beauty, beautiful to him I will seem]. Following Ficino's formulation, she reads beauty and ugliness as indices of moral goodness, and while beauty

[89] *La Diffinition*, fol. 21v.
[90] Lynn Enterline, *The Rhetoric of the Body from Ovid to Shakespeare* (Cambridge University Press, 2000).
[91] Women who engaged directly in the *querelle des femmes* did not accept such terms. See Anne R. Larsen, "Paradox and the Praise of Women: From Ortensio Lando and Charles Estienne to Marie de Romieu," *SCJ* 28:3 (1997): 759–74.

is not ostensibly about appearance, it "rend le corps de femme transparent" [renders the woman's body transparent].[92] At times, she trusts that her love is different because it is reciprocal.[93] She does not think her beloved deceives her or wants anyone else. After all, he has explained the importance of reason and the elevating effects of love. She understands that salvation is the appropriate end of love that lifts the soul to God.[94]

Doubts meld with gender conventions built into the sexual tensions inherent to Neoplatonism. Because she is a woman, Amye is wary of carnal desire and the consequences of physicality. As a wife, her social transgression of loving another man is considered adultery. Although she fears being reproached for her disloyalty to her husband, Amye justifies herself with a vociferous condemnation of forced marriage and the subjection of women in it.[95] Submission to a master ("A la mercy d'ung maistre suis submise") is unlike voluntary submission of body and soul to her lover. The cross-voicing is also revelatory: the male poet uses Amye's persona to carve a space for male sexual license. He then suggests that women have an advantage with respect to understanding love in that they are familiar with subjection. Héröet has Amye articulate the prescriptive presumption that women are less apt in matters of love because they are more vulnerable to physical desire. Amye is a good girl because she fears pleasure as a "une furie" [a fury] that "Laissent au corps ung esbahissement" [Leaves the body invaded].[96] Implicitly, men are less susceptible and ironically, capable of resisting "bad" desire even while engaging in it.

Gender-coding produces Amye's re-instantiation in sexual norms, now claimed as Neoplatonic and transcendent. As a woman, Amye understands

---

[92] The quotations are from Antoine Héröet, *La Parfaicte amye*, ed. Christine M. Hill (University of Exeter, 1981), ll. 60, 260, 181–2, 471, and 1397. See also ll. 1211, 1379–1400, 1402–25 for comments about beauty and l. 268 about disguise. Héröet has been relatively neglected compared to most other significant French Renaissance poets. For background, see Jules Arnoux, *Un précurseur de Ronsard: Antoine Héröet, néo-platonicien et poète* (Digne: Imprimerie Chaspoul, 1912). See also W. A. R. Kerr, "Antoine Héröet's *Parfaite Amye*," *PMLA* 20:3 (1905): 567–83; and Marie Madeleine Fontaine, "Débats à la cour de France autour du *canzoniere* et de ses imitateurs dans les années 1533–1548," in *Les Poètes français de la Renaissance et Pétrarque*, ed. Jean Balsamo (Geneva: Droz, 2004), 104–35. Héröet is discussed on pp. 131–5.

[93] Héröet, *Parfaicte amye*, ll. 31, 144, 202, 562–75. Eventually, reciprocity comes to mark true love: "Que vraye amour n'ayt esté reciproque" (l. 1655).

[94] Héröet, *Parfaicte amye*, ll. 37–8, 121–82, 1183–4. The language sounds much like Corrozet's *Satire contre fol amour* in *Cents considerations*, unpaginated. Part of the *Satire* is reproduced in Festugière, *Philosophie*, 164–5.

[95] Nonetheless, in the mouth of Amye, Héröet says that women injure their lovers under the cover of love (ll. 535–6), ignoring the structural supremacy of men. In an abject moment, Amye says that she derives her perfection from her lover (l. 488). For her ruminations on marital disloyalty, see ll. 229, 291, 297–304, 395–403.

[96] Héröet, *Parfaicte amye*, ll. 331, 357–8, 207 (fury) and 588. (See also ll. 584, 1311 for divine fury. She is even anxious about the limiting touching that "Bembo" considers acceptable in *The Courtier*. For expressions along these lines, see *Parfaicte amye*, ll. 597–8: "Sans y penser se mettent à leur ayse, / Que la main touche, ou que la bouche baise." See also the anxiety about "volupté" (ll. 1142–3; 1159–61).

love relative to procreation. Héroët describes procreation as making one's own likeness. Héroët's position is close to Léon Hébreu's, who argued for the centrality of sexual reproduction in love. Hébreu argues that sex creates universality through the desire to procreate and depends on the divine Intellect. In framing his version of astrological Aristotelian elemental theory linking the microcosm of human sex to the macrocosm of the universe, Hébreu argues that God takes his love for himself (which is "female" or Matter) and turns that love towards his creation (which is active, "male" and Form). Earth and the stars inseminate like man and woman. The perfect (male) heavens provide the seminal material that is nurtured by the (female) earth in sensual terms.[97] Love holds the universe together by means of the instrumental reality of reproduction. Intercourse – spiritual or physical – allows for the crucial concept of participation. Héroët adjusts Hébreu's reading so that Amye understands sacrifice as a necessary part of love and it occurs through procreation. Willingness to accept the sacrifices entailed in procreation may mean that love is ordained.[98]

Although steeped in derogatory and limited views of women, Héroët has Amye engage in an imaginative exercise meant to help her see past the limitations of carnal love: she imagines that her lover has died.[99] Meditating on her responses to this idea leads "her" – or leads Héroët to articulate – a possible resolution of the desire/beauty problem. Amye understands death as the separation of the body and soul, and she envisions her soul reunited with her beloved in God. Imagining this purified, non-corporeal condition, Amye now understands that beauty of the body is an "estincelle" [spark] of the divine.[100] The remainder of that spark in the physical body is the result of souls

---

[97] Hébreu, *Dialogues*, 77–81, 86. For more on this understanding of the universe, see also above, Chapter 2 (Astrology). On the hierarchical organization of sex, see also Hébreu, *Dialogues*, 90–1, 111, 174–5, 198–201, 251, and 93 for the feminine earth. The male contribution is key: "Tout le ciel la produit avec son continuel mouvement, ainsi comme tout le corps de l'homme en commun produit le sperme et semence virile" (p. 91). Hébreu returns to Aristotle as the authority who confirms the scientific basis of generation as a cosmological principle. See pp. 145–8.

[98] Héroët, *Parfaicte amye*, ll. 1129–32; 1169–70; 1620–40. On the other hand, Amye/Héroët condemns Petrarchan expressions of pain in love as mistaken. True love is happy in sacrifice. Stories of unhappy love are many because few are capable of higher, true love (ll. 1512–45).

[99] Sperone Speroni, *Dialogi di M. S. Speroni. Nouvamente ristampati, & con molta diligenza riveduti, & corretti* (Venice: Aldine, 1543) suggests that love is only perfected by separation. See especially "Dialogo del Cathaio," fols. 156v–165r. Death as the ultimate form of separation recurs in French Renaissance poetry.

[100] Héroët, *Parfaicte amye*, ll. 818–52; 871–7. For similar imagery see Joachim Du Bellay, *Œuvres poétiques*, ed. Henri Chamard and Henri Weber, 9 vols. (Paris: Nizet, 1961–1982), vol. II, 192. From *Les Regrets* (1558), sonnet CLXXVI:

> Ta seule nourriture & ton accroissement,
> Et qui de tes beaux raiz en nostre entendement
> Produis ce hault desir, qui au ciel nous r'appelle,
> N'apperçois-tu combien par ta vive estincelle
> La vertu luit en moy?

contemplating beauty in heaven before birth ("Depuis tombés en ces terrestres corps" [Before falling into these earthly bodies]).[101] The spark of beauty creates the desire for unity with the lover; desire is the beauty of two souls seeking each other.[102] Amye can only comprehend spiritual unity through permanent physical separation, and it seems that the relationship between spiritual and physical unity remains complicated.

And, for some, "complicated" necessarily meant sexual. For worse or better, the key to the locus of women in Neoplatonic terms was sex. This inspired outrage on occasion. The *Louenge des femmes* (1551) blames women for all errors in love, linking female beauty to bad sexual behavior.[103] The author denounces women for ensnaring men with false beauty and leading them to "bestial" sexual love. Even when female beauty is a good thing, it causes men to stray:

C'est un desire de ce qu'on oyt nommer	It is a desire for this that one can call
Beauté, qui touché oeil, esprit, et aureille,	Beauty, which touches the eye, the soul, and the ear.
Mais touchant l'oeil, moins fait à estimer.	But touching the eye does less than is imagined.[104]

The author emphasizes that misguided "love" is always sexual:

Ce n'est donq pas, cest impudiq desir	This is thus not, this unchaste desire
Qui femme tient, de corps et cul conjoindre.	Which women have for body and cunt to conjoin.[105]

See also Pierre de Ronsard, *Œuvres complètes*, ed. Jean Céard, Daniel Ménager, and Michel Simonin, 2 vols. (Paris: Gallimard, 1993), vol. I, 116 (*Amours*, 1552, sonnet CLXXIV), in which Ronsard refers to being guided by a woman while "inflammed" with desire. In *Le premier livre des sonnets pour Hélène*, she leads him out of "voluptez" to higher love as well. See vol. I, 368–9, sonnet LIII (1578).

[101] Héroët, *Parfaicte amye*, l. 901. Kerr, "Antoine Héroët's *Parfaite Amye*," 579, argues that the spark of beauty is always awakened by women. Héroët's text supports this, but it is a misreading of Plato, which Kerr emphasizes throughout his analysis, to see this as generally about female beauty.

[102] Héroët, *Parfaicte amye*, ll. 1105–9. Héroët clearly read Bembo, as this section of Héroët's poem follows on an extended riff on the episode of the Queen of the Fortunate Isle (ll. 1061–1100). In an unannounced test of the purity of their thoughts, visitors to the island are invited to sleep, and the queen reads their dreams. If they dream of anything other than the queen's beauty, they are sent away from the island. Santina C. Val, "Equicola and the School of Lyons," *Comparative Literature* 12:1 (1960): 19–32, argues that Héroët derived this idea from Mario Equicola's *Libro di natura de amore*. Héroët's language is quite similar.

[103] Anon., *La Louenge des femmes. Invention extraite du Commentaire de Pantagruel, sus l'Androgyne de Platon*, ed. M. A. Screech, intro. Ruth Calder (London: S. R. Publishers, 1967), v–vi. There were two editions. The facsimile is from the first edition of 1551. A second edition appeared in 1552. The work was probably by Thomas Sébillet and definitely an attempt to capitalize on the popularity of Rabelais's *Gargantua* and *Pantagruel*.

[104] *Louenge des femmes*, 31–2.   [105] *Louenge des femmes*, 32.

Others were more moderate even while allowing that sex was problematic. Louys Le Roy admits that desire for beauty can have a sexual dimension, but insists that procreation is a divine act.[106] Desire for beauty has utility for Le Roy, but he concedes that physical beauty is unreliable because it is

subjette necessairement à plusieurs vehementes perturbations, come sont volupté, douleur, hardiesse, crainte, ire, esperance.	necessarily subject to many vehement perturbations such as voluptuousness, sadness, harshness, fear, anger, hope.

Much as he insists on the heuristic value of physical beauty, Le Roy is no fool:

L'Amour des personnes belles est incertain, d'autant que leur beauté dur peu, & leur volonté est variable.	Love of beautiful people is uncertain, as much as their beauty does not last and their will is variable.[107]

The limited corrective is that readers can hold out for the "lumière spirituelle" [spiritual enlightenment] that accompanies eternal beauty to tell them when they have gone astray.[108] Le Roy wants women to be legible; he wants beauty to be reliable; he wants desire to be for the good. But he knows that sometimes – and it is hard to know which times – none of these holds true.

Whether the angry dismissal of women as sexual reprobates in texts like the *Louenge* or worried unease of the type that permeates Le Roy's commentary, adding women to Neoplatonism significantly altered the dynamics of homosocial, salvific love. Given the centrality of the *querelle des femmes* in public discourse, French encounters with Neoplatonism from Champier forward were heavily engaged with the gender complications raised by Marsilio Ficino. Attempts both within texts and across the corpus to come to grips with the gender implications of Ficino's claims for desire and beauty resulted in an infusion of concern about sex. Almost all warn that feminine beauty is deceptive. Nearly as many insist that women are easily deceived by physical beauty. Most believe that male desire for women must be treated with extreme caution.

---

[106] Le Roy, *Sympose*, fols. 104v–109r. Generation is an "oeuvre divin & immortel" on fol. 105r. As did Héroët, Le Roy follows Hébreu in moving from human generation to cosmic copulation. Le Roy also cites Bembo on the value of conception and generation.

[107] Le Roy, *Sympose*, fols. 153r and 176r.

[108] Le Roy, *Sympose*, fols. 159v, 171r. Recall that Castiglione's Bembo could only convey his understanding of love under such an influence. See Castiglione, *The Courtier*, *The Book of the Courtier*, trans. and intro. George Bull (Harmondsworth: Penguin, 1976), 343. Le Roy offers another supposedly reliable marker – one that he derived from Castiglione and which got some play when Neoplatonism enjoyed resurgent popularity in the 1570s largely through Philippe Desportes. Le Roy dedicates the third book (which is on perfect beauty) of his commentary to Mary, Queen of Scots. For Le Roy, Mary represents the unification of physical and intellectual beauty. Castiglione assumed that proper love would be appropriate to class; Le Roy contends that royal love, educated toward intellectual higher ends, will be productive and beneficial to society. Ironically, the higher end is procreation: Le Roy hopes Mary's beauty will inspire sexual desire in her husband. See Le Roy, *Sympose*, fols. 68r–69r, 135v–36v.

All take it as a given that female desire is prone to disorder. The gender hierarchy of the *querelle des femmes* shaped the reception of Neoplatonic concepts even while French Neoplatonists struggled to make heterosexual desire into the answer to Ficino's homosociality. But adding women to Neoplatonism meant adding Neoplatonism to women, and too often, women were deceptive, inferior, horny, passionate, incapable of higher reason, or just plain distracting. What, if anything, could be done to make love between women and men functional in philosophically responsible ways?

Crazy love

For French Neoplatonists, heterosexual desire had to be made plausible. As an aid to salvation, if only just, desire could facilitate procreation. But it was only one possible outcome, and the other effects of desire were troubling. Desire between men might lead to altruistic self-sacrifice, but it might also lead to unnatural, and yet apparently quite appealing vice. Homoerotic attachment was not the answer. Heterosexual love did not, and does not, preclude either misogynous dismissals of women or homosexual desire, but some tried to imagine that it could. For others, love in its form as desire threatened marriage and social stability. Love, after all, was not likely to be directed toward one's spouse. As Neoplatonism seeped into French culture, the questions about its implications multiplied. Ficino opened up the discussion of love; the French ended up finding that very expansiveness at once supportive of notions of French fecundity and deeply threatening.

The roots of these sentiments go back again to Ficino, who reluctantly allowed for instrumental heterosexual love. Sexual desire between men and women, Ficino opined, has a natural purpose:

Oportebat autem animadvertere partis illius incitamenta non irritum hac iacture opus, sed serendi et procreandi officium affectare atque a masculis ad feminas eam traducere.	It is proper, however, to acknowledge that the stimuli of that part are not an activity [that] leads to no result by this act of squandering, but that it tries to accomplish the duty of begetting and procreating and to move it from men to women.[109]

Not simply Pauline channeling of sexual desire to avoid damnation, Ficino sees value in sexual reproduction within his theological schema. As Kristeller observes, Ficino locates generation as part of his ontological understanding of inferior substances generated by superior ones and seeking union with them. All organisms – and for Ficino, humans are organisms more perfect than other

---

[109] Ficino, *De amore*, 230. The Italian text added, "It is not pleasant to do . . . " (that is, talk about sexual matters, especially involving two men). See Ficino, *Commentary on Plato's Symposium*, 208 and note.

animals – propagate in search of perfection. Ficino vacillated between this idea and the notion that humans reproduce out of fundamental egotism.[110] Natural though it is, sexual desire is narcissistic:

desiderium hoc perfectionis proprie propagande cunctis ingenitum, latentum et implicatam cuiusque fecunditatem explicat.	This desire, which is innate, for propagating one's own perfection explains the fecundity, latent and implicit, in all things.[111]

Inherent even in non-corporeal entities such as the arts and the stars, procreation in these terms is both fundamental and mundane.

Procreation was acceptable as an outcome of love for Ficino, but it was always inferior to pure, rational love. For Ficino, heterosexual reciprocity follows the economy of coitus in which men give, women receive, and giving is always better because men do it.[112] Moreover, misdirection in love resulting in lust and sex is a frequent problem. In the dedication of his Italian translation, Ficino wrote to Bernardo del Nero and Antonio Manetti:

tutti quasi amiamo male, et quanto più amiamo tanto peggio amiamo...Questo mostruoso errore guai a noi c'aviene perchè temerariamente entriamo prima in questo faticoso viaggio d'amore, che impariamo el termine suo et modo di camminare et e pericolosi passi del cammino, et però quanto più andiamo, tanto più oimè miseri a nostro grande danno erriamo.	almost all of us love wrongly, and so the more we love, the worse it becomes...We fall into this great error, unfortunately for us, because we boldly start out upon this difficult journey of love before we know its destination or how to travel the perilous path of the journey. The farther we go, the farther we stray.[113]

While Ficino is emphatic about physicality having (and being kept in) its correct place, he acknowledges that it is easy to lose track of what the order of things ought to be.

French reactions to and reformulations of Neoplatonism took up Ficino's vacillations between assuming desire operated toward the good and acknowledging that it did not. In his analysis of the differences between French and Italian attitudes and responses to the *prisca theologia*, D. P. Walker comments, "it can be said that on the whole the French are more cautious than the Italians and more patriotic."[114] Walker's interest is in the transmission of

---

[110] Kristeller, *Philosophy*, 136–8. For Ficino, procreation was a practical matter as well in that it ensured the continuation of humanity. Consult *Philebus Commentary*, p. 245: "...videlicet per Venerem ad salutem speciei."

[111] Ficino, *De amore*, 165. Elsewhere, Ficino recognizes that narcissism is a powerful support for love. See for example *Letters*, vol. I, 144–5; vol. II, 56.

[112] Ficino, *De amore*, 174.

[113] Marsilio Ficino, *Supplementum Ficinianum*, ed. Paul O. Kristeller, 2 vols. (Florence: Leonis S. Olschki, 1937), vol. I, 90.

[114] Walker, "The *Prisca Theologica* in France," 204.

the pre-Christian philosophical texts, including Plato and the *Orphica*. Walker excavates the French insistence on the authority of the Druids as a source of ancient authority through which the French asserted their philosophical independence from Italian Neoplatonism.[115] French reworkings of Neoplatonism furthered nationalistic claims in the course of parsing procreative heterosexuality (of the type described in French astrological discourse above in Chapter 2). The emphasis on heterosexual desire caused palpable discomfort: sexual desire might be a way toward salvation, but it was also the source of *fol amour* (crazy love). There would be no resolution of the disagreements about desire. Both impulses came to mark French culture through the copious amount of talk about sex and love and through the persistence of the option of imagining a sexualized intellectual life.

Sheer volume was evident in the attention to *fol amour* that peppered the *querelle des amyes* of the 1540s. Staples included worrying about lascivious desire impairing good judgment, the loss of reason in the presence of corporeal beauty, and how easy it was to endanger the soul by failing to distinguish carnal from spiritual love. Antoine Héroët's *Parfaicte amye* prompted several replies that dealt with these concerns. Using the cross-voicing technique, Bertrand de La Borderie's *Amye de Court* satirically attacked women by creating a protagonist with a highly mercenary approach to love and marriage.[116] La Borderie's *amye de court* seeks rich, gullible men and seduces them. Eschewing the sort of higher aspirations for love supported by advocates of Neoplatonism, she just wants to have fun. Her "doctrine" is, "Assés de joye, & de tristesse point" [Enough of joy and of sadness, nothing].[117] Twisting Neoplatonic logic in knots, she announces that her beauty is perfection, which inspires many men to love her. She resists concupiscence by refusing to succumb to desire unless there is something in it for her.[118] When she does get what she wants, love is physical. She commends her lovers to her body:

---

[115] Symphorien Champier, *De Triplica Disciplina* (Lyon: no pub., 1508), unpag. after sig. ddd iv makes the point about distance from Italian ideas: "Dicis enim licet corpore gallus sim: anima tamen non solum ficinus sed italus: nedum gallus sum. Non miseris me gallum: & in philosophia: medecine: atque theologia multa scribere" [It is said for instance that a Gaul is similar of body: the soul however is not only Ficino but Italy: Not to say I am a Gaul. Do not pity me a Gaul, and fine things are written on philosophy, medicine and theology]. On the Druids, see esp. Walker, "*Prisca Theologia* in France," 214–16.

[116] Antoine Héroët's *Compleincte d'une dame surprinse nouvellement damour*, in *La Parfaicte Amye* (Troyes: Nicole Paris, 1542), 85–96, was perhaps the catalyst for La Borderie's satirical intervention. Like *La Parfaicte Amye*, the less philosophically elaborate *Compleincte* is in a female voice, and that of an unmarried woman, so the *Compleincte* was perhaps more vulnerable to attacks on its female protagonist. As with the *querelle des femmes*, dismissing the *querelle des amyes* as merely rhetorical exercises and bravura displays of verbal pyrotechnics ignores the ideological import of the controversy.

[117] Bertrand de La Borderie, *L'Amie de court. Nouvellement inventée par le Seigneur de la Borderie* (Lyon: Estienne Dolet, 1543), 6. [First edition: 1542.]

[118] La Borderie, *L'Amie de court*, 8, 9, 14, 16.

Figure 12. School of Fontainebleau (sixteenth century), *Venus and Mars*, canvas, Musée du Petit Palais.

The rendering of images of Love in normative terms is apparent in the decision to feature Mars as sexually intimate with Venus, while Cupid is near by but less sexually implicated. That Mars and Venus found physical love and found it in adultery is congruent with Neoplatonist concerns about the attractions of physical desire.

En la partie en moy la plus parfaicte, Au tetin ferme, ou la cuisse refaicte.	In the part of me that is the most perfect, To the firm breast, or the well-made thigh.[119]

M. A Screech has emphasized that La Borderie meant the piece as a satire.[120] It is not simply satire, however. La Borderie's issues with Héroët's Amye are resolved in an entirely pragmatic, carnal fashion. The bold carnality of La Borderie's heroine exemplifies the dangers of Neoplatonic desire let loose.

The dialogue between and among poets and prose writers took shape around such claims for and disavowals of sexual desire. Héroët weighed in again in his *Aultre invention extraicte de Platon de n'aymer point sans estre aymé*, maintaining that true love could only grow when men loved women who had to facilitate that love by encouraging the men at every turn.[121] Finding Héroët's versions inadequate, Charles Fontaine allows that beauty can be created:

Le jeune esprit est comme un frais tableau	The young spirit is like a blank canvas
Ou ny a rien qui soit painct, laid, ou beau:	Where there is nothing except paint, ugly or beautiful:
Mais toutesfois ou le painctre paindra	But nevertheless where the painter will paint
A son plaisir, & tout ce qu'il vouldra.	For his pleasure and all that he will want.

Vociferous in his condemnation of mercenary "love," Fontaine insists that unvarnished, untainted love by a woman for a good man leads to good things. The key is to love a worthy object: "Le sot espoux en fin t'abysmera: / L'espoux scavant en fin t'elevera" [The foolish husband in the end falls into ruin: / The wise husband in the end elevates himself]. Fontaine spends much of his text explaining to women that they must not seek a man for his money or position, but instead, must recognize the attributes of his heart and soul. The teleology of this education is not just heterosexual love, but marriage:

Mais un cueur noble a l'amour pour thresor.	But a noble heart has love for its treasure
... Cela faisoit l'amour d'honnesteté,	This is made of love of honesty,
De Vertu, Foy, & vraye Liberté.	Of Virtue, Faith, and true Liberty.
Et ce pendant ...	And in the meantime ...
Tu te rendz serve en riche mariage.	You render yourself to serve in rich marriage.[122]

---

[119] La Borderie, *L'Amie de court*, 23.

[120] M. A. Screech, "An Interpretation of the *Querelle des Amyes*: A Study of the Exchange of Poems between B. de La Borderie, G. des Autelz, Charles Fontaine, Paul Angier, Héroet, A. du Moulin, Sébillet, Papillon and François Habert, together with certain attitudes of Rabelais's," *Bibliothèque d'Humanism et Renaissance* 21 (1959): 103–30.

[121] Antoine Héroët, "Aultre invention extraicte de Platon de n'aymer point sans estre aymé," in *Œuvres poétiques*, ed. Ferdinand Gohin (Paris: Cornély, 1909), 96. Originally published in 1542.

[122] Charles Fontaine, *La Contr'amye de court par Maistre Charles Fontaine Parisien* (Lyon: Sulpice Sabon pour Antoine Constantin, 1543), 13, 34, 43.

For Fontaine, marriage, in which earnest, honest devotion displaces the possibility of false desire, can control *fol amour*. Transcendent on this model feels rather more prosaic, despite the emphasis on virtue, faith, and liberty. These are the result of dutiful service rather than contemplation of, or desire for, divine beauty.

Fontaine was not the only one troubled by the implications of Neoplatonic desire. Paul Angier's *Honneste Amant* (1544) reacts more pointedly than Fontaine against Héroët's Amye finding love outside of marriage. For Angier, marriage without concupiscence or worldly desire, is the goal: "A assembler l'homme avecques la femme, / Pour eviter la paillardise infame" [To assemble the man with the woman, / In order to avoid infamous lechery]. The mechanism is marriage, which Angier assures his readers can be "loyal" and "perfect" if chastity is maintained and love reserved only for one's spouse.[123] Angier is joined by François Habert, whose *La Nouvelle Vénus* (1547) also reacts against the subversive suggestions of the *Parfaicte Amye*. For Habert, marriage is the only acceptable locus of physical desire and the goal is children. The power of generation is central to love, Habert maintains, but it must all take place within marriage: "C'est vous à qui sert la conionction / D'Eve & Adam, où gist perfection" [It is you [renowned and chaste women] to whom the conjunction / Of Eve and Adam wherein lies perfection].[124] Only Habert suggests that procreative desire offers anything remotely resembling – and it is quite remote – Ficino's rational transcendence through desire for beauty.

But marriage was not entirely satisfying. The warnings against *fol amour* and the incorporation of marital love as a corrective to it in philosophical discourse were never entirely sufficient. In the midst of the *querelle des amyes*, Maurice Scève published his *Délie* (1544), which as a whole vacillates between expressions of unrequited desire in the mode of Francesco Petrarch and attempts

---

[123] Paul Angier, *L'expérience de M. Paul Angier, Carentennnois, contenant une brefve defence en la personne de l'honneste Amant pour l'Amye de court contre la Contreamye*, in *Opuscules d'Amour par Heroet, La Borderie et autres divins poëtes*, intro. M. A. Screech (Paris: Mouton, 1970), 212. See also p. 232. The text is a facsimile of Jean de Tournes's edition (Lyon, 1547). There were at least nine variant editions of the main poems in the *querelle des amyes* in the sixteenth century, in addition to single editions of the principal poems. For more on marriage, see pp. 203–4, 207, 213. Chronology matters with respect to the sexual content of the *querelle des amyes* as a whole. Despite overlapping themes with the *querelle des femmes*, the *querelle des amyes*, as M. A. Screech has argued, was a distinct literary event. See Screech, "An Interpretation of the *Querelle des Amyes*." Screech understands Angier as reacting only to La Borderie and seems to ignore that Fontaine was also clearly troubled by Héroët's Amye. Screech thus avoids the ways that the *querelle* was a multi-vocal attempt to grapple with the implications of Neoplatonic sexual politics.

[124] François Habert, *La Nouvelle Vénus* (Lyons: Jean de Tournes, 1547), 35. Similar sentiments appear in the *Louenge des femmes*, 31–2. Habert's argument, unlike the one in the *Louenge*, is that there are good, chaste women who love in the Platonic way: "Car ma Venus ayme parfaictement. / Parfaict amour est divine & celeste" (p. 2).

to intellectualize love in Neoplatonic terms.[125] As Thomas Hunkeler notes, the extent and nature of Scève's Neoplatonism have been analyzed several times, although not in entirely satisfactory terms. Hunkeler argues that Scève's interest in *spiritus* is derived from Neoplatonic sources in ways that have been obscured by the tension throughout the *Délie* between love and aversion.[126] Perhaps this is Scève struggling with his cultural context and its concerns about extramarital desire. At the same time, Scève is not shy about articulating the physicality of the protagonist's love for a married woman he can not have. Scève depicts frustrated desire with an earthy lasciviousness, as in this dizain describing his jealousy as he imagines Délie being fondled by her husband:

Seul avec moy, elle avec sa partie:	Alone with myself, her with her part [husband]:
Moy en ma peine, elle en sa molle couche.	I in my pain, her in her soft bed.
Couvert d'ennuy je me voultre en l'Ortie,	Wrapped in grief, I wallow in nettles,
Et elle nue entre ses bras se couche.	And she naked in his arms lies.
Hà (luy indigne) il la tient, il la touche:	Ha! (unworthy him) he holds her, he touches her
Elle le souffre: et, comme moins robuste,	She suffers it: and, as the less robust,
Viole amour par ce lyen injuste,	Violates love by this unjust lien,
Que droict humain,et non divin, a faict.	Which human right, and not divine, has made
O saincte loy à tous, fors à moy, juste,	O holy law, just to all, except to me,
Tu me punys pour elle avoir meffaict.	You punish me for the misdeeds she has made.[127]

---

[125] On the Petrarchan ties, see for instance Richard Sieburth, "Introduction," *Emblems of Desire: Selections from the "Délie" of Maurice Scève* (Philadelphia: University of Pennsylvania Press, 2003), xxiv–xxx. See Joann Dellaneva, *Song and Counter-song: Scève's "Délie" and Petrarch's "Rime"* (Lexington: French Forum, 1983) for analysis of the differences and similarities in their poetic projects. See also Terence Cave, "Scève's *Délie*: Correcting Petrarch's Errors," in *Pre-Pléiade Poetry*, ed. Jerry Nash (Lexington: French Forum, 1985), 112–24. All citations are from Maurice Scève, *Délie. Object de plus haulte vertu*, ed. Defaux. All poems will be referred to by number and line numbers as appropriate. For the quotation, see X, 3–4. For a few of the many instances of Petrarchan expression, see for instance XXIV, XLIII, CCXXXIX, CCLXV, CCCXXXII, CCCLVII, and CCCLXXXVIII (which includes specific reference to Petrarch and Laura). Elements of the courtly love tradition are also legible throughout. Scève's beloved was widely thought to be Pernette Du Guillet. On her poetic production as responding to his, and to his love, see Lawrence D. Kritzman, "Pernette du Guillet and a Voice of One's Own," *The Rhetoric of Sexuality and the Literature of the French Renaissance* (Cambridge University Press, 1991), 11–28.

[126] Thomas Hunkeler, *Le Vif du sens: corps et poésie selon Maurice Scève* (Geneva: Droz, 2003), 137–70. On Ficino's influence, see also Jean-Claude Margolin, "Du *De amore* de Ficin à la *Délie* de Maurice Scève: lumière, regard, amour et beauté," in *Ficino e il ritorno di Platone*, ed. Gian Carlo Garfagnini 2 vols. (Florence: Olschki, 1986), vol. II, 587–614. Jacqueline Risset, *L'Anagramme du désir* (Rome: Bulzoni, 1971) makes a case for Hébreu's influence on Scève.

[127] Scève, *Délie*, CLXI. Other expressions of lascivious desire may be found in CXXXIX (conquest language) and CCCLXVII (which ends: "Sentant ses mains, mains celestement blanches, / Avec leurs bras mortellement divins / L'un coronner mon col, l'aultre mes hanches" [Feeling her hands, hands celestially white, / with their fatally divine arms / one the crown of my neck, the other my hips]).

For Scève, true love is above marriage, a position that would seem to be consistent with Neoplatonic notions of love as the higher good and an intellectual enterprise that leads to spiritual salvation. Despite the sexually explicit language, he insists that true love is not *fol amour*. Scève's protagonist reasons his way to higher understanding, denouncing carnal love and distinguishing good from bad desire in Neoplatonic terms.[128] He chooses a beautiful woman whose "vertu" [virtue] is both physical and moral. In an uncomplicated way, her beauty is a good thing: "Celle beauté, qui embellit le Monde" [This beauty which embellishes the World] because it leads his soul upward to participation in heavenly love.[129] As a man, he suffers from physical yearning. He is alternately restless, listless, self-contained, and verging on fury because of it.[130] And yet he struggles to contain his desire, expressing the hope that once he is united with his beloved, their desire will be resolutely chaste:

Et abhorrir pour vil contentement	And to much abhor as vile contentment
Le bien qu'Amour (Amour lasscif) conseille.	The good which Love (lascivious Love).[131]

For Scève, love can create irrational, physical responses. It can be, perhaps must be, found outside of marriage.[132] Yet it can still transcend.

Expressions of the complications of desire such as Scève's fed into the attacks by authors in the *querelle des amyes* against *fol amour*. While the critiques undermined the reception of Neoplatonism, they also provided the obvious corrective: Love inside marriage cast as the way to rational transcendence. Louys Le Roy tries to recuperate Neoplatonism as the philosophy of chaste, rational, and marital love. Layering his argument, Le Roy sets up the abstract universal

---

[128] Scève, *Délie*, CLXI.

[129] Scève, *Délie*, VII, 1. See CXXXV and CCCVI for articulations of heavenly love.

[130] Scève, *Délie*, XLVI, CCCXXXIV, and CCCXXXIX. The last includes a specific reference to the pedagogy of Diotima.

[131] Scève, *Délie*, XXVIII, 7–8. See also XXXI, 2–4: "Quand au plus doulx serain de nostre vie / Desdaing s'esmeut pour honneste deffence / Contre l'ardeur de nostre chaste envie" [When at the more sweet evening of our life / Disdain to be moved by honest defence / Against the ardour of our chaste envy]. Chaste desire is further described in CCCCXIII. For reciprocity, see XLIX, 7, 10.

[132] In *The Heptameron*, Dagoucin makes a case for perfect love that is also outside of marriage. See Marguerite de Navarre, *The Heptameron*, trans. P. A. Chilton (London and New York: Penguin, 1984), 113. In addition to her own engagement with Neoplatonism, Marguerite encouraged others. See above n. 9 (translations and commentaries dedicated to her or commissioned by her) and n. 10 (Des Périers dedicated his *Lysis* to her). Héroët's *L'Androgyne* (1536) was presented to François I in 1536 through Marguerite's intervention. See Pierre Jourda, *Marguerite d'Angoulême, duchesse d'Alençon, reine de Navarre (1492–1549): étude biographique et littéraire*, 2 vols. (Paris: Champion, 1930), vol. I, 209. On Marguerite's patronage more broadly, see Barbara Stephenson, *The Power and Patronage of Marguerite de Navarre* (London: Ashgate, 2004); Anne Funke, "Marguerite de Navarre et son influence spirituelle sur les vitraux de la cathédrale Sainte-Marie d'Auch," in *Patronnes et mécènes en France à la Renaissance*, ed. Kathleen Wilson-Chevalier (Université de Saint-Etienne, 2007), 321–40.

conditions that require marital love. When the physician, Erysimachus, offers speech describing diseases of excessive or immoderate love, Le Roy comments that the universe is held together by the attraction of complementary opposites at all levels. From the cosmos to the body; from the seven planets to the four humors, love is necessary in a cosmic sense.[133] Le Roy emphasizes this idea by reading Agathon's discourse describing love as a paean to notions of cosmic harmony through rational attraction. Then Le Roy reads Aristophanes' fable of the androgyne as a tale about creating the conditions for successful love and generation through properly directed desire in marriage.[134] Le Roy closes the first book by echoing one of Bembo's arguments from *Gli Azolani* that heterosexual procreative desire makes civilization possible, insisting that "Amour est tousjours utile & plaisant" [Love is always useful and pleasant].[135] Good love is now recognizable by virtue of its utility: heterosexual reproduction has utility; therefore, heterosexual love is good. *Fol amour* can be banished if Plato is rendered (somewhat improbably, if one considers the original source) as an active supporter of marriage and sexual desire restricted to and contained by it.

As Le Roy's insistent rewriting of Plato indicates, skepticism about heterosexual love remained. Precisely because (sexual) love outside of marriage was so easily imagined, some rejected Neoplatonic claims that aspiring to love – any love – was a good thing. Etienne Jodelle wrote 300 sonnets, a handful of which he published, under the title *Les Contr'amours*. Using a variety of Platonic tropes (the notion of transcendent love, invocations of deceptive beauty, excoriations of Eros as actually Anteros), Jodelle heaped scorn on the notion of Neoplatonic love as a good thing.[136] In the fourth dialogue of the *Contr'amours* (1581), "Paradoxe contre l'Amour," Thomas Sébillet uses a variety of examples to emphasize that Neoplatonic ideas about love are dangerous. All the problems of the world, including, "la haine, la discorde, & l'inimité," [hate, discord, and emnity] jealousy, political instability, and domestic strife, Sébillet lays at the hands of "fol & faux Amour" [crazy and false love] and the "lascives affections" [lascivious affections] it inspires. Only familial love – potentially dangerous marital love transformed by the duties of family – can reliably

---

[133] Le Roy, *Sympose*, fols. 27v–37v. Hébreu is not cited here, but appears later in connection with a recapitulation of these ideas about generation. See fols. 104v, 109r. See also Chapter 2 on the astrology of sex as universal.

[134] Le Roy, *Sympose*, fol. 44v ("se integrent en mariage"); 46v ("les superfluitez & delices voluptueuses"). On the lascivious uses of the androgyne as part of its trajectory in French philosophical discourse, see Katherine Crawford, "The Impossibility of Indeterminacy: The Androgyne in Renaissance France" (in preparation).

[135] Le Roy, *Sympose*, fol. 67r. Le Roy does not mention Bembo at this juncture, but he does cite him elsewhere in the text. See fols. 104v, 109r.

[136] See Etienne Jodelle, *Les Oeuvres et meslanges poétiques d'Estienne Jodelle*, ed. Charles Marty-Leveaux, 2 vols. (Paris: Lemerre, 1868), vol. II, 91.

safeguard against the follies of love.[137] Sébillet argues that men and women in the grip of *fol amour* are worse than animals. He shapes his readings of nature toward his larger purpose:

Le mesme Eléphant aime & honnore sa fémelle; jusques a luy garder, comme une foy maritale: ne se joinant iamais avéq autre, que celle qu'il avoit amoureusement choisie.	Even the Elephant loves and honors his female, as far as guarding her; as marital faithfulness, never joining with other than the one he has amorously chosen.[138]

When in love, men who are supposed to be superior are brought low. Despite the efforts of Le Roy, Sébillet vilifies Plato's androgyne as an image that incites "copulation d'effrénée & libidineuse volupté" [unrestrained copulation and libidinous voluptuousness] by encouraging people to seek their other half through carnal satisfaction rather than in chaste marriage.[139] Sections denouncing claims that the heavens determine love and examples of the damage done in the name of love follow. Among those who embody bad love are Sardanapalus, Semiramis, Jocasta, and Orpheus (who is dismembered for inventing "denaturé plaisir" [denatured pleasure]). In the end, only chaste married couples attending to their spouses and parents can "réduire les coeurs pervertis, & les esprits dépravez" [reduce the perverted hearts and depraved spirits] of love.[140] Rejecting the heteronormative apologetics of Le Roy, Sébillet dismisses Neoplatonism as utterly deserving of condemnation. Unlike the earlier interventions of the *querelle des amyes*, Sébillet excoriates not just *fol amour* but all love outside the familial setting. Any other kind of love is inherently and thus perilously sexual.

While Sébillet's rejection of *fol amour* as the necessary result of Neoplatonic love is in tune with the moral clamp-down after the Council of Trent, his summary rejection did not entirely prevail. Catholics and Protestants, in competition for the moral high ground, made the play around sex in Neoplatonism suspect. Cautious impulses in French Neoplatonism came to the fore. Cultural conservatives like Jean Aubery advocated prayer to counter lust and the lascivious incitements of love talk.[141] For more worldly

---

[137] Thomas Sébillet, "Paradoxe contre l'Amour," in *Contramours . . . Paradoxe, contre l'Amour* (Paris: Gillez Beys, 1581), 263–8. For Sébillet's work as translator of the other dialogues, see Screech, "Querelle des Amyes," 100. The original of the other dialogues is Battista da Campo Fregosa (or Fulgosus), *Baptistae C. Fulgosi Anteros* (Milan: Pachel, 1496). The work attacks Petrarchan idealism in matters of love. On Anteros in the Renaissance, see Robert V. Merrill, "Eros and Anteros," *Speculum* 19:3 (1944): 265–84.

[138] Sébillet, "Paradoxe," 271. The section on the virtues of animals compared to men runs to p. 273.

[139] Sébillet, "Paradoxe," 275.   [140] Sébillet, "Paradoxe," 303, 307.

[141] Jean Aubery, *L'Antidote d'amour* (Paris: Claude Chappelet, 1599), fols. 133r, 135v. Aubery trained as a physician at Montpellier. In addition to his writings on love, he wrote a history of the baths at Bourbon-Lancy and Bourbon l'Archembault and a defense of physicians, *Joannis Auberii . . . restituenda et vindicanda Medicinae Dignitate* (Paris: J. Cottereau, 1608).

members of high society, poets elaborated a classed theory of love to protect against improper desire. When he invoked Neoplatonic love, for instance, Philippe Desportes emphasized that the nobility of the female love-object ensured perfect love through attraction to their inherent transcendent beauty and desire.[142]

Much of the ambivalence about love was built into Florentine Neoplatonism as adapted by French Renaissance authors. Some of that ambivalence was diffused for poets such as Desportes through class as a corrective for possible misinterpretations of beauty and desire. But for others, inviting contemplation of love by means of something as potentially deceptive as beauty and as easily corrupted as desire was all but guaranteed to cause disaster for body and soul. Only love built on obligation, responsibility, duty to family; only desire – sexual desire especially – in service of the requirements of marriage and family was acceptable. Fertility as a marker of "good" love also indicated the beneficence of French abundance. For the French, "good" love was articulated through instrumental sexual desire, which is exactly why many who encountered it in that guise wanted something else. Desire outside of duty was not just about having a bit on the side; it was the possibility of much more. And if that pressure wasn't enough, the stakes were salvation or damnation.

Fragile desires

Let us be clear on the story here: a philosophy that posited male homosocial love as the path to transcendence and salvation in French hands became instead definitional of instrumental heterosexual duty. Attracted to Ficino's aim of revitalizing Christianity through the infusion of Plato into Catholic theology, French interlocutors grappled with Ficino's precepts from the outset. The French were neither the first nor the only readers of Ficino who attempted to resolve the conundra around the sexual problems raised by Neoplatonism. Both utilizing and repudiating Italian ideas, French Neoplatonists worked toward descriptors of interpersonal and sexual relationships that were not about identity in the modern sense, but in which object choice (same sex or opposite sex) did matter. The figurations of desire that emanated from Ficino's vision propagated, rather than resolved, around problematic forms of desire and object choice in Neoplatonically inflected texts. As discomfort with Ficino's homosociality developed, French Neoplatonists reconfigured Ficino's epistemology by dwelling on the gender issues created by the presence of women in a

---

[142] See for instance Philippe Desportes, *Elégies*, ed. Victor E. Graham (Geneva: Droz, 1961); "Elégie VII," 57, and *Cléonice dernières amours*, ed. Victor E. Graham (Geneva: Droz, 1962), "Sonnet XVIII," 31. The elegy dates from the 1573 collection. *Cléonice* is from 1583.

philosophy developed initially without them in mind. Inserting women into Ficino's homosocial model enabled French apologists to restructure homosociability into heterosexual compatibility. The French retained Ficino's central notion that love is defined as seeking the divine, but took quite seriously the ways in which physicality persistently complicated the move toward philosophical transcendence.

All the talk, all the controversy meant that Neoplatonism, reworked simultaneously to encourage and deny heterosexual desire, loomed large in the culture. Because people were unreliable – their desire too fickle and their notions of beauty too fungible – the promises of Neoplatonic transcendence had to be tempered. That it could sometimes be made to serve the cause of generation and could prove its instrumental value through procreation made Neoplatonism congruent with imaginings of France as a fertile and abundant nation (see also Chapter 5). The fantasy of sex marked by love as an unmitigated good, however, receded. Sex was too powerful. The disruptions it could cause meant that philosophical fragility remains embedded in heterosexual, marital love.

4   Cupid makes you stupid: "bad" poetry in the French Renaissance

On September 8, 1533, poet Maurice Scève announced that he had located the tomb of Francesco Petrarch's beloved, Laura, at the convent of Saint-François in Avignon. While the find was soon discredited, the poetic and political appropriations it inspired had more lasting effects. Interested in Italian art and poetry, François I (r. 1515–1547) encouraged the poets to link the French king with the Italian master.[1] In 1532 to 1533, the king had supported the publication of Italian court poet Luigi Alamanni's *Opere toscane* in Lyon.[2] Scève's "discovery" faded into obscurity, but its political claims continued to refract through the poetic competition that surrounded the absorption of Petrarch in Renaissance France. The links between and among François and Petrarch and poetry were intriguing enough that the king, upon visiting the site of the tomb, purportedly composed an epitaph for Laura on the spot. François I later wrote a second epitaph, and for years after the discovery, French poets (at court, and more local ones, such as Lanteaume de Romieu, a gentleman from Arles who collected poems written for the occasion) generated memorials of the event.[3] In addition to the poetic output, literary historians have noted that the François/Francesco conceit supported constructions of the Valois king in terms of *translatio studii et imperii*. Perhaps the most explicit articulation of this was a sonnet written by Mellin de Saint-Gelais well after the fact:

---

[1] On the dynamics at the time, see for instance Enzo Guidici, "Bilancio di un 'annosa questione': Maurice Scève e la 'scoperta' della 'tomba di Laura'," *Quaderni di filologia e lingue romanze* (Rome: Ed. dell'Ateneo, 1980), vol. II, 7–70.

[2] Luigi Alamanni, *Opere toscane* (Lyon: Gryphe, 1532–1533). On Alamanni's influence, see Jean Balsamo, "Marot et les origines du pétrarquisme français (1530–1540)," in *Clément Marot, "Prince de poëtes françois," 1496–1996. Actes du Colloque international de Cahors en Quercy, 1996*, ed. Gérard Defaux and Michel Simonin (Paris: Champion, 1997), 323–37.

[3] When the tomb was discovered, poets produced verses in conjunction with the king's visit to the region between August 29 and September 12, 1533, and another flurry when François returned to Avignon on November 15–16. Memorials persisted for over a decade. Jean Balsamo, "Pétrarque en France à la renaissance: un livre, un modèle, un mythe," in *Les Poètes français de la Renaissance et Pétrarque*, ed. Jean Balsamo (Geneva: Droz, 2004), 13–32. See pp. 23–4.

Rien ne se faict des grans en ces bas lieux
Que du hault Ciel le cours n'ayt ordonné,
Et s'on vous veoit, Monsieur, tant adonné
Au vray tuscan, c'est ouvraige des dieux.
A qui pourroit ce langaige seoir mieulx
Qu'à vous, qui seul au monde avez donné
Certain espoir de vois veoir couronné
Roy d'Italie hault et victorieux?
Donques lisez avec heureux presaige
Le los de Laure, espérant par vos faictz
De vert laurier les honneurs plus
    perfaictz.
Illustrez tant de triumphes nostre age
Que cest honneur advienne à ce Petrarque
D'appartenir au grand Charles Monarque.

Nothing great is done in these low places the course of which the high Heavens had not ordered. And if one views you, Monsieur, so devoted to the true Tuscan, this is the work of the gods. To whom could this language become better, than to you, who alone in the world have given a certain hope to see you crowned, high and victorious King of Italy? Therefore, read with happy presage the fate of Laura, hoping by your deeds to make the honors of the green laurel more perfect. You illustrate so many of the triumphs of our age, that this honor happened to this Petrarch to belong to great King Charles.[4]

François I's efforts at cultural appropriation – importing not just Italian art, but Italian artists – were not simply admiration of Italian artistic skill, but political policy.[5] The poets at his court understood this. Clément Marot, for instance, offered an epigram that linked the king and Petrarch through Laura:

O Laure, Laure, il t'a esté besoing
D'aymer l'honneur et d'estre vertueuse,
Car Françoys Roy sans cela n'eust prins
    soing
De t'honnorer de tumbe sumptueuse,
Ne d'employer sa dextre valureuse
A par escript ta louenge coucher;
Mais il l'a faict, pour aultant
    qu'amoureuse
Tu as esté de ce qu'il tient plus cher.

O Laura, Laura, you have needed to love honor and to be virtuous. Because King François would not have taken care without this, honoring you with a sumptuous tomb, nor employ his brave right hand to lay his praises in writing, but he made them for as much of the love you had as that which he holds more dear.[6]

Marot was responding to the impetus from the top, which was to absorb, remake, and outdo Italian art and culture as part of international competition for

---

[4] Mellin de Saint-Gelais, *Sonnets*, ed. Luigia Zilli (Geneva: Droz, 1990), 16. This version was produced for the death of Charles d'Orléans, François I's oldest son, which occurred on September 8 or 9, 1545. The poem had been written earlier with a different final line and several variants have been located. See Marie-Madeleine Fontaine, "Débats à la cour de France autour du *Canzoniere*," 111–12.

[5] See Knecht, *Renaissance Warrior and Patron* for the intertwining of politics and patronage.

[6] Clément Marot, *Œuvres poétiques complètes*, ed. Gérard Defaux, 2 vols. (Paris: Bordas, 1990), vol. II, 363.

status. Francesco Petrarch's poetic corpus became central to this competition, especially because of his links to France.[7]

This is the pragmatic context, but why Petarchanism? There were other possibilities. The French knew Roman poets such as Catullus, Tibullus, and Ovid,[8] but Petrarch resonated more extensively. Petrarch was considered the master poet of love.[9] His formulations of unrequited desire formed a significant skein of poetic language articulated in early modernity. Poets and diplomats, often overlapping groups, utilized Petrarchan poetry in political negotiation.[10] As Roland Greene has argued, Petrarchan lyric poetry figures prominently in the construction of New World society, and in notions of resistance to European imperialism.[11] Petrarch's central themes – an unhappy lover, unable to satisfy or consummate his love because of resistance from his (female) beloved, suffers from unrequited desire – formed the template for one mode of love poetry in the Renaissance. The other mode, Neoplatonism, also features unsatisfied love, but Neoplatonic lovers are happy, despite their often vexed relationship to heterosexuality.[12] (See Chapter 3 above.) Where the Neoplatonic lover takes pleasure in trying to transcend corporeality, the Petrarchan lover is typically rather more miserable. Petrarch's source for unrequited love, articulated in paradoxical metaphors (burning cold, for instance), was his thirty-one-year poetic obsession with Laura. Thirty-one years of sighing, crying, fretting, and being frustrated by a woman. Of course Petrarch's Laura was a figure, an idol, but she was, in 1533, also a corporeal presence of sorts. Tombs typically contain bodies, and the discovery of Laura's tomb

---

[7] Etienne Pasquier, *Les Recherches de la France, Reveuës & augmentees de quart Livres* (Paris: Jamet Mettayer & Pierre L'huillier, 1596), fol. 240r. See also 229v for claims that Dante and Petrarch learned their poetic craft in France.

[8] Gaisser, *Catullus and His Renaissance Readers*. Hutton, *The Greek Anthology in France*, traces the educational uses of Catullus' epigrams in France.

[9] In order to understand Petrarch's influence in France, it is worth considering his importance in early modern England. See for instance Heather Dubrow, *Echoes of Desire: English Petrarchism and Its Counterdiscourses* (Ithaca, NY: Cornell University Press, 1995); Gordon Braden, "Shakespeare's Petrarchism," in *Shakespeare's Sonnets: Critical Essays*, ed. James Schiffer (New York and London: Garland, 1999), 163–83; and Richard Strier, "The Refusal to Be Judged in Petrarch and Shakespeare," in *A Companion to Shakespeare's Sonnets*, ed. Michael Schoenfeldt (Oxford: Blackwell, 2007), 73–89. The direction of influence was from France to England for the most part. See Anne Lake Prescott, *French Poets and the English Renaissance: Studies in Fame and Transformation* (New Haven: Yale University Press, 1978), which traces English borrowings.

[10] See for instance Gabriele Morelli, *Hernando de Acuna: un petrarchista dell'epoca imperiale* (Parma: Studium parmense, 1977).

[11] Greene, *Unrequited Conquests*.

[12] Peter Ure, "The 'Deformed Mistress' Theme and the Platonic Convention," *Notes and Queries* 193/13 (June 1948): 269–70, points out that Platonism supported the subversive convention of the paradoxical encomium. I would add that, as is often the case, the satirical form supported the normative straight reading.

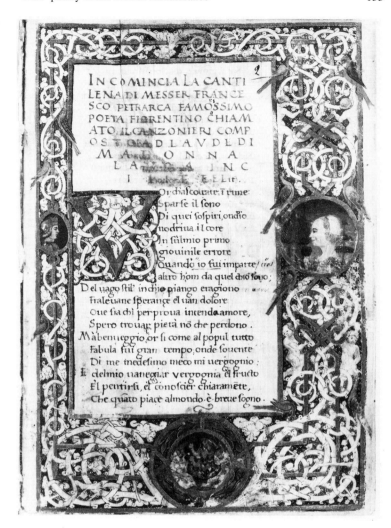

Figure 13. Petrus von Middlebourg (fifteenth century), *Song Praising Laura* from Petrarch's *Sonetti I Canzoni*, Bibliothèque Inguibertine, Carpentras, France, MS 392, fol. 1.

This is from one of the many editions of Petrarch circulating in Renaissance France. "Laura" is depicted in a tondo in the margin, chastely separate from Petrarch's poem about his love for her.

helped to bring out the ambivalence of French (male) poets around the female body.

The story of sex in French Renaissance poetry begins over the fictive dead body of Laura. The adoption and integration of Petrarchan poetics, skepticism about Petrarch's desire, and masculine imperatives associated with the consummation of sexual desire, form the narrative core of my argument. From the early sixteenth to the early seventeenth century, French poets absorbed Petrarch's idioms, ideas, and poetic forms deploying them to produce a native love poetry tradition.[13] Borrowing the sonnet and appropriating the vernacular, many French poets relished Petrarchan unrequited desire and paradoxical formulations. But others reacted against Petrarchanism.[14] Rather than returning to what Petrarch rejected – Dante's spiritualized, incorporeal Beatrice as a path to salvation – some reworked Petrarchan themes in highly somatic ways.

The somatic is central to French Renaissance poetry, as it is the locus of competition over the relationship of love and desire to masculine poetic prowess. Several intersecting themes emerge within a broadly Petrarchan frame: masculinity, self-control, and poetic power; the emergence of trite love tropes around the female body; the slippage from "bad" poetry that says little because it relies on such tropes to "bad" poetry that moves from trope to parody around sexually explicit representation. We know that poems are "bad" in the second sense when they appear in collections of dirty ditties that began circulating at the end of the sixteenth century. French publishers produced at least seventeen collections of salacious, scabrous, graphically sexual poetry.[15] Authorities periodically harassed and occasionally executed writers involved in these enterprises. The pursuit of the libertine poet Théophile de Viau (1590–1626) drove the production of such volumes out of view. Théophile fell afoul of the Catholic Church when *Le Parnasse des poètes satyriques* (1621) appeared in print. Although he denied contributing to it, friends at court, including Jean-Louis Guez de Balzac (1597–1654) abandoned him.[16] The government imprisoned Théophile in the insalubrious Conciergerie for two years for attempting to flee the country. Sentenced to ten years' banishment in 1625, he survived only one,

---

[13] There were other influences, such as Medieval troubadour poetry. Infinite regress is always possible, but the French felt that Petrarch was a crucial influence, and occasionally despaired about the dearth of great French poets in the Medieval period. This is apparent in the discussions of language and poetics below.

[14] For discussion, see Robert J. Clements, "Anti-Petrarchism of the Pléiade," *Modern Philology* 39 (1941): 15–21.

[15] For a general account, see Frédéric Lachèvre, *Les Recueils collectives de poésies libres et satiriques publiés depuis 1600 jusqu'à la mort de Théophile (1626)* (Geneva: Slatkine, 1968 [1909–1928]). For a brief list, see pp. 390–1. The descriptions of the contents and identifications of contributors of individual volumes are sometimes inaccurate, but the overall picture is helpful.

[16] Selected for the Cardinal de Richelieu's Académie française in 1634, Guez de Balzac was linked in the early 1620s to the Cardinal de La Valette, for whom he was an agent.

his health destroyed by his incarceration.[17] Théophile's demise signaled the end of the golden age of the bawdy ditties: the last new collection appeared in 1625, although reprints of older volumes continued to circulate.

The collections appear toward the end of our story, but the poems are largely from Renaissance poets, and often quite famous ones. Philippe Desportes, Pierre de Ronsard, Etienne Jodelle, Jean Antoine de Baïf, Joachim Du Bellay, and Clément Marot are among the prominent names. This chapter traces the movement from love poetry to sex poetry in the work of respectable court poets, less famous outsiders, and satirists, many of whom remain anonymous or obscure. All utilized the idioms of Petrarchan Renaissance love poetry to formulate articulations of desire. Poets created a world that tried to fix sex through the iterations of gender. That is, they fashioned vocabularies of love, sex, and desire that were always about gender, power, and subjectivity. The story of this chapter ends with *La Parnasse* and its counterparts; it begins with the emergence of Petrarchan poetics at the court of François I, traces the contestation over and rejection of Petrarchanism, and argues that the fragmentation of Petrarchan poetics encouraged the impulse toward distinguishing French poetics as a matter of masculine achievement defined in part as French sexual mastery and accomplishment.

Ambivalence and assurance

For many poets, Neoplatonic complications around gender, object choice, and the reliability of salvific markers such as beauty and desire were not entirely satisfying. The figure of Francesco Petrarch, in his guise as the steadfast lover of Laura, seemed to provide a more reliable gender politics of desire and sexual difference. French poets and poetic theorists were sure that Petrarch's example of poetic achievement through chaste desire – as well as his model use of the vernacular in the sonnet form and his ability to earn renown for his poetic corpus – could provide a suitable model for poetic accomplishment. In many ways, Petrarch's poetic persona did just that. "Petrarch's" love for Laura modeled unrequited desire as the source of poetic agency. But over time, concerns about Petrarch's veracity, particularly about consummation, led French poets to articulate physicality as a marker of masculine poetic prowess.

French poets adopted Petrarch as the exemplary lyric poet in the early sixteenth century. Petrarch's works were more cited than incorporated in any meaningful way until the reign of François I. Then court poet and companion

---

[17] Malherbe, Théophile de Viau, and Marc-Antoine Gérard, sieur de Saint-Amant, *Malherbe, Théophile, and Saint-Amant: A Selection*, ed. R. G. Maber (Durham, UK: University of Durham, 1983), xix–xx. For an exhaustive account, see Frédéric Lachèvre, *Le Procès du poète Théophile de Viau*, 2 vols. (Paris: Champion, 1909–1924).

of the king, Clément Marot, included Petrarch in a list of masters of poetry in 1515.[18] Petrarch was associated with Boccaccio's story of Griselda from the *Singulier et proufitable exemple pour toutes femmes mariées*.[19] French editions of the *Triumphs* began to appear in 1514.[20] Nicole Oresme's adaptation of *De Remediis utriusque fortunae* appeared in 1524, followed seven years later by a collection of sayings drawn from Petrarch's prose writings.[21] Although many French readers took to Petrarch in Italian, the move to translate his work and appropriate the sonnet form rapidly gained support. Marot translated six sonnets in 1539, and Jacques Peletier produced an edition that included extracts.[22] The influence of Petrarchan poetry took a leap forward in 1548, when a jurist from Avignon, Vasquin Philieul, published a vernacular French edition of 229 of the 366 poems that made up the *Rerum vulgarium fragmenta*.[23] The original, personalized, feminized title disappeared with subsequent editions – the 1555 expanded edition was entitled *Toutes les euvres vulgaires de Françoys Petrarque*. Philieul's sonnets followed the language, form, and meter of the original Italian as closely as possible, with the expected losses in subtlety and beauty of language that often attend such textual fidelity.[24] The poems nonetheless provided a sense of the power of vernacular poetry to convey emotional complexity in beautiful ways. Philieul's translation filled out what had been mere glimpses of Petrarch's central themes for most French readers.

[18] Marot, "Le Temple de Cupido," in *Œuvres poétiques*, vol. I, 36. On the relationship between François I and Marot, see Stephen Bamforth, "Clément Marot, François I et les muses," in *Clément Marot, "Prince des poëtes françois", 1496–1996: actes du colloque international de Cahors en Quercy 21–25 mai 1996*, ed. Gérard Defaux and Michel Simonin (Paris: Champion, 1997), 225–35.

[19] [Petrarch], *Singulier et proufitable exemple pour toutes femmes mariées qui veullent faire leur devoir en marriage envers Dieu et leurs marys et avoir louenge du monde* (n. p. [Lyon?]: no pub., n. d. [c. 1500]). Its affinity with Medieval moral literature aimed at women is signaled by its form: it was printed in gothic type and engraved with wood cuttings.

[20] The first version was *Les triomphes messire Françoys Petrarcque translatez de langaige tuscan en francois*, trans. Georges de La Forge (Paris: B. Vérard, 1514). A second edition appeared in 1519. It was expanded in 1520. A Lyon edition appeared in 1531. Denys Janot undertook a new printing in Paris in 1539, and a 1554 edition (printed in Paris by E. Groulleau) included additional works about Petrarch.

[21] Francesco Petrarch, *Messire François Petrarcque, des Remèdes de l'une et l'autre fortune prospère et adverse* (Paris: Galliot du Pré, 1523); *Les Parolles joyeuses et dictz mémorables des nobles et saiges homes anciens rédigez par le gracieulx et honneste poète messier Francoys Petrarcque* (Lyon: Par Denys de Harsy, pour Romain Morin, 1531).

[22] Clément Marot, *Six sonnets de Pétrarque* (Paris: Corrozet, n. d. [1539]); Jacques Peletier du Mans, *Les Oeuvres poétiques* (Paris: Vascosan, 1547).

[23] On the iterations of Philieul's translation project, see Giovanni Bellati, "La traduction du *Canzoniere* de Vasquin Philieul," in *Les Poètes français de la Renaissance et Pétrarque*, ed. Jean Balsamo (Geneva: Droz, 2004), 203–28; and "Il primo traduttore dal *Canzoniere* petrarchesco nel Rinascimento francese: Vasquin Philieul," *Aevum* (1985): 371–98.

[24] Petrarch's Italian was in hendecasyllabic meter; Philieul (and most early modern French poets) used decasyllabic. Not without irony, Catullus was the proponent of hendecasyllabic lyric poetry. Philieul followed Marot's rhyme scheme in the tercets (CCDEED).

Nor was this elaboration of Petrarch's poetry simply increased volume. Whatever its flaws, Philieul's translation offered Petrarch as a poet and as an actor in a love drama. Philieul introduced many of the sonnets, organizing them into a romance between Petrarch and Laura grounded in time and place. In narrating the story, Philieul described Petrarch battling his desire. Before Sonnet XXV, the argument reads: "Il se plaint, oultre de desdaings de sa dame, de se veoir surmonté de l'appetit & sensualité" [He complains, indignant with the disdain of his lady, overcome with appetites and sensuality]. The argument before Sonnet LI is that "fureur amoreuse" [amorous fury] is the subject of the subsequent poems.[25] The effects of desire are devastating:

Par sensualité & voluntez charnelles est adhiré, & perdu tout plaisir à contempler les choses haultes & spirituelles.	By sensuality and the hold of whims of the flesh all pleasure in contemplating high and spiritual things is lost.

The narrative arc resolves with Philieul describing Petrarch leaving behind his "fantaisies amoureuses" [amorous fantasies] through prayer and by honoring God.[26]

Philieul's stitched-together tale of physical desire left traces in the conceptualization of sonnet sequences that followed. Du Bellay cited Philieul's work, and both he and Ronsard benefited from its example when they set to work on *L'Olive* (1549) and *Les Amours* (1552) respectively.[27] Several sonnet sequences with a central female love object (Ronsard featured Cassandra, Helène, and two women named Marie at various times;[28] Jean-Antoine de Baïf's Francine poems; the Diane poems by Philippe Desportes, to name a few) were cast with an awareness of narrative.[29] The sequences told stories

---

[25] All page references are from [Petrarch], Vaisquin Philieul, *Laure d'Avignon, au nom et adveu de la royne Catherine de Médicis, royne de France* (Paris: Jacques Gazeau, 1548). A facsimile reprint was prepared under the direction of Pierre Lartigue and Jacques Roubaud (Paris: Actes Sud, 1987), fols. 16r and 32r for the quotations. See also fol. 44r.

[26] Petrarch [Philieul], *Laure d'Avignon*, fols. 69v. See also fols. 94r and 115r.

[27] Jean Balsamo, *Les Rencontres des Muses: italianisme et anti-italianisme dans les lettres françaises de la fin du XVIe siècle* (Geneva: Slatkine, Bibliothèque Franco Simone, 1992), 222–3.

[28] Donald Stone, Jr., *Ronsard's Sonnet Cycles: A Study in Tone and Vision* (New Haven and London: Yale University Press, 1966) offers a reading of Ronsard's corpus in terms of how the poet moved past the stylistic limitations of Petrarchan sonnets to more personal, emotional engagement.

[29] The question of narrative in sonnet sequences has been considered extensively with respect to William Shakespeare's sonnets. The literature is vast, but for an overview, see James Schiffer, "Reading New Life into Shakespeare's Sonnets: A Survey of Criticism," in *Shakespeare's Sonnets: Critical Essays*, ed. James Schiffer (New York and London: Garland, 1999), 3–71. See also Hilton Landry, *Interpretations in Shakespeare's Sonnets* (Berkeley and Los Angeles: University of California Press, 1963); Heather Dubrow, *Captive Victors: Shakespeare's Narrative Poems and Sonnets* (Ithaca, NY and London: Cornell University Press, 1987), 171–90; Margreta de Grazia, "The Scandal of Shakespeare's Sonnets," in *Shakespeare's Sonnets: Critical Essays*, ed. James Schiffer (New York and London: Garland, 1999), 89–112; and the essays in Michael Schoenfeldt, ed., *Companion to Shakespeare's Sonnets* (Malden, MA: Blackwell, 2007).

of fidelity and betrayal figured in the construction of the poetics of desire and masculine poetic subjectivity.

The utility of Petrarch as the spokesman for unrequited love provided material that crystallized French concerns about their native poetic tradition. French rhetoricians, poets, and critics debated the place of the French language within the European tradition with vernacular poetry as a primary field of discussion.[30] Interest in Horace's *Ars poetica* had shaped poetry theory in France since the twelfth century, and a focus on French, rather than Latin, dated from at least Eustache Deschamps's *Art de dictier* (1392). Pierre Fabri and Gratien Du Pont offered advice on poetic forms, metrical structures, and pronunciation.[31] These treatises articulated the preoccupations of the *rhétoriqueur* aesthetic that was maligned by later proponents of French poetry.[32] Regarding *rhétoriqueur* habits such as punning heavily, having entire poems begin with the same letter, and the insertion of riddles within poems as absurd, French poets turned in part to Italian theorists for guidance. Du Bellay's *La Deffence et illustration de la langue françoyse* (1549) looked to such seminal works on the vernacular as Dante's *De vulgari eloquentia* (1303–1304) and Pietro Bembo's *Prose della volgar lingua* (1525) for ways to imagine reform of French through the study of ancient languages.[33] Despite his borrowings (or perhaps because of them), Du Bellay envisioned French having the same cultural effects as Italian had on France, but in reverse.[34] Writing in a period in which the monarchy aspired to expand aggressively in Italy, Du Bellay imagined a conquering monarchy and a conquering French language working hand in hand. Italian was a source of information, but also the primal site of reaction.

Where Italian advocates of the vernacular provided material, Thomas Sébillet provided a point of departure. Sébillet's *Art poétique françoys* (1548) insisted on French poetry as the continuation of the best poetic traditions. French poetry had is own integrity, Sébillet insisted. French poetic forms were just alternative versions of other forms (the rondeau was the French sonnet; Medieval morality tales were restructured ancient tragedies). Sébillet acknowledged the

---

[30] See for instance, William M. Purcell, *Ars Poetriae: Rhetorical and Grammatical Invention at the Margin of Literacy* (Columbia: University of South Carolina Press, 1996); Peter Rickard, *A History of the French Language* (London: Hutchinson, 1974); François Rigolot, *Poésie et Renaissance* (Paris: Seuil, 2002).

[31] Gratien Du Pont, *Art et science de rhetoricque metriffiee* (Toulouse: Nicolas Vieillard, 1539); Pierre Fabri, *Le grant et vray art de pleine rhetoricque* [1521], ed. A. Héron, 3 vols. (Rouen: Lestringent, 1889–1890). Reprint: 1 vol. (Geneva: Slatkine, 1969).

[32] On the *rhétoriqueurs*, see Ernest Langlois, ed., *Recueil d'arts de seconde rhétorique* (1902; reprint Geneva: Slatkine, 1974); François Rigolot, *Le Texte de la Renaissance: des rhétoriqueurs à Montaigne* (Geneva: Droz, 1992).

[33] For these influences, see Balsamo, *Rencontres des Muses*, 133–7.

[34] Jean-Charles Monferran, "Preface," Joachim Du Bellay, *La Deffence, et illustration de la langue francoyse pour l'instruction des jeunes studieus et encor peu avancez en la poésie françoise* (Geneva: Droz, 2001), 17, 24, 40. Monferran indicates, following others, that Du Bellay also borrowed heavily from Sperone Speroni's 1542 *Dialogo delle lingue*.

vernacular Italian sonnet, but he argued that French was the culmination of ancient poetics.[35] Although he mentioned Petrarch, Sébillet's favorites were Virgil, Ovid, Alain de Lille, and Jean de Meung. Sébillet was adamant that contemporary French authors, including Hugues Salel, Antoine Héroët, and Marot, were as good as ancient authors. Sébillet stressed that good poetry was the result of divine inspiration, and only good poetry should serve as the basis of imitation. The way to know the good from the bad was to study Greek and Roman masterpieces in the original languages, but he allowed that translation was an acceptable mode of imitation.

Translation as pedagogy created some controversy. Du Bellay regarded translation as inadequate for teaching the nuances of poetry. Poets ought to look to the great authors (Ovid, Horace, Virgil, Catullus, and Petrarch are among those he names), but the goal, he maintained, should be immersion to absorb style and content (*elocutio* and *inventio*).[36] Direct translation, especially of poetry, is doomed to failure because each language has unique nuances. While celebrating French traditions, Du Bellay rejected much of French poetry. Lemaire and Marot had some positive attributes, but most of the poetry celebrated by Sébillet ought to be jettisoned in favor of ancient or Italian models read in the original languages. Du Bellay's stated intention was to expand the poetic repertoire of French poets, and his defense of the French language was an appeal to transform it by creating a French poetics based on assimilating foreign traditions. Poetic forms (such as the sonnet) and language (words borrowed and modified), along with metrical and syntactical innovations, were all fair game. Absorbed and reworked within French idioms, poetic formulations would enhance French and then French poetry would enrich the traditions from which they were originally borrowed.

Petrarch was central to Du Bellay's project, and to the reform projects of the Pléiade more broadly.[37] While the amount and quality of Petrarchan

---

[35] Thomas Sébillet, *Art poétique françoys*, ed. Félix Gaiffe (Paris: Droz, 1932). See p. 14 for poetic models, and pp. 115–18 regarding the sonnet. Sébillet was probably writing in part in response to Jacques Peletier du Mans, *L'Art poétique d'Horace* (Paris: Vascosan, 1545), which translated Horace with minor adaptations for French. A more technical treatise preceded Sébillet's: Etienne Dolet, *La manière de bien traduire d'une langue en aultre*. Among the more influential works after Dolet were Charles Fontaine, *Le Quintil Horatian sur le premier livre de La Defense, et illustration de la langue françoyse, et la suycte* (Paris: veufve Françoys Regnault, 1555); Jacques Peletier, *Dialogue de l'orthographe e prononciation Françoise, departi en deus livres par Jacques Peletier du Mans* (Poitiers: Jan e Enguilbert de Marnes, 1550) and *L'Art Poëtique, departi en deus livres*; Pontus de Tyard, *Solitaire premier, ou Dialogue de la fureur poétique* (Paris: Galiot du Pré, 1575), originally 1552; and Ronsard, *Abrégé de l'art poëtique françois*. For the context of French debates, see Cave, *The Cornucopian Text*, esp. 3–167.

[36] G. W. Pigman, "Versions of Imitation in the Renaissance," *RQ* 33: 1 (1980): 1–32.

[37] When Henri II succeeded in 1547, Sébillet and Du Bellay vied for the new king's attention and patronage. Henri's patronage went largely to poets of the "Brigade," later to become the "Pléiade." Within the "Brigade," Pierre de Ronsard's *Les Quatre premiers livres des odes de Pierre de Ronsard, Vaudomois; Ensemble son Bocage* (Paris: G. Cavellat, 1550) was a bid for leadership in the form of actual poetry instead of discussion about it. M.-E. Balmas,

influence has been disputed by literary criticism and historians, the efforts by the
French monarchy to encourage Italian and Petrarchan forms and themes seem
evident.[38] In 1533, Marot published "Le Chant des visions de Petrarque." The
opening line, "Une jour estant seulet à la Fenestre," cites Petrarch's "Standomi
un giorno solo a la fenestra."[39] Poetic competitions sponsored by François I
encouraged poets to emulate particular sonnets.[40] As Marie-Madeleine
Fontaine has discovered, exchanges of poems, particularly epigrams, encouraged the spread of Petrarchan forms. Rhyme schemes and metrical patterns
often followed Petrarch's models so closely that different authors utilized the
same rhyming couplets. Among the specific competitions Fontaine cites were
ones set up in 1534 around "Piaga per allentar d'arco non sana" (Sonnet XC)
and the evidently quite inspiring "Standomi un giorno," around which François
I himself generated a ballad, "Estant seulet à la fenestre."[41] Such borrowings
remained standard. "A une Dame," by Mellin de Saint-Gelais, began, "Au temps
heureux que ma jeune ignorance," a reworking of Petrarch's "Nel dolce tempo
de la prima etade."[42] Du Bellay's use of the name Olive played on Petrarch's
Laura/laurel conceit. Throughout his sequence, Du Bellay imitates Petrarch's
use of antitheses to articulate the effects of love. In Sonnet XXVI, for instance,
the speaker is overjoyed and tortured by his beloved; he wants to run, but
he is frozen in place: "Desir m'enflamme, & crainte me rend glace" [Desire
enflames me, and fear renders me as ice].[43] In addition to creating Cassandra
on the model of Laura, Ronsard borrowed liberally from the image archive

"De la Brigade de la Pléiade," in *Lumières de la Pléiade*, ed. Pierre Mesnard (Paris: Vrin,
1966), 13–20, argues that both the Brigade and the (changing) group of seven who constituted
the Pléiade were created by Ronsard. The literature on the Pléiade is vast, but the classic remains
Chamard, *Histoire de la Pléiade*.

[38] Stephen Minta, *Love Poetry in Sixteenth-Century France: A Study in Themes and Traditions*
(Manchester University Press, 1977) rejects claims for Petrarchan influence. Minta argues that
love poetry was widely circulating from several sources, and trademark formulations attributed
to Petrarch had antecedents in Medieval courtly love poetry. While most critics recognize that
Medieval and ancient traditions were in play, specifically Petrarchan elements did enter French
poetic culture in the 1530s.

[39] Marot, "Le Chant des visions de Petrarque, translate de Italien en Françoys," in *Œuvres
poétiques*, vol. I, 347–9. Originally published in *La Suite de l'Adolescence clementine* in
late 1533 or early 1534. Petrarch is also cited as a master along with Ovid in "L'adolescence
Clementine" (1515), vol. I, 36, ll. 323–24.

[40] Jean Balsamo, "Marot et les origins du pétraquisme français," 323–37.

[41] Fontaine, "Mellin de Saint-Gelais," 108–11. The original by Petrarch may be found in Francesco
Petrarca, *Canzoniere*, ed. Gianfranco Contini (Turin: Einaudi [1964], 1992), 397–9.

[42] Francesco Petrarca, *Canzoniere, Trionfo, Rime varie*, ed. C. Muscetta and D. Ponchiroli (Turin:
Einaudi, 1958), 26. Saint-Gelais, *Œuvres poétiques françaises*, vol. I, 203–4. Originally published in *La Fleur de poesie francoyse* (1543).

[43] Du Bellay, *Œuvres poétiques*, ed. Chamard, vol. I, 49 (Sonnet XXVI, l. 6). See also Sonnet V,
vol. I, 30–1 and Sonnet XXVII, vol. I, 50 for direct borrowings from Petrarch. Petrarch also
appears in *L'Olive* and in "L'Anterotique de la vieille et de la jeune amye." See p. 131 and n.
("Cheveux, qui d'un fil delé / M'ont à eux si tresfort lïé" is derived from Petrarch's sonnet, "O
chiome bionde, di che'l cor m'annoda").

and the syntax of the *Canzoniere*.[44] François Rouget has identified thirty-two close imitations of Petrarch's *Canzoniere* and *Trionfi d'Amore*.[45] The frustrated lover tormented by opposite sensations (hot/cold; despair/elation), being tossed on the sea, or admiring the beloved in various guises (compared to flowers or the sun, likened to exquisite objects, as a collection of perfect body parts or precious stones) became standard topoi.

But the same group of admiring imitators and adaptors also attacked Petrarch, especially over the quality and nature of his relationship with Laura. Robert J. Clements has argued that wariness of Petrarchanism among French Renaissance poets was a function of distrust of Petrarch's sincerity. The French found Petrarch's claims that his love for Laura lasted thirty-one, chaste years difficult, if not impossible, to believe. Petrarch's tears and sighing over his beloved when she was alive seemed false or insincere, and more so after her death.[46] Rejection came first at the hands of Neoplatonists. One might expect the idealizing propensities of Neoplatonism to condition its proponents to see Petrarch's treatment of Laura as an extension of Dante's idealized love for Beatrice. Instead, French Neoplatonists likened Petrarch's attachment to Laura to ineffectual flailing. Antoine Héroët's 1542 *Parfaite Amie* complained:

Tous les scripts et larmoyants autheurs,	All the words and teary authors, all that
Tout le Pétrarque et ses imitateurs,	Petrarch and his imitators who fill the
Qui de souspirs et de froydes querelles	air with sighs and cold quarrels if
Remplissent l'air en parlant aux estoilles.	speaking to the stars.[47]

Héroët sees Petrarch as overly devoted to his own emotional responses. True love is not about histrionics. The physicality of Petrarchan love offends Héroët, whose protagonist seeks transcendence of corporeality through love. All the sighs and tears and quarrels impede the possibility of achieving rational love. Love was difficult enough without the myriad distractions described in Petrarch's poems. In 1553, Joachim Du Bellay, who remained dedicated to Petrarchan sonnets and to the vernacular, rejected Petrarchan love conceits on Neoplatonic grounds. Du Bellay attacked the fragmentation of the female body as a poetic imperative, arguing instead for an understanding of beauty in universal terms:

---

[44] André Gendre, "Pierre de Ronsard," in *Les poètes français de la Renaissance et Pétrarque*, ed. Jean Balsamo (Geneva: Droz, 2004), 229–51.

[45] François Rouget, "Philippe Desportes, médiateur du Pétrarquisme français," in *Les Poètes français de la Renaissance et Pétrarque*, ed. Jean Balsamo (Geneva: Droz, 2004), 331–51. See esp. 344–5. See also Charles Dédéyan, "Ronsard et Bembo," in *Ronsard e l'Italia / Ronsard in Italia* (Fasano: Schena, 1988), 27–51.

[46] Robert J. Clements, *Critical Theory and Practice of the Pléiade* (Cambridge, MA: Harvard University Press, 1942).

[47] Antoine Héroët, *La Parfaicte amye*, ed., ll. 1511–14.

De voz beautez je diray seulement,	Of your beauties, I will say only that my
Que mon oeil ne juge folement,	eye does not judge foolishly, your
Vostre beauté est joinct egalement	beauty is joined equally to your good
A vostre bonne grace: . . .	grace: . . . But if however Petrarch
Si toutesfois Petrarque vous plaist mieux,	pleases you more . . . I will choose one
Je choisiray cent mille nouveautez,	hundred thousand novelties of which I
Dont je peindray voz plus grandes beautez	will paint your greatest beauties
Sur la plus belle Idee.	according to the most beautiful idea.[48]

Du Bellay objects to the propensity to reduce the beloved object/female body into fragments that Nancy Vickers has identified as the result of Petrarch's reliance on Ovidian narratives of dismemberment in the *Rime sparse*. The story of Actaeon and Diana as retold by Petrarch, Vickers notes, conjoins, "Seeing and bodily disintegration," a trope that reappears several times in Ovid, but each time with the man (Actaeon, Orpheus, Pentheus) dismembered for seeing.[49] In reversing Petrarch, Du Bellay seeks to create the whole rather than reduce it to a part. Offering a vision of command over the poetic creation, implicitly, he suggests he will not end up morcelized like his Ovidian forbears.

Where Du Bellay asserted a form of masculine bravado as poetic creation, Ronsard rewrote the Petrarchan story – and rewrote it and rewrote it. Ronsard experimented with different endings to the unrequited desire story in his major sonnet sequences. Self-consciously Petrarchan in *Les Amours*, Ronsard cast Cassandra as his Laura.[50] Where Petrarch is left mourning Laura, Ronsard is sure he is going to die for love. One sonnet begins, "Quand ces beaux yeux jugeront que je meure" [When these beautiful eyes judge that I die] and ends with Ronsard's projected epitaph:

Ci dessous gist un amant Vandomois,	Here below lies a lover from the Vandomois,
Que la douleur tua dedans ce bois	That anguish killed you in this thicket
Pour aimer trop les beaux yeux de sa dame.	For loving too much the beautiful eyes of his lady.

In the next poem, love actually brings death, and ends with the thought that the happiest lover is the one who dies for his beloved ("Et plus heureux

48 Joachim Du Bellay, "Contre les Petrarquistes," in *Divers jeux rustiques*, ed. Verdun L. Saulnier (Geneva: Droz, 1947), ll. 193–96, 201, 206–8. This is a reworking of "A Une Dame" (1553). The *Divers jeux* appeared in 1558.
49 Nancy J. Vickers, "Diana Described: Scattered Woman and Scattered Rhyme," *Writing and Sexual Difference*, ed. Elizabeth Able (University of Chicago Press, 1982), 95–109, esp. pp. 96–9. For Petrarch's version of the Actaeon story, see *Rime sparse*, 23.
50 See for instance Ronsard, *Œuvres complètes*, ed. Céard, Ménager, and Simonin, vol. I, 60–1, Sonnet LXXII (*Les Amours*).

qui meurt pour l'amour d'elle" [And more happy is he who dies for love of her]).[51] Ronsard aims for the ultimate sacrifice for love initially, but in the narrative of his sonnet sequences, he does not die of his love for Cassandra. Instead, he goes on to write more sequences to other women, in the course of which Ronsard develops his disbelief that Petrarch remained chaste for so long. Despite his intensely emotional language, Petrarch must be lying:

Et que le bon Petrarque un tel peché ne fist,
Qui trente et un ans amoureux de sa dame,
Sans qu'un autre jamais luy peust eschauffer l'ame:
Respons-luy je te pri,' que Petrarque sur moy
N'avoit authorité de me donner sa loy,
Ny à ceux qui viendroyent après luy, pour les faire
Si long temps amoureux sans leur lien desfaire.
. . .
Pour ester sot trente ans, abusant sa jeunesse
Et sa Muse au giron d'une vieille maistresse:
Ou bien il jouyssoit de sa Laurette, ou bien
Il estoit un grand fat d'aimer sans avoir rien.
Ce que je ne puis croire, aussi n'est-il croyable.

And that the good Petrarch such a sin did not make, who thirty-one years loving of his lady, without any other ever who could warm his soul: I pray you respond to him, that Petrarch does not have authority over me to give his law, nor to those who come after him, to make them in love such a long time without their bonds undone . . . For to be foolish for thirty years, abusing his youth and his Muse at the bosom of an old mistress: Either he plays with his little Laura, or he was a great fool for loving without having any. This I cannot believe because it is not believable.

Ronsard's choice of language (*giron*, *jouir*, *fat* – which connote foppishness) suggests he thinks Petrarch is lying about chastity, rather than love. For Ronsard, some pursuit is reasonable, but if the beloved remains difficult or unavailable, he advises, "On s'en doit esloigner, sans se rompre la teste" [One must distance oneself, without breaking one's head]. Women, he goes on, should be

---

[51] Ronsard, *Œuvres complètes*, vol. I, 55–6, Sonnets LXII and LXIII (*Les Amours*). See variant reading c, p. 1240. Evidence suggests that Ronsard had narrative intentions. See the discussion of the revisions to the commentaries on his poems studied in Isidore Silver, *Three Ronsard Studies* (Geneva: Droz, 1978), 109–67. The movement of poems within categories in Ronsard's later collected works, overseen by Ronsard, indicates attempts to arrange the stories. On the practice of setting out the conditions of reading in the opening of Renaissance sonnet sequences, see Roberto Fedi, *La memoria della poesia: canzonieri, lirici e libri de Rime nel Rinascimento* (Rome: Salerno, 1990), 74–7.

wooed, to be sure, but they also lead men on and cannot be trusted. If a man should be lucky enough to find one who is "Humble, courtoise, honneste, amoureuse et gentile, / Sans fard, sans tromperie, et qui sans mauvaitié / Garde de tout son coeur une simple amitié" [Humble, courteous, honest, loving, and gentle, / Without make-up, without deception, and who is without evil / Guard with all his heart such simple love], he should love her beyond measure. While Ronsard condemns the man "Qui trompe une pucelle..." [Who fools a maiden], he says he loved another woman while waiting for his beloved Cassandra to return his love.[52] Desire in a man is normal and expected; waiting for consummation is reasonable only to a point. Petrarch's three decades of unrequited love without satisfaction are far beyond that point. Consummation of desire is what men do. Ronsard is frank about having loved, written about, and written for several women in succession, and by the time he writes the sonnets for Marie, Ronsard admits that he was not steadfast in his love for any one woman:

J'avois au-paravant, veincu de la jeunesse,	I had previously vanquished in youth
Autres dames aimé (ma faute je confesse).	Other women I loved (my fault, I confess).[53]

Ronsard revisits the Petrarchan narrative by recurrently asserting his own veracity as a matter of physical intimacy.[54] Perhaps more than any other French poet, Ronsard elides the poetic persona (usually "je") with his autobiographical self. This is in keeping with the construction of a body of work that rested heavily on Ronsard's integrity, which was demonstrated by confessing that his desire was neither constant nor unrequited.[55]

Skepticism about chastity did not have to be in the context of sorting out a poetic narrative on Ronsard's scale. More locally, Mellin de Saint-Gelais rejected the extremities of Petrarchan language about love:

[52] Ronsard, "Elegie à son livre," in *Œuvres complètes*, vol. I, 167–72, ll. 38–44, 47–50. From *Le Second livre des amours* (1560). See also his confession that he mocked Petrarch for waiting so long. *Les Amours*, Sonnet CXXIX (*Œuvres*, vol. I, 139).

[53] Ronsard, "Elegie," in *Œuvres complètes*, vol. I, 258, ll. 25–6. The larger sequence, "Sur la mort de Marie," is analyzed relative to Petrarch's treatment of Laura's death in Sara Sturm-Maddox, *Ronsard, Petrarch, and the Amours* (Gainesville: University of Florida Press, 1999), 128–58.

[54] See also Ronsard, "Discours en forme d'élegie," in *Œuvres complètes*, vol. II, 307: "Maintenant je poursuy toute amour vagabonde: / Ores j'aime le noire, ores j'aime la blonde... / Je cherche ma fortune où je la puis trouver" [Now I pursue all vagabond love: / Now I love black, now I love blond... / I seek my fortune wherever I might find it] (ll. 143–6).

[55] Ronsard, *Œuvres complètes*, Sonnet XX, *Le Second Livre des Amours*, vol. I, 188 insists, "Je ne suis variable... / Que tost je n'oubliasse et Marie et Cassandre" (ll. 1, 4).

Il n'est point vray que pour aymer on
  meure,
Car je serois ja mort et mis en terre,
Si grand douleur en moy faict sa
  demeure.
Il n'est point vray qu'un Amant puisse
  acquerre
Bien ne repos pour peine qu'il endure,
Car je serois en paix et non en guerre.
Il n'est point vray que loyauté qui dure
Se puisse voir jamais recompensée,
Puisq'une m'est encores estrange et dure.
. . .
Il n'est point vray que jamais autre amye
Puisse en mon coeur loger ny trouver
  place
Loyauté n'est en moy si endormie.
Mais il est vray que qui a veu sa face,
Ne peut avoir que de mourir l'attente
Bien heureux est qui du mal se contente
Mais plus heureux qui a sa bonne grace.

It is not true that one dies for love, because I would be already dead and in the ground if great sadness in me made its abode. It is not true that a Lover can easily acquire repose for the pain he endures because I am at peace and not at war. It is not true that loyalty that lasts will ever see itself recompensed, because mine is still unknown and strong . . . It is not true that never can another beloved find a place in my heart. Loyalty is not so sent to sleep. But it is true that I who saw her face can only die from the wait [and] very happy is he who with evil contents himself. But more happy is he who has good grace.[56]

For Saint-Gelais, Petrarchan language about devotion is literally and affectively untrue. One does not die from unrequited love, and lovers move on. Saint-Gelais rejects the subordination of the male lover to the pains of endless, futile desire.[57] At the same time, Saint-Gelais's poetic persona articulates the precarity of masculine agency in this poem and the ones following it in the manuscript. The speaker wills himself to leave off destructive devotion in terms that articulate an awareness that this is a difficult prospect. He alternates language of desolation and pride in having maintained a sense of self. Elsewhere, Saint-Gelais suggests additional moves away from Petrarchan chaste, miserable desire, including an attempt to test for truth:

Si l'on me monstre affection,
S'oit pour vray ou par fiction,
A aymer aussi je consens,
Mais je n'ay pas si peu de sens
Que je ne mecte en divers lieux
Aussi bien le coeur que les yeux.

If one shows me affection,
Whether it is true or fiction,
To love also I consent
But I do not have so little sense
That I do not put in diverse places
The heart as well as the eyes.[58]

[56] "Leger chappre: pour le Luth, a double repos," BN MS fr 878, fol. 28r–v; MS fr 885, fol. 26v. Mellin de Saint-Gelais, Œuvres poétiques françaises, ed. Donald Stone, Jr., 2 vols. (Paris: Société des Textes Français Modernes, 1993), vol. I, 69–70.

[57] The opposite response – embracing endless, futile desire – had its proponents as well. See for instance Philippe Desportes, Œuvres de Philippe Desportes, ed. Alfred Michiels (Paris: Adolphe Delahays, 1858), 68, Sonnet III (Amours de Diane II) ends, "Pour rendre mon desir et ma peine eternelle." The poem was first published in 1573. BN MS fr 868, fol. 91.

[58] BN MS fr 878, fol. 81r; MS fr 885, fol. 79r; Saint-Gelais, Œuvres poétiques, vol. II, 43.

In part because of the Neoplatonic warnings with respect to desire, poets allowed for the possibility that love could be false. The range of Petrarchan love language increased such caution. Saint-Gelais's version is to insist on the need to agree to the terms of engagement, rather than to be pulled along hopelessly as the Petrarchan model seemed to indicate. Once love has been verified, the beloved had best not rely too closely on the Petrarchan model either. The poet warned women against assuming love stories as scripts for a relationship:

Si vous voulez estre aymee et servie,	If you want to be loved and served,
Faictes qu'Amour quelque bien nous propose,	Make that which Love proposes to us some good,
Et n'estimez que pour perdre la vie,	And do not consider that, in order to lose life,
A servir personne se dispose.	preparing oneself to serve no one.
Je ne voy point que l'on cherche la Roze	I have not seen one search for the Rose
Pour n'y trouver qu'espine et cruauté.	Only to find it with thorns and cruelty.
On en faict cas pour bien meilleure chose,	One can make a case for a much better thing,
Car sa douceur respond a sa Beauté.	For its sweetness responds to its Beauty.[59]

On the one hand, Saint-Gelais constructed a version of masculine control over love by way of distinguishing his poetic persona from the comparatively hapless Petrarchan speaker. On the other hand, Saint-Gelais in his anti-Petrarchan moments (not unlike Ronsard in his) suggested that the woman was largely to blame. If she refused to reciprocate in love or consummate physical passion, Saint-Gelais advised the male lover to move on and find satisfaction elsewhere. It was not mentally or physically healthy for a man to delay gratification.

The struggles of Ronsard and Saint-Gelais point to the difficulties created by the simultaneous desire for and dependence on the (female) beloved in poetic love discourse. Attempts to direct and shape the expression of desire in poetic terms were part of the gender dynamics in French culture. In the agonistic tradition of Renaissance poetry with respect to poetry, one way to demonstrate mastery was to do so over other men. In gendered terms, this is most apparent in the *blason* "competitions" organized by Marot.[60] As in the *querelle des amyes* (see Chapter 3), the *blason* was in part rhetorical competition. In

---

[59] BN MS fr 878, fol. 90v; MS fr 885, fol. 91v; Saint-Gelais, *Œuvres poétiques*, vol. II, 80.

[60] In 1535, the exiled Marot made a bid for a return to favor by announcing a literary contest in which poets were to describe the parts of the (female) body. Marot declared Maurice Scève's "Blason du sourcil" the winner, but really, *blasons* allowed poets (mostly, but not always, men) to demonstrate wit and facility with language. *Blasons Anatomiques des Parties du Corps fémenin* (1536) appeared the next year. For especially cogent discussions, see Lecercle, *La Chimère de Zeuxis*, 79–165, which articulates a typology of *blasons*; Nancy J. Vickers, "Members Only: Marot's Anatomical Blazons," in *The Body in Parts: Fantasies of Corporeality in Early Modern Europe*, ed. David Hillman and Carla Mazzio (London and New York: Routledge, 1997), 3–21; and Sawday, *Body Emblazoned*, for the larger cultural impulses at work.

the combative mode, French poets occasionally mocked Petrarch. Du Bellay parodied an Italian love sonnet by Francesco Berni by exaggerating standard Petrarchan language. Du Bellay demonstrates his command of language and implicitly the emotions behind them as superior to the Petrarchan original. The imagery and the punctuation markers of Du Bellay's Sonnet 91 from *Les Regrets* signal the poet's intentions by amplifying the elements of the *blason* to absurd lengths:

O beaux cheveux d'argent mignonnement retors!	O beautiful silver hair, daintily twisted!
O front crespe & serein! & vous face doree!	O face veiled and serene! And you, golden in appearance,
O beaux yeux de crystal! ô grand' bouche honoree,	O beautiful eyes of crystal! O great mouth honored
Qui d'un large reply retrousses tes deux bords!	With a large crease turned up from your two borders.
O belles dentz d'ebene! ô precieux tresors,	O beautiful ebony teeth! O precious treasures,
Qui faites d'un seul riz toute ame enamouree!	That make an enamored soul laugh a single time!
O gorge damasquine en cent pliz figuree!	O the damascene throat figured with a hundred folds!
Et vous beaux grands tetins, dignes d'un si beau corps!	And your great big breasts, worthy of such a beautiful body!
O beaux ongles dorez! ô main courte & grassette!	O beautiful golden fingernails! O short and fat hands!
O cuisse delicate! & vous gembe grossette,	O delicate thigh! And your large leg,
Et ce que je ne puis honnestement nommer!	And that which I cannot honestly [without lasciviousness] name!
O beau corps transparent! ô beaux members de glace!	O beautiful transparent body! O beautiful limbs of ice!
O divines beautez! pardonnez moy de grace,	O divine beauty! By your grace, pardon me,
Si, pour estre mortel, je ne vous ose aymer.	If, being mortal, I do not dare love you.[61]

Berni's original is serious about serving love by describing the beauties of his mistress. Du Bellay tipped standard imagery over the line into ridicule, rewriting typical elements using the Petrarchan penchant for paradox for comic effect. Du Bellay made her hair silver (that is, she is an old woman) rather than gold. The details speak to the grotesque, rather than inviting: the wrinkled

---

[61] Du Bellay, *Œuvres poétiques*, vol. II, 122 (Sonnet XCI). From *Les Regrets* (1558). The original model is Francesco Berni, *Tutti le Opere di Berni* (Venice: B. Zanetti, 1542). See BN Rés. Y4 1277, fol. 60v. See also Dubrow, *Echoes of Desire*, 54–5, 196 on Du Bellay's move.

throat and ebony teeth prompt revulsion. Praise for unattractive attributes such as the woman's ugly, indelicate hands and cold body deliberately wrenched Petrarchan expectations out of their sockets. The expression of repulsion in the idiom of the unworthy lover crowned the parodic effect.

Parody often borders on belligerence, and as the Du Bellay poem indicates, French poets relied on Petrarchan forms, metaphors, and ideas, but also appropriated the poetic tradition to more aggressive ends. French poets questioned the premises of chaste, unrequited love. They implied that Petrarchan abstinence was absurd. While the anxiety that the beloved object might not believe the insistent lover was palpable, several poets offered reassurances that they were not lying. Rémy Belleau began one sonnet, "Maistresse, croyez moy, je ne suis point menteur" [Mistress, believe me, I am not a liar] before assuring her that his desire, "Avez plongé mon ame en extreme fureur" [Has plunged my soul in an extreme furor]. In *La seconde journee de la bergerie* (1572), Belleau was adamant,

Je n'en mentiray point, quand ce baiser je pris	I have not lied, when I took this kiss
Sur les bords rougissans de ceste leure tendre,	on the red banks of this tender lure,
Je restay si transi que je ne puis apprendre.	I remain so benumbed that I cannot tell.[62]

Etienne Jodelle insisted that his poems were truthful because he hated ones that were not:

Sans pleurer (car je hay la coustumiere feinte	Without crying (because I detest the fake custom of our lovers, who have
De nos amans, qui n'on que leurs pleurs pour sujet).	nothing but their tears as a subject).[63]

In 1573, Philippe Desportes began the *Les Amours de Diane*,

Je n'agrandiray point, riche d'inventions,	I will not aggrandize with rich inventions
Vos beautez, vos dédains, ma foy, mes passions:	Your beauty, your disdain, my faith, my passions:
Il suffira qu'au vray mon crayon se rapporte.	It will suffice for my pen to report the truth.[64]

By insisting on the veracity of their emotional responses, French poets claimed moral superiority over their Italian models.

[62] Rémy Belleau, *Œuvres poétiques de Rémy Belleau*, ed. Charles Marty-Laveaux, 2 vols. (Geneva: Slatkine, 1878), vol. I, 146, vol. II, 89.
[63] Jodelle, *Les Oeuvres et meslanges poetiques*, ed. Marty-Laveaux, vol. II, 19. Jodelle died in 1573. Most of his poetry was published after his death.
[64] BN MS fr 868, fol. 59, no. 1; Philippe Desportes, *Les Amours de Diane. Premier livre*, ed. Victor E. Graham (Geneva: Droz, 1959), 26 (Sonnet I).

Part of the truth of love poetry was that sometimes the lover was satisfied, but making corporeal satisfaction admirable could be difficult. Poets worked to maintain modest language while describing physical intimacy. In *Les Amours*, Ronsard tells his beloved, "Tout une nuit je le puisse embrasser"[65] [All night, I can kiss it]. More coy is the suggestive sonnet that begins "Quand au matin ma Deesse s'habille" [When in the morning, my Goddess dresses herself]. The luxuriant description of her beauty that follows indicates a very intimate night.[66] But physicality could explode beyond the bounds of decorum. Sonnet CIII is explicit: "Sur le sablon la semence j'épan"[67] [On the sand, I scatter my seed]. Kisses, entwined limbs ("Et ne m'oste quand je sommeille / Ma Cassandre d'entre mes bras" [And do not deprive me when I sleep, my Cassandra of being in my arms]), memories of nights spent together, and the lingering remains of touch pepper Ronsard's love poems.[68] Ronsard struggled to assert physical fulfillment artfully.

Ronsard was not the only one. Olivier de Magny ended one sonnet,

Et desormais d'une douce liqueur	And henceforth a sweet liqueur
Soigneusement arrosez vostre cueur,	Carefully soaks your heart,
Sans vous monstrer si durement rebelle.	Without showing you as so harshly rebellious.[69]

Magny conjoined the effects of physical intimacy with the language of the heart to convey consummation. Marot was more playfully blunt, noting that Ysabeau is beautiful no matter whether she is dressed as a maid or a princess. Nonetheless, "Mais il me semble, ou je suis bien trompé, / Qu'elle seroit plus belle toute nue"[70] [But it seems to me, unless I am much mistaken, / that she would be more beautiful entirely nude]. The lasciviousness is more insistent for culminating the poem. Rémy Belleau is one of many who dwelled on kissing:

Ta bouche en me baisant me versa l'ambrosie...	Your mouth in kissing me pours me ambrosia...
Sus donc approche toy & me baise mignonne,	Under, therefore, I approach you and kiss me, mignonne,
Suçons & ressuçons l'un & l'autre à son tour.	Suck and suck more one and the other in turn.[71]

---

65 Ronsard, *Œuvres complètes*, Sonnet XXX, *Les Amours*, vol. I, 40.
66 Ronsard, *Œuvres complètes*, Sonnet XLI, *Les Amours*, vol. I, 45.
67 Ronsard, *Œuvres complètes*, Sonnet CIII, *Les Amours*, vol. I, 76.
68 See for instance Ronsard, *Œuvres complètes*, Sonnet XLVI, *Les Amours*, vol. I, 47–8, "Je veux mourir pour tes beautez, Maistresse," which ends, "Toute une nuit au milieu de tes bras." See also *Vᵉ Livre des Odes*, vol. I, 985 (Ode XXX).
69 Olivier de Magny, *Œuvres poétiques*, ed. François Rouget (Paris: Champion, 1999), 109, Sonnet LXXXI.
70 Marot, *Œuvres poétiques*, vol. II, 379.
71 Belleau, *Œuvres poétiques*, vol. I, 129. "A Sa maistresse." See also his descriptions of kissing, vol. I, 147–8 and from *La seconde journée de la bergerie*: "Donne moy la bouche tienne: / Approche, voila la mienne, / Succe & ressucce le bout / De ma bouchette succree," vol. II, 125.

Pontus de Tyard takes the Neoplatonic acceptance of kissing as a potential guide to salvific desire articulated in *The Courtier*, but describes kissing in highly corporeal terms: "A celle bouche où d'enrose et s'embame / Un baiser sec et un baiser humide"[72] [At this mouth where I enroll myself and avail myself / A dry kiss and a wet kiss].

When combined with sexual description, agonistic truth-telling in the name of appropriating Petrarchan love could get out of hand. Ronsard, whose descriptions occasionally got quite explicit, rebuked other poets for their licentiousness:

L'on nous depeint une Dame paillarde	One paints us a lewd woman
L'un plus aux vers qu'aux sentences regarde,	One regards more his verses than his meaning
Et ne peut onq tant se sceut desguiser,	And he can never hide
Apprendre l'art de bien Petrarquiser.	His learning of the art of Petrarchising well.[73]

But for the most part, physicality was honest in the modern sense of the term: It was real and realistic to expect bodies to respond to each other. Petrarchan "honesty" in its early modern meaning as chastity or sexual probity might be admired, but it was not believable. Or so was the argument of Petrarch's French interlocutors, who positioned themselves as poets and lovers within and against the frame of physical consummation. In other words, real men – even fictional, poetic ones – did it.

Getting dirty

Ah, but Ronsard lied too.[74] Despite his insistence on propriety, Ronsard had his raunchy side. Published anonymously in 1553 but attributed to Ronsard at the time and since, the *Livret de Folastries* included several explicitly sexual poems. Consider this one:

Lance au bout d'or qui sais et poindre et oindre,	Lance with a tip of gold which shocks and breaks and anoints,
De qui jamais la roideur ne defaut,	Of which the grinding never defaults,
Quand en camp clos bras à bras il me faut	When, on the battlefield, I grasp arm in arm

---

[72] Tyard, *Erreurs Amoureuses*, part 3, sonnet I, p. 265. Although warning that kisses might be overly sensual, Baldessare Castiglione, *The Courtier*, trans. and intro. Bull, 336–7, puts similar words about kissing in the mouth of Pietro Bembo, whose *Gli Asolani di messer Pietro Bembo* (Venice: Aldo Romano, 1505) indicated that some physicality between men and women might facilitate transcendent love. (See also Chapter 3.)

[73] Ronsard, *Œuvres complètes*, vol. I, 145, ll. 41–4. From *Les Amours*, "Elegie à Cassandre."

[74] Cave, *Cornucopian Text*, 223–70, argues that Ronsard's prolix proliferations can be read as poetic strategy. That I have called one element of Ronsard's rewritings and suppressions "lies" supports Cave's point.

Toutes les nuis au dous combat me joindre.	All the nights in sweet combat join me.
Lance vraiment qui ne fus jamais moindre	Lance which can truly never be least
À ton dernier qu'à ton premier assaut,	From your last to your first assault
De qui le bout bravement dressé haut	Of which the tip bravely high erect
Est toujours prest de choquer et de poindre.	Is always ready to strike and to shock.[75]

The patina of anonymity did not obviate the reveling in Priapic imagery. Love-making, rather than love, is central, with Ronsard punning on images of war to depict sexual combat. "Love" in the Petrarchan sense withers away, as the masculine poetic subject takes over with his performance of militaristic sexual fortitude. "Love" and the woman get lost in the skirmish that is sex. Making the world safe for a poetics of love, it seems, could lead down some unforeseen paths.

Ronsard lied about his own decorum, but he did so to reveal that achieving sustained, transcendent desire was not realistic. In addition to Ronsard, many French poets articulated the idea that consummation was part of poetic practice. This reminded readers that purity of love was suspect and that the effects of desire were unruly. At the same time, Petrarchan poetics, especially in the French narrative version, emphasized the ways that poetry revealed the truth about the poetic subject. How could a poet maintain honesty and assert control over the discourse of desire? One solution was to attempt frankly and unrepentantly to inspire and direct arousal. Some poets, and many of the same poets who labored within the constraints of the Petrarchan idiom, turned their attention to explicit articulations of sexual desire. Scoffing at the priority of chaste desire and rejecting the presumption that the proper locus of sex is within socially and religiously sanctioned confines, these poets churned out reams of "bad" (dirty, lascivious, intentionally arousing) poetry.[76] The truth of this "bad" poetry at times outweighed the scruples of the most eminent poets.

---

[75] Pierre de Ronsard, "Sonet," in *Œuvres complètes*, vol. I, 571. From *Livret de Folastries* (1553). This and similar poems appeared in later editions of Ronsard's work published during his lifetime.

[76] Collections include Anon., *La Muse folastre. Recherchée des plus beaux esprits de ce temps* (Paris: Pour Anthoine de Brueil, 1600) with variant versions in 1603, 1607, 1611, 1615, and 1621; Anon., *Le Labyrinthe d'amour ou suite des Muses Folastres* (Rouen: chez Claude le Vilain, 1610) with two variant editions in 1611 and 1615; Anon., *Le premier, second et troisiesme livre du labyrinthe de Recreation. Recherché des plus beaux Esprits de ce temps* (Rouen: chez Claude de Vilain, 1602); Anon., *Les Muses incognues ou la seille aux bourriers plaine de desires et imaginations d'amour* (Rouen: Imprimerie de Jean Petit, 1604); Anon., *Le Sandrin ou verd galand où sont naïfvement deduits les plaisirs de la vie rustique* (Paris: Anthoine du Brueil, 1609); Anon., *Les Muses gaillardes recueillies des plus beaux esprits de ce temps* (Paris: Par A. D. B. [Anthoine du Brueil], 1609) with a second, expanded printing in 1609 and editions in 1611 and 1613; Anon., *Les Satyres du sieur Regnier. Derniere edition, reveuë corrigee, et de*

Such poetry was part of the libertine impulse in the sixteenth century, the nature of which has sparked some debate. Because of its hedonistic celebrations of sex, some historians have considered lascivious early modern poetry to be a form of pornography.[77] Scholars who have focused on the wide range of explicit writings sometimes found such categorizations too reductive. In his analysis of late-seventeenth-century erotica, Roger Thompson divided explicit material into four categories: pornography, obscenity, bawdy, and erotica. Pornography is aimed at inspiring a sexual response in the reader or viewer; obscenity is "intended to shock or disgust" and relies on reference to physical or moral taboos; bawdy is humorous references to sex; and erotica refers to sex within love relationships marked by mutuality.[78] The distinctions sound better than they work for two reasons. First, many early modern works of literature or art are so hybrid that they defy categorization. Consider François Rabelais's story of Panurge getting revenge on a Parisian woman who turned him down by sprinkling her with a powder made from the genitals of a bitch in heat. The lady is then chased and pissed on by 600,014 male dogs.[79] Is this obscenity or merely bawdy? Second and more importantly, we know very little about what early modern people made of such materials – except that the volume of them suggests their popularity.

Given the problems of definition and reception, Ian Frederick Moulton rejects pornography as a category altogether for the sixteenth and early seventeenth centuries. He argues that pornography did not emerge until the nineteenth century, when modern visual technologies were developed. Before

---

beaucoup augmentée, tant par les sieurs de Sigogne, et de Berthelot, qu'autres des plus signalez Poëtes de ce temps (Paris: L'Imprimerie d'Anthoine du Brueil, 1614) with editions in 1616, 1617, 1621, and 1625. There also was a knock-off, Anon., Les Satyres du sieur Regnier. Dediées au Roy (Paris: Anthoine Estoc, 1619). See also Anon., Les Bigarrures et touches du Seigneur des Accords (Paris: Jean Richer, 1614); Anon., Les satyres bastardes et autres oeuvres folastres du Cadet Angoulevent (Paris: B. A. et Cabinet de M. P. Louÿs, 1615); Anon., Recueil des plus excellans vers satyriques (Paris: Anthoine Estoc, 1617); Anon., Le Cabinet satyrique ou recueil parfaict des vers piquans et gaillards de ce temps (Paris: Anthoine Estoc, 1618), with editions in 1619, 1620, 1621, 1623 [misprinted as 1613], and 1632 (printed in Rouen). Subsequent editions appeared in 1666, 1667, 1700, 1859, and 1864; Anon., Les Delices satyrique [sic] ou suite du cabinet des vers Satyriques de ce Temps (Paris: Anthoine de Sommaville, 1620); Anon., Le Parnasse des Poëtes satyriques (n. p. [Paris?]: no pub., 1622), with editions in 1623, 1625, 1627, and 1633 under slightly variant titles; Anon., La Quint-Essence satyrique, ou seconde partie, du Parnasse des Poetes Satyriques de nostre temps (Paris: Anthoine de Sommaville, 1622); and Le second livre des délices de la poesie françoise Ou, nouveau recueil des plus beaux Vers de ce temps (Paris: Toussainct du Bray, 1620). Many poets appear in multiple volumes, and poems (sometimes attributed, sometimes anonymous) are reused frequently. For details, see Lachèvre, Les Recueils collectives de poesies libres.

[77]   See for instance Benoît L'Hoest, L'Amour enfermé. Sentiment et sexualité à la Renaissance (Paris: Olivier Orban, 1990), 194.

[78]   Roger Thompson, Unfit for Modest Ears (London: Macmillan, 1979), ix–x.

[79]   François Rabelais, Pantagruel, in Œuvres complètes, ed. Mirelle Huchon (Paris: Gallimard, 1994), chs. 21–2 (p. 291–7).

that, writing was broadly erotic, he maintains, rather than pornographic. Maintaining that pornography is about sex without other representational frames, Moulton sees the explicit writings of early modernity as far too embedded in context to qualify for the single-minded purpose of pornography.[80] On Moulton's terms, the lascivious poetry that French Renaissance poets produced does not qualify as pornography, and might be considered erotic. But seeing dirty poetry as primarily erotic diminishes the startling impact of its highly charged sexual politics. These poems are saturated with concerns about masculinity, feminine agency, and sexual desire. The dirty poems feature an obsessive focus on pleasure, frankly sexual attention to body parts, and contestation over sexual power. Often these are presented as resolutions to some of the problems raised by the tamer erotic poetry corpus that was "respectable." That is, the unresolved anxieties around male control over corporeal indeterminacy, about the truth of unrequited love, and concerning male self-restraint were addressed in poems that foregrounded physicality and virility as sexual achievement. Dirty poetry exposes sexual practices to public scrutiny in a collective process that is not erotic, but is powerful enough to define sexual performance from a variety of angles.

French poets, like their Italian and English counterparts in the Renaissance, wrote many forms of dirty poetry. Scatology, class transgression, and religious satire all figure prominently. This common tradition was the result of the circulation of joke collections, or *facetiae*. Giovanni Francesco Poggio Bracciolini's collection, published in 1450 in Latin, was translated at least twice into French between 1514 and 1525, again in 1549, and once more in 1574.[81] Other collections circulated as well. Ludovico Carbone composed and circulated his *Facezie* between 1466 and 1471, although it remained in manuscript. Barbara Bowen notes that the *Facecies et motz subtilz* (1559) is considered the first vernacular joke collection generated originally in French, although it was preceded by compilations appended to other texts.[82] Often focused on sexual pursuits, jokes used stereotypes and satire to skewer the sexual antics of their subjects.

[80] Ian Frederick Moulton, *Before Pornography: Erotic Writing in Early Modern England* (Oxford University Press, 2000). Part of Moulton's purpose is to locate pornography in historically specific terms as a way of moving past the feminist "sex wars." The feminist literature pro and contra is vast. For an introduction, see Drucilla Cornell, ed., *Feminism and Pornography* (Oxford University Press, 2000).

[81] There are indications of a printed edition in French in the 1490s, but it is now lost. On it and the other French editions, see Guillaume Tardiff, *Les Facecies de Poge: Traduction du "Liber facetiarum" de Poggio Bracciolini*, ed. Frédéric Duval and Sandrine Hériché-Pradeau (Geneva: Droz, 2003), 53–7. Poggio is discussed in David O. Frantz, *Festum Voluptatis: A Study of Renaissance Erotica* (Columbus, OH: Ohio State University Press, 1989), 10–27.

[82] Ludovico Carbone, *Facezie e Dialogo de la partita soa*, ed. Gino Ruozzi (Bologna: Commissione per i Testi de Lingua, 1989). Barbara C. Bowen, ed., *One Hundred Renaissance Jokes: An Anthology* (Birmingham, AL: Summa Publications, 1988), 16–19, includes a few of Carbone's jokes. For the *Facecies*, see pp. 87–9.

Women were insatiable, husbands were stupid, and intercourse caused all manner of (humorous) trouble. Bawdy jokes insisted that sex (whether attempted or achieved) made its practitioners ridiculous. The dirty poetry of late-sixteenth-century France took themes and tonal cues from the *facetiae*. Scatological subjects – "La constipé de la cour," for instance, satirizes the pursuit of patronage by analogy to seeking a reliable purgative – abound.[83] In one of the many poems that feature class transgressions, a young man (entering from behind) hurries to penetrate the maid, only to have her comment when he finishes that he aimed too high.[84] Nor was class antagonism the only social problem on display. Etienne Jodelle's "Epitaphe du membre viril de frere Pierre" decries clerical incontinence by recounting how the ostensibly celibate Pierre used his penis to death.[85]

Attacks on sexual misbehavior of all sorts figure prominently, but the story of this chapter is French poets taking on the Petrarchan lie about chaste desire. Instead of painful non-consummation and despairing desire, poets offered sexual fulfillment and virile achievement. The dirty version of the love poem made a virtue of the Petrarchan detritus of desire. Getting the girl, or sometimes the boy, enabled the poet to reassert mastery over the conditions of sexual expression. Of course, with mastery came subversions of a new order, but first things first.

Dirty poems often derived their humor from twisting the standard tropes derived from the Petrarchan vocabulary of love. A sonnet entitled, "Pour escrire dessus le luth d'une damoiselle," rewrites the *blason*, the association of Petrarchan sonnets with music, and specific intertextual references to love poems featuring lute playing:

Sy vostre main blanche et legere	If your hand, white and nimble
Anime et donne au luth la voix,	Animates and gives the lute its voice,
Jugez ce qu'elle pourroit faire	You judge what she could do with an
D'un instrument que de bois.	instrument made of wood.
Croyez, belle menestriere,	Believe, beautiful minstrelless,
Pendant que vous avez le choix,	while you have the choice,
Remuez un peu le derriere,	Arouse a little the derriere,
Et non pas sy souvent les doigts.	And not so often the fingers.
Le luth pour un temps vous peut plaire,	The lute for a time can please you,

---

[83] Anon., *Cabinet satyrique*, vol. II, 161–4.

[84] Anon., *Cabinet satyrique*, vol. II, 225–6. Other class-based satires include, "Contre une vieille riche," and "Panégire de l'amour des chambrières," in Anon., *Satyres bastardes*, 24–5, 100–2.

[85] Jodelle, *Œuvres complètes*, vol. II, 428–31. Jodelle was reasonably well connected. In 1553, his play, *Cléopatre*, was performed before Henri II at Rheims. See Pasquier, *Recherches de la France*, fol. 233v. Jodelle also wrote *Le Recueil des inscriptions, figures, devises, et masquarades*.

Mais ce plaisir ne dure guiere:	But the pleasure will not last forever:
Il ennuye et lasse par fois;	It bores and fatigues sometimes;
Mais un V. fait tout le contraire,	But a cock is always to the contrary,
Car son entretien ordinaire	Because everyday maintenance of it
Faict que les ans semblent des mois.	Makes the years seem like months.[86]

Playfully inverting the usually transitory (sex) and transcendent (good music), the move from hands on the musical instrument to hands on the sexual instrument invokes Pontus de Tyard's "Chant a son luth," in which the speaker offers a *blason* of his beloved. Tyard's telos is Petrarchan lack of fulfillment:

Tout ce parfait que l'honnesteté cele.	All this perfection which honesty conceals.
Que craintif j'ayme et sans espoir desire.	That I love fearfully and desire without hope.[87]

Unlike the unconsummated original, love in the dirty version depends on the fulfillment of sexual desire. Sex, rather than lack of it, will make love last. An epigram puts the relationship between love and sex succinctly:

Amour est une affection	Love is an affection, which enters the
Qui par les yeux dans le coeur entre,	heart through the eyes. Then, by a
Puis, par une defluction,	de-inflammation, a movement of blood
S'escoule par le bas du ventre.	down or away that flows out by the
	base of the belly.[88]

The medical connotations of the language enable the physicality expressed to undermine the notion that the lover who looks but does not touch is necessarily chaste. One immediate and no doubt intended result was that "straight" poems that dwelt on the beloved's physical beauty no longer looked so innocent.

Strategic deployment of a brief trope could destabilize the presumptions of love poetry. An epigram by Pierre Motin described the "beaux yeux" of the speaker's mistress coaxing his penis out like a snail emerging from its shell.[89] The choice of the eyes evokes both the Neoplatonic emphasis on sight as crucial for salvation (but here, for physical deliverance) and standard Petrarchan

---

[86] Sieur de Regnier, "Pour escrire dessus le luth d'une mademoiselle," in Anon., *Cabinet satyrique*, vol. I, 48–9.

[87] Tyard, *Les Erreurs amoureuses*, part 2, "Chant à son luth," 246–8, ll. 47–8. From *Continuation des Erreurs amoureuses* (Lyon: Jean de Tournes, 1551). At least one modern commentator has seen Tyard's version as teetering on the brink of parody. See Lecercle, *Chimère de Zeuxis*, 133. See also Ronsard, *Œuvres complètes*, vol. I, 962 (Ode XXX, "A son lut"). Ronsard, like Tyard, was the musician. In Ronsard's version, he seeks poetic inspiration to praise Cassandra by dispensing with all other subjects.

[88] Sieur de Regnier, in Anon., *Cabinet satyrique*, vol. I, 72 (untitled).

[89] Pierre Motin, "Epigramme," in Anon., *Cabinet satyrique*, vol. I, 58. Pierre Motin (1566?–1613?) was a friend of Regnier, Berthelot, and Sigognes. See Frédéric Lachèvre, *Le Libertinage au XVIIe siècle*, 11 vols. (Paris: Champion, 1909–1924), vol. V, 308.

178   The Sexual Culture of the French Renaissance

language. Another trope takes a cue from the poets who questioned Petrarch's veracity. This lover swears he is not lying:

Alize, ma chere verveille,
Sur mon ame, je ne ments pas
Quand je vous dis que vos appas
Font que jamais je ne sommeille;
Que si, malgré tous les propos
Tesmoins de mon peu de repos,
Vous croyez que je dissimule:
Couchez ceste nuict avec moy,
Et vous verrez, belle incredulle,
Combien je suis digne de foy.

Alice, my lively dear, on my soul, I do not lie when I tell you that your charms are such that I never sleep; that yet, despite all the resolutions, witnesses of my lack of repose, you believe that I dissimulate. Sleep with me tonight, and you will see, beautiful incredulous one, how I am worthy of faith.[90]

Unchastity becomes the marker of truth. Rather than trumpet unfulfilled desire and frustration, the persona offers sex as a demonstration of his veracity. Sex reveals the truth that has been hidden by the insistence on unrequited desire. A different play on this theme featured dishonesty (in the modern sense) leading to satisfaction:

Un bon mary, des meilleurs que l'on face,
Venu de loing plustost qu'il ne devoit,
Sa femme void, dormant de bonne grace,
Qui ses reins frais sur la plume convoit;
Il y prend goust, d'un masque se pourvoit,
Il juche et jouë, elle le trouve doux.
Quand le bon Jean eust tiré ses grands
     coups,
Se demasqua; lors, le voyant, la belle:
Et: qu'est cecy, mon mary, ce dit-elle,
Je pensois bien que fust autre que vous.

A good husband, one of the best that one could fashion, coming from far away where he could not see his wife, found her sleeping gracefully on the feather bed such that his fresh loins lusted after her. To acquire a taste, he supplied himself with a mask. He perched and played, she found it sweet. When the good Jean had taken his great strokes, he demasked; then, seeing him, the beautiful one said: "Is that you, my husband? I was certain it was someone other than you."[91]

The joke is partly about cuckoldry because the wife is expecting her lover, but the husband becomes the (good) lover by donning the mask. Masquerade, Joan Riviere points out, allows the individual to be who s/he really is.[92] Riviere's context is different – she is interested in exploring the ways that wearing femininity is how women construct themselves as women in psychoanalytic terms – but the concept helps articulate how the story functions. The joke works because the husband is able to be the good lover because the wife does not know

[90] Motin, untitled, in *Cabinet satyrique*, vol. I, 81.
[91] Anon., untitled, in *Les Satyres bastardes* (1615), 178.
[92] Joan Riviere, "Womanliness as Masquerade," in *Female Sexuality: Contemporary Engagements*, ed. Donna Bassin (London and Northvale, NJ: Jason Aronson, 1999), 127–37. (Originally 1927.)

it is him. The double "because" is not sloppy, but rather, structurally necessary. Masquerade succeeds because the person in the mask adopts the behaviors and the person confronted with the assumed identity will accept them only under the false conditions. The result of the fiction is truth: the husband becomes the identity he assumes.

Most sexually explicit poetry concerned with honesty worked more simply. One common joke was to move a seemingly idealized encounter toward sexual fulfillment. A sonnet that begins with kissing rapidly becomes tongue-kissing: "S'entre-meslent les langues dans la bouche" [Intermingling of their tongues in the mouth]. Bodies in the abstract start engaging in physical play ("Flanc dessus flanc, redoubler escarmouche . . . On soit saisy d'un doux ravissement" [Thigh upon thigh, redoubling the skirmish . . . One is well seized with a sweet ravishment]). Whether or not true love is involved, the poem ends with pen-etration: "Dedans son C. j'ay mis mon V. refait, / Je suis lasché, ne l'ay-je pas foutue?" [In her cunt I have left my cock set up / I am wanton, have I not fucked you?][93] Sensuality and ease of satisfaction replace the tortured expressions of self-restraint in the name of unrequited love and obviate con-cerns about consummation. Sex is not a problem, and it could be a positive social good. A poem that opened, "Chacun . . . ut à sa guise, et le peuple de France / Repeuple tous les jours tant de bourgs desolez" [Each fucks in his way, and the French people / repopulate every day in the desolated towns]. Some-times the imagery is blunt: "Ores, tous C. sous C. et chaque V. s'y plonge" [From the edge, all cocks in cunts and each prick plunges itself]. Elsewhere in the poem, it is more metaphorical: "V. qui n'a desdaigné, d'une masle pointure, / Enfoncer les cachots de ceste ample jointure" [Prick which has no disdain for a male pointer, / Thrust in the secret places of this ample joint]. Recurring to the theme of populating empty places, the author allows that one should "s'eslance à l'adventure, / Quatre fois, voire cinq" [rush to adventure, / Four times, maybe five].[94] Lingering descriptions are not the preferred mode. References to pricks, cocks, cunts, and asses do the abbreviated work of establishing the sexual context. Brevity is part of the point: achieving physical union need not be arduous.

Achievement, moreover, was good for the male ego battered by Petrarchan conceits that featured submission to female whims. The explicit versions of love poetry tropes allowed masculine failures to be revised. Loss of self-control becomes instead the triumph of sexual prowess. In "Voeu d'une dame à Venus," a woman prays for "ce gros Priape carnu" which will "d'une abondante liqueur, / M'arouser le flanc er le coeur" [this large Priapic flesh . . . by an abundant

---

[93] BN MS 884, fols. 234v–235r.
[94] Anon., "Fantaisie," in Anon., *Cabinet satyrique*, vol. II, 206–9, esp. 207–8.

Figure 14. Engraving after Guilio Romano (1499–1546), associated with
Pietro Aretino, *I Sonetti Lussuriosi di Pietro Aretino* (1524).
    While this particular image is from the eighteenth century, it is a depiction
based on the sixteenth-century engravings that Romano made and for which
Pietro Aretino wrote lascivious sonnets. The combination of words and pic-
tures was quite notorious, and many versions, all more or less based on the
original engravings, circulated widely.

liquor, will arouse my womb and my heart].[95] While reworking the idea that all women are lusty, this poem appears in a collection dedicated to skewering the pieties of unrequited love. Another features a male speaker crowing about his ability to do it ten times a night.[96] The combat lost in Petrarchan love poetry is won, and handily, in the explicit version of the amorous encounter:

Mais à quoy sert tant de finesse	But what is the point of so much finesse,
Qui tend rien qu'à m'abuser?	which tends at nothing but
Car, après tout, belle maistresse,	self-deception? Because, after all,
Mon V. n'est point à refuser.	beautiful mistress, my dick is by no
	means to be refused.

The poetic persona exclaims that he, elided syntactically with his penis, is "Brave, courageux, et vaillant" [Brave, courageous, and valiant]. He/it will rise to the touch, enjoying the "combat." In fact:

Son escrime est toujours gaillarde	His sword is always lusty
Il n'est jamais las ny perclus,	It is never soft nor impotent,
Et fait dire à la plus paillarde:	And makes the most wanton woman say:
Monsieur le V., je n'en plus rien!	Mr. Penis, I don't want anything
	more![97]

The poet conflates the poetic persona and himself through the appropriation of the penis within the epideictic idiom. The poetry of praise is turned onto the self, or onto the part of the self that defines masculine sexual accomplishment.

Foregrounded as it is, is the penis a synecdoche for the male body or for the masculine poetic persona, or perhaps both? The subjectivity of the (male) poet is at issue in the context of the claims made for masculine prowess through sex. Again, this is not about modern subjectivity as a matter of sexual identity, but it is an argument about the construction of versions of the self through poetic practice. Literary critics have seen early modern sonnet sequences as especially fertile ground for such construction. Joel Fineman, for instance, argues that William Shakespeare "invents a genuinely new poetic subjectivity" with his sonnets by disrupting the "normative nature of poetic person and poetic persona."[98] An often brilliant argument, Fineman's premise is that, through the paradox of praise, Shakespeare's sonnets develop a new first-person subjectivity out of the rather tired Petrarchan tradition: "[T]he poetry of praise inscribes upon the ego of the praising poet the specific features of its ideal ego, and this epideictic ego ideal entails specific psychological

---

[95] Anon., *Cabinet satyrique*, vol. I, 132–3. This poem is anonymous.

[96] Sieur de Maynard, untitled, in Anon., *Cabinet satyrique*, vol. I, 54–5.

[97] Motin, "Stances," in Anon., *Cabinet satyrique*, vol. II, 204–5.

[98] Joel Fineman, *Shakespeare's Perjured Eye: The Invention of Poetic Subjectivity in the Sonnets* (Berkeley: University of California Press, 1986), 1.

Figure 15. Engraving after Guilio Romano (1499–1546), associated with Pietro Aretino, *I Sonetti Lussuriosi di Pietro Aretino* (1524).

Images such as this one reflect the association of some love poetry with promiscuity and sex by the later sixteenth century. The trope of two lovers embracing is rendered in lascivious terms by the frank depiction of the genitals in an aroused state.

consequences for the character or the characterology of the praising poet."[99] While Fineman sees Shakespeare as the originary moment in creating a new poetic subjectivity, a version of this reconfiguration is evident in the French poems that take on the problem of masculine performance in the Petrarchan tradition. Poets who assert poetic agency through corporeal achievement fuse subjectivity and sexuality in response to Petrarchan norms that resisted articulation.

Lest this story sound like a triumph of male subject formation, the process was not without serious complications. For one thing, the reworking of the epidiectic tradition involved a move that made masculine sexuality interdependent with female corporeality. Explicit poetry reworked the focus on the female body, not simply by inverting the terms (a negative portrait paired with a positive one) or by shifting from female to male as the primary object. French poets moved toward explicit description of the penis. Recall that, in 1553, Ronsard wrote of "his" gold-tipped lance. The metaphor was both coy and obvious. By 1617, an epigram, probably by François Maynard, described a friend's penis as "Un V. de deux pieds et demy / Qui . . ut six coups tout d'une haleine"[100] [A penis of two and a half feet / Which comes six times full of wind]. Usually veiled in visual or poetic imagery, the penis is revealed – or almost revealed, as many poets resort to the transparent abbreviation, "V." – in rewriting Petrarchan corporeal representation.[101]

The evasions were mild, however, and the graphic physicality was insistent. Akin to the anatomical *blason*, the explicit poems collectively *blason* the fit between penis and vagina. One poem announces that the speaker's penis is so large that no matter how big the woman, he will feel tight. Another makes fun of small ones lost in cavernous "cunts."[102] In Pierre Motin's poem, the speaker likes a large vagina:

J'ayme les C. les belles marges,	I love cunts with beautiful scope,
Les grands C. qui sont gros et larges.	The great cunts which are big and wide.
Où je m'enfonce à mon plaisir.	Where I bury myself to my pleasure.
Les C. si estroits de closture	Cunts with tight closings
Mettent un V. à la torture.	Are torture for a dick.

In response, a second poem answers:

---

[99] Fineman, *Shakespeare's Perjured Eye*, 14.

[100] Anon., *Cabinet satyrique*, vol. I, 50. The poem is anonymous, but has been identified for stylistic reasons with Maynard.

[101] Commenting on the lack of attention to the penis in their own volume, David Hillman and Carla Mazzio suggest that the absent presence is worth taking seriously. See David Hillman and Carla Mazzio, eds., *The Body in Parts: Fantasies of Corporeality in Early Modern Europe* (New York and London: Routledge, 1997), xx.

[102] Sigognes, "Stances," in Anon., *Cabinet satyrique*, vol. I, 56–7.

Ces grands C. dont vous faites feste,	The great cunts of which you celebrate,
Qui ont oreille et double creste,	Which have ears and double crests,
Ne me viennent point à plaisir;	Do not give me my pleasure;
J'ayme ces C. de fine sarge . . .	I love cunts of fine serge . . .

The poems argue over the superiority of plenty of space versus the pleasures of a tight fit.[103] Another sonnet maintains that a tight vagina, "Donne appetit de foutre" [Gives an appetite to fucking]; while the subsequent epigram moans, "Qu'un V. moindre qu'un festu / Y seroit à la torture" [That a prick less than a pin makes for torture].[104] The poetics of consummation provided a new space for competitive creation.

Rewriting the Petrarchan narrative to include consummation meant that men had to perform well. Prowess mattered in the doing and in the writing. But achievement and accomplishment in sex were tricky. Who gets to say if the man has sexual prowess? The issue of "fit" in poetic discourse puts under stress the long-standing (and decidedly gentle on most male egos) medical wisdom that a medium-sized penis is best. Physicians maintained that too small a penis inhibited delivery of semen into the womb.[105] Large penises, medical texts claimed, allowed the sperm to cool too much before it reached the womb. In a clear violation of moderation described by Todd W. Reeser as the dominant principle behind masculinity, in the poems, bigger is better.[106] One poem insists that fecundity depends on size: "Vous eussiez eu de la semance / D'un V. dont la grandeur immence" [You have had semen / From a prick whose size is enormous].[107] At once satirizing moderation and asserting dominance, the size question points to a double anxiety lurking close to the surface: the obvious one about measuring up, but also the fear that for women, size might be a matter of taste. The woman, lusty though she presumably is, might not be willing, an outcome that causes one poet to pronounce: "Car, après tout, belle maistresse, / Mon vit n'est point à refuser" [Because after all, beautiful mistress, / My prick is not to be refused]. Descriptions of his well-shaped, ever-ready, always courteous penis follow.[108] Methinks the poet doth protest too much.

One cannot be sure that such bluster is symptomatic of anxiety, but collectively, the poems rehearse so many modes of failure that the insistence on prowess becomes suspicious. Men who put their penises in the wrong place or

---

[103] Anon., *Cabinet satyrique*, vol. I, 67–8.

[104] Anon., "Sonnet," and Motin, "Epigramme sur Jeanne" in Anon., *Cabinet satyrique*, vol. I, 70–1.

[105] Jacques Bury, *Le Propagatif de l'Homme et secours des femmes en travail d'enfant* (Paris: Chez Melchior Mondiere 1623), 29.

[106] Reeser, *Moderating Masculinity*.

[107] Maynard, "Stances satyriques contre une courtisane," in Anon., *Cabinet satyrique*, vol. I, 109. See also Anon., "Sur un quidam," in *Satyres bastardes*, 87, in which Priapus is jealous of an especially large penis.

[108] BN MS fr 884, fol. 158r.

did it with the wrong person, invitations to the reader to compare his own organ to the poet's were common. Occasionally, the worry was that perhaps a penis was not necessary at all:

Elle succeroit bien la goutte	She would suck the drop from a big,
De quelque gros V. reboulé,	stroked penis, but I want a cad to fuck
Mais je veux qu'un goujat la . . . te	her with a peeled cucumber.[109]
Avec un concombre pelé.	

Despite its vindictive rage, this poem allows that artificial means were available – apparently in any kitchen that could afford fresh vegetables. This knowledge was not welcome. Poets found self-sufficiency among women, whether masturbatory or lesbian, unsettling. Pontus de Tyard claimed he could not imagine the idea of female intimacy in the course of a long poem about two women in love. He insisted he could recount plenty of examples of men with other men; cited love between men when it served higher Neoplatonic ends approvingly; and love between a man and woman, he allowed, was commonplace. A woman in love with a woman, however, was at least an oddity:

Mais d'une femme à femme, il ne se trouve encor	But a woman with a woman, one does not still find this
Souz l'empire d'Amour un si riche thresor.	A so rich treasure under the empire of Love.

In the manner of the kettle defense, Tyard allows that, in any case, women in love with each other interfered with finding love that could save the soul. Love between women is counter to love, and causes the woman beloved by a man to "embrase une autre ardeur" [embrace another ardor].[110] The Neoplatonist Tyard sees same-sex female love as perverting the possibility of (heterosexual) transcendence through desire.

Tyard articulates a version of the antipathy toward female–female erotics that Valerie Traub has analyzed in the English Renaissance. Traub argues that women operating outside the erotic economy of heterosexual patriarchy came to be seen as threatening to prevailing gender dynamics.[111] In Traub's account, "innocent" representations of same-sex female erotics disappeared as medical and legal discourses started labeling transgressive individuals

---

[109] Sigognes, "Epigramme," in Anon., *Cabinet satyrique*, vol. I, 193. Pierre de L'Estoile recorded many explicit ditties posted around Paris during the reign of Henri III, including one that ended with a reference to a dildo: "Sapho et Sodome revit / Un gaudemichi et un vit." See Pierre de L'Estoile, *Journal pour le règne de Henri III*, ed. Louis-Raymond Lefèvre (Paris: Gallimard, 1943), 435 (Pièces diverses).

[110] Pontus de Tyard, "Elégie pour une dame enamourée d'une autre dame," in *Œuvres poétiques complètes*, ed. John C. Lapp (Paris: Librairie Marcel Didier, 1966), 246–50, ll. 65–6, 89.

[111] Traub, *Renaissance of Lesbianism*.

as hermaphrodites, tribades, or female sodomites. In England, amidst acute concern over heterosexual chastity, female–female intimacy was initially regarded as protecting chaste women from sexual contact with men. But fears about the misuse or abuse of female pleasure, particularly after the "redis-covery" of the clitoris by anatomists, coalesced into assumptions that women would infringe on male sexual prerogatives. While criminality was usually reserved for cases that insistently outraged communal norms, tacit approval of same-sex female erotics disappeared from view.[112] In keeping with Traub's argument, female homoeroticism in medical texts, travel narratives, and imag-inative literature (which Tyard or his poetic persona apparently missed) is plainly evident.[113] Tyard is among those who worked to turn same-sex female desire into monstrosity.

What if a penis was necessary or at least useful, but women were not? Sodomy was supposed to be a terrible thing, but one poet noticed it provided much pleasure:

Fouté Bouches, Culs, Cons, et d'une main lubrique,	Fucking mouths, asses, butts, and by a lubricious hand given you by Venus
Donnés vous de Venus le savoureux Plaisir...	the savory pleasure . . . I know that you
Je sçai que vous dires que le Grand Juppiter	say that the great Jupiter does nothing in heaven but fuck asses and cunts, and
Ne fait rien dans le Ciel que Culs et Cons fouter,	that for all this, he does not lose his crown.
Et que pour tout cela il ne perd sa Couronne.	

Despite the gesture toward heterosexual copulation, sodomy is the problem. By way of condemnation: "Vostre Semance chet en terre qui n'est bonne" [Your semen dumped on the ground is not good].[114] This poem, one of many recorded by Pierre de L'Estoile attacking Henri III and his favorites, excoriated sodomy. Poets linked political power and sexual corruption through sodomy, and yet, suggestions of pleasure break through the negative rhetoric. The appeal of men to other men meant that women might be left out. The Bacchantae who dismembered Orpheus come to mind when the poet notes that sodomites burned with desire for men, "Et que feront les pauvres femmes?" [And what will

---

[112] On the criminality of homosexuality, see for instance Tom Betteridge, ed., *Sodomy in Early Modern Europe* (Manchester University Press, 2002), and Puff, *Sodomy in Reformation Germany and Switzerland, 1400–1600*. While the rhetoric was dire and punishments for those convicted were brutal, carrying through was not terribly common.

[113] See for instance the homoerotic self-sufficiency of Muslim women described in Sébastien Münster, *Cosmographie Universelle de Tout le Monde*, trans. François Belleforest, 3 vols. (Paris: Michel Sonnius, 1575), vol. III, 1208–9. Originally 1556.

[114] BN MS n. a. f. 6888, p. 136 (marginal note to the long poem). For other poems condemning (presumed) male homosexual sodomy at court, see pp. 85–9, 128, 131, 137, 158.

the poor women do]?[115] An anonymous epigram entitled "Un soupçonné de sodomie" [One suspected of sodomy] suggested that "Antoine" should conceal his desire more effectively:

Antoine, je ne sçai pourquoi Tu escris souvent au femelles, Mais je sçai que pas une d'elles N'a point affaire aveques toy.	Antoine, I do not know why you write often to women, but I know that not one of them has had an affair with you.[116]

A man who desires other men is not necessarily a problem, but not wanting women had to be disguised. Negative representations allowed and feared that sodomy had its attractions. One poet described sodomy as "contre les loix de Nature" [against the laws of nature], but confessed that in doing it: "Vous plongez dedans leurs délices" [You plunge amidst its delights]. The concern again is that the lover will quit women altogether. In another poem, a man who wants another man is effeminate: "Prenez la robbe d'une femme / Puis que vous en avez le coeur"[117] [Take the dress of a woman / Because you already have the heart of one]. The gender politics of sodomy meant that men who engaged in it, especially men who sought it out, were overly sexual and hence like women. "Contre les sodomites" opens, "Sodomite enrage, ennemi de nature" [Enraged sodomite, enemy of nature] and goes on to depict the man who seeks satisfaction from other men as weak and dependent.[118] Sodomites were marked by sexual excess – a typically feminine trait in Renaissance culture.[119] While discussing sodomy revealed it, poets structured radical condemnations to dissuade men from risking their masculinity.

At the same time, heterosexual love discourse needed protection from heterosexuals. Earnest lovers cheated. Wives and fiancées made men into cuckolds apparently at the drop of a hat. Echoing Panurge's concerns that drove him to consult an astrologer in the opening of Chapter 2, one poem observed that many were dubious about marriage because they feared getting cuckolded. Fear turned men into beasts, made them sick, caused them to become jealous fools, and ruined all happiness.[120] A sonnet entitled "Remede pour le cocuage" encouraged the reader to let go of the fear because cuckoldry was inevitable:

---

[115] Sieur de B., "Epigramme," in Anon., *Cabinet satyrique*, vol. I, 223.
[116] Anon., *Le Cabinet secret du Parnasse*, ed. Louis Perceau, 3 vols. (Paris: Au Cabinet du livre, 1928–1932), vol. I, 235.
[117] Sigognes, "Satyre," in Anon., *Cabinet satyrique*, vol. I, 224. See similarly Sigognes, "Satyre contre un courtisan à barbe rasée," vol. I, 280–6, in which an overly fastidious courtier is called Ganymede and likened to an hermaphrodite. Esp. p. 283; BN MS fr 884, fol. 49r.
[118] Anon., *Quint-Essence satyrique* (1622), 277.
[119] See the discussion in Reeser, *Moderating Masculinity*, 187–214.
[120] See for instance BN MS fr 884, fol. 49r; Anon., *Cabinet satyrique*, vol. I, 296–8: Sigognes, "Stances sur la crainte du cocuage."

"Les cornes, pour certain, suyvent le marriage"[121] [Horns, for certain, follow marriage]. In another, the persona understands when Madelon looks for another lover:

Car il faut, pour vray, confesser	Because one must for true confess
Que le navire bransle et flotte	That the ship shakes and flutters
Quand le mast ne peut plus dresser.[122]	When the mast cannot stay erect.

Another, noting the affair of Venus and Mars, commented that if a man marries, his prick will languish or his wife will be too lascivious. He will want to give his wife to the neighbor so he himself can enjoy the chambermaid.[123] The problem with cuckoldry in the poems is not that a father will raise some other man's children; the poems focus on the competition for pleasure. Shame for having been cheated on can be ameliorated by cheating as well. The economy of sexual competition vaults winning over love or marriage.

Cheating was not the only threat to marriage or indeed to (heterosexual) sex. Venereal disease and impotence were well-nigh epidemic, if the dirty poems are an index. Jean-Antoine de Baïf joked that his friend was wise for going back to the brothel so frequently. How better to find the nose he had lost there?[124] Philippe Desportes's nephew, Mathurin Regnier, sardonically referred to venereal disease ("la chaude pisse") as "Une fleche de Cupidon" [A shaft of Cupid].[125] Another poem, "Le Testament d'un vérolé," satirizes a deathbed confession, with the speaker giving away bits of his infected body instead of his worldly goods.[126] Claude d'Esternod's satire features the protagonist seeking relief from recurrent syphilis, by consulting a Jesuit, a doctor of Latin, and a confessor. Repentant and suffering, he is nonetheless enraged that the woman who infected him has been going about her business without interruption.[127] Venereal disease simultaneously proclaimed one's sexual prowess and threatened it. In the competition for masculine supremacy, that would hardly do.

In the combative context of French poetry, impotence was catastrophic. Who wanted the truth to be the collapse of virility? Even reassurances recalled failure:

---

[121] La Roque, "Sonnet," in Anon., *Cabinet satyrique*, vol. I, 298. See also BN MS Dupuy 843, 193r, "Cocuage;" Anon., *Satyres bastardes*, 85–7, 131, 168 for a selection of cuckoldry poems.
[122] Sieur Berthelot, in Anon., *Cabinet satyrique*, vol. I, 294.
[123] Anon., *Cabinet secret*, vol. II, 115–18.
[124] "De Galin," in Anon., *Cabinet secret*, vol. I, 175.
[125] Anon., *Cabinet secret*, vol. II, 16–17. See also "Contre une vielle sempiternelle," in Anon., *Satyres bastardes*, 69–71.
[126] Anon., *Cabinet satyrique*, vol. I, 252–5.   [127] Anon., *Cabinet secret*, vol. II, 168–78.

On se remuë, on se jouë, on se hoche,	One moves, one plays, one shakes oneself,
Puis, quand ce vint au naturel devoir:	Then, this comes to its natural duty
'Ha! dit Catin, le grand degel s'approche,	Ha, says Catin, the great thaw approaches,
— Voire, dit-il, car il s'en va pleuvoir!"	— See, he says, because it is going to rain.[128]

The anxiety is evident in the attempts of the protagonist in a poem attributed to Rémy Belleau to excuse and explain. The poem features a man in despair when, after extensive foreplay,

Mon V. faict le poltroon, estant en mesme sorte	My prick makes like a coward, being of the same kind
Qu'un boyau replié de quelque chevre morte:	as a gut filled with some dead goat;
Bref, il reste perclus, morne, lasche, et faquin.	In brief, it rests, an impotent, dejected, slack rascal.

Previously, he swears, he never had a problem, but now his penis is "couard et craintif" [cowardly and fearful]. He is like a cannon without a ball, "un manche sans marteau, un mortier sans pilon, un navire sans mast" [a handle without a hammer, a mortar without a pestle, a ship without a mast]. Embarrassed, he imagines it will only be good for pissing.[129] Temporary inability indicated permanent failure to come. Florent Chrestien penned a long poem in which a young woman at court tries to overcome the impotence of her elderly lover. Excited by his advancement at court, she tries to arouse him to no avail:

Bruloit mes yeux; ses bras, blancs comme albastre,	My eyes burn; her arms like alabaster,
M'embrassoient tout, et ses embrassemens	Kiss me all over, and her embraces
M'estoient, hélas! autant d'embrazemens.	They are to me, alas, so many conflagrations.

She tries masturbating him and lying on the bed naked, but in the end, "Me laissant là et haïssant du tout / Le V. qui meurt et qui faut par le bout" [They leave me there and hating everything / the prick which dies, and by the end, must].[130] The danger in the poems is not to heterosexual propriety, but to successful satisfying consummation. Non-consummation is not about Petrarchan love; it is mechanical failure.

---

[128] Marot, "Epigramme," in Anon., *Cabinet satyrique*, vol. I, 164.
[129] Belleau, "Impuissance," in Anon., *Cabinet satyrique*, vol. I, 273–6.
[130] BN MS fr 1662, fols. 16v–20r, "D'une Courtisanne Greque sur l'impuissance d'un vieil Ambassadeur François;" also in Anon., *Cabinet secret*, vol. I, 220–31.

Perhaps the most subversive rewriting of the Petrarchan tradition was the deliberate mocking of the narrative construction of poetic subjectivity that occurred through the sonnet sequence. The starkest example of this is Etienne Jodelle's sonnet sequence, which destabilizes the Petrarchan persona of the lover in radical ways. Jodelle's brief, ten-poem sequence includes several themes that have marked the contested sexual politics of French Renaissance love poetry. Instead of ruminating on unrequited love, the first poem indicates the locus of satisfaction which eludes the Petrarchan lover: "Bague fatale atteinte de la Lance, / Mise en l'arrest de deux pertuis marbrins" [Fatal ring attacked by the lance, / Made in the suspension of two marbled openings]. Jodelle sets the tone with clear references to Petrarchan language: his sapling ("planson") is "doucement furieux" [sweetly furious] and in the *blason* tradition, it is the colors of "corail et d'ivoire" [coral and ivory]. Entering his lover is "mon plaisant travail" [my pleasant travail].[131] The second sonnet utilizes the combat metaphor, but alters its trajectory. The opening feels like a standard reference to love as combat:

En quelle nuict, de ma lance d'ivoire,	In which night, from my ivory lance /
Au mousse bout corail rougissant.	With the foam tip reddening coral
Pourrai-je ouvrir ce bouton languissant,	Can I open this languid knob / In the
En la saison de sa plus grande gloire?	season of his most great glory
Quand verserai-je, au bout de ma victoire.	When will I pour out, leading up to my victory.

But instead of conquest, the speaker finds that he needs the woman to complete the experience: "Puisse elle tost à bonne heure venir" [She can come soon at a good hour] (Sonnet 2). Paradox marks the next sonnet, in which the speaker is at once on fire and refreshed by his desire because of his "douce lancette" [sweet lancet]. Where Sonnet 3 ends with the speaker waiting for the "la lutte tresbuchée" [stumbling struggle], Sonnet 4 opens with an imperative: "Touche de main mignonne, frétillarde" [Mignon, touch my wriggling thing with your hand]. This is followed by instructions for masturbating him: "Pince et blandist mainte corde à l'entour, / Et l'animant d'agile brusque tour" [Pinch and caress now the cord around / and animate it with an agile, brusque turn]. Once he comes, he settles for a "long repos" [long rest] (Sonnet 4). Sonnet 5 uses the metaphor of the ship at sea, here reworked so that he drops his anchor "en son port favorable" [in a favorable port]. Ejaculation ("C. qui va distillant une moiteuse colle" [Cunt that releases a moist paste]) and satisfaction turn into concern over performance in Sonnet 6. The speaker knows that any well-endowed man will satisfy his beloved, while "petit bagage" will not be received.

[131] Etienne Jodelle, *Œuvres complètes*: I: *Le Poète chez les hommes*, ed. Enea Balmas, 2 vols. (Paris: Gallimard, 1965), vol. I, 431–2. Five of them are in BN MS fr 1662, fols. 20r–21r. All the quotations in this paragraph are from the Balmas edition, pp. 431–6.

Jodelle's dismissal of the under-endowed is not convincing. The problem with consummation is that anyone can do it. The specificities of the Petrarchan romance drop away. Interchangeability means the ambivalence is acute: The speaker is aware that it does not matter whose penis satisfies a woman's wanton desires. He consoles himself with the knowledge that he did, which means he is large and capable. Performance may not be enough, however. In Sonnet 7, in which sex results in venereal disease ("Bosses Chancreuses, / Pisses chaudes . . . ou vérolles rongeuses" [Battered chancres, / syphilis, or gnawing pox]). These are the flowers of dirty sex, and they are "pour garir Sathan quand il se sent malade" [for healing Satan when he feels sick]. Lest this be taken as a moral tale about the superiority of chaste love, the speaker suggests the discomfort is worth it. Rejecting the notion that sexual pleasure is only for procreation, the eighth sonnet says there is honor in being a good whore:

| D'estre chaude, lassive, impudique, lubrique, | To be warm, lascivious, impudent, lubricious, |
| Et d'estre à tous venants la pute et le bordeau. | And to be a whore to all comers and at the bordello. |

This, he allows, is natural, but he draws the line at sodomy:

| Mais de prester le C . . . l au bougre sodomiste, | But to squeeze the cock as a buggering sodomite, |
| Ha, ma foy! par ma foy! cet acte n'est pas beau! | Ha, my faith! by my faith! This act is not beautiful. |

Jodelle is not finished turning Petrarch upside down. The penultimate sonnet is a *countreblason*, in which the woman smells like old cheese. After describing her decrepit and diseased body, the speaker allows that the rest of her, meaning apparently her feet, is beautiful.[132] While neither as elaborate nor as long as other sonnet cycles, Jodelle's sequence has a logic that is emphasized in the closing lines:

| Tant le Ciel, se moquant de l'amour et de moy, | Even Heaven mocks love and me |
| Dévoroit les beaux ans de ma verte jeunesse. | Devouring the beautiful years of my green youth. |

The speaker's desire is requited, he loses his delusions. Love is not transcendent. Desire makes a man fear for his sexual abilities; women are not beautiful and

---

[132] Unlike most painted or written portraits, the speaker deliberately goes below the waist: "En descendent plus bas, un trou sanglant on void, / De peaux moites autour, un landi qui paroist / De chancres revestu, de farcins pleins des bords" [In going lower, one sees a bloody hole, / moist skin around a heath which appears / clothed again in chancres, of sausage filling the edges.] Artists depicted women in baths to frame the body discreetly and maintain some decorum. See for instance Ecole de Fontainebleau, *Gabrielle d'Estrées et une de ses soeurs* (1594).

yet they are irresistible, perhaps especially when the lover has no special attachment to them. Where Ronsard broke apart the Petrarchan devotion to one unconsummated romance with his succession of sonnet sequences to various (mostly unchaste) women, Jodelle created a persona so enmeshed in physicality that love disappeared entirely.

Subjectivity is reduced to the demands of the penis. The speaker's beloved body part gets satisfaction and does so in the vernacular idiom and syntactic frame of Petrarchan love. In true Priapic form, the male speaker creates an architecture of his body centered on his own solipsistic desire. If the *blason* of the female body is a kind of violence, the satirical celebration of the male member is also a sonnet narrative based explicitly on mutation and metamorphosis of the male sex organs. The penis sonnets offer an erotics of function and achievement under the threat of failure in the form of collapse, rejection, disease, or just insufficiency. The truth of the story is not unconsummated love, but how to aspire to arousal and satisfaction knowing that it is always imperiled.

Love, sex; subjection, subjectivity

Sexual performance is far distant from poetic pieties about the health of the chaste soul. The tussle with Petrarch over his veracity resulted in a logic of performative success, and it seeped into French poetic practice. This is not to say that poetry lied before the French took on Petrarch and was entirely honest after the encounter. The French reaction to Petrarch, however, was profoundly corporeal. The commitment to embodied desire as the marker and maker of poetic subjectivity shaped the concern about truth that was a recurrent preoccupation in French Renaissance poetry.

In a sense, the attraction to rational, transcendent love along Neoplatonic lines with its concomitant confusions over beauty and desire facilitated both the French embrace of Petrarch and the almost immediate focus on whether the poet is chaste or lascivious. Many of the intersections of these issues are apparent in a comparison of two poems by Phillipe Desportes. Consider this sonnet:

Si parfaite beauté n'est pas une fontaine	Such perfect beauty is not a fountain
Où chacun puisse aller pour se desalterer.	Where one can go to be quenched of thirst.
Si le plus grand des Dieux vouloit vous adorer,	If the greatest of the gods want to adore you,
Contre luy de fureur mon ame seroit pleine:	Against him the fury of my soul will fall:
Comment donc souffrirois-je une personne humaine?	How then will I suffer as a human being?

Les Rois et les Amans veulent seuls
  demeurer.
Descouvrez à nos yeux quel est vostre
  courage,
Gardant celuy des deux qui vous plaist
  davantage
Sans ainsi feintement l'un et l'autre
  abuser.
J'ayme mieux n'avoir rien, que si j'estois
  le maistre
De la moitié d'un bien qui tout à moy
  doit ester.
Une si belle fleur ne se peut diviser.

Kings and lovers can wish to remain
  alone.
You discover what your courage is to our
  eyes,
Keeping the one of the two who you love
  more
Without so faintly deceiving one another.

I prefer having nothing than if I was the
  master
Of the half of good which ought to be all
  to me.
Such a beautiful flower cannot be
  divided.[133]

Like much love poetry, Desportes deploys familiar imagery. The speaker
employs hyperbolic language of love and standard tropes: Perfect beauty is
a fountain; his soul is in a furor or madness; the gods are his rivals; in the
end, he would rather have nothing than have to share. The poet's articulation
of his desire demonstrates his mastery of his art, and implicitly of his (female)
subject. He is also bound by this love and if not powerless before it, certainly
diminished in his command over the conditions of it. The Petrarchan elements
are evident, but this is also Desportes in his Neoplatonic guise, especially
when he yearns for this love to transcend. As an expression of male prowess –
amorous or poetic – the poem masks its unsettledness. Uncertainty lurks in its
metaphors.

In some ways, then, Desportes is more honest in the modern sense of straightforward and truthful when he describes Lize, whose beauty has faded, in
"Mespris d'une dame devenue vieille:"

En fin, mes voeux sont exaucez:
Lize, tes beaux jours sont passez,
Tu deviens laide et contrefaite;
Le temps ton visage a changé,
Et, ce qui me rend mieux vengé
Tu fais la jeune et la doucette.
Avec des apas degoustans,
Et quelque vieux mot du bon temps,
Tiré d'une bouche blesmie,
Tu pense esveiller nos esprits,
Mais la desdaigneuse Cypris
Prez de toy languit endormie.

Finally, my wishes are granted:
Lise, your beautiful days have passed,
You are becoming ugly and counterfeit;
Time has changed your face,
And, this which renders me more avenged
You play young and sweet.
With disgusting feminine charms,
And some old word of good times
Drawn from a blemished mouth,
You think to enliven our spirits,
But the disdainful Cyprus
Next to you languishes sleeping.

---

[133] Philippe Desportes, *Diverses Amours et autres oeuvres meslées*, ed. Victor E. Graham (Geneva:
Droz, 1963), 17, Sonnet IV, ll. 3–14.

The poem goes on to fill in the suggestions of the first two stanzas. Lise and the speaker were lovers, and Desportes alternates between bucolic imagery of young love and horrified reaction to Lise, now "Mauvaise, inconstante et lascive" [Evil, inconstant, and lascivious].[134] While not the dirtiest of poems, it is explicit about sexual activity and the collapse of sexual desire. It is "bad" in that it is focused on carnal desire and physical responses. It is also honest in its grounding in the corporeal, in its choice to shun steadfast non-consummation as improbable and accept the disappointment of aging and loss. Desportes may not have intended it as a "dirty," "bad" poem – he originally entitled it *Imitation d'Horace* in his *Diverses amours* – but others evidently took it so: It was included in the compilations of dirty poetry that mark the end of this story.[135]

In this story, Petrarch offered much to French poets, as did antiquity. Both ended up as elements in the project of poetic self (and national) creation in which sexual success included achievement and integrity in matters of desire. Desportes uses the poetic persona and his reactions to desire and its fulfillment to define male mastery of the flawed, fungible, persistently irresistible female object. The precariousness of mastery produced by dependence on subjection is built into the sexual choices in both of Desportes's poems. As Renaissance poetry gave way to the controlled containment of the classical, the disciplinary structures that marked that transition displayed their force. Recall that Viau was done to death by his association with dirty poetry and Cardinal de Richelieu's Académie took up linguistic regulation and decorum in part against libertine poetic impulses, in part to carry out the national promise of French language (albeit in rather different form) extolled by the Pléiade. At that point, the physical intimacy in French Renaissance poetry that blurred the line between the "clean" and the "dirty" poems dissipated.

To get from the constraints of Medieval poetics to the new constraints of French language in service of king and country under the Bourbons, Renaissance poets embraced and engaged with the ancient past and the vernacular (near) present. I am not saying that French libertine poetry was only a reaction against Petrarch, but the striving to make the *translatio studii* culminate in France by outdoing Petrarch was central to the dynamic in which caustic, blunt, often misogynous, frequently indecorous and impious, ribald wit became the stuff of sexual subjectivity.

---

[134] Entitled "Mespris d'une dame devenue vieille" in libertine poetry anthologies such as the version in Anon., *Cabinet satyrique*, vol. I, 417–19.
[135] On the original title, see Desportes, *Diverses Amours*, 210–12.

5 Politics, promiscuity, and potency: managing the king's sexual reputation

What about that king in that formulation "king and country?" Kings have hovered mostly in the background thus far. François Habert dedicated his translation of Ovid's *Metamorphoses* to Henri II, François I swooned over the discovery of "Laura's tomb," and Orpheus made appearances on the décor for royal entrée ceremonies. Louys Le Roy addressed his commentary on Plato's *Symposium* to François II and his wife, Mary, Queen of Scots.[1] All the Valois kings engaged with, at times relied on, astrological prediction. And the monarchy (although, as we shall see, not all the Valois kings) benefited from the national claims for French and France within the vibrant culture of the European Renaissance. The management of the sexual forces at play – some of which kings unleashed – amplifies and complicates our story. The central issues in managing the monarch's sexual reputation were circumscriptions around male homosociality, the requirements of productive and reproductive masculine achievement, and the force of sexual polemic as "truth." By the end of this story, normative constraints articulated in Renaissance discussions of the sexual determined the narrow range within which monarchs as different as childless, effeminate, hapless Henri III and promiscuous, manly, opportunistic Henri IV could operate.

The pieces we have seen developing throughout this story determined that range. Renaissance kings used sexualized myth, consulted the stars, relied on Neoplatonic philosophy, and enjoyed (sometimes suffered) poetry in the service of conveying sexual reputation. For kings, this meant presenting themselves as procreatively potent, moderate in their desires and habits, and aggressive as circumstances warranted. Each aspect of the king's sexual reputation was only partly up to the king. Generation was the work of two and subject to the opinions of many. Defining the proper lineaments of moderation depended on external factors that were often in flux. Context determined when martial

---

[1] Le Roy, *Le Sympose de Platon*. Habert similarly dedicated his reflections on the Dauphine as the feminine ideal of heterosexual, Neoplatonic love. See Habert, *La Nouvelle Vénus*, 3–6, 15, for explicit equivalencies. Habert was the first to translate the entire Ovid's *Metamorphoses* into French (see above, Chapter 1). For Orpheus, see Jodelle, *Le Recueil des inscriptions, figures, devises, et masquarades*, fols. 15v–16r.

aggression became a masculine virtue. Add to these difficulties the dynamic of the monarchy's own dialectic in which each king had to grapple with the inheritance of the Renaissance as his predecessors had deployed it.

The argument that follows briefly traces the development of sexual politics around the king in terms of forces put in play by the Renaissance. The well-known factional machinations around royal mistresses receive less attention than a few of the central representational practices developed for François I and Henri II to convey sexual ideas about the king. My choice of examples is guided by an effort to be representative of the thematic choices that were particularly congruent with the Renaissance. Art, poetry, and royal performance that recalled the ancient past located the king in terms of national competition, generative fecundity, heterosexual desire, and poetic truth. Rather than an exhaustive catalogue, I highlight exemplary moves each king made that established expectations and parameters for understanding royal sexuality. These would come into play after Henri's death in 1559, when the youth of François II (r. 1559–1560) and Charles IX (r. 1561–1574) shifted the emphasis from erudite Renaissance play to the pragmatic issue of generation. The pieces – presumptions about the mythological associations with potency and procreative success – were in place when Henri III ascended the throne in 1574. Caught between the profligate splendor of his grandfather's and father's courts and the failure to reproduce of his brothers, Henri III was in a difficult situation. He had to convey mastery of himself and his court while convincing his subjects that he was endowed with masculine potency. Because he remained childless, he chose to convey his image through his patronage of his male favorites and assertions of his procreative potential. In so doing, Henri created a homosocial environment that proved dangerously susceptible to sexualized critique. His successes and failures must be seen within the longer trajectory of the Valois court, just as those of Henri IV must be understood as establishing the context of Bourbon sexual politics. The repudiation of Henri III's male homosociality as a political model and the policing of Henri IV's generative gallantry in turn combined to create the classical ethos of royal sexual politics that prevailed in the seventeenth century.

(Renaissance) sex rules for kings

The Most Christian kings of France observed two informal "rules" regarding royal sexuality – enjoy many girlfriends and have many children – and two important sub-clauses: be certain several of those children are legitimate and as many as possible are boys. Additional tenets created some problems. The first corollary about girlfriends was not to let them get out of control. Ceding control to a mistress reflected badly on the king. The second corollary was that having mistresses was a way to demonstrate sexual virility. Satisfying a woman (thought to be sexually voracious by nature) without succumbing to either fatigue or feminine wiles asserted the king's sexual prowess. Royal masculinity and procreative potency had to be balanced, maintained, and performed. The king's sexual abilities permeated the political order.

Generally, historians have not considered the sexual escapades of French kings in such terms. Sex is usually a minor part of other, implicitly more important stories. Mistresses, for instance, sometimes appear in order to be blamed for the king's bad decisions, but the sexual politics of mistresses and factions are subordinated to monarchical politics as if sex must serve politics and not the other way around. The prominence of civil war and religious strife further reduced consideration of the impact of sexuality (except with respect to Henri III) on the functioning of the monarchy in the Renaissance. Furthermore, sexual reputation was often articulated by later, unreliable observers. As Janet Cox-Rearick has established, François I's reputation was largely the work of nineteenth-century artists and writers.[2] Finally, the concern that twenty-first-century understandings have obscured contemporary notions of sexuality in the Renaissance must be added to the effects of posthumous reputation-building. No French king, perhaps no king ever, has suffered in his sexual reputation as much as Henri III has. Assumptions of deviance formulated in his lifetime have been used ever since to explain the problems of his reign, which ended with his assassination in 1589. Among the recent iterations of the negative image of Henri is Shekhar Kapur's 1998 film *Elizabeth*, which represents Henri, then duc d'Anjou, as a cross-dressing fop more interested in the men of his entourage than in courting the queen of England. The film conflates Henri, who never visited England, with his younger brother, François, duc d'Alençon, who did court Elizabeth in person but was not renowned for flamboyant sexual behavior. In Patrice Chéreau's 1994 film *La Reine Margot*, based upon Alexandre Dumas's 1845 novel of the same name, Henri displays incestuous desire for his sister and a preference for male company. French history textbooks include Henri III's alleged sexual "misdeeds." James B. Collins describes him as cross-dressing and asserts, "Henry's contemporaries believed him to be bisexual."[3] In all these cases, Henri's sexual deviance is not merely fact, but explanatory fact: He was a bad king because he was deviant.

As analysis goes, that does not take us very far. Let us begin by allowing that we should take sex in politics seriously not least because kings worked hard to shape the readings of their sexual actions. They did not entirely succeed because, like all men, kings were subject to the indeterminacies of masculinity (about which, see also Chapter 4). The contingency built into masculinity,

[2] Janet Cox-Rearick, "Imagining the Renaissance: The Nineteenth-Century Cult of François I as Patron of Art," *RQ* 50:1 (1997), 207–50.
[3] James B. Collins, *From Tribes to Nation: The Making of France 500–1780* (Toronto: Nelson Thomson Learning, 2002), 252–3.

particularly around the undefined requirement of moderation identified by Todd W. Reeser, presented acute problems, and perhaps especially for kings.[4] The performative qualities of royal power required the display of the king and his magnificence in everything from prints that record decorating choices at the royal palace to highly staged royal entrées. The king's performance could not be moderate because he had to be more spectacular than those around him. The story of sexual display, of how to be moderate and superior at the same time, was a problem of masculinity that took shape around the intertwined issues of royal favorites (female and male) and royal generation. The factional effects of mistresses and *mignons* are well known; less understood is how the claims for the king's (unbounded) sexual prowess prompted response, reaction, and counter-assertion.

Beginning with the vocabulary and grammar of sexual expression around François I, this chapter traces the emergence of a disciplinary critique of royal masculinity centered on favorites and fertility. Throughout the sixteenth century, royal masculine performance proved increasingly perilous as literacy in the representational claims around the king's sexuality became more widespread. Over time, public appropriation and redeployment made sexual critique a powerful curb on the king. Sexual scandal was not just a recurrent issue, but to use Carla Freccero's term, a haunting.[5] The monarchy was haunted by recycling its own sexual vocabulary. Homologies enabled re-use of the same images to make claims about the king's subjectivity and subjection. To invoke Henri III again, the extensive, sexualized references to male favorites allowed his contemporaries to label Henri as deviant – as a sodomite given to excessive desire for men. Freccero argues powerfully that difference (in this instance, the alleged difference of sodomitical desire as deviant) and identification can be seen in operation in the public condemnations of the king. Accusations of deviance were not always named as "sodomy," but as Jonathan Goldberg has suggested, such charges worked because sodomy was seen in relational terms, as a marker of (deviant) homoerotic desire within and across texts.[6] The rhetoric of deviance became a synecdoche for a mode of political polemic, which in Henri III's case employed a capacious definition of sodomy. Put plainly, what the king actually did mattered, as when he fathered sons (or failed to do so); but what the court and the country believed the king did often mattered more.

The task, then, is to separate not "fact" from "fiction," but rather, to understand how fictional facts or factual fictions about the king's sexual reputation grew out of and were transformed by the intellectual impetus of the Renaissance. Consider the controversial issue of François I's relationship with his sister. Contemporary perceptions shaped by Renaissance love language and

---

[4] Reeser, *Moderating Masculinity.*   [5] Freccero, *Queer/Early/Modern.*
[6] Goldberg, *Sodometries.*

Neoplatonic philosophy combine readily with François I's reputation for womanizing to suggest that the intense attachment expressed by the king's sister, Marguerite, for her brother was inappropriately intimate. Marguerite indicated her "love" for François repeatedly, which is not in itself terribly interesting. She also deployed a level of physicality in some of her language that is both interesting and unsettling. After François died, she wrote:

O la presence a tous yeulx agreable,	Oh, presence to all eyes agreeable,
La plus parfaicte et la meilleur grace	The most perfect and the best grace
Qui fut jamais et la plus amyable!	That ever was and the most amiable![7]

While "tous" diffuses the intensity of a single love object, the Neoplatonic invocations of loving the more perfect being were not free of the complications around desire in Renaissance interpretations of Plato (see above, Chapter 3). Marguerite was aware of this. Later, the response to François's death, *La Navire ou Consolation du Roi François Ier a Sa Soeur Marguerite* (1547) featured the persona "Marguerite" lamenting her brother's death in physical terms. "François" responded, rejecting her carnal preoccupations and chiding her for indulging them. None of this constitutes evidence of incest, especially of incest consummated physically.[8] But the ambiguity around the corporeal manifestations of desire in Neoplatonic philosophy troubled Marguerite enough for her to compose *La Navire* in part to exorcise them. "Did they or didn't they" matters less than the tangle of possibilities that François and Marguerite left behind. All we "know" about what happened is the stories that remain.

This leads us back to the rules for kings. François I was very much a man of his time in his approach to love and sex. According to the great court gossip, Pierre de Bourdeille, seigneur de Brantôme, François insisted that noblemen at court should have mistresses:

Or ne pensez pas que ce grand roy fust si abstraint et si reformé au respect des dames qu'il n'en aimast de bons contes qu'on luy faisoit sans aucun escandale . . . J'ay ouy conter à aucuns qu'il voulait fort que les honnestes gentilhommes de sa cour ne fussent jamais sans des maistresses; et	Now do not think that this great king was so restrained and reformed with respect to the ladies that he only loved good stories about them, that one told him without any scandal . . . I have heard it reported that to some he said he very much wanted the honest gentlemen

---

[7] Marguerite de Navarre, *La Navire ou Consolation du Roi François Ier à sa sœur Marguerite*, ed. Robert Marichal (Paris: Champion, 1956), 242, ll. 121–3.

[8] Jourda, *Marguerite d'Angoulême*, vol. I, 64 insists that "un secret hideux" referred to greed. Jourda dismisses other possibilities, along with an episode in 1521 in which Marguerite was sufficiently concerned about her intimate correspondence with François to ask him to destroy it: "sy vous plet ensevelir mes lettres au feu et la parolle en silense aultrement vous renderyes." See François Génin, ed., *Nouvelles lettres de la Reine de Navarre addressées au Roi François Ier son frère* (Paris: Jules Renouard et Cie., 1842), 26, letter 1.

s'ils n'en faisoyent il les estimoit des fats et des sots.

of his court to never be without mistresses; and if they [the men] didn't have them [mistresses], he considered them [the men] to be cretins and idiots.[9]

Whether or not François said any such thing, he behaved as if he did.

François conformed to the trends in contemporary articulations about sex. As an infant, his mother believed in his destiny, including its sexual aspects. Advised that he would father at least two sons and a daughter, he was also told he would marry, experience love "during the said marriage," and enjoy "inseparable love," but the astrologer who prepared the horoscope evaded committing to whether or not it was for his wife.[10] In 1517, a spectacle designed for the king's entertainment at Rouen featured Ovid's *Metamorphoses*, and invited the king and the rest of the audience to identify François with the powerful and promiscuous king of the gods, Jupiter.[11] François and his sister were exposed to Neoplatonic philosophy as part of their education and through literary productions at court.[12] Clément Marot made his bid to return after being exiled by François by collecting poems cataloging the female form in *blasons*, a response to Petrarchan poetics that proffered morcelized female body parts as idealized and sexualized objects.[13] At François I's court, the gender politics included an ethos of visible sexual pleasure enjoyed by men in the company of women.

As for the requirement that he father many children, François took care of that with his first wife, Claude (d. 1524). To be sure, François fretted initially about not having a son. His first two children were girls: Louise, born August 19, 1515 and Charlotte, born October 23, 1516. He undertook a penitential walk to the shrine of St. Martin of Tours to pray for a son in November of 1516. Whether the prayers worked or not, a dauphin, François, was born on

[9] Pierre de Bourdeille, seigneur de Brantôme, *Les Dames galantes*, ed. Maurice Rat (Paris: Garnier, 1955), 297–8. Brantôme was born in about 1540, so the "recollections" of François I's court were of necessity not Brantôme's own.
[10] BN MS fr 5106, fols. 22v–23v. Such predictions were given a boost when Luca Gaurico predicted François's victory at Marignano. See Luca Gaurico, *Tractatus astrologicus in quo agitur de praeteritis multorum hominum accidentibus per proprias eorum genituras ad unguem examinatis* (Venice: Curtium Troianum Navò, 1552), 54v: "Corporatura obesus, statura Giganteus, & Herculeus . . . Gauricus vero sub tertia Cancri parte, ex qua, tempore Leonis X publicae praedixerat, & victoriam contra Eluetios in oppido Marignani prope Mediolanum" [Stout in build, like a giant in stature, and Herculean, in fact according to Gauricus, subject to the influence of the third region of Cancer, from which, in the time of Leo X, he [Gaurico] had also proclaimed the victory against the {H]elvetii in the town of Marignano near Milan.]
[11] Lecoq, *François Ier imaginaire*, 269.
[12] Antoine Héroët's *Androgyne* was presented to François in 1536. Héroët was on Marguerite's payroll.
[13] Anon., *Les blasons Anatomiques du Corps fémenin. Ensemble les Contreblasons de nouveau composez & aditionez* (Paris: Nicolas Chrestien, 1554). Originally published in shorter form in 1536. For Marot's relationship to Petrarch, see Balsamo, "Marot et les origines du pétrarquisme français." On the gender politics of the *blason*, see for instance Vickers, "Members Only."

February 2, 1518. Another son, Henri, was born on March 31, 1519, another daughter, Madeleine on August 10, 1520, a third son, Charles, on January 22, 1522, and a fourth and final daughter, Marguerite, on June 4, 1523. Lest this seem excessive, only Henri and Marguerite outlived their father.

More complicated was the king's extramarital life. François took pleasure in the beauty and company of the female retinues of his mother (Louise de Savoie), sister, and wife. His first official mistress, Françoise de Foix (d. 1537), dame de Châteaubriant, was a lady-in-waiting to Queen Claude. Married to Jean de Laval, sire de Châteaubriant in 1509, Françoise was influential at court by 1516 in part because of her family connections in Brittany.[14] François gradually moved Françoise aside after meeting Anne de Pisseleu in 1526. By the following year, Anne routinely joined royal hunting expeditions and soon took over as the king's preferred mistress. The king had her marry Jean de Brosse, seigneur de Penthièvre, and gave the couple the county of Estampes in 1534. Over the remaining years of the king's life and their relationship, Anne enjoyed much influence. She collected perquisites for her family, the king raised the county of Estampes to a duchy, and Anne engaged in elaborate maneuvers at court that affected policy. For instance, her opposition to Anne, connêtable de Montmorency, led her into conflict with Prince Henri and his favorite, Diane de Poitiers. Diane supported Montmorency, whose disgrace Madame d'Estampes helped engineer in 1541. Increasingly, as François aged, Anne used her alliances to counter those of Henri, his wife (Catherine de' Medici), and Diane.[15] Machinations based on sexual alliances swirled around the royal court in the 1540s, shaping everything from internal issues around religion (Madame d'Estampes encouraged toleration of "Lutherans;" Diane de Poitiers supported repression) to external policy (in 1544, Anne pressed anti-Hapsburg intervention in Europe against the advice of Claude d'Annebault, Admiral of France).

As R. J. Knecht has pointed out, and allowing that much of what was said was amplified later, critics castigated François I for his sexual behavior:

As is well known, Francis was a great womanizer. Some of the stories about him are hard to swallow. For example, it has been alleged that he had a mistress at the age of ten, that his relations with his sister were incestuous, and that he built Chambord to be near one of his mistresses. Some of these tales can be traced to late sixteenth-century works by authors associated with the house of Bourbon, who wanted to blacken the king's reputation. Yet Francis was undoubtedly a libertine.[16]

[14] For her portrait, see the drawing by Jean Clouet, *Françoise de Foix, comtesse de Châteaubriant*, Musée Condé, Chantilly; for narrative about her, see Pascal Arnoux, *Favorites et "Dames de cœur" d'Agnès Sorel à Mme de Pompadour* (Paris: Rocher, 2005), 43–58.
[15] Arnoux, *Favorites*, 59–89; Paulin Paris, *Etudes sur François Premier, roi de France, sur sa vie privée et son règne*, 2 vols. (Paris, 1885; reprint: Geneva: Slatkine, 1970), vol. I, 204–323.
[16] Knecht, *Renaissance Warrior and Patron*, 112.

Affairs with married women, rowdy visits to Parisian brothels, and his loud insistence that his wife and mother include many pretty women among their ladies-in-waiting were among the charges leveled at the king. Knecht quotes Antonio De Beatis, who visited France in 1517: "The king . . . is a great womaniser and readily breaks into other gardens and drinks at many sources." The king contracted syphilis, probably by 1524, and the effects plagued him until his death. In 1543, courtiers were still complaining about the king's skirt-chasing.[17] Fifty years after François died, Brantôme reported,

Le roy François une fois voulut aller coucher avec une dame de sa cour qu'il aimoit. Il trouve son mary l'espée au poing pour l'aller tuer; mais le roy luy porta la sienne à la gorge et luy commanda, sur sa vie, de ne luy faire nul mal, et que s'il luy faisoit la moindre chose du monde, qu'il le tueroit ou qu'il luy feroit trencher la teste; et pour cette nuict l'envoya dehors, et pris sa place.

King François wanted one time to sleep with a woman of the court he loved. Finding her husband, sword in hand, ready to kill her, instead the king put [his weapon] on his throat and commanded him, on his life, to do her no evil, and that if he did the least thing in the world, he would kill him and cut off his head, and for this night, he sent him out and took his place.[18]

Even if this "memory" of François I was distorted, his reign and reputation were marked by his sexual exploits.

Much of Francois I's sexual reputation stems from the art he supported during his reign. While tracing all of the Renaissance entanglements of the king's sexuality in art, architecture, and the remains of performance would be well-nigh impossible, some examples point to ways that sexual politics in the mythological mode made for ambiguity and tension. Consider the theme of Venus (Love) conquering Mars (War). While seemingly an image of feminine triumph, the depiction of Mars as reluctant can been read as advice for François: he must appear to submit, in his case, to marriage with Eleanor, the sister of his adversary and captor, Holy Roman Emperor Charles V. Apparent submission, however, does not mean that Mars/François has to relinquish genuine power.[19] The more obvious reading is that François is subject to Venus, which might seem more apt, given the king's notorious womanizing. In 1529 or 1530, Rosso Fiorentino offered François a rendering of the theme in which a youthful Mars is recoiling from an aggressive Venus. Surrounded by nymphs, Mars is identified by his armor piled in the corner. A small figure, probably Cupid, tugs at Mars'

[17] R. J. Knecht, *Francis I* (Cambridge University Press, 1982), 428. See also p. 86 regarding the syphilis rumors. See Lucien Romier, *Les Origines politiques des Guerres de Religion*, 2 vols. (Paris: Perrin, 1913; reprint Geneva: Slatkin, 1974), vol. I, 22 for 1543.

[18] Brantôme, *Les Dames galantes*, 12.

[19] See Jean Adhémar, "Aretino: Artistic Advisor to Francis I," in *Journal of the Warburg and Courtauld Institutes* 17 (1954): 311–18, for this argument about the meaning of these images. Rosso Fiorentino's given name was Giovanni Battista di Jacopo.

Figure 16. Rosso Fiorentino (1494–1540), *Mars and Venus, with Nymphs and Cupids* (c.1529), drawing, Louvre, Paris.

This image was sent to François I by the artist at the behest of Pietro Aretino (see Figures 12 and 13). Framed by sensual imagery, Venus beckons Mars, a version of the familiar idea of Love conquering War. Observers consider the image appropriate for the moment, as Rosso seems to have prepared it around the time of the Treaty of Cambrai, also called the Paix des Dames, which included provisions to resolve the conflict between the Hapsburgs and the Valois by marrying François to Charles V's sister, Eleanor of Portugal.

cloak, increasing his off-balance pose as Venus gestures for him to approach. The lavish profusion of foliage, fruit, and flowers underscores the theme of sexual abundance. Despite the possibly problematic criticism the image contained, François did not take it amiss: he took Rosso into his employ and sexual themes congruent with Rosso's image inspired several related portrayals on the walls of the *Appartement des bains*.[20] While the paradox of submission to the weak was the kind of double-thinking that delighted French Renaissance readers,[21] mastery through subjection would seem to threaten the king whose dominance could be seen as illusory if those around him were using apparent abjection to manipulate him.

As Kathleen Wilson-Chevalier makes clear, artists at Fontainebleau gradually dampened the ambiguity around the king by emphasizing the dangers presented by women.[22] Relatively subtle subversions in Rosso's image were largely eliminated in the 1535 decoration of the portico of the Porte Dorée. Executed by Francesco Primaticcio, the Porte Dorée featured Hercules, Omphale, and Ovid's passage from the *Fasti* in which Faunus inadvertently attempts to copulate with Hercules.[23] Faithful to the Renaissance Ovidian tradition, the image denounces Omphale's feminization of Hercules as producing misplaced desire that is sterile and unnatural. The actions of women, the images suggested, were at the root of the problematic desires of men. By the 1540s, images by Primaticco drawn from the *Iliad* illustrate Zeus' ham-fisted threats directed at Hera for distracting her husband and meddling in the Trojan War. But claiming that men enjoyed sexual power over and through women brought the question of the relationship between the two into the open. Collectively, the effect of all this gender competition was to foreground the link between political and sexual power at François I's premier palace.

Assertions of masculine mastery were particularly necessary because of the sumptuous framing devices that prompted feminine gender associations. As Rebecca Zorach argues, the decoration of the palace at Fontainebleau begun after 1527 showed preoccupation with erotic abundance. Decorative motifs were often elaborate, indexing ancient objects and visual formulae with explicit reference to sex, desire, and generation. Cupid and Venus appear frequently.

[20] Waddington, "The Bisexual Portrait of Francis I." The images from the *Appartement des bains* are preserved largely in engravings.

[21] For discussion of engagement with paradox, see Jacqueline Boucher, *Société et mentalités autour de Henri III*, 4 vols. (Paris: Champion, 1981), vol. III, 861–77.

[22] I am relying on the juxtaposition of the images discussed in Kathleen Wilson-Chevalier, "Women on Top at Fontainebleau," *Oxford Art Journal* 16:1 (1993): 34–48. See also Sara Matthews Greico, *Ange ou diablesse: le représentation de la femme au XVIᵉ siècle* (Paris: Flammarion, 1991), 386–7, on the anxiety about the informal power of women expressed in sixteenth-century images.

[23] On Primaticcio in France, see Louis Dimier, *Le Primatice: peintre, sculpteur et architecte des rois de France* (Paris: Leroux, 1900).

Figure 17. Rosso Fiorentino (1494–1540), *Venus Frustrated*, fresco and stucco decoration, Gallery of François I, Château de Fontainebleau.
   Both the central image and the surrounding decoration focus on the association of Love/Venus with abundance and generation. The stucco in particular features male and female figures supporting bounteous profusion.

Extravagant foliage, heaping fruit baskets, comely nymphs, and randy satyrs recur throughout the palace. Zorach demonstrates that the profusion of ornament associated with generation was part of a nationalistic claim that France, by virtue of its natural abundance, was superior to artful, artificial Italy.[24] This is another version of the cultural competition engaged in by French poets and specifically aimed at Italy. But politics and art were a bit trickier than poetry. Not only did François rely on Italian artists; the emphasis on decoration as expressing fertile abundance contributed to the association of Fontainebleau with the feminine.[25] The king deepened this association by relying on his mother as his regent when he was captive in Spain after the

---

[24] Zorach, *Blood, Milk, Ink, Gold*.

[25] Kathleen Wilson-Chevalier "Femmes, cour et pouvoir: la chambre de la duchesse d'Etampes à Fontainebleau," in *Royaume de fémynie: pouvoirs, contraintes, espaces de libertés des femmes, de la Renaissance à la Fronde*, ed. Kathleen Wilson-Chevalier and Eliane Viennot (Paris: Champion, 1999), 203–36.

Figure 18. Francesco Primaticcio, The Room of the Duchess d'Estampes (now the Escalier du Roi), *The History of Alexander the Great* (1541–1544), fresco and stucco, Château de Fontainebleau.

Prepared for François I's most important mistress, the decoration refers to Alexander the Great's relationships with women. The satyrs between the legs of the caryatids are a symbol of sensuality in the Renaissance, and combined with the images of fruit and fertility throughout the setting, they suggest the increasingly programmatic association of generation and abundance with French style.

disastrous loss at Pavia (1525) and on the advice of his sister throughout his life.[26]

Other appropriations of the classical inheritance highlighted the links between and among the feminine, mythological invocations of the erotic, and the king. Consider the decoration of the Chamber of the Duchesse d'Estampes decorated by Francesco Primaticcio. Sculptures of naked caryatids "hold up" the entablature around a sequence of images devoted to the relationships of ancient heroes with women. Alexander the Great and his encounters with

[26] In addition to Jourda, *Marguerite d'Angoulême*, see Leah Middlebrook, "'Tout Mon Office': Body Politics and Family Dynamics in the *verse epîtres* of Marguerite de Navarre," *RQ* 54:4 (2001): 1108–41, and Elizabeth McCartney, "The King's Mother and Royal Prerogative in Early Sixteenth-Century France," in *Medieval Queenship*, ed. John Carmi Parsons (New York: St. Martin's, 1993), 117–41.

Thalestris, Campaspe, and Roxane loom large. Thalestris was the Amazon queen who, legend has it, brought 300 women to Alexander so that he might father a superior race of warriors by impregnating them. The Bactrian Roxane was married to Alexander in order to secure his conquests in central Asia. Campaspe was Alexander's mistress. Her story is that when Apelles painted her, he fell so in love with her that Alexander gave her to the artist as payment for the painting. Collectively, the images foreground virile superiority, military/marital conquest, and royal magnanimity. Putti play among the abounding fruits that cascade around the image. The framing of the picture is set off by caryatids flanking half-sized satyrs to evoke generation and sexual abundance. A quintessential emblem of lust in Renaissance iconography, the satyrs face out into the room, challenging the gaze of the viewer. All of this, again, was designed for the king's mistress. Whatever it may say about the king, it put him in the midst of fertile, generative, erotic abundance when he visited her.

Without abandoning his father's taste for luxurious ornament, Henri II (r. 1547–1559) shaped his patronage in a more public direction in part to curb perceptions of sexual excess that marked François I's reign. The scheme at Fontainebleau was erudite and largely consumed by the court. The expansion of royal sexual representation to wider audiences became programmatic under Henri II. As Françoise Bardon has documented, Henri II's primary mistress, Diane de Poitiers, was honored in poetry, prose, sculpture, painting, tapestries, and objets d'art. Royal planners celebrated her in entrées at Lyon (1548), Paris (1549), and Rouen (1550), as well as for the program in honor of the birth of Henri's II son in 1549. Bardon lists just those examples which feature Diane de Poitiers, rather than the attributes of the goddess Diana. The addition of those cultural products includes images of Diana as goddess of the moon, Diana the huntress, and Diana and Acteon, mythological referents that were familiar before Diane de Poitiers inspired the profusion of artistic representations.[27] The long history of Ovid's *Metamorphoses* in France provided extensive knowledge of Diana's mythology.[28] Diana the huntress, with her phallic arrows, defending her sexual purity against Acteon, rejecting Callisto after she was raped by Jupiter, and Diana's association with the Moon, which for astrologers, was crucial for women and childbirth – all fed and fed off the sexualized image of the king's mistress.[29]

---

[27] Françoise Bardon, *Diane de Poitiers et le mythe de Diane* (Paris: Presses universitaires de France, 1963) argues that Diane de Poitiers provided the inspiration for allegorical art of glorification at the French court. See esp. pp. 39–103.

[28] Bardon, *Diane de Poitiers*, focuses on the *Ovide moralisé* and Boccaccio. The more fulsome tradition around Ovid that is traced relative to Orpheus in Chapter 1 above is also relevant.

[29] For associations with the Moon, see Jacques Peletier du Mans, *L'Amour des amours* (Lyon: Jean de Tournes, 1555).

While still renowned for his lavish court,[30] Henri II's support for images of Diane de Poitiers differed from his father's generalized patronage of erotic abundance. Artists set up Henri's mistress to evoke purity and chastity. François Habert invoked sex in order to deny Diana's part in it:

Mais peu à peu Venus s'abolira,	But little by little, Venus will be abolished,
Et en son nom Diane on publiera,	And in her place one will publish Diane
Que toute fable ha dict estre pudique,	Who all fables say is chaste,
Contraire en tout au vouloir vénérique.	Contrary in all ways to venerian desire.[31]

Much of the imagery for Diane de Poitiers made this double move. At the entrée at Rouen in 1550, the song of Orpheus opens with an invocation of chastity:

Ne seras-tu pas compagne	Will you not be the companion,
O Diane	O Diane
A louer la majesté	To commend the majesty
Du Roi, qui ton croissant porte	Of the King to your crescent door
Et supporte ta vertu de chasteté.	And support your virtue of chastity.[32]

Repeatedly, royal image-makers likened Diane de Poitiers to the cold, inaccessible Moon, at once dampening the association of sex with heat and recalling the association of the Moon with fertility and reproduction.

This balance between devotion to one woman as a sign of self-controlled moderation and the claims for royal magnificence proved difficult to maintain. The image of Diane de Poitiers was the fulcrum upon which the king's reputation balanced. The 1549 entrée ceremony at Lyon ostensibly celebrated Catherine de' Medici, but included images associating Diane with peace and abundance. The first major decorative element was an obelisk adorned with an interlaced "H" and "D" symbol, and the first triumphal arch depicted Diana

[30] Niccolò Tommaseo, ed., *Les relations des ambassadeurs vénitiens sur les affaires de France au XVIe siècle*, 2 vols. (Paris: Imprimerie Royale, 1838), vol. I, 404: "Talmente che in tempo di pace tanto manco vien ad esser l'entrata, allo incontro delle quale, se bene a proporzione vi sia ano una grossa spesa... come quei che sanno che la grandezza, la richezza, e li tesori loro consistono nella larga distribuzion del suo a' suoi... non sia mai stato re, di quanti s'ha memoria, che spendesse nè tenisse maggior casa del re Enrico" [To such an extent that in peace time not even the income comes to be, on the contrary of that which, though in proportion there may be a big expense... as they who know that their greatness, their wealth, and their treasure consist in the wide distribution of one's property to one's followers... there has never been a king, for as long as can be remembered, who spent [more] or kept a bigger household than King Henry.]

[31] François Habert, *Déploration poétique de feu M. Antoine du Prat* (Lyon: J. de Tournes, 1545), 45.

[32] Anon., *Les pourtes et figures du sumptueux ordre, plaisantz spectacles et magnifiques théâtres, dressés et exhibés par les citoiens de Rouen* (Rouen: Jean Dugort, 1557). The events took place on October 2, 1550.

presiding over chaste abundance represented by her band of nymphs.[33] Artists displayed her crescent Moon symbol with the king's.[34] The ceremony itself featured images of peace as crucial for French fertility of the land and people.[35] Other elisions of Diana with Venus as the goddess of love and Minerva as councilor to the king advertised Diane de Poitiers melding her roles.[36] The effect, like all the images of a comely Diana bathing or hunting, was simultaneously to acknowledge and deny the sexual importance of the royal mistress. The implicit claim for the king is that his love is not carnal, but transcendent. Ironically, Henri II, who expressed the desire that his court would be more orderly and less morally loose than his father's,[37] served as the primary patron of images that defined his court by a central sexual connection outside of marriage.

These examples from the images developed for François I and Henri II demonstrate the monarchical habit of presenting the king and the monarchy on multiple levels congruent with other Renaissance practices. Recall, for instance, that the treatments of Orpheus made clear that the main narrative had several alternative possible meanings some of which suggested polymorphous perversity. (See above, Chapter 1.) Royal image-makers defined the sexuality of the king by locating him in relation to similarly sexually elaborate myths of the ancient deities and legendary or historical characters. Readings of the relationship of Mars and Venus, of Alexander the Great's heterosexual encounters, of Diane as Diana, and of the erotics of material abundance were not entirely transparent and were not meant to be. The king might be responsible for the increase

---

[33] Anon., *La magnificence de la superbe et triomphante entrée de la noble et antique cité de Lyon au Treschrestien Roy de France Henry, deuxiesme de ce nom, et à la Royne Catherine son Espouse, le xxiii de Septembre M.D.XLVIII* (Lyon: Guillaume Rouillé, 1549), sig. D3r, E3r. See also the Paris entrée. Anon., *C'est l'ordre qui a este tenu a la nouvelle et ioyeuse entrée, que treshault, tresexcellent, & trespuissant Prince le Roy Treschrestien Henry deuzieme de ce nom à faicte en sa bonne ville & cité de Paris, capitale de son Royaume, le sezieme jour de Iuin M. D. XLIX* (Paris: Iacques Rosset, 1549), 33. Diane de Poitiers is less obvious, but pointedly accompanies the queen.

[34] I. D. McFarlane, ed. *The Entry of Henri II into Paris 16 June 1549* (Binghamton: Medieval and Renaissance Texts and Studies, 1982), 64, notes that master joiner Clément Delaire was paid for preparing a crescent/fleur-de-lys design for a mock naval battle.

[35] See for instance Anon., *C'est l'ordre*, 6v–7r, explaining the image of "Gallia Fertilis;" and 8r for "Gaule" surrounded by gardens of plenty.

[36] See for instance Jean-Antoine de Baïf, *Poésies choises de J.A. de Baïf suivies de poésies inédites*, ed. L. Becq de Fouquières (Paris: Charpentier et Cie., 1874), 177: "Diane chasseresse au veneur donne aïde, / Et Venus flateresse à l'amoureux préside: / Diane porte l'arc, Venus aussi le porte" [Diane the huntress gives aid to the hunter / And Venus the flateress presides over love: / Diane carries an arrow, Venus carries one also.] It seems likely that Diane shaped some of these images. Her own patronage emphasized her status as a widow and a servant of the royal dynasty. See Sigrid Ruby, "Diane de Poitiers: veuve et favorite," in *Patronnes et mécènes en France à la Renaissance*, ed. Kathleen Wilson-Chevalier with Eugénie Pascal (Université de Saint-Etienne, 2007), 381–99.

[37] Knecht, *The French Renaissance Court*, notes the observation by ambassadors that Henri's court was more formal and that the king issued sumptuary legislation to make social ranks readily legible. See pp. 69 and 310–11.

of his realm, but the dangers presented by women, the effects of male desire, the possibility (or probability) of damaging sexual entanglements abounded.

François I and Henri II could present themselves as effective kings and as inhabiting the presumptions of masculine performance because they fulfilled the basic Renaissance rules for kings. After Henri died in 1559, the representational supports had to change for François II, who was only 15 when he became king. Humanists who aspired to royal patronage knew that antiquity was potentially troubling in its sexual messages. That did not stop them from trying to frame the thinking about the ancient past in productive ways. One offering to the young king was a new script centered on procreative potentiality by means of an attempt to harness Neoplatonism in the service of royal generation. Louys Le Roy's commentary on Plato's *Symposium* as a wedding gift for the future François II and his wife drew on the common assumption that kings were models for their people. Le Roy argued for and demonstrated the utility of heterosexual love through the royal couple by willfully misreading Plato to fit his marital theme. In the dedication to the second book, Le Roy tells François II that Plato,

recommande l'honneste Amour qui consiste principalement en mariage, & celebre la perfaitte beauté . . . en mesme perfection & purité divine.

recommends honest [chaste] love which is composed principally in marriage and celebrates the perfect beauty . . . in the same perfection and divine purity.[38]

Le Roy explains that Plato teaches how to avoid getting distracted by false human beauty by means of marital union. Marc Schachter observes that this dedication shapes the text in the direction of French political logic. The interchange between Socrates and Diotima in Le Roy's third book, for instance, makes the transcendence of *eros* always a matter between husband and wife, rather than (male) lovers. By marrying and having children, François will not only continue his line, but also expand the French monarchy through its ties to Scotland.[39] But Le Roy uses the utility of the royal marriage to argue that Platonic love is consonant with the reproduction of the social order. Love excites,

incessement en l'humanité appetit d'engendrer qu'elle a meslé expressement de plaisir, nous invitant tous d'un commun instinct à perpetuer les humains.

in humanity the appetite to engender incessantly, which it has mixed with pleasure, inviting all of us with a common instinct to perpetuate humanity.

[38] Le Roy, *Sympose*, sigs. a iir–v.
[39] Schachter, "Louis le Roy's *Sympose de Platon*." See esp. 430–1. Of course, the marriage between a close heir to the English throne and the French king had greater aspirations than Scotland. Henri II and his advisors knew that Mary Tudor was unlikely to have an heir, and if (or when) her Protestant sister, Elizabeth, became queen, Mary Stuart was Elizabeth's closest heir.

Neoplatonic insistence on the higher good has been transferred from individual salvation to society as a whole. With society in the place of beauty, marriage is the safe place for desire. Outside of marriage, bad sex threatens:

Au contraire tout Amour hors mariage illicite, & les enfans qui en naissant bastardz, incapables d'honneurs, & dignitez.

To the contrary, all Love outside of marriage is illicit, and the children born there are bastards, incapable of honors and dignities.[40]

Implicitly rejecting the sexual complications in the invocations of antiquity at the courts of François I and Henri II, Le Roy offers Neoplatonic support for marital procreation as beneficial to the kingdom through the reproduction of the royal line and as an example of orderly, natural sex. The script for a boy king, then, was both in line with and a departure from the basic rules for kings. The insistence on producing heirs in legitimate unions was familiar; the locating of the king in terms of potential rather than actual procreative success was new.

François II died before he had time to either fulfill or ignore Le Roy's injunctions. For Charles IX, the sexual was held in abeyance during his youth, but the need for royal sexual productivity did not abate. King at 10 years old, Charles was cast both in sexual imagery that recalled Henri II and in terms of procreative potentiality. Following a painting by François Clouet of a rider with Charles's features approaching the goddess Diana bathing, artists depicted Charles as Henri's heir in matters of erotic, but chaste, abundance. The comely goddess surrounded by her naked attendants indicated sexual bounty; putting Charles above it all on horseback lessened, but did not eliminate, the suggestion that he was a voyeur (Figure 19).[41] The message is not transparent in this image or another by Clouet. Sometimes called *Lady in her Bath*, sometimes called *Diane de Poitiers*, Clouet painted it around 1570, and it may situate Charles relative to his own mistress. The identifications are tentative in part because the influence of Charles's mistress, Marie Touchet, was limited. Unlike Diane de Poitiers and Anne d'Heilly, Marie was from a minor noble family. Her father held the relatively insignificant post of Lieutenant-General of Orléans.[42] The obscurity of Charles's extramarital love life suggests that someone (Catherine de' Medici is usually credited with such things) wanted to keep that aspect of the king's life circumscribed.[43]

---

[40] Le Roy, *Sympose*, fol. 69v.

[41] André Chastel, *French Art: The Renaissance, 1430–1620*, trans. Deke Dusinberre (Paris and New York: Flammarion, 1995), 234, notes the persistence of the image with Charles as the rider.

[42] Jean Castarède, *Les Femmes galantes du XVIᵉ siècle* (Paris: France-Empire, 2000), 124, asserts that Catherine de' Medici chose Marie because of her comparatively humble origins.

[43] The evidence is circumstantial, but Catherine continued to express antipathy toward her husband's mistresses long after his death. In a letter dated April 25, 1584, to Pomponne de Bellièvre, Catherine explained that she put up with her husband's "whore." See Catherine de' Medici,

Figure 19. François Clouet (c.1515–1572), *Diana at Her Bath* (1558–1559?), oil on wood, Musée des Beaux-Arts, Rouen, France.

The central feature of this image is the frank sensuality of the goddess Diana, who is associated with Henri II's mistress, Diane de Poitiers. In addition to the group of very partially clad nymphs, the satyrs also indicate the sexual nature of the depiction. The identification of the rider is problematic, but later images derived from this one sometimes featured the face of Charles IX.

Picking up on the message of François II's reign rather than his father's, Charles encouraged dissemination of his procreative potential as the sign of his inhabiting of the masculine and sexual norms of kingship. Hope in this vein developed early on: a reassuring horoscope promised Charles many sons.[44] In the end, the horoscope was rather off the mark: Charles had only one illegitimate son and a posthumous daughter. By the 1570s, the gap between the claims for the king's generative power and the reality of royal infecundity was all too visible. The 1571 Paris entrée of Charles and his wife Elizabeth attempted to associate the king with generation in a positive manner. The ceremony

Lettres de Catherine de Médicis, ed. Hector de La Ferrière, 11 vols. (Paris: CDI, 1880–1943), vol. VIII, 181. See also vol. X, 494. Catherine detested Henri II's other mistresses as well. In 1564, Catherine ordered a search of Lady Fleming's belongings. See Paul Van Dyke, *Catherine de Médicis*, 2 vols. (New York: Charles Scribner's Sons, 1923), vol. I, 42, based on BN MS fr 6618, fol. 20.

[44] BN MS fr 14772, p. 74.

was designed to celebrate what was hoped (wrongly) would be lasting peace between the warring Catholics and Protestants. The triumphal entrée emphasized the marriage alliance with the Hapsburgs that many hoped would diminish war between France and the Holy Roman Empire.[45] The entrée presented aspirations to royal generation throughout. After recounting the marriage of the legendary progenitor of the kings of France, Pharamond, with the daughter of the "Emperor of the Germans" [Empereur des Allemaignes], a Ronsard poem claimed Trojan origins for France:

Feit alliance à la fille d'un Roy	Make an alliance with the daughter of a king
Qu'il laissa grosse & enceinte...	Whom he leaves fat and pregnant...
Long temps apres de ceste Roine enceinte,	Long after this pregnant Queen,
Vint une race au faict des armes craincte,	Came a race feared because of its arms,
...Ce Pharamond qui avoit pris naissance	...This Pharamond who was born
De la Troienne, & Germaine alliance,	of the Trojan and German alliance,
...Les Roys François sont descendus de luy	...The French Kings are descended from him
De pere en filz d'une immortelle suitte.	From father to son in an immortal series.[46]

The poem extols the benefits of marriage and celebrates the paradox that peace will come by the union of France and Empire. Later in the program, the king's device, surrounded by exuberant flowers and foliage, joins two columns labeled "Pietate et Iusticia" [Piety and Justice]. The key to the king inhabiting these qualities is his procreative future with his wife:

En l'une des ioües de cest arc estoit un tableau de riche & excellente peinture, representant une femme couchee & appuyee sur son coulde, ayant plusieurs mammelles & petis enfans à l'entour d'elle.	And one of the works of this arch was a tableau of a rich and excellent painting representing a woman lying down and supported on her elbow, having many breasts and small children surrounding her.[47]

The audience is told that "grandeur & fertilité" [grandeur and fertility] will soon repair the realm after ten years of troubles. A map of France labeled

---

[45] Perhaps the planners felt that celebrating a peace that resolved civil war was inappropriate. The king's marriage provided a useful positive element that distracted from the complications of commemorating civil strife.
[46] Simon Bouquet, *Bref et sommaire recueil de ce qui a esté faict, de l'ordre tenüe à la ioyeuse & triumphante Entree de...Charles IX. Avec le couronnement de...Princesse Madame Elizabeth d'Austrice son espouse, le Dimanche vingtcinquiesme* (Paris: Denis du Pré, 1572), fols. 10r–v.
[47] Bouquet, *Bref et sommaire recueil*, fol. 11v.

"GALLIA" and festooned with dolphins makes for an unsubtle suggestion that the king needed to provide a dauphin.[48] The language of generation as procreative potential recurs throughout the program, with invocations of Henri II and his predecessors as exemplars of royal fecundity, praise for Catherine de' Medici as the mother of kings, and didactic explanations of Platonic notions of immortality through "le succes de generation" [success in generation] appearing at regular intervals.[49]

The claims that stemmed from the as-yet-unfulfilled procreative potential were expanding as well. The entrée depicted France as the heir to the Roman Empire and the new and better home of the Renaissance demonstrated by erudite invocations of the classical heritage. The monarchy furthered the centrality of generation by carrying out the coronation of Elizabeth in conjunction with the entrée. Elizabeth's coronation was the glaring exception to the rule that queens of France were crowned after they had provided an heir.[50] Crowning the queen as if she were already a mother highlighted the generative potential of the royal couple.

The emphasis on potential created its own perils, especially when kings failed to pull it off. French kings did not have a choice but to demonstrate virile success through procreation, but, in France, the problem was more acute because of the male-only succession. When the king did his job, the monarchy sexualized his efforts as part of the politics of masculine display. While their intentions are lost to us, perhaps François I and Henri II recognized that their power as secular rulers could be served by asserting the importance of a dimension that Christian morality repudiated and condemned. Sexualizing the king offered a figure of virility and potency less tied to the constraints of religious sexual norms. Under the boy kings, sexual performance as an integral aspect of court life continued, but it necessarily followed a different script. That both fertile abundance and procreative potentiality were unstable foundations upon which to rest the sexual reputation of the king would soon become apparent.

---

[48] Bouquet, *Bref et sommaire recueil*, fol. 13v for the fertility claims; 14r for the dolphins. See also 33r–35r and 52v–53v, which describe a gift to the king of a representation of Cybele as an image of French fecundity. (The dais holding Cybele's chariot is supported by dolphins.) The lineages of generation are also highlighted, with references to previous French kings named Charles, including Charlemagne.

[49] Bouquet, *Bref et sommaire recueil*, fol. 20v, 22v, and 28v. These are just three of many iterations.

[50] For details of Elizabeth's coronation, see Theodore and Denys Godefroy, *Le Ceremonial François*, 2 vols. (Paris: Sebastien Cramoisy, 1649), vol. I, 519–38. On the historical meanings of the coronation of French queens emphasizing the comparison between the ceremonies for kings and queens, see Fanny Cosandey, *La Reine de France: symbole et pouvoir, XVᵉ–XVIIIᵉ siècle* (Paris: Gallimard, 2000), 127–62.

Controlling sexual reputation

More than his father or grandfather, Henri III tried to set the terms of debate around the king's sexual reputation. Far more than his brothers, Henri did so relative to his reproductive life with his wife and his intimate relationships with his male favorites, the *mignons*. Despite his efforts to present himself as a potent and effective king, Henri's own reproductive failure and the multiplicity of readings of the king's image worked against him. So too did the troubled times. The monarchy Henri III inherited in 1574 was deeply in debt. Religious civil war was well-nigh endemic. Protestants viewed Henri as their particular enemy for his role in the St. Bartholomew's Day massacres. Many were inclined to follow his younger brother, François, duc d'Alençon. Rivalries at court, especially between the ultra-Catholic Guise and the Protestant Bourbons, had reached a high pitch. Catherine de' Medici had been left in charge after Charles IX died because Henri was in Poland, where he had been elected king on February 21, 1574. Many regarded her as duplicitous and inclined to effeminize her royal sons,[51] and the failure of her sons to produce children seemed to support such charges.

In addressing the twin pressures of court rivalry and religious conflict, Henri III set the initial terms for discussions of his sexuality by making a controversial marriage. The context for Henri's rapid assertion of his procreative intentions through marriage is significant. Three months elapsed between Charles IX's death (May 30) and Henri's return from Poland (September 4). As Henri wended his way home, Alençon, using his status as heir to the throne, allied himself with moderate Catholic and Protestant "Malcontents," who sought a greater voice for the nobility as a way to break the religious deadlock.[52] To assert his control over events, Henri combined his coronation (*sacre*) with his marriage. In the eyes of contemporaries, both *sacre* and marriage conferred masculine authority. The *sacre* made Henri "the father of his people," and marriage

---

[51] On Catherine's reputation, see Katherine Crawford, "Constructing Evil Foreign Queens," *JMEMS* 37:2 (2007): 393–418. On effeminacy and lack of reason, see for instance Rebecca Bushnell, "Tyranny and Effeminacy in Early Modern England," in *Reconsidering the Renaissance*, ed. Mario A. Di Cesare (Binghamton: Medieval and Renaissance Texts and Studies, 1992), 339–54. On early modern understandings of sexual characteristics, see for instance Phyllis Rackin, "Historical Difference/Sexual Difference," in *Privileging Gender in Early Modern England*, ed. Jean R. Brink (Kirksville, MO: Sixteenth-Century Essays and Studies, 1993), 37–63.

[52] The Malcontent program is illustrated by a piece issued in Alençon's name, *Brieve remonstrance a la noblesse de France sur le faict de la Declaration de Monseigneur le Duc d'Alençon* (n. p.: no pub., 1576). For the setting, see Arlette Jouanna, "Un programme politique nobiliare: les Mécontents et l'Etat (1574–1576)," in *L'Etat et les aristocraties (France, Angleterre, Ecosse) XIIe–XVIIe siècle*, ed. Philippe Contamine (Paris: Presses de l'Ecole normale supérieure, 1989), 247–77.

gave him (as it did other men) legal and social powers as a husband.[53] In what was becoming a familiar – and thus perhaps unsettling – claim, Henri offered the optimistic prospect of generative potency and paternal power to a country that had not had a king father a legitimate heir in a quarter century.[54]

The marriage was also part of a political strategy to reintegrate the noble families of the realm through the person of the king.[55] Henri wrote to his uncle, the duc de Savoie:

J'ai reçu vostre conseyl... qui estoit de prandre une famme quil feust de bonne maison, et pour me contantter.	I received your counsel... which was to take a wife of a good family and for my contentment.[56]

Henri settled on Louise de Vaudemont. According to the romantic version, he had seen Louise on his way to Poland and found her beautiful and gracious.[57] More pragmatically, Louise was a member of the ultra-Catholic Guise clan, which Henri wanted to enlist against Alençon and his Huguenot allies. The marriage took place on February 14, 1575, the day after Henri's coronation at Rheims. The marriage contract was brief and signed on the spot; decoration used for the coronation was recycled for the wedding.[58] The *sacre* allowed Henri to touch for scrofula, which demonstrated his potency as a divinely appointed monarch. The royal marriage asserted Henri's intention to provide the realm with heirs, and while no marriage precluded other sorts of sexual relationships, by situating his wedding in proximity to the *sacre*, Henri emphasized his commitment to the monarchy's divine (Catholic) heritage.[59]

---

[53] On the *sacre*, see Richard A. Jackson, *Vive le Roi! A History of the French Coronation from Charles V to Charles X* (Chapel Hill: University of North Carolina Press, 1984).

[54] Ironically, given his later reputation, Henri pressed the marriage issue in part to address anxiety over his now largely forgotten heterosexual escapades with the Venetian courtesan, Veronica Franco. See Antonio Maria Salviati, *Correspondance du nonce en France Antonio Maria Salviati, (1572–1578)*, ed. Pierre Hurtubise and Robert Toupin, 2 vols. (Rome: Université pontificale grégorienne, 1975), vol. II, 41, August 23, 1574. Jacqueline Boucher, *Deux épouses et reines à la fin du XVIᵉ siècle: Louise de Lorraine et Marguerite de France* (Université de Saint-Étienne, 1995), 123–4, argues that Henri had affairs with women of the court, which upset Louise de Lorraine. If so, the evidence is lost.

[55] This strategy has been analyzed in Le Roux, *La Faveur du Roi*.

[56] Henri III, *Lettres de Henri III, Roi de France*, ed. Michel François, 4 vols. (Paris: Klincksieck, 1965), vol. II, no. 1222.

[57] Jacques-Auguste de Thou, *Histoire universelle de Jacques-Auguste de Thou, depuis 1543, jusqu'en 1607*, 15 vols. (London [Paris]: no pub., 1734), vol. VII, 167. On the marriage possibilities, see vol. VII, 76, 158.

[58] BN MS fr 15598, fols. 186r–88v.

[59] Published accounts include Anon., *L'Entrée triomphante et magnifique du Tres-Chrestien Roy de France et de Pologne Henri III en sa ville et cité de Rheims, venant en son sacre et couronnement* (Rheims: Chez Jean de Foigny, 1575). See also Nicolas Du Mont, *Advertissement venu de Rheims du sacre, couronnement et marriage de Henry III, très chrestien roy de France et de Pologne* (Paris: D. Du Pré, 1575). A pamphlet of the same title was also published in Lyon, and at least four other pamphlets recounting the sacre and marriage were prepared, including one in Latin.

Despite Henri's efforts, the marriage and the alliance it created with the Guise raised concerns about his authority. Henri had sought to tie the Catholic aristocracy to him; rival noble families claimed the king had married beneath his dignity. The papal nuncio echoed the criticism, and several observers expressed apprehension about the precipitous nature of the marriage.[60] Succumbing to impetuous desire, although it was legitimated by marriage, raised questions about the king's masculine self-control. Henri's use of proxies in his battles at court further damaged his attempt to define himself in terms of masculine prowess.[61] When Guise harassed the Malcontents, Alençon moved closer to the Protestants and stepped up criticism of Henri's government for failing to address the religious crisis with vigor. When Catherine de' Medici tried to reconcile her sons, Alençon associated her strategy with Henri's efforts to hide behind Guise, complaining that both feminized royal authority. In a sense, Alençon's behavior was evidence of the veracity of his charges: his running amok reflected poorly on Henri's ability to control his own family. Using Guise to harass Alençon made it easy to cast Henri as deficient in masculine honor.[62] Alençon's status as Henri's heir compounded the problem. As the papal nuncio observed,

la difficultà del Re ... [e] sin che il Re havesse figliuoli, . . . il Re donasse a un suo fratello un stato di qualche importanza, mediante il quale paresse ad Alanson di esser' il primo in Francia dopo il Re.	the difficulty of the king [is] that until the King has children [or sons], . . . [he] must give his brother an estate of some importance, by means of which he deems Alençon to be the first in France after the King.[63]

The onus thus fell upon Henri.

Weakness and effeminacy continued to be attributed to Henri after – and because – he and Alençon had made their peace in November 1575. Their reconciliation, which Catherine helped effect, enabled Alençon to take the lead in settling the fifth War of Religion. The terms of the Edict of Beaulieu, which ended the war on May 6, 1576, rewarded Alençon with the duchy of Anjou. (He will hereafter be referred to as Anjou in keeping with contemporary practice.) His elevation and his appearance as the peacemaker made the king's younger brother a force with which to be reckoned.[64] The terms of the settlement, commonly called the "Peace of Monsieur," persuaded many committed

---

[60] Salviati, *Correspondance*, vol. II, 162–3. See also *Calendar of State Papers, Foreign Series, of the Reign of Elizabeth, 1575–1577*, ed. Allan James Crosby (London: Longman, 1880), vol. XII, 350 (February 13 and 14, 1575); L'Estoile, *Mémoires-Journaux*, vol. I, 51.

[61] In March, Guise was stirring up enmity between Alençon and Henri de Navarre, a move which benefited no one except Henri III. *Calendar of State Papers*, vol. XII, 29–31 (March 18, 1575).

[62] Thou, *Histoire*, vol. VII, 285–6.   [63] Salviati, *Correspondance*, vol. II, 236 (May 30, 1575).

[64] For the treaty and the conflict with Alençon over it, see Louis de Gonzague, duc de Nevers, *Les Memoirs de Monsieur le Duc de Nevers, Prince de Mantouë* (Paris: Jolly, 1665), 92–135.

Catholics that the king was dominated by his brother ("Monsieur") and his mother.[65] The Catholic polemicist Clément Marchant charged Henri with refusing to impose Catholicism on his wayward Protestant subjects because of his own intemperance. For Marchant, Henri failed to embrace masculine moderation, and the continuing religious violence was divine retribution for his effeminacy. Marchant invoked the destruction of Sodom, linking it to sexual license and then excoriating Henri's court as a den of licentiousness.[66] The king's sexual reputation was already suffering at the hands of a hostile public.

Henri seems to have been aware of the criticism, and he insisted on his conformity with masculine norms. He told Philippe Hurault, comte de Chiverny, that,

il vouloit prendre & chercher une femme agreable, disant qu'il en desiroit une pour la bien aimer & en avoir des enfans, sans aller à d'autres femmes, comme beaucoup de ses predecesseurs, avoient fait.

he wanted to take and find a pleasant woman, . . . stating that he wanted one he could love well and with whom he could have children, without going to other women, as many of his predecessors had done.[67]

Henri wanted to fulfill his generative obligation and to do so without marital infidelity. On the one hand, Henri would not be taken to task as his father and grandfather had been for their mistresses. On the other, Henri was violating the unspoken rule that kings were to demonstrate their virility through sexual performance. Henri tried to assert his manly fortitude in other ways. In June, Henri let it be known that he was actively trying to father an heir:

The King with a very few is gone to Gallion in Normandy, and thence to go to Dieppe with the intention that the young Queen [Louise] may be bathed in salt water the sooner to conceive with child.[68]

Henri also went hunting, a routine activity for noblemen at the time, but not one of his preferred activities. The king's vigor received favorable comment, indicating that he was making headway.[69]

But Henri created a new, more intractable problem for himself. The Peace of Monsieur required him to pay off the mercenaries the Protestants had hired, a

[65] See for instance *Calendar of State Papers*, vol. XII, 333 (May 23, 1576); Salviati, *Correspondance*, 489 (July 24, 1576).
[66] Clément Marchant, *Remonstrance aux francoys, sur les vices qui de ce temps regnent en tous estats avec le remede à iceux* (Paris: Chez Nicolas Chesneau & Jean Poupy, 1576), 30v, 34v.
[67] Philippe Hurault, comte de Chiverny, *Mémoires de Mre. Philippe Hurault, comte de Chiverny, Chancelier de France sous les rois Henri III & Henri IV*, 2 vols. (The Hague: Chez T. Johnson, 1720), vol. I, 58.
[68] *Calendar of State Papers*, vol. XII, 346 (June 25, 1576).
[69] Guillaume le Riche, *Journal de Guillaume et de Michel le Riche, avocats du roi à Saint-Maixent (de 1534 à 1586)* (1846; reprint Geneva: Slatkine, 1971), 266 (June 2, 1576).

provision Catholic militants regarded as outrageous.[70] When many refused to pay the required tax subsidies, Henri visited the parishes of Paris accompanied by his *mignons* to present his case. According to L'Estoile, reporting in July 1576,

Le nom de Mignons commença, en ce temps, à trotter par la bouche du peuple, auquel ils estoient fort odieux, tant pour leurs façons de faire qui estoient badines et hautaines . . . Leurs exercices estoient de jouer, blasphémer, . . . paillarder, et suivre le Roy partout.	The name *Mignons* began, at this time, to travel by word of mouth through the people, to whom they were very odious, as much for their ways which were jesting and haughty . . . Their occupations are gambling, blaspheming . . . fornicating and following the King everywhere.

The king, his critics complained, lavished attention and money on these rowdy young men,

que pour leurs fards et accoustremens effeminés et impudiques . . . portoient leurs cheveux longuets, frisés et refrisés par artifices, remontans par dessus leurs petit bonnets de velours, comme font les putains du bordeau et leurs fraises de chemises de toiles d'atour empezées et longues de demi-pied que ce fust le chef Saint-Jean dans un plat.	that by their make-up and effeminate and lewd accoutrements . . . wore their hair long, curled and recurled by artifice, with little bonnets of velvet on top of it like whores in the brothels, and the collars are of starched finery and the ruffles on their linen shirts are one half foot long so that their heads look like St. John's on a platter.[71]

L'Estoile's account may be exaggerated, but it is confirmed in part by the English ambassador, who told Burghley: "Monsieur is gone towards Bourges and the King returned to Paris with a number of 'monkyes and papagayes' [popinjays]."[72]

The king offended by bringing bedecked young men to plead poverty and caused alarm by mixing power, politics, and sexuality. Having male favorites was not in itself a problem. As Nicolas Le Roux has demonstrated, Henri II had several, selected from eminent families.[73] But Henri III's favorites were drawn from relatively obscure families of the secondary noblesse, and raising them

---

[70] BN MS fr 23295, pp. 53–4. Claude Haton complains about the king's dealings over the "foreigners," as he called the Protestant mercenaries. See BN MS fr 11575, fols. 702v–3r. L'Estoile, *Mémoires-journaux*, vol. I, 143–9, includes poems about this episode.

[71] L'Estoile, *Mémoires-journaux*, vol. I, 142–3. On aspects of the polemical configurations throughout the pamphlet literature of the Wars of Religion, see Philip Benedict, "Of Marmites and Martyrs: Images and Polemics in the Wars of Religion," in *The French Renaissance in Prints from the Bibliothèque nationale de France*, ed. Karen Jacobson (Los Angeles: Grunwald Center for the Graphic Arts, 1994), 108–37. Zorach, *Blood, Milk, Ink, Gold*, 219–26 points out that criticism of the *mignons* often focused on sartorial excess.

[72] *Calendar of State Papers*, vol. XII, 350 (July 15, 1576). The court was in Paris at the time. See Boucher, *Société*, vol. II, 843.

[73] Le Roux, *Faveur du roi*, 33–8.

to great heights through physical intimacy with the king added to fears about the stability of the social order.[74] The culturally conservative Parlement of Paris echoed the noise from the streets when it complained that the patronage the *mignons* received was inappropriate given the dire financial situation.[75] Several delegates at the Estates-General at Blois complained that the *mignons* undermined Henri's resolve.[76] The language all around implied that the king let himself be led – itself indicative of his effeminacy – into spendthrift extravagance usually associated with women.

Structurally, the king inserted the *mignons* into the space usually occupied by female favorites, and rather than protect him from charges of succumbing to undue feminine influence, the *mignons* inspired sexual attacks on a grand scale. Poems circulating in Paris during January 1577 attacked the *mignons* for giving the king bad advice, complained about their financial wrong-doings, and accused them of exploiting the king's love:

Passer outre Venus, perdre ce qu'on labeure,	To take no notice of Venus, to lose that which one works for,
Doubler Ganimedès, renverser la nature,	Deceitful Ganymedes, reversing nature,
Aux pauvres affligés faire tousjours le sourd.	To the afflicted poor to always be deaf.[77]

The poem goes on to accuse the *mignons* of cravenly betraying their country. These poems retained a notion that the king was innocent and deceived, but to identify the *mignons* with Ganymede, the paradigmatic figure of homosexual youth in Renaissance art, was to associate Henri with Jupiter.[78] The active partner in his relationship with Ganymede, Jupiter could be read as subject to his passions and out of control.[79] Several poems relied on facile substitutions. A poem referring to one favorite as a sodomite used the Ganymede language to circle back to the king.[80] Other poems complained that serfs (read: low-born

---

[74] On the convergence of fears about social disruption and sodomy, see Alan Bray, "Homosexuality and the Signs of Male Friendship in Elizabethan England," in *Queering the Renaissance*, ed. Jonathan Goldberg (Durham, NC: Duke University Press, 1994), 40–61. The context is English, but many of the issues applied in France.

[75] See Nancy Lyman Roelker, *One King, One Faith: The Parlement of Paris and the Religious Reformations of the Sixteenth Century* (Berkeley: University of California Press, 1996), 324.

[76] *Calendar of State Papers*, vol. XII, 476; Salviati, *Correspondance*, vol. II, 594–5; BN MS fr 23295, 65, 77–8.

[77] L'Estoile, *Mémoires-journaux*, vol. I, 172. The king was at Blois from January until May of 1577 (Boucher, *Société*, vol. II, 843).

[78] Saslow, *Ganymede in the Renaissance*.

[79] See Rocke, *Forbidden Friendships*, 87–111, for the implications of the passive and active roles in terms of the male life-cycle and masculinity.

[80] L'Estoile, *Mémoires-journaux*, vol. I, 173. [Barnaud], *Le Cabinet du Roy de France*, 299, includes a poem with similar language. With respect to the production of pamphlets, the number produced remained in the teens and twenties until 1587, at which point the number jumped to 78 and then roughly doubled in 1588 and doubled again to 362 in 1589. The number

mignons) were in command, that women (read: not just Catherine de' Medici, but also sartorially extravagant male favorites) were acting as councilors, and that all of France was miserable.[81]

Where there was scrutiny of the king, the inevitable misreadings ensued. A month after the verses appeared, L'Estoile reported,

Ce pendant le Roy faisoit jouxtes, tournois, ballets et force masquarades, où il se trouvoit ordinairement habillé en femme, ouvroit son pourpoint et descouvroit sa gorge, y portant un collier de perles et trois collets de toile, deux à fraize et un renversé, ainsi que lors portoient les dames de sa Cour.

Nevertheless, the king made jousts, tournaments, ballets and a great many masquerades, where he was found ordinarily dressed as a woman, working his doublet and exposing his throat, there wearing a pearl necklace and three collars of linen, two ruffled and one turned upside down, in the same way as was then worn by the ladies of the court.[82]

The timing of this report is significant: it was February 24, the beginning of Carnival. Other sources confirm that Henri planned festivities for Carnival, and he enjoyed playing pranks, although he never again appeared to be cross-dressing.[83] If Henri did cross-dress for Carnival, he had terrible timing. Given the stress of the moment, the usual joke of cross-dressing as simultaneously subverting and confirming the "natural" order was difficult to relish. If he did not cross-dress, that his subjects thought he would is perhaps more telling. Consider too the ball Catherine de' Medici threw at Chenonceau in May 1577, after royal forces defeated the Protestants at La Charité. The English ambassador remarked matter-of-factly:

In the Queen Mother's banquet of the 12th the King, Monsieur [Anjou], and all the other great Estates were served with ladies apparelled by two and two in

---

was back down to 26 in 1592. See Denis Pallier, *Recherches sur l'imprimerie à Paris pendant la Ligue (1585–1594)* (Geneva: Droz, 1976), 55.

[81] L'Estoile, *Mémoires-journaux*, vol. I, 174–5. Barnaud, *Cabinet*, 306–7, includes the same themes.

[82] L'Estoile, *Mémoires-journaux*, vol. I, 180 (February 24, 1577). For the slippage of *mignons* into women, see also Scévole de Sainte-Marthe, *Les oeuvres de Scevole de Sainte-Marthe. Derniere Edition* (Paris: Jacques Villery, 1619), 171. The original edition was 1579. The phrasing, "Ces jeunes gens frisez, goldronnez, parfumez, / Fards qui de nostre temps n'estoient accoustumez, / Nous feroient bien mesprendre à discerner les Dames / D'entre les Chevaliers, qui ressemblent aux femmes" [The young men curled, bedecked, perfumed / Making those who in our time are not accustomed blush, / To us they quite misapprehend to discern the ladies / From the knights, who resemble the women] is virtually identical to language L'Estoile recorded.

[83] See Boucher, *Société*, vol. IV, 1184, for Henri's behavior in other years. See also "Extraits des comptes," vol. X, 427–8, for dressing the king and his intimates for Carnival in 1580. Expenses include silks of various colors, forty-three masks, ribbons, nineteen outfits for musicians, and a special suit for Henri's fool. On cross-dressing and carnival inversion, see Sylvie Steinberg, *La Confusion des sexes: le travestissement de la Renaissance à la Révolution* (Paris Fayard, 2001), 19. On the competitive nature of clothing display at Henri's court, see Jacqueline Boucher, *La Cour de Henri III* (Rennes: Ouest France, 1986), 74–6.

sundry colours. Madame de Retz representing the great Master, and four other ladies supplying the places of the four maitres d'hotel with white staves in their hands.[84]

In Paris, reports described two separate balls, one with cross-dressed women and the other with women of the court appearing half-nude.[85] The papal nuncio mentioned the serving women in passing after describing his congratulations to the king for his efforts on behalf of Catholicism.[86] What seemed reasonable to those present was transformed in Paris into sexual scandal. Sexual polemic was becoming a shorthand for a wide range of anxieties, many of which focused on the young men Henri had "made."

While scholars have noted that Henri presented himself in ways that caused public uproar, they have made few attempts to explain why he did so. Joseph Cady locates Henri's actions as an incipient sexual identity formation. Whether one accepts the possibility of thinking in those terms in sixteenth-century France or not, Cady begs the question of intentions.[87] Henri's persistence points to something more than throwing his favorites in the proverbial face of a suspicious French public. Why would Henri deliberately attract attention to himself in ways that were evidently taken against him? Given the sexual structures in which French kings operated, Henri had little choice. Since he had not fathered any children, he had to find another way to show he was a potent king. While leading his court was a way to do this, making public displays that were readily taken as sexually ambiguous may seem unpromising to us, but perhaps not to Henri. In an intellectual culture that reveled in ambiguity and paradox, poets routinely blurred the line between chaste desire and lascivious fulfillment. In addition to their various turns at serious and scabrous verse, poets such as Pierre de Ronsard and Philippe Desportes (who also served as an advisor to one of Henri's favorites) incorporated what Malcolm Quainton calls "ordered chaos" in their work.[88] The cultivated court loved word games and turning one phrase into another, which speaks to a willingness to read,

[84] *Calendar of State Papers*, vol. XII, 586. C. Chevalier, *Histoire de Chenonceau, ses artistes, ses fêtes, ses vicissitudes* (Lyon: Imprimerie Louis Perrin, 1868), 323–27, confirms that the ball took place, but relies for details entirely on L'Estoile, who was not there. See BN MS fr 26154, fol. 65, for extraordinary expenses in May 1577.

[85] L'Estoile, *Mémoires-journaux*, vol. I, 188 (May 15, 1577).

[86] Salviati, *Correspondance*, vol. II, 638. Although the sources are silent, it is possible that Catherine used her women to serve rather than the gentlemen of her sons, who were in conflict as discussed below.

[87] Cady, "'Masculine Love'."

[88] Malcolm Quainton, *Ronsard's Ordered Chaos: Visions of Flux and Stability in the Poetry of Pierre de Ronsard* (Manchester University Press, 1980).

as it were, on multiple levels.[89] Henri III located himself within a lineage of ambiguity and multiplicity.

The responses to displays of sexual ambiguity were unpromising, but Henri III did not have much to work with. For one thing, he was not conventionally masculine in his deportment (as the chronic criticism of it suggests). For another, he was unable to demonstrate his sexual prowess categorically because he remained childless. Consequently, he had to assert his male potency in different ways. His attachment to his *mignons* offered a model of love and reciprocity in a Neoplatonic mode to counter the proclivity toward sectarian violence in his kingdom. Henri tried to use male homosocial ties to move above the fray and beyond the reach of malefactors. Homosocial love became the way to transcend violence. This is most apparent in 1578, after Henri's *mignons* engaged a series of armed skirmishes around the court.[90] The leader of Henri's favorites, Jacques de Lévis, comte de Quélus (or Caylus) and another *mignon*, Maugiron, were mortally wounded and several others badly injured. Henri visited the injured daily, accepted poems from Ronsard and Amadis Jamyn written in their honor, erected funerary monuments for them, and commissioned Arnauld Sorbin, the orator who had eulogized Charles IX, to celebrate the dead.[91]

---

[89] On the arts at Henri's court, see Boucher, *La Cour*, 127–50. Anagrams would later be used against Henri, whose name was turned into "Vilain Hérodes" and "de Valois" into "O le Iudas." See David A. Bell, "Unmasking a King: The Political Uses of Popular Literature under the French Catholic League, 1588–89," *SCJ* 20 (1989): 371–86. See p. 377. For examples, see Anon., *Les Admirables et justes anagrammes de Henry de Valois* (Edinburgh [Paris]: Guillaume Petit, 1589). Discussed in Keith Cameron, *Henri III: Maligned or Malignant King?* (University of Exeter Press, 1978), 22–3. Anagrams on the names of *mignons* also appeared. See Jacqueline Boucher, "Culture des notables et mentalité populaire dans la propagande qui entraîna la chute de Henri III," in *Mouvements populaires et conscience sociale, XVIe–XIXe siècles* ed. Jean Nicolas (Paris: CNRS, 1985), 339–49. See p. 342.

[90] The disorder at court attracted much contemporary attention. See *Calendar of State Papers*, vol. XIII, 502 (February 15, 1578) and 658–60 (May 3, 1578); Salviati, *Correspondance*, vol. II, 746–53 (February 13 and 15, 1578); Abel Desjardins, ed., *Négociations diplomatiques de la France avec la Toscane. Documents recueillis par Giuseppi Canestrini et publiées par Abel Desjardins*, 6 vols. (Paris: Imprimerie nationale, 1876), vol. IV, 137–65 (February 1578); and Thou, *Histoire*, vol. VII, 724–8. Contemporaries expressed concerns about perceptions of the king's authority because of the quarrels.

[91] Pierre de Ronsard, "Epitaphe du seigneur de Quélus en dialogue," *Œuvres complètes*, vol. II, 958–61; "Pour le mesme," vol. II, 961. See also Philippe Desportes, "Sur la mort de Jacques de Levy," *Œuvres de Philippe Desportes*, intro. Alfred Michiels (Paris: Adolphe Delahays, 1858), 476–77, in which Desportes describes Quélus as "beauty most perfect" and compares him to great warriors and ancient paragons of beauty such as Adonis. Jamyn was listed as receiving annual wages from the Queen Mother's household accounts. See AN KK 116 (1579), 27v. He had been in Henri's *maison* earlier. See AN K 134, 31r (1574). Whether Henri commissioned these pieces remains unclear. They may have been offered on spec. See Boucher, *La Cour*, 142. The Jamyn pieces and others are reproduced in L'Estoile, *Mémoires-journaux*, vol. I, 245–54.

By reabsorbing the *mignons* in language of love and affection, Henri was trying to shape his image as a king and following the traditions he knew. One recurrent theme in the French Renaissance, invoked in the decoration of Fontainebleau and rehearsed by Charles IX in reference to his marriage, was the idea that violence, usually in its quintessential form as war, could be overcome by love. Many of Henri's contemporaries believed that love held people together: love was the source of order and deference in the family; love for king and country inspired service and devotion; a ruler's relationship to his subjects was cast as paternal or marital love. If we remember that the court and the country had been ripped apart since 1562 by increasingly brutal violence, that this violence, with its overtones of expiation and purification, had usually been met with more violence, and that such responses had solved nothing, then Henri's attempt to present himself as the figural embodiment of love makes some sense.[92]

However, as the angst over Neoplatonism's relationship to corporeal desire suggests, contemporaries believed that love tainted by carnal desire could destroy the soul. (See above, Chapter 3.) Henri's critics saw his love as more carnal than pure. Henri's use of love language made criticism not just possible, but likely. By the 1570s, the Neoplatonic notion of desire between a (male) lover and a (male) beloved had been largely displaced by formulations of heterosexual love. Scurrilous commentary in the poetic mode that made its truth claims through sexually explicit language swelled to fill the gap between the king's expressions of idealized love and the carnal presumptions about it:

Quélus n'entend pas la manière	Quélus not knowing how
De prendre les gens par devant;	To take men from the front;
S'il eust pris Bussy par derrière,	If he'd taken Bussy from behind,
Il lui eust fourré bien avant.	He'd have stuffed it to him well before.[93]

The poem suggestively linked the sexual implication of "from behind" to the cowardly act of attacking from behind. Such images painted Henri's public association with Quélus as effeminate and sodomitical. Other verses made a mockery of the image archive Henri had developed in praise of his *mignons*. One poem utilized the classical references of Mars and Venus to charge Maugiron with sodomy and Henri with involvement in it:

---

[92] On ritual violence in early modernity, see Natalie Zemon Davis, "The Rites of Violence" in *Society and Culture in Early Modern France* (Stanford University Press, 1975), 152–87; René Girard, *La violence et le sacré* (Paris: B. Grasset, 1972).

[93] L'Estoile, *Mémoires-journaux*, vol. I, 232. I have followed Cady's translation, "'Masculine Love'," p. 149, n. 21. For other reports of the complaints about the *mignons* at this juncture, see Thou, *Histoire*, vol. VII, 727–8; BN MS fr 23295, 108–9.

Vénus son beau devant, et Priapus aura	Venus [had] his beauty in front, and Priapus had
Le derriere pour soi, qui le devant n'empire.	the derrière for himself, which the front of him did not make worse.
Mars, frustré de son droit,	Mars, frustrated in his rights,
forcenoit en son ire,	furious in his ire,
Et qu'il auroit son ame en partage il jura!	And that he would share his soul he swore![94]

For his critics, Henri's attention to the dead *mignons* was excessive: "Quélus est doncques mort, . . . / Trop aimé de son Roy" [Quélus is therefore dead . . . / Too much loved of his King]. The historian Jacques-Auguste de Thou observed that Henri's behavior was taken amiss, as did the Catholic Claude Haton and the Protestant Agrippa d'Aubigné.[95] The logic was starting to circle on itself: Excess was effeminate; effeminacy was sexually suspect; the king was excessive and effeminate.

Given all the criticism, the homosocial strategy seems an obvious failure, but it is important to note that it almost succeeded. The deaths among the *mignons* in 1578 enabled the emergence of two *archmignons*, Jean-Louis Nogaret de La Valette, later *duc et pair* of Epernon, and Anne de Joyeuse, baron d'Arques and later *duc et pair* of Joyeuse. Henri showered both men with honors and titles. Epernon, in his mid-twenties, became governor of La Fère in 1580, colonel-general of the infantry, governor of Metz and Provence, and a peer in 1581. In 1579, 19-year-old Joyeuse received command of a *compagnie d'ordonnance* and the government of Mont-Saint-Michel. After elevation to the peerage, Joyeuse became admiral of France, chevalier of the order of Holy Spirit, governor of Normandy, and governor of the duchy of Alençon.[96] The spectacular success of Joyeuse and Epernon indicated in material terms that loving the king could be very rewarding.

Henri insisted homosociality could be combined with royal generation. In September 1581, Henri arranged for Joyeuse to marry Marguerite de Lorraine, the half-sister of Queen Louise. With this wedding the *archmignon* became a member of the royal family, and the suspected sodomite was transformed

---

[94] L'Estoile, *Mémoires-journaux*, vol. I, 249. Maugiron's tomb in the church of St. Paul was among several destroyed by Parisian mobs on January 2, 1589, when news of the Guise murders reached the capital. See vol. III, 230–1, and the discussion in Chevallier, *Henri III*, 680. An engraving of Maugiron's tomb made in 1588 is reproduced in Boucher, *La Cour*, 61.

[95] Thou, *Histoire*, vol. VII, 727. For Haton's complaints about the "noise" caused by the king, see BN MS fr 11575, fol. 743r. See also BN MS fr 23295, p. 109. For d'Aubigné, see *Les Tragiques*, in *Œuvres*, ed. Henri Weber (Paris: Gallimard, 1969), 72–3 esp.

[96] Both men also provided for their families: Epernon's brother, Bernard, received valuable government posts, and Joyeuse's brother secured a cardinal's hat. Arlette Jouanna, "Faveur et favoris: l'exemple des *mignons* de Henri III," in *Henri III et son temps actes du colloque international du Centre de la Renaissance de Tours, octobre 1989*, ed. Robert Sauzet (Paris: Vrin, 1992), 155–65; Pierre Chevalier, *Henri III: roi shakespearean* (Paris: Fayard, 1985), 425–31.

into the (ostensibly) conventional husband. The wedding took place at court with great pomp and circumstance. Festivities included masquerades, sword contests, jousts, music, and dances and ballets.[97] Henri participated in and helped plan the wedding program, which included entertainments that presented the king as a potent figure. One theatrical cast Henri as the God of Marriage surrounded by a group of boys dressed in matching outfits. A performative version of Henri's practice of dressing his *mignons* to display their status, the skit unwittingly suggested homosocial generation through sartorial excess. In a staged combat, after Henri's "troops" conquered Love, the king united the opposing troops, led by the Duke of Guise, with his own.[98] Gaining peace through love of a superior being (read: Henri) illustrated the Neoplatonic ideal of unity with the divine, but the combat context meant that integration came at the risk of war and death. And the artificiality of the performance is striking. Henri III's appearance in the combat literally staged his masculine prowess.[99] The artificiality highlighted Henri's distance from the real thing.

It would seem that performance was all. A ballet Queen Louise hosted on October 15 pulled out all the stops to present the king as effectively masculine in his procreative potentiality. The central figure was Henri (by mythological association) as master of the court and its potent ruler. Set on Circe's island and featuring lavish set pieces about fertility and reproduction, the climax featured Jupiter and Minerva defeating Circe.[100] At the ballet's conclusion (after five and a half hours), Louise

approchant du Roy son seigneur, le print par la main, & luy feit present d'une grande medaille d'or, où il y avoit dedans un Daulphin qui nageoit en la mer:	approaching the King, her lord, and took by the hand and presented him with a large gold medal which had on it a Dolphin swimming in the sea: then everyone took

---

[97] Thou, *Histoire*, vol. VIII, 551. Other commemorations include Ronsard, "Epithalame de monseigneur de Joyeuse, admiral de France," *Œuvres complètes*, vol. II, 297–9. Paintings commemorating events were prepared as well. See Lucienne Colliard, "Tableaux représentant des bals à la cour des Valois," *Gazette des Beaux-Arts* 61 (1963): 147–56, and Louis Dimier, *Histoire de la peinture de portrait en France au XVIᵉ siècle*, 3 vols. (Paris and Brussels: G. Van Oest et Cie., 1924–1926). For accounts of the festivities, see Frances Yates, "Poésie et musique dans les 'Magnificences' au mariage du Duc de Joyeuse," in *Musique et poésie au XVIᵉ siècle* (Paris: CNRS, 1954): 241–60; Jacques Lavaud, "Les noces de Joyeuse," *Humanisme et Renaissance* 2 (1935): 44–52; and Margaret McGowan, "1581: The Spectacle of Power," in *A New History of French Literature*, ed. Denis Hollier (Cambridge, MA: Harvard University Press, 1989), 243–8. The collective biography by Pierre de Vaissière, *Messieurs de Joyeuses (1560–1615)* (Paris: Albin Michel, 1926) includes an account of the wedding. See pp. 60–83.

[98] BN MS fr 15831, fols. 90v–91r, "Nopce de M. de Joyeuse."

[99] To be fair, Henri II also sometimes just watched. See Anon., *La magnificence de la superbe et triomphante entrée*, sig. C1v, for Henri II observing combat theatricals.

[100] Balthazar de Beaujoyeulx, *Le Balet Comique, 1581. A Facsimile with an Introduction*, ed. Margaret M. McGowan (Binghamton: Center for Medieval and Renaissance Studies, 1982), fol. 55r.

lors chacun print pour augure asseuré de
celuy que Dieu leur donnera pour la bon-
heur de ce royaume.

it for an assured omen of the happiness
God would give them for this kingdom.[101]

The ballet re-appropriated the Jupiter image in ways that brought out Henri's
ambiguous position, but asserted the king's triumph: Henri was the source of
order, enabling Jupiter to triumph over the chaos represented by Circe.

What Henri offered was the hope that he would fulfill his reproductive
role. Henri coupled the reproductive claims of the festivities for Joyeuse with
renewed efforts to demonstrate his generative capacity. As François I had done,
Henri participated in religious processions aimed at securing an heir.[102] As he
explained,

c'est le seul moyen par lequel je doibs
esperer tirer mes sujets des calamitez et
miseres qui les affligent, lesquelles je con-
fesse proceder de mes vices et pechez; et
quand il plairoit a sa divine bonté que
seul j'en portasse la penitence pour le
salut et redemption de tant de pauvre et
desolé peuple qu'il a sousmis sous ma
puissance, lequel succombe sous la faix,
je m'estimerois tres heureux.

it is the only way by which I can hope
to extract my subjects from the calamities
and miseries which afflict them, which I
confess originated from my vices and sins;
and when it would please his divine bounty
that I alone should bring them penitence
for the welfare and redemption of such a
poor and desolate people that he has sub-
jugated under my power, which succumbs
under the burden, I will deem myself very
happy.[103]

On January 23, 1579, he went to Olinville to be purged and then to Chartres,
where

et y prist deux chemises de Nostre-Dame
de Chartres, une pour lui, l'autre pour la
Roine sa femme. Ce qu'aiant fait, il revinst
à Paris, coucher avec elle, en espérance de
lui faire un enfant, par la grace de Dieu et
de ses chemises.

he took two chemises to Our Lady of
Chartres, one for himself, the other for
the Queen his wife. Having done this, he
returned to Paris, slept with her in hope of
giving to him a child, by the grace of God
and of the chemises.[104]

In January 1582, the king and queen walked from Paris to Chartres, praying for
an heir to the throne. Six months later, the royal couple repeated the journey.[105]
Processions to pray for an heir were organized in Paris in December, and in

---

[101] Beaujoyeulx, *Le Balet Comique*, 63v. For an image of the medal, see 65r. Much of the same
imagery was used for a ballet in March, 1585. See BL Additional MS 8719, fol. 17r–18v.
[102] Henri required the court to follow him on his penitential devotions as early as December, 1574.
See BN MS n. a. f. 7225, fols. 35r–84v; Thou, *Histoire*, vol. VII, 165. The Cardinal de Lorraine
caught his death of cold on one of them.
[103] Henri III, *Lettres*, vol. IV, 285 (no. 3541), Henri to Arnaud du Ferrier (October 9, 1579).
[104] L'Estoile, *Mémoires-journaux*, vol. I, 306–7.
[105] BN MS Italien 1732, pp. 341–6 (June, 1582); BN MS fr 11575, fol. 1008v (Claude Haton).
Boucher, *Deux épouses*, 138–40, notes additional actions of Louise.

January 1583, Queen Louise went alone on a pilgrimage to Nôtre-Dame de Liesse to pray for a son. In April 1583, the king and queen walked to Chartres and Cleri, again praying for an heir.[106] At some point, Henri sought reassurance from an astrologer, who told him:

Sire vostre fils vivra aage d'homme, regnera plys que vous – mais lui & vous serez tous differens en inclinations & humeurs.	Sire, your son will live to be a man, and reign longer than you, but you and he will be entirely different in inclinations and humors.[107]

Speaking of his hopes to procreate, Henri remarked that, "with this shot my powder will catch fire, something that would astonish my detractors."[108] Elsewhere, Henri cast himself as a sinner who could be healed by God's mercy, earning some respect from Catholics.[109] To be sure, his abject, penitential demonstrations highlighted his failure to produce an heir of his body,[110] but his efforts provided some hope.

Emphasizing his interest in fruitful generation combined with strategic deployment of the *archmignons* helped dampen criticism for a time. As Nicolas Le Roux has demonstrated, the *archmignons* protected the king by acting as interlocutors for anyone who sought the king's favor. Henri utilized his favorites to forge a political position distinct from either the ultra-Catholic one staked out by Guise or the Protestant one represented primarily by Henri de Navarre. Henri III sent Joyeuse as his Catholic champion to do battle with Navarre's troops while directing Epernon to make overtures to Navarre and the Protestants.[111]

---

[106] L'Estoile, *Mémoires-journaux*, vol. II, 95, 97–8, 121. A month before, the duc de Guise recommended an empiric from Dauphiné to help the queen conceive. See Boucher, *Deux épouses*, 135.

[107] BN MS Dupuy 588, fol. 205v.

[108] Quoted in Anita M. Walker and Edmund H. Dickerman, "The King Who Would Be a Man: Henry III, Gender Identity and the Murders at Blois, 1588," *Historical Reflexions / Réflections historiques* 24 (1998): 252–81. They discuss this admission in conjunction with an apparent collapse in Henri's confidence more generally. See pp. 274–5. The source is Henri III to Villeroy, [Undated, 1586?], BN MS n. a. f. 1245, fol. 148.

[109] René de Lucinge, sieur des Allymes, *Lettres sur la cour d'Henri III en 1586*, ed. Alain Dufour (Geneva: Droz, 1966), 243 (June 18, 1585). Claude Haton, often highly critical, commented approvingly on Henri's efforts. See BN MS fr 11575, fol. 1008v.

[110] See *Calendar of State Papers*, vol. XV, 463 (January 27, 1582); vol. XVI, 249 (August 15, 1582); René de Lucinge, *Lettres sur les débuts de la Ligue (1585)*, ed. Alain Dufour (Geneva: Droz, 1964), 242–3 (November 19, 1585); Lucinge, *Lettres, 1586*, 130 (March 25, 1586). This last example was in part to escape pressure from Catholic militants about the Protestants. Penitence could have several uses. On Henri's efforts lapsing into disillusion, see for instance Lucinge, *Lettres de 1587. L'année des reîtres*, ed. James J. Supple (Geneva: Droz, 1994), 116 (April 6, 1587).

[111] Le Roux, *Faveur du roi*, 461–504, especially. On Epernon in deliberate conflict with Guise, see Lucinge, *Lettres, 1586*, 41, 121, 130. Henri also got to play the peace-maker between the two; see p. 117.

But it was a fragile structure. Anjou's death on June 10, 1584, left the Protestant Henri de Navarre as heir apparent. The extremist Catholic League reconstituted itself, and its members were determined to exclude Navarre. It is no accident that, within months, sonnets appeared highlighting the king's reproductive failure: "Le Roy na poinct d'enfant pour succeder en france" [The King has no child to succeed in France].[112] Henri was still childless when Joyeuse died at Coutras (October 20, 1587), precipitating the collapse of the king's attempt to build a Catholic alternative to the League.[113] Because Epernon had negotiated with Navarre, suspicious Catholics attacked him. The earlier storms around the *mignons* reappeared as critics fused Henri's history of love language, demonstrations of favor, and childlessness as evidence of his unnatural love for Epernon.[114] After May 12, 1588, the Day of the Barricades, when Henri lost control of Paris to the duc de Guise, League polemicists attacked the king for all the ways his masculine deportment had been found insufficient. Henri's decision to flee Paris rather than to stand up to Guise prompted further derision.[115] In August, the League sponsored the printing of *L'Histoire de Pierre de Gaverston*, which compared the ill-fated English monarch Edward II and his *mignon* (and alleged partner in sodomy) to Henri and Epernon.[116] After Henri arranged for the murders of Guise and his brother, the

---

[112] BL Additional MS 8719, fol. 2r. The manuscript includes *Discours faict au mois D'Avril 1585 sur les troubles qui arriverent en ce temps. du regne du Roy Henry de Vallois iiime de ce nom* (fols. 2r–3r) as well.

[113] Le Roux, *Faveur du roi*, 620, 681, remarks that Catholics developed a narrative of Coutras as a plot by the supposedly Protestant Epernon to eliminate Joyeuse. Henri's granting of Joyeuse's governments to Epernon made this belief seem credible.

[114] Charles Pinselet, *Le martyre des deux freres*, in *Archives curieuses de l'histoire de France, depuis Louis XI jusqu'à Louis XVIII, ou Collection de pièces rares et intéressantes, telles que chroniques, mémoires, pamphlets, lettres, et vies*, ed. L. Cimber and F. Danjou (Paris: Beauvais, 1834–1837), ser. 1, vol. I, 57–107. Henri is described as sodomitical, "denatured," and effeminate because of Epernon. The original pamphlet was published in 1589. Henri continued to sponsor lavish court spectacles as well. See the description, "Ballet faict par le Roy Henry de Vallois iiiem de le nom le jour de Caresme," (1585), which was thrown to honor the English and Flemish ambassadors. BL MS Additional 8719, fols. 17r–18r.

[115] Louis de Saint-Yon, *Histoire tres-veritable de ce qui est advenu en ceste ville de Paris, depuis le septiesme de May 1588, jusques au dernier jour de Juin ensuyvant audit an* (Paris: Michel Joüin, 1588), 24. Henri was also described taking counsel from his mother in derisive terms (6) and his flight was contrasted with Catherine's fortitude when she, at 78, went to the Sainte Chapelle the day after Henri left and before the barricades were dismantled (30).

[116] Jean Boucher, *Histoire tragique et memorable de Pierre de Gaverston* (n. p.: no pub., 1588). Boucher's work provoked several responses, including Anon., *Reponce à l'Antigaverston de Nogaret* (n. p.: no pub., 1588), and Anon., *Réplique à l'Antigaverston, ou response faict à l'histoire de Gaverston, par le Duc d'Espernon* (n. p.: no pub., 1588). See pp. 24–5 of the latter for reference to sodomitical acts. Gaverston also leaked into other pamphlets condemning Henri. See for instance Anon., *Les Choses horribles, contenues en une lettre envoyée à Henry de Valois, par un Enfant de Paris, le vingthuitiesme de Janvier 1589* (Paris: Jacques Gregoire, 1589), 9, and Anon., *Dialogue du Royaume; auquel est discourse des vices et vertus des Roys, et de leur Etablissement* (Paris: Chez Didier Millot, 1589), 119.

cardinal de Lorraine, at Blois on December 23–4, 1588, League pamphleteers called Henri a "bugger" and a "tyrant" in the same phrase.[117] Henri became a character in "autobiographical" pamphlets, confessing to adultery, fornication, lechery, incest, and sodomy along with tyrannical impulses.[118] Sexual excess became political excess. The positive images of masculine comportment that Henri had tried to cultivate were inundated by counter-assertions of effeminate lack of control over self, sex, and subjects.

Polemics do not kill people, but people inspired by polemics do. On August 1, 1589, the monk Jacques Clément stabbed Henri III, who died the next day. The accusations against the king that inspired Clément came out of the sexualized representational environment that Henri helped create but could not control. Homosocial ties all too easily enabled assumptions about inappropriate intimacy to be turned into ungenerative, sinful sodomy. Henri III's inability to procreate combined with the sexualized homosocial context he created to negate the notion that the king could overcome violence with love. The Neoplatonic valences Henri employed to create his patronage ties became markers of prurient and deviant misdeeds that remain to this day the "facts" of his reign.

The politics of heterosexual constraint

Henri IV contrasted his own potent womanizing (he had at least six illegitimate children in addition to six legitimate ones) with Henri III's impotent sodomy. Heterosexual potency, however, could have serious drawbacks. Because he had not broken the pattern of royal reproductive failure when he came to the throne, Henri IV was susceptible to some of the same charges with respect to his sexual reputation. And Henri IV had some additional complications. Not only was Henri without legitimate offspring, he was married to Henri III's sister, Marguerite. They separated unofficially in 1586 and she stayed away from court until 1605. Contemporaries blamed the couple's infertility on Marguerite who had no children despite rumors (now much disputed by historians) that she was promiscuous.[119] Henri himself enjoyed a series of mistresses, and the need

---

[117] L'Estoile, *Mémoires-journaux*, vol. III, 241–2; 284.

[118] Anon., *Les Propos lamentables de Henry de Valois, tires de sa confession, par us remords de conscience, qui tousjours tourmente les miserables* (Paris: Pierre Mercier, 1589), 10. See also André de Rossant, *Les Meurs humeurs et comportemens de Henry de Valois representezx au vray depuis sa naissance* (Paris: Anthoine le Riche, 1589). Both are discussed in Cameron, *Henri III*, 17–18 with respect to League depictions of Henri as a tyrant. David Potter, "Kingship in the Wars of Religion: The Reputation of Henri III of France," *European History Quarterly* 25 (1995): 485–528, points out that Rossant had no qualms in 1589 about listing Henri's alleged misdeeds with both sodomitical *mignons* and nuns in the same paragraph. See p. 501.

[119] The origins, implications, and points of veracity or otherwise are discussed in Eliane Viennot, *Marguerite de Valois: histoire d'une femme, histoire d'un mythe* (Paris: Payot, 1993).

to assert his masculinity and proper functioning as a monarch by producing children perhaps pushed him toward a more public and aggressive presentation of his sexual prowess. If Henri III's failure to procreate undermined his access to masculine modalities of representation, Henri IV's ability to do so would facilitate his assertions of masculine efficacy. That is why, despite his marriage, Henri had a habit of promising his mistresses he would marry them if they gave him children, particularly sons.[120]

But sons by mistresses could also be problematic. Henri's behavior with his mistresses, especially Gabrielle d'Estrées, raised troubling questions. Henri's conundrum was that the potency and masculinity he succeeded in demonstrating by getting Gabrielle pregnant did him little good since she was not his wife. Henri needed to find a way to marry her, and to persuade his subjects that doing so was a good idea. While he might appear to be returning to a mode of heterosexual performativity in the manner of François I and Henri II, Henri IV had to negotiate the history of royal mistresses who absorbed criticism about the king's sexuality, royal representations of fecundity, the repeated disappointments around royal procreative potentiality, and the anxiety produced by Henri III's ambiguous masculinity.

Henri IV's negotiations began when he met Gabrielle d'Estrées in November 1590. Despite finding Henri physically off-putting, by the following April, she apparently allowed the king into her bed.[121] Gabrielle was twenty years Henri's junior and unmarried. In August 1592, Henri arranged for Gabrielle to marry to Nicolas d'Amerval, seigneur de Liancourt.[122] Traditionally, brief flings might involve unmarried women, but long-term liaisons with married or widowed women were less threatening to the king's legitimate family. Moreover, the king's participation in double adultery seemed slightly less reprehensible than if he was the only culpable party. Gabrielle was a married woman committing

---

[120] After Gabrielle d'Estrées died, Henri promised Henriette d'Entraigues that he would marry her within six months of October 1, 1599, if she gave him a son. See Henri IV, *Recueil des Lettres Missives*, ed. Berger de Xivrey and J. Gaudet, 9 vols. (Paris: Imprimerie nationale, 1843–1876), 5: 224–7 (Letters to Henriette d'Entraigues and her father, both dated April 21, 1600); Maximilien de Béthune, duc de Sully, *Mémoires des sages et royales oeconomies d'estat, Nouvelle collection des mémoires pour servir à l'histoire de France*, ed. Michaud and Poujoulat, 32 vols. (Paris: Imprimerie d'Edouard Proux, 1836–1839), 2nd ser., vol. II, 320. Sully claimed he retrieved the promise from Henriette's father and destroyed it. Marguerite de Valois, *Mémoires de Marguerite de Valois*, ed. Ludovic Lalanne (Paris: P. Jannet, 1858), 173–80, reported that Henri made a similar promise to marry another mistress, Françoise de Montmorency-Fosseux ("Fosseuse") in 1582.

[121] The narrative of their early relationship is discussed in Desclouzeaux, "Le mariage et le divorce de Gabrielle d'Estrées d'après des documents nouveaux," *Revue historique* 30 (1886): 49–106.

[122] Desclouzeaux, "Le mariage," 65–75, claims that Gabrielle's father arranged the marriage. Inès Murat, *Gabrielle d'Estrées* (Paris: Fayard, 1992), 75–81, argues that it was Gabrielle's idea – so she could maintain her clandestine relationship with Roger de Bellegarde.

adultery with a married man. The symmetry of the illicit extramarital behavior dampened moral criticism of the king.

Then Gabrielle gave birth to César on June 7, 1594, providing Henri with a son he wanted to acknowledge as his own. César meant that the king, for the first time in two decades, was not childless. Henri IV had proven his virility and potency, but what good was that to the realm if the king could not recognize his own son? Counting on the desire for a settled succession, Henri embarked on an unprecedented course: he sought to clear the path to marry Gabrielle. Paradoxically, given that the impetus was fatherhood, Henri's actions brought his masculinity into question. Henri's apparent willingness to ignore or subvert the religious and political constraints against such an action raised concerns about his having lost control of his reason. On August 27, 1594, Gabrielle filed for an annulment at Amiens. Despite the objections of Liancourt, the French Church (under pressure from Henri) granted it on December 24, 1594. Leaning on the Church in France was one thing, but Henri also needed the Papacy to annul his marriage to Marguerite. Despite Henri's conversion, Gregory XIII remained suspicious of the twice-relapsed heretic and was not about to help Henri marry his mistress. The refusal of the Papacy to accede to Henri's wishes inspired expressions of unease about the king's moral position. Clerics harangued Henri with pointed references to Biblical examples of kingdoms destabilized by family concerns.[123]

Henri responded by trying to present his own set of imperatives, initially in symbolic and artistic terms. As soon as César was born, court artists began producing images of Gabrielle and César in conjunction with portraits of other members of Henri's immediate family.[124] These images, combined with engravings pairing Gabrielle with Henri, located the king's mistress in the royal family and announced her location to the court and observers of it. The king had "HG" carved in the frieze of the Grande Galerie of the Louvre and Guillaume Dupré executed a medal with Henri on the face and Gabrielle on the reverse.[125] Contemporary understanding of the images or messages on the reverse was that

[123] Jean de Serres, *Voeu pour la prosperité du Roy & du royaume* (Paris: J. Mettayer 1597), 25–6, 65. The speech was delivered in November, 1596.

[124] Cynthia Burlingham, "Portraiture as Propaganda: Printing during the Reign of Henri IV," *The French Renaissance in Prints from the Bibliothèque nationale de France*, ed. Karen Jacobson (Los Angeles: Grunwald Center for the Graphic Arts), 138–51, notes the shift in subject matter, but primarily characterizes it around the sitters. That is, after 1595, portraiture shades off from court images into family depictions. Jean Adhémar, "Thomas de Leu et les portraits gravés d'Henri IV," *Maso Finiguerra* 2 (1937): 219–26, notes the emphasis on the succession question in court portraits around 1598.

[125] The medal was completed in 1597. Sylvie Béguin, "Contribution à l'iconographie d'Henri IV," in *Avènement d'Henri IV quatrième centenaire, V: Les arts au temps d'Henri IV* (Pau: J. & D., 1992), 41–61.

they expanded on the theme or portrait on the obverse.[126] Henri was the primary figure, with Gabrielle supporting him.

Where Henri used royal symbolic traditions, his subjects used popular ones to indicate their worries. Henri cast his virility as integral to the stability of the realm; contemporaries read his excessive devotion to Gabrielle as causing him to compromise the future. Scurrilous verses called Gabrielle a whore and compared Henri to Sardanapalus, the ancient Assyrian monarch who was so depraved that his army rebelled against him.[127] Critics questioned whether Henri had the requisite reason to control his appetites. Henri seemed to be the captivated lover who had succumbed to his desires and was about to make a serious mistake. When word spread that Henri wanted to marry Gabrielle, opponents left verses on the king's bed calling César, "un fils de putain" [a son of a whore] and Gabrielle:

Putain dont les soeurs sont putantes,	A whore whose sisters were whores
Comme fut la mère jadis,	Like their mother before them
Et les cousines et les tantes.	And their cousins and aunts.[128]

The poems warned Henri that it would be better for his realm to be invaded than for a bastard to inherit. Welcome as a generative king might be, rational sexual self-control was necessary as well.

In reply, Henri emphasized that his devotion to the public good was greater than his love interest. At court, Henri pointedly displayed his control over his physical desires. In March 1597, the king and court were enjoying festivities when news of a Spanish attack on Amiens arrived. After commenting that this news was a scourge from Heaven, Henri announced to Gabrielle, "Ma maistresse, il faut quitter nos armes, et monter à cheval, pour faire une autre guerre" [My mistress, I must lay aside our arms, and mount a horse, to make

---

[126] Joanna Woods-Marsden, "Portrait of a Lady, 1430–1520, " in *Virtue and Beauty: Leonardo's Ginevra de' Benci and Renaissance Portraits of Women*, ed. David Alan Brown (Princeton University Press, 2001), 62–87, esp. pp. 82–3.

[127] L'Estoile, *Mémoires-journaux*, vol. VII, 89: "Ha! vous parlez de vostre Roy! / –Non fais, je vous jure ma foy! / Par Dieu! j'ai l'âme trop réale: / Je parle de Sardanapale. / Non sempre sta in bordello: / Hercule! non se fare immortello / Au roiaume de Conardize, / Où pour Madame la Marquize, / Les Grands Mons sont mis à Monceaux, / Et toute la France en morceaux, / Pour assouvir son putanisme. [Ha! You speak of your king! / I am not doing so, I swear on my faith / By God! I have a soul too real: / I speak of Sardanapalus. / Not always staying in the bordello: / Hercules! One is not made immortal / In the realm of the Nags, / Where, for Madame the Marquise, / the Great Mounds are at Monceaux, / And all of France is torn apart, / In order to satisfy her whoring.] On Sardanapalus, see Rachel Weil, "Sometimes a Scepter is Only a Scepter: Pornography and Politics in Restoration England," in *The Invention of Pornography: Obscenity and the Origins of Modernity, 1500–1800*, ed. Lynn Hunt (New York: Zone Books, 1993), 124–53. The figure was also used against Henri III, and seems to have been well known. See for instance [Barnaud], *Le Cabinet du Roy*, 305.

[128] L'Éstoile, *Mémoires-journaux*, vol. VII, 178.

another war].[129] His commitment to the masculine virtues of command and his willingness to part from Gabrielle signaled to observers that he put duty before his lady love. Henri's actions emphasized his most central masculine role, and announced his priorities: Love was subordinate to war.[130]

When Henri situated Gabrielle so as to perform her designated place in the monarchy's future, dissent became correspondingly obvious. Having made Gabrielle duchesse de Beaufort in July 1597, Henri recognized César and raised the toddler to the peerage as duc de Vendôme. Critics castigated the king for his single-minded devotion to Gabrielle.[131] Despite continued opposition – L'Estoile reported that some people started calling Gabrielle "La Duchesse d'Ordure" [the duchess of filth][132] – Henri indicated that he considered a duchess to be of a plausible rank to be his wife. Henri commissioned matching pendant portraits that compared himself to Mars and Gabrielle to Minerva as goddess of wisdom and of the art of war. Significantly, he did not have Gabrielle cast as Venus.[133] Within Renaissance modalities of representation, she was situated as supporting the king, rather than distracting him.

By the spring of 1598, Gabrielle's prominence prompted rumors that the king and his mistress were betrothed. Henri displayed Gabrielle for all intents and purposes as his wife in conjunction with the Treaty of Vervins, which ended the war with Spain. At a dinner celebrating the peace in June, Gabrielle and the king led the festivities. Gabrielle's status was indicated by the service at dinner:

La collation y fust faire magnifique, où Madame de Guise servist la duchesse de Beaufort, qui estoit assise dans une chaise: à laquelle Madame de Guise, avec de grandes révérences, présentoit les plats.	The collation there was magnificent, where Madame de Guise served the duchesse de Beaufort, who was seated in a chair, and to whom, Madame de Guise presented the dishes with great reverences.[134]

With consternation, L'Estoile observed that Henri had always respected decorum by leaving his wife's seat empty or filling it with his own sister. Gabrielle now occupied the queen's position and one of the most exalted families in

---

[129] L'Estoile, *Mémoires-journaux*, vol. VII, 84. See also Henri's speech before the Parlement of Paris of April 19, 1597 in Henri IV, *Lettres Missives*, vol. IV, 743. Henri discussed his efforts against the Spanish, and emphasized his readiness to defend the state (*l'état*).

[130] Henri sought advice on the issue of marrying Gabrielle. See BN MS fr 15599, fols. 483r–487r; MS fr. 23301, pp. 13–46. For the context and an extended discussion, see Crawford, "The Politics of Promiscuity."

[131] BN MS fr 23301, 143, satirizes Henri by having him complain of needing a divorce among his accomplishments.

[132] L'Estoile, *Mémoires-journaux*, vol. VII, 99.

[133] The portraits and surrounding events are discussed by Burlingham, "Portraiture as Propaganda," 144; Adhémar, "Thomas de Leu," 224. Gabrielle did appear as the goddess Diana in a painting at Chenonceaux. Ambroise Dubois, *Gabrielle d'Estrées en Diane*. Reproduced in Bardon, *Diane de Poitiers*, pl. XXXI.

[134] L'Estoile, *Mémoires-journaux*, vol. VII, 122.

France served her. In December 1598, Gabrielle's daughter by Henri was baptized at Saint-Germain-en-Laye with a prince of the blood as a godfather and a cardinal performing the ceremony. One of Henri's most devoted courtiers, Maximilien de Béthune, duc de Sully, was shocked.[135] Henri's persistence had been a positive quality while he pacified the realm, but now it became an unsettlingly stubborn insistence on Gabrielle.

Because Gabrielle died on April 10, 1599 in the midst of her fourth pregnancy, conflict over the king's mistress did not become more serious.[136] With one of the principals gone, the disagreement between the king and the critics was reconfigured. As soon as Gabrielle was dead, Marguerite de Valois requested that the annulment of her marriage with Henri, a topic of discussion since at least 1592, go forward. Her case moved quickly through the curia, where the new Pope, Clement VIII, no longer had to be concerned about encouraging the king's aspirations for his mistress.[137] On December 17, 1599, both parties were pronounced free to remarry.[138] The speed with which the marriage was terminated supports the observation that Marguerite had stalled during Gabrielle's lifetime.[139] Whether to avoid the indignity of being replaced as queen by the

---

[135] Sully, *Oeconomies royales*, vol. II, 295–8. Sully disliked Gabrielle, not least because of the potential problems she might cause Henri. See vol. II, 317 for Sully's views and Desclozeaux, "Gabrielle d'Estrées et Sully," *Revue historique* 33 (1887): 241–95, for comment.

[136] L'Estoile, *Mémoires-Journaux*, could not contain his relief: "la Duchesse de Beaufort mort miraculeuse et de conséquence pour la France, de laquelle elle estoit désignée Roine . . . disoit tout haut qu'il n'y avoit que Dieu et la mort du Roy qui l'en peust empescher" [The duchess of Beauford died miraculously and as a consequence for France, of which she had been designated to be Queen, it was said loudly that no one but God and the death of the King could have prevented it.] *Mémoires-journaux*, vol. VII, 185–6. See also Catherine de Bourbon to Henri IV (April 12, 1599) printed in *Lettres d'amour et écrits politiques*, ed. Jean-Pierre Babelon (Paris: Fayard, 1988), 239–40. Catherine expressed her sympathies, but made it clear she was relieved.

[137] The bulk of Marguerite's various procurations may be found in BN MSS fr 23301, 47–109 and fr 15598, fols. 287r–97r. One of the earlier ones include reference to "ledict seigneur et ses subjectz doivent avoir qu'il a y des enfans comme seul et plus asseuré moyen de resstablir cet estat" [the aforementioned lord and his subjects ought to know that having children is the most assured way to reestablish this state] (MS fr 15598, fol. 287v). This language disappears in later versions. Marguerite refused to base her petition on non-consummation of the marriage because that would allow the possibility that Henri's children by Gabrielle could be recognized as Henri's legitimate heirs. On the change of personnel at the Papacy, see Cardinal de Florence, *Lettres du Cardinal de Florence sur Henry IV et sur la France, 1596–1598*, ed. Raymond Ritter (Paris: Bernard Grasset, 1955), esp. 212, 219.

[138] L'Estoile, *Mémoires-journaux*, vol. VII, 198–9; BN MS fr 18529, fol. 156. On December 22, 1599, the dissolution of the marriage was published by the Parlement of Paris, and Marguerite publicly commended Henri.

[139] Henri's representatives to Marguerite recognized this, but were at a loss about what to do. See BN MS fr 15599, fols. 490–2. See BN MS fr 23301, pp. 118–20, for possible arguments to be made to the Pope. Plans to claim Henri would continue to stray and to accuse Marguerite of adultery were rejected as "honteux à la maison royale." For Marguerite stalling, see BN MS fr 15599, fols. 490–2 and 502, a decoded memoir expressing Marguerite's reasons for refusing to proceed in March, 1599 and then her consent under the exact same terms in May

king's mistress or because she recognized dangers that opposition to Gabrielle's rise had precipitated, the effect was the same: Marguerite had delayed until the problem was gone.

Henri, however, was as void of plausible heirs as before. He immediately sought to remedy this. For several years, Henri had engaged in intermittent talks with the Florentines about marrying Marie de' Medici, niece of the Grand Duke of Tuscany. When Gabrielle was alive, the Florentines had remained skeptical about Henri's intentions.[140] Despite the show on Gabrielle's behalf, Henri perhaps recognized that he might not be able to get what he wanted: he sent an ambassador to Florence in January 1599 on unspecified business, but probably to explore the marriage possibilities. After Gabrielle died, these negotiations proceeded rapidly and the marriage contract was signed on April 25, 1600.[141]

The king's artists incorporated Marie into Henri's representational scheme, but finding mutually sustaining images of the king and his wife proved somewhat difficult. Despite conventions that allowed for some idealization, contemporaries expected images to be basically honest depictions. Entirely suppressing well-known facts about one's life or appearance exceeded the rules that guided portrait composition. Henri's new family had to contain the detritus of his complicated sex life. In fact, the presence of Henri's new mistress, Henriette d'Entraigues, kept the remainders of his randy past very much present. Several artists heightened the tensions by portraying Henri and Marie as properly procreative even before Marie reached France. On October 5, 1600, Henri married Marie by proxy in Florence. Officials at the proxy ceremony fired cannons in imitation of the tradition that accompanied the birth of a dauphin. A *tableau vivant* with women playing the parts of Juno and Minerva signified the roles Marie was to inhabit.[142] The choices located Marie in a gendered economy of references that illustrated Henri's roles as well. Minerva/Marie took over the role Gabrielle had occupied in facilitating the military prowess of Mars/Henri. Juno/Marie paired with Jupiter/Henri indicated domestication of the promiscuous king of the gods by marriage:

after Gabrielle's death. The annulment was granted on the basis that Marguerite was coerced by her mother and brother.

[140] The Florentines were aware of Henri's efforts on Gabrielle's behalf, and as late as February of 1599, Marie's uncle thought about marrying her to one of her Austrian Hapsburg cousins. See Sully, *Oeconomies royales*, vol. II, 276, and David Buisseret, *Henry IV* (London and New York: Routledge, 1984), 79; Michel Carmona, *Marie de Médicis* (Paris: Fayard, 1981), 12–17; and Murat, *Gabrielle d'Estrées*, 380, for context.

[141] Henri IV, *Lettres Missives*, vol. V, 83; vol. VIII, 734. In March, Villeroy and Gondy were sent to Florence to reassure Ferdinand de' Medici of Henri's good will. See Henri IV, *Lettres Missives*, vol. V, 101.

[142] The festivities continued from Friday until Monday. See L'Estoile, *Mémoires-journaux*, vol. VII, 239–41.

Dieux! que de fruicts naistront de son sein plantureux,	Gods! That the fruits they give birth from his generous bosom,
Quand nostre Juppiter, d'une Junon seconde.	When our Jupiter [marries] a second Juno.[143]

Given the widespread understanding of Jupiter's chronic infidelity, the reference implied the expectation that Marie would be relatively tolerant concerning Henri's sexual infidelities, and it presumed she knew his history.

Festivities at Avignon celebrating the marriage on November 19, 1600 focused on procreative potentiality. Artists depicted the seven labors of Hercules on seven arches throughout the city with the story configured to emphasize marital sexuality as an heroic attribute. In a reference harking back to the images in Florence, Jupiter explains that Henri will "Semez au Jardin de Florence" [Fertilize the Garden of Florence].[144] The fourth arch also referred to the Florentine imagery, with Minerva articulating Marie's role as the wife who will render Henri/Hercules immortal by providing him with heirs.[145] The last of the seven labors was the marriage of Hercules/Henri to Hebe/Marie, captioned "UXORE ACCEPTA."[146] While Henri's ability to fulfill his promise as Hercules still depended on a woman and the succession still remained unsettled, accounts of the Avignon entry were markedly hopeful. Henri had a wife who could inhabit the appropriate dynastic role.

Tensions nonetheless remained. Though Marie was the legitimate wife who produced legitimate sons, the existence of Henri's various families remained a potential source of disorder. In the eyes of her partisans, Henriette d'Entraigues had a binding promise that made the king's marriage to Marie void.[147] Henri had implied marriage to Gabrielle and promised it to Henriette while negotiating the contract with the Florentines. Representations such as Léonard Gaultier's 1602

---

[143] Gabriel du Peyrat, *Stances au Roy faictes avant son mariage* (n. p.: no pub., 1601?), 5. See also Hercules marrying Hebe in Jean Passerat, *In nuptias Henrici IIII Gallicae Navarraeque regis et Mariae Medicieae* (n. p.: no pub., 1600), 2–3. The references were not new in French ceremonial practices. See Lecoq, *François Ier Imaginaire*; Lawrence M. Bryant, *The King and the City in the Parisian Royal Entry Ceremony: Politics, Ritual and Art in the Renaissance* (Geneva: Droz, 1986).

[144] Anon., *Labyrinthe Royal de l'Hercule Gaulois Triomphant sur le suject des Fortunes, Batailles, Victoires, Trophées, Triomphes, Marriage, & autres faictes heroiques* (Avignon: Chez Jacques Bramereau, 1601), 35. For fulfillment of this promise, see Léonard Gaultier, engraving, *L'Olympe des françois ou sont representez au naturel le Roy, la Royne et les Enfans de France* (1607).

[145] Anon., *Labyrinthe Royal*, 35–6.

[146] Capitalization in the original. Anon., *Labyrinthe Royal*, 12–13. The plan of the seven labors is depicted as a gallery with seven steps, the top one being marriage. For negative associations around Hercules and marriage, see Marc-René Jung, *Hercule dans la littérature français du XVIe siècle: de l'Hercule courtois à l'Hercule baroque* (Geneva: Droz, 1966), 137–57.

[147] Henriette's involvement in the 1604 plot against Henri hatched by Charles de Gontaut, maréchal de Biron and utilizing Spanish money seems to have been prompted by her ambitions for her children. See Buisseret, *Henry IV*, 112–15, 125–6.

Figure 20. Léonard Gaultier (1561–1641), *Henri IV and His Family* (1602), engraving, Musée national du Château du Pau, Pau, France.

This image features Henri IV reaching out to the Dauphin (the future Louis XIII) who is sitting on his nurse's lap in front of Marie de' Medici. Standing apart from the legitimate family is César de Vendôme, the son of Henri's mistress, Gabrielle d'Estrées. In addition to the gesture toward Louis, Henri has a phallic protrusion from his breeches in the direction of his legitimate family. This, coupled with César's isolation, illustrates the importance the king attaches to his legitimate offspring. Henri's children by Henriette d'Entraigues are not even present. By inclusion and omission, Henri's illegitimate offspring served to delineate and underscore the significance of his legitimate one.

engraving, *Henri IV et sa famille*, recalled the problems of Henri's sexual past as much as dispelled them because the king had to acknowledge the problem in order to regulate it.[148] A seated Henri reaches across the front of his wife to take the dauphin's hand as he sits on a nurse's lap. Henri turns away from César de Vendôme who stands hat in hand, isolated from his father, while

---

[148] For a brief comment on this image, see Karen Jacobson, ed., *The French Renaissance in Prints from the Bibliothèque nationale de France* (Los Angeles: Grunwald Center for the Graphic Arts, 1994), 429. Gaultier was another of Henri IV's favorite engravers.

Henriette's son, born a month after the dauphin, is not even shown. César's presence allows Henri to indicate his priorities, and to underscore his ability to produce sons. Four gentlemen, one of whom leans toward Henri as if to speak to him, accompany the royal family. Given the high quality of the image, the gentlemen probably stand in for the court. The court, then, participates in a private moment in which the king defines the status of his various families. Henri seems to manage aspects of his life previously criticized as out of control. Remarkably, in the center of his breeches is the royal phallus in the form of what appears to be a protruding codpiece protecting the royal member. Henri's sexual prowess is on display. Visibility asserts prowess, but simultaneously reveals vulnerability. The caption text referring to the linkage between Henri's heroic and procreative selves implies the uncertainties:

Dieu vueille que de tout a son Pere il ressemble,	God wants that the son resembles the Father
Affin q'uil soit l'hercule et le mars des francois,	In order that he can be the Hercules and the Mars of the French,
Qu'a ses septres acquis des conquis il assemble,	That he assemble his scepters acquired by conquest,
Les gaignant par son bras les gardant par ses lois.	Winning then with his arms and guarding them by his laws.[149]

The unproblematic heroic future is deferred to the next generation. In the end, Henri's abundant legitimate family and his death by assassination combined to obscure the contestation over the king's sexual behavior. Because Louis XIII succeeded peacefully in 1610, French royal fecundity prevailed. Royal reproductive failure receded until the salient, simplified remains were "gay" Henri III and "gallant" Henri IV.

Making the classical phallus

Henri IV marks the end of one story and the beginning of another. His reign was the culmination of Renaissance sexual play around the king. Beginning with François I, kings of France incorporated Renaissance representations – iconography from antiquity, evocations of philosophical and "scientific" strains of thought, word play as refined by the ethos of humanistic study of Greek and Latin – as part of their repertoire of imagery about royal sexuality. The balancing act between generation and sexual reputation became a more public, prominent aspect of monarchical life. In part this was a practical matter. The technology of print made information far more susceptible to sustained discussion, allowing circuits of innuendo, rumor, and fiction to multiply. The monarchy contributed

[149] Léonard Gaultier, *Henri IV et sa famille*, BN, Paris, Ed 12h, (1602).

by making reproductive success part of the ethos of cultural competition that surrounded the absorption of the new learning and its emanations. Renaissance invocations of the past brought sex front and center in art, poetry, and political staging. At the same time, foregrounding sexual performance opened it up to public policing. François I and Henri IV might look the same – both had a string of mistresses and a reputation for gallantry – but the optimism of François I's encounter with Renaissance modalities of sexual expression gave way to anxiety and a type of surveillance that shaped royal body politics until the end of the Old Regime and beyond. When royal image-makers presented Henri IV in ways that signaled monarchical potency, Renaissance play and multiplicity gradually transformed into concerns about incipient sexual disorder at the apex of French society.

The story of the transition from the Valois to the Bourbon is also the story of the change from Renaissance to classical corporeal aesthetics, with political consequences to match. The dialectic of sexual performance from François I through Henri IV produced the priority on control and containment that only became more pronounced in the reigns of Louis XIII and Louis XIV. The son of Henri IV subordinated desire to duty, sacrificing his evident pleasure in the company of men to political expediency. Henri Coiffier de Ruzé, marquis de Cinq Mars discovered this most brutally when he was executed in 1641; but so too did Charles d'Albert, duc de Luynes to a degree when the king's favor waned before Luynes' death in 1621; and Claude Henri de Rouvroy, comte de Saint-Simon, who survived the cooling affection of the king. Although renowned early in his adulthood for his "gallantry," the grandson of Henri IV, Louis XIV, adamantly relegated pleasures to circumscribed places and times. Louis XIV made love as he did everything else: on a schedule. Talk of his affairs and rumors of his morganatic marriage to Madame de Maintenon abounded, but the king made sure that his performative self-control limited the disruptive potential.

Louis XIII and Louis XIV were heirs of the complicated negotiations over masculine self-presentation as a sexual problem in the Renaissance monarchy. Abundance, fertility, and frivolity of décor remained to associate the king with bountiful generation. Sexualized scepters and well-formed legs presented in formal portraits indicated monarchical potency, eliding the sexual referents and the messy detritus. But one legacy of the Renaissance was that the rules had changed. Kings could still have girlfriends and still had to have children (especially boys), but asserting control began with the self and became part of political policy. Containing incipient sexual disorder through heroic masculine comportment took the place of the erudite but fragile Renaissance prince.

Conclusion: dirty thoughts

Born to poor parents, Jacques Amyot (1513–1593) made his way to the University of Paris and worked his way through school as a servant to wealthier students. He was recommended to Marguerite de Valois, who helped get him appointed professor of Greek and Latin at Bourges. His service to the royal family continued when he was chosen as a tutor for Charles IX and the future Henri III, and appointed Grand Almoner in 1561. Named Bishop of Auxerre in 1571, he served there until his death, continuing his work as a translator and commentator. His lucid prose style earned a very favorable review by Michel de Montaigne, and Amyot is still considered an important stylist of French language.[1]

Amyot was very much a product of and a contributor to the French Renaissance, but what about sex? Despite his clerical status, Amyot engaged in discussions of all sorts of sexualized discourses. He had advice about chaste and reciprocal marriage:

Mais il faut que le mary domine la femme, non comme le seigneur fait son esclave & ce qu'il possede, mais comme l'ame fait le corps, par une mutuelle dilectation & reciproque affection . . . sans s'asservir aux voluptez, ny aux appetits desordonnez.

But the husband must rule the wife, not like a lord over his slave whom he possesses, but like the soul over the body, through mutual delectation and reciprocal affection . . . without submitting either to sensual pleasures or to disorderly appetites.

He supported his arguments about sex and intimacy with evidence from antiquity. Amyot contrasts Paris and Helen with Odysseus and Penelope, and, dropping all the problematic bits, Amyot subscribes to the view that Orpheus' main value was his devotion to Eurydice.[2] Amyot understood the stars to

---

[1] Montaigne, *Complete Essays of Montaigne*, II, 4 (Let business wait till tomorrow), 262: "I give, and it seems to me with reason, the palm to Jacques Amyot over all our French writers, and not only for the naturalness and purity of his language, in which he surpasses all others; or for his perseverance in so long a work; or for the depth of his knowledge . . . (but I see throughout his translation a sense so beautiful, coherent and sustained, that either he has clearly understood the real thought of the author, or at least, having by long acquaintance implanted vividly in his own soul a general idea of Plutarch's soul, he has attributed to him nothing that belies or contradicts him)."

[2] Plutarch/Amyot, *Les Oeuvres morales*, vol. II, 375v. See also vol. II, 372v; vol. III, 674v.

govern generation and fertility, with Venus, the Sun, and the Moon having special importance.[3] Poets, he notes, have used divine inspiration to help human beings understand the beauty of love and "generation."[4] Amyot presented a user-friendly Plato and Neoplatonism in his *Les Oeuvres morales et meslees de Plutarque* (1574). One section, entitled "Les questions Platoniques," addressed everything from Plato's idea of the Daimon ("Le naturel de l'homme est un Demon?" [Is the nature of man a Demon?]) to questions about Plato's conception of the heavens ("Comment est-ce que Timaeus dit, que les ames sont semees parmy la terre, parmy la lune, & parmy les autres instruments du temps?" [How does Timaeus say that souls are strewn among the Earth, the Moon, and the other instruments of time?]).[5] The "Questions" was a prelude to a long section entitled "De l'amour," in which Autobulus, the son of Plutarch, discusses love with Flavianus, Protogenes, and several others. The invocation of Ficino's *De amore* and Plato's dialogic format notwithstanding, Amyot's Plutarch is resolutely French in his priorities. The dialogue centers on how to combine love and "espouser legitimement" [marrying legitimately].[6] Acknowledging Platonic homoeroticism, Protogenes allows that marriage is for generation, but loving women is at best irrational concupiscence, and "ceste passion . . . pour le moins fera-ce un amour effeminé & bastard" [this passion, at the least, makes for an effeminate and bastard love].[7] The problem is that a man submitting to another man is either the result of violence or "une lascheté effeminee" [an effeminate weakness]. Better to seek the "natural" submission of women to men with results in "une tranquilité calme du loyale mariage" [a calm tranquility of loyal marriage].[8] Despite extolling the values of friendship between men (it makes men invincible in battle if they love each other),[9] the rational choice is marital love. Marital love in moderation and productive:

toutesfois ce grand & admirable chef d'oeuvre principal de Venus & accessoire de l'Amour, qui est la generation . . . la Deesse Venus, par le moien de l'Amour, engendre une amitié & meslange de deux en un.

nevertheless, this great and admirable principal masterpiece of the goddess Venus, and the accessory of Love is the generation through the means of love engenders a friendship and the blending of two in one.[10]

---

[3] Plutarch/Amyot, *Les Oeuvres morales*, vol. III, 678v–680v.

[4] Plutarch/Amyot, *Les Oeuvres morales*, vol. III, 681r.

[5] Plutarch/Amyot, *Les Oeuvres morales*, vol. II (part 2), 465v–66v; 468v; 475r–76v.

[6] Plutarch/Amyot, *Les Oeuvres morales*, vol. III, 655r.

[7] Plutarch/Amyot, *Les Oeuvres morales*, vol. III, 657r. See also love of women is "chose basse, sale & vile" (657v). For more on the benefits of generation in marriage, see 659r, 684v.

[8] Plutarch/Amyot, *Les Oeuvres morales*, vol. III, 658r–v. Desire between men is called "une boisson flatueuse," (vol. III, 659v) and neither passion for women nor affection between men "ny l'un ny l'autre n'est amour." (686v).

[9] Plutarch/Amyot, *Les Oeuvres morales*, vol. III, 669r–74r. Love can also cure illnesses such as melancholy. See vol. III, 675v–76r.

[10] Plutarch/Amyot, *Les Oeuvres morales*, vol. III, 666v.

Amyot renders Neoplatonic intricacies in bottom-line, generative terms with the emphatic exclusion of homoeroticism in a pitch-perfect reflection of the dynamic of adoption and adaptation of Neoplatonism.

Amyot the bishop, royal servant, philosopher, translator, humanist, was very much a man of his time. To be sure, his brief mentions of poetry are earnest, rather than satirical, farcical, or prurient. He generally avoids direct commentary on political questions, but he was a man engaged with the questions of sex that permeated Renaissance France. Amyot's terms, like those utilized by authors and in contemporary texts throughout this project, were not at all about either acts or identities, but about interpersonal functions understood in language. That is, the domains that have recurred throughout the chapters past, products of a specific time, place, and set of cultural collisions, resulted in formulations of sexual meaning that depended on and defined the social and cultural space of France.

Michel Foucault is the obvious theoretical referent in several ways. Despite numerous, often valid arguments that he ignored the material conditions of the past and questions about his claim that sexual identity was a modern invention, Foucault made a case for the centrality of language, of discourse for creating meaning. He also asserted that the Renaissance was a time of sexual play – before the repressions of modernity and the coalescing of sex into identity categories came to accrue their modern normative weight. The interlocutors in the French Renaissance do exhibit play around sexuality, but only in the course of defining normative practices and expectations. The play around sex inspired and revolted at turns. The narrative of this project along these lines could be read as the gradual occluding of alternatives. The straightening out of Orpheus is an elaborate version of making the past "safe" for consumption. In astrological discourse, the procreative imperative permeated popular and erudite explanations of the operations of the stars such that claims for France as singular took shape as part of the astrological description of the orderly universe. The remaking of Neoplatonism as heterosexual marital desire, brought together the rewriting of the classical in a "safer" sexual register, the insistence on generative heterosexuality (in marriage), and a fresh synthesis of love language. Sexual desire – almost always expressed by men about women – provided a semantic field on which poets especially could express masculine self-possession as coherent with sex. French poets claimed the superiority of both France and their poetry by telling the truth about desire. That this led to immoderate expressions of physicality, articulations of anxiety about women and sex, and bad (meaning trite or raunchy or both) formulations did not undo the claims for poetic prowess as a function of masculine sexuality. Because of its sexual requirements, masculinity as a disciplinary structure was deployed against kings. Scurrilous poetry and other sexualized commentary helped form one of the channels within which kings of French operated. Too much, not enough, not "right," all mattered to a public that had opinions about sex and acted on them the arena of monarchical politics. In Renaissance France, in short, there was play to a point, but past that, there might be dragons.

The move from normative to disciplinary is a space in which the ideological import of French Renaissance sexual culture gets solidified. I suggested at the outset that part of my purpose was to emphasize the "obviousness" of ideology in order to see its historical specificity under construction. It is the trick or trap of ideology that recognition does not mean one is free of ideology, but it is my contention that recognition of the impulses, reactions, leaps of faith, and cascades of doubt that produce sexual ideology can provide critical distance and open up wider recognition of the structural imbrication of sex in cultural loci of power.

This is not free-floating ideology construction. Although the early modern social structure precluded many possibilities by gender and what we would call class, sexual culture was written and performed by a wide group of people who took their cues from an array of cultural locations. The circuits were at once tight (the same personnel dealt with multiple discourses of sex) and widespread (ties among and between interlocutors cover the geographic space of France and link to an array of social settings). Starting somewhere in the middle, in addition to *La Parfaicte amye*, Antoine Héroët as part of the circle of François I's sister, Marguerite de Navarre, wrote Neoplatonic texts Louys Le Roy embedded in his commentary on the *Symposium*. Le Roy relied on Pietro Bembo and Léon Hébreu in addition to Ficino for his commentary, which he dedicated to François II and Mary, Queen of Scots. Le Roy invoked Joachim Du Bellay's arguments about translation and French language to justify his interpretations of Plato, as well as his conformity with the French practice of erasing of polymorphous perversity from Ovid's Orpheus. Pierre de Ronsard, who cast himself as the French Orpheus and wrote several astrological poems, was a friend of Du Bellay and of Jean-Antoine Muret, whose relationship to Orphic pederasty got him into hot water with French authorities. Ronsard was also part of the household of the dauphin, François (d. 1536), moved to François I's third son, Charles, and then served Henri II, François II, Charles IX, and Henri III. Through the Palace Academy,[11] Ronsard interacted with Henri III, along with Jean-Antoine de Baïf, Jacques Davy Du Perron, Pontus de Tyard, Agrippa d'Aubigné, and Philippe Desportes, among others. Neoplatonism, which was revived at court by Desportes at the end of the century, spawned further connections. Marguerite de Navarre's *valet de chambre*, Jean de La Haye, translated Ficino into French. Another of Ronsard's friends, Pontus de Tyard, translated Leone Ebreo's Neoplatonic *Dialogues d'amour*, wrote several astrological texts (including an ephemeris), attended the Palace Academy, and was Maurice

---

[11] Yates, *The French Academies of the Sixteenth Century.*

Scève's student. Scève "discovered" Laura's tomb, contributing to the absorption of Petrarchan love conceits and the poetic developments that followed. Scève was introduced to Symphorien Champier in Lyon some time before Champier died in 1539 and after Scève's arrival in 1534.[12] Champier originated much of the Neoplatonic discussion of love and sex in France, themes taken up by Gilles Corrozet, who refers to the Italian Neoplatonic love treatises and recommends them to his (female) readers. This advice prompted the satires of the *Louenge des femmes*, which also exploited the ribald wit of Rabelais. Scève was also a friend of Charles de Sainte-Marthe, who wrote poems to Etienne Dolet, who was the publisher of Héroët. The list could multiply not quite infinitely, but close enough.

The larger ideological frame created by this web of people in this time and place defined aspects of France at the beginning of modernity. The normative impulses in straightening out queer Orpheus were local and "French." As humanists standardized education in Renaissance France, Ovid figured prominently in the *quatrième classe*, in which students studied Latin grammar utilizing Terence, Cicero, and Virgil, in addition to Ovid. The *Metamorphoses* continued as featured text in the *troisième* and *seconde* levels. As George Huppert emphasizes, humanist schools were at once widespread geographically and increasingly bound to the standardization emanating from Paris.[13] In the school curriculum, Orpheus the pederastic misogynist gave way to the husband who, in the end, was devoted to his wife. The interplay of risqué sexual values and bog-standard social responsibility became a marker of French sexual culture.

One resolution of sorts of the potential incoherent aspects of this interplay was the emphasis on fertility, profusion, and natural abundance as especially French. The figure of Venus provides an index for such claims. The routine astrological invocations of Venus and the Moon assisting in matters of generation ranged from erudite treatises to popular fiction to high art to public ephemera. The *Traicté sommaire des Planettes et de leurs effects selon l'opinion des anciens Autheurs, qui en on Escript*, for instance, blamed and praised at once: "Venus denote la volupté de chair, et de mariage, curiosité des habits, lamour" [Venus denotes voluptuousness of the flesh, and of marriage, curiosity of habits, love].[14] In his satirical prognostication, Rabelais defined Venus as responsible for prostitutes, pimps, all manner of sexual deviants, and for the spread of venereal diseases ("de verolle, de chancre, de pisses chauldes").[15] Regardless of her bad influences, Venus was crucial for

---

[12] Festugière, *La Philosophie de l'amour*, 76.
[13] George Huppert, *Public Schools in Renaissance France* (Urbana and Chicago: University of Illinois Press, 1984). See pp. 53–4 for a Parisian-inflected program in Auch.
[14] BN MS fr 2083, fol. 7v.
[15] François Rabelais, *La Pantagrueline prognostication*, ed. François Bon and Louis Dubost (Charente: Le Dé bleu, 1994), 27.

the formation of "semence de generation" [seed of generation].[16] Venus was seemingly everywhere. Images ranged from Rosso Fiorentino's *Venus Frustrated* at Fontainebleau (Figure 16), to Léonard Limosin's enamel, *Venus and Cupid* (Figure 10), to the School of Fontainebleau images such as *Venus and Mars* and *Venus at her Toilette*, to an image of Diane de Poitiers as Venus – and Henri II as Mars – in a fresco at Château Tanlay (Figure 21). Venus festooned public processions, was invoked to encourage lust, love, and childbirth, and figured as an emblem of national fertility by implication in Pierre de Ronsard's *Franciade*.[17]

The simultaneity of positive and negative sexual readings is both a Renaissance formation and a French one. To take the Renaissance case first, consider Petrarchan love language, which seeped into the available vocabulary of love and intimacy all across Europe. Late Petrarchanism has been the subject of much study, especially in the English Renaissance. Joel Fineman's Lacanian reading of Shakespeare's sonnets takes the belatedness of Petrarchan love poetry as central to his argument. Fineman reads the first 126 of Shakespeare's sonnets, the ones to the young man, as using epideictic poetry in service of homosexual sameness (the Lacanian "Imaginary"). Heterosexual difference through poetry of mock praise and satire locates poems 127 to 154 in terms of the Lacanian "Symbolic." Fineman regards Shakespeare's sequence as the invention of modern poetic subjectivity through this movement.[18] Fineman does not particularly consider continental sequences that make the same move, although perhaps not so neatly, long before Shakespeare. Priority, however, is less important than the association of love poetry and subjectivity in the Renaissance. The process was neither limited to Shakespeare nor entirely positivistic. As Heather Dubrow has argued, poetry in the Petrarchan mode must be read in conjunction with critics, revisionists, and resistors to Petrarch's original templates.[19] Rejecting love in favor of spiritual fulfillment, exceeding the frame of unrequited love, and indulging in anti-Petrarchan conceits such as exaggeration of terms or parodic poetic syntax were among the common ploys.

Starting with poetry, simultaneity in French Renaissance sexual thought produced the contours of French particularlity. The French were interested in honesty (in the modern sense), and finding Petrarch wanting enabled the assertion of French sexual priorities that included frank engagement with sex. Paradoxically, then, French libertine poetry had an ethical agenda, albeit in an

[16] Ferrier, *Des Jugemens astronomiques*, 110–11. See also pp. 134–5.
[17] In Book II, Venus sends Cupid to bless and "rendre amoureuse" Hyante and Climene, the daughters of King Dicée. See Pierre de Ronsard, "La Franciade," in *Œuvres complètes*, vol. I, 1061–3 (ll. 709–82). In addition to the images previously reproduced in Chapters 5 and 3 respectively, see School of Fontainebleau, *Venus and Mars* (Fontainebleau, sixteenth century; currently in the Musée du Petit Palais, Paris, France); *Venus at her Toilette* (Fontainebleau, sixteenth century; currently in the Louvre, Paris, France).
[18] Fineman, *Shakepeare's Perjured Eye.*   [19] Dubrow, *Echoes of Desire.*

Figure 21. School of Fontainebleau (sixteenth century), *The Hall of the Conspirators, Henri II as Mars and Diane de Poitiers as Venus*, fresco, Château Tanley, France.

    With its invocation of both antiquity and contemporary Renaissance political issues, this fresco recalls a number of the themes throughout this project: The ancient references, the association of Venus and Mars with astrology, the Neoplatonic theme of the dangers of sensual love, the conflation of love and consummation that preoccupied so many poets, and the monarchical context of the image.

often disconcerting moral register. That the French linked their ethics to sex by the end of the Renaissance was by no means true only in poetry. From the claims for national priorities in the re-writing of Orphic sexuality, to the development of French as a language capable of philosophical nuance, to the political claims around Italian territory and patronage, French interlocutors defined their Renaissance in national and linguistic terms. In many ways, the monarchy reflected the national priorities more than it directed them. François I's art patronage was largely intended to decorate his court by bringing superior artists from Italy (and occasionally, as with Jean Clouet, from elsewhere). In this sense, the monarchy led the way, and as Rebecca Zorach has pointed out, cheaper, more accessible reproductions, particularly engravings that captured the style of abundance, circulated far beyond the court.[20] While art patronage was top-down, the message of sexual license embedded in much that emerged from that art encouraged the development of a dynamic of commentary on royal sexuality. The assertions and assumptions about the king as the royal embodiment of France connected royal generation with the status of the realm. Since royal reproductive failure and success were matters of public interest, kings had to negotiate their actions in public terms. Sex was only one factor in the controversies that swirled around the French Renaissance monarchy, but the entanglements around royal sexual practices figured prominently because of the insistent linkage of an image of France that rested on its sexual character.

In the Renaissance tradition of paradox, let me close with the claim that the national is at once insignificant and central to my larger argument. The specificities of French absorption and transformation of ancient texts, astrology, Neoplatonism, poetry, and politics in the Renaissance are interesting, but not terribly important. How much does it matter that the French became known (and are still) for their delicate ornamentation in design? Perhaps the fact that France has been associated with a kind of blasé acceptance of normative sexual practices and concerns about fertility since the Renaissance figures in much later understandings of French obsessions about population, but that is too large a leap to take without filling in the interim, and one I am not prepared to take on mere conjecture. But if "Frenchness" is unique, that is important in another, larger way. What makes this important rather than just nationally idiosyncratic is that I chose France with an eye to the larger frame of the emergence of modern sexuality. The fact that "Renaissance" archives produce radically different effects around sexuality is actually tremendously important. That the moves to assert heteronormativity were widely variable in the Renaissance, that masculinity had an astonishing range of unstable parameters, that sodomy meant so many different things – these are the kinds of general observations about sexuality that emerge from analysis of different Renaissance sexual cultures throughout Europe. The French version is not the only one, and that is very much a point worth remembering as the battles over sexual meaning continue unabated.

[20] Zorach, *Blood, Milk, Ink, Gold*, esp. pp. 144–52.

Bibliography

MANUSCRIPTS

AN KK 116 (Henri III's household)
AN KK 134 (Henri III's household)
Bibliothèque Mazarine, MS 3876 (591) (Bersuire)
BL Additional MS 8719 (ballet of March, 1585)
BL Additional MS 8719 (*Discours faict au mois D'Avril 1585* and Henri III documents)
BL Additional MS 10324 (Ovid)
BL Burney 224 (Arnulf d'Orléans)
BL Harley 1014 (*Allegorie librorum ovidii* (Exposito moral fabulam extram ex methamorfoseo ovidii))
BL MS Royal 12.E.XI (Arnulf d'Orleans)
BL MS Sloane 2030, "Tractatus astrologicus de iudiciis sive de interrogationibus"
BN MS 884 (poetry)
BN MS Dupuy 588 (Gabriele Simeoni to Catherine de' Medici; Henri III horoscope)
BN MS Dupuy 843 (poetry)
BN MS fr 667 (table of conjunctions)
BN MS fr 868 (poetry)
BN MS fr 878 (poetry)
BN MS fr 884 (poetry)
BN MS fr 885 (poetry)
BN MS fr 1351 (*Livre des elections*)
BN MS fr 1355 (astrology treatise)
BN MS fr 1355 (Zodiac positions)
BN MS fr 1662 (poetry)
BN MS fr 2047 (Zodiac positions)
BN MS fr 2083 (*Traicté sommaire des Planettes et de leurs effects selon l'opinion des anciens Autheurs, qui en on Escript*)
BN MS fr 2489 (Horoscopes)
BN MS fr 5106 (Horoscope of François I)
BN MS fr 6618 (Catherine de' Medici)
BN MS fr 9531 (eclipses, conjunctions)
BN MS fr 11575 (Claude Haton)
BN MS fr 12287 (foldout calendar with the rising and setting of the stars)
BN MS fr 12290 (geniture collections; *Instruction fort utile et necessaire pour l'astrologie judiciare*; planetary positions)

BN MS fr 12293 (geniture collections)
BN MS fr 14769 (geniture collections)
BN MS fr 14772 (geniture collections; horoscope of Charles IX)
BN MS fr 14773 (prognostications for 1570–1572 with calculations)
BN MS fr 15598 (Henri III marriage contract; Procurations of Marguerite de Navarre)
BN MS fr 15599 (Henri IV and Gabrielle d'Estrées)
BN MS fr 15831 (Wedding of M. de Joyeuse)
BN MS fr 18529 (Marguerite de Navarre)
BN MS fr 19934 (calculating positions for 1589)
BN MS fr 23295 (Agrippa d'Aubigné; poetry)
BN MS fr 23301 (Henri IV and Gabrielle d'Estrées)
BN MS fr 26154 (Expenses for May 1577)
BN MS Italien 1732 (Henri III devotions)
BN MS lat. 7996 (Arnulf d'Orléans)
BN MS lat. 8001 (Arnulf d'Orléans)
BN MS lat. 8008 (Guillelmus de Thiegiis/John of Garland)
BN MS lat. 8010 (Guillelmus de Thiegiis/John of Garland; Arnulf d'Orléans)
BN MS lat. 8019 (Bersuire)
BN MS lat. 8020 (Bersuire)
BN MS lat. 8123 (Bersuire)
BN MS lat. 8253a (Bersuire)
BN MS lat. 9323 (Fulgentius)
BN MS lat. 14135 (Arnulf d'Orleans)
BN MS lat. 14136 (Bersuire)
BN MS lat. 15145 (Bersuire)
BN MS lat. 16787 (Bersuire)
BN MS n. a. f. 1245 (Henri III letters)
BN MS n. a. f. 6888 (poetry)
BN MS n. a. f. 7225 (Henri III devotions)
BN MS nouv. acq. lat. 1830 (Bersuire)
Mellon MS 25, Yale University Beinecke Rare Book and Manuscript Library (*Centiloquium*)
Reims, Bibliothèque municipale MS 1262 (Arnulf d'Orleans)
Saint-Omer, Bibliothèque municipale MS 662 (Bersuire)
Saint-Omer, Bibliothèque municipale MS 670 (Arnulf d'Orléans)
Saint-Omer, Bibliothèque municipale MS 678 (Arnulf d'Orléans)
Troyes, Bibliothèque municipale MS 1627 (Bersuire)
Troyes, Bibliothèque municipale MS 1634 (Bersuire)

PRINTED PRIMARY SOURCES

Aeschylus. *Agamemnon, Libation-Bearers, Eumenides, Fragments*, ed. and trans. Herbert Weir Smith, appendix Hugh Lloyd-Jones (Cambridge, MA: Harvard University Press, 1996).
Agrippa, Henri Corneille. *Declaration de la Noblesse et Preexcellence du sexe feminin*, trans. Martin Le Pin (Lyon: François Juste, 1537).
Alamanni, Luigi. *Opere toscane* (Lyon: Gryphe, 1532–1533).

Alençon, duc d'. *Brieve remonstrance a la noblesse de France sur le faict de la Declaration de Monseigneur le Duc d'Alençon* (n. p.: no pub., 1576).

Alighieri, Dante. *Vita Nuova. Italian Text with Facing English Translation*, trans. Dino S. Cervigni and Edward Vasta (Notre Dame, IN and London: University of Notre Dame Press, 1995).

Al-Qabisi. *Al-Qabisi (Alcabitius): The Introduction to Astrology*, ed. Charles Burnett, Keiji Yamamoto, and Michio Yano (London and Turin: Warburg Institute / Nino Aragno Editore, 2004).

Anacreon. *Anacreonis Teii Odae. Ab Henrico Stephano luce et Latinitate nunc primum donatae* (Paris: Henri Estienne, 1554).

Angier, Paul. *Expérience de Maistre Paul Angier, Carentenoys, contenant une brieve deffence en la personne de l'honneste Amant pour l'Amye de Court contre la Contre Amye*, in *Opuscules d'Amour par Heroet, La Borderie et autres divins poëtes*, intro. M. A. Screech (East Ardsley: S. R., 1970).

Anon. *Les Admirables et justes anagrammes de Henry de Valois* (Edinburgh [Paris]: Guillaume Petit, 1589).

Anon. *Les Argonautiques orphiques*, ed. Francis Vian (Paris: Société d'édition, 1987).

Anon. *Astrologie naturelle, Par lequelle un chacun pourra sçavoir par sa nativité ce qui luy doit arriver suivant le cours des Planettes* (Paris: Michel Daniel, 1619).

Anon. *Les Bigarrures et touches du Seigneur des Accords* (Paris: Jean Richer, 1614).

Anon. *Les blasons Anatomiques du Corps fémenin. Ensemble les Contreblasons de nouveau composez & aditionez* (Paris: Nicolas Chrestien, 1554).

Anon. *Le Cabinet satyrique ou recueil parfaict des vers piquans et gaillards de ce temps* (Paris: Anthoine Estoc, 1618).

Anon. *Le Cabinet secret du Parnasse*, ed. Louis Perceau, 3 vols. (Paris: Au Cabinet du livre, 1928–32).

Anon. *C'est l'ordre qui a este tenu a la nouvelle et ioyeuse entrée, que treshault, tresexcellent, & trespuissant Prince le Roy Treschrestien Henry deuzieme de ce nom à faicte en sa bonne ville & cité de Paris, capitale de son Royaume, le sezieme jour de Iuin M. D. XLIX* (Paris: Iacques Rosset, 1549).

Anon. *Les Choses horribles, contenues en une lettre envoyée à Henry de Valois, par un Enfant de Paris, le vingthuitiesme de Janvier 1589* (Paris: Jacques Gregoire, 1589).

Anon. *Le Compost et kalendrier des bergiers* (Paris: Guiot Marchant, 1493; 1500).

Anon. *Cy est enseigne et demonstre le kalendrier et compost des bergiers* (Rouen: chez Raulin Gaultier, 1505).

Anon. *Les Delices satyrique* [sic] *ou suite du cabinet des vers Satyriques de ce Temps* (Paris: Anthoine de Sommaville, 1620).

Anon. *Dialogue du Royaume; auquel est discourse des vices et vertus des Roys, et de leur Etablissement* (Paris: Chez Didier Millot, 1589).

Anon. *L'Entrée triomphante et magnifique du Tres-Chrestien Roy de France et de Pologne Henri III en sa ville et cité de Rheims, venant en son sacre et couronnement* (Rheims: Chez Jean de Foigny, 1575).

Anon. *Le grand calendier et compost des bergiers compose par le bergier de la grand montaigne* (Lyon: Jehan Canterel, 1551).

Anon. *Le grant kalendrier et compost des Bergiers* (Paris: Payot, 1525).

Anon. *Le grant kalendrier et compost des Bergiers avecq leur Astrologie* (Troyes: Nicolas le Rouge, 1529).

Anon. *The Kalender of Shepherdes. The Edition of Paris 1503 in Photographic Fac-simile, A Faithful Reprint of R. Pynson's Edition of London 1506*, ed. Heinrich O. Sommer (London: Kegan Paul, 1892).

Anon. *Le Kalendrier des bergieres* (Paris: en l'ostel de beauregart en la rue Cloppin a lenseigne du roy Prestre jehan, 1499).

Anon. *Le Labyrinthe d'amour ou suite des Muses Folastres* (Rouen: chez Claude le Vilain, 1610).

Anon. *Labyrinthe Royal de l'Hercule Gaulois Triomphant sur le suject des Fortunes, Batailles, Victoires, Trophées, Triomphes, Marriage, & autres faictes heroiques* (Avignon: Chez Jacques Bramereau, 1601).

Anon. [Thomas Sébillet?]. *La Louenge des femmes. Invention extraite du Commentaire de Pantagruel, sus l'Androgyne de Platon*, ed. M. A. Screech, intro. Ruth Calder (London: S. R., 1967).

Anon. *La magnificence de la superbe et triomphante entrée de la noble et antique cité de Lyon au Treschrestien Roy de France Henry, deuxiesme de ce nom, et à la Royne Catherine son Espouse, le xxiii de Septembre M.D.XLVIII* (Lyon: Guillaume Rouillé, 1549).

Anon. *La Muse folastre. Recherchée des plus beaux esprits de ce temps* (Paris: Pour Anthoine de Brueil, 1600).

Anon. *Les Muses gaillardes recueillies des plus beaux esprits de ce temps* (Paris: Par A. D. B. [Anthoine du Brueil], 1609).

Anon. *Les Muses incongnues ou la seille aux bourriers plaine de desires et imaginations d'amour* (Rouen: Imprimerie de Jean Petit, 1604).

Anon. *Ovide moralisé en prose* (Texte du quinzième siècle), ed. C. de Boer (Amsterdam: North-Holland Publishing, 1954).

Anon. *Ovide moralisé, poème du commencement du quatorzième siècle, publié d'après tous les manuscrits connus*, ed. Cornelius de Boer, Martina G. de Boer, and Jeanette Th. M. van't Sant, 5 vols. (Amsterdam: J. Müller, 1915–1938).

Anon. *Le Parnasse des Poëtes satyriques* (n. p. [Paris?]: no pub., 1622).

Anon. *Les pourtes et figures du sumptueux ordre, plaisantz spectacles et magnifiques théâtres, dressés et exhibés par les citoiens de Rouen* (Rouen: Jean Dugort, 1557).

Anon. *Le premier, second et troisiesme livre du labyrinthe de Recreation. Recherché des plus beaux Esprits de ce temps* (Rouen: chez Claude le Vilain, 1602).

Anon. *Les Propos lamentables de Henry de Valois, tires de sa confession, par un remords de conscience, qui tousjours tourmente les miserables* (Paris: Pierre Mercier, 1589).

Anon. *La Quint-Essence satyrique, ou seconde partie, du Parnasse des Poetes Satyriques de nostre temps* (Paris: Anthoine de Sommaville, 1622).

Anon. *Les quinze signes addressez es parties d'Occident vers les Royaumes d'Escosse, & Angleterre, significatifz de la ruine, fin, & consommation du monde* (Paris: Michel Buffet, 1587).

Anon. *Recueil des plus excellans vers satyriques* (Paris: Anthoine Estoc, 1617).

Anon. *Réplique à l'Antigaverston, ou response faict à l'histoire de Gaverston, par le Duc d'Espernon* (n. p.: no pub., 1588).

Anon. *Reponce à l'Antigaverston de Nogaret* (n. p.: no pub., 1588).

Anon. *Le Sandrin ou verd galand où sont naïfvement deduits les plaisirs de la vie rustique* (Paris: Anthoine du Brueil, 1609).

Anon. *Les satyres bastardes et autres oeuvres folastres du Cadet Angoulevent* (Paris: B. A. et Cabinet de M. P. Louÿs, 1615).

Anon. *Les Satyres du sieur Regnier. Dediées au Roy* (Paris: Anthoine Estoc, 1619).

Anon. *Les satyres du sieur Regnier. Derniere edition, reveuë corrigee, et de beaucoup augmentée, tant par les sieurs de Sigogne, et de Berthelot, qu'autres des plus signalez Poëtes de ce temps* (Paris: L'Imprimerie d'Anthoine du Brueil, 1614).

Anon. *Le second livre des délices de la poesie françoise. Ou, nouveau recueil des plus beaux Vers de ce temps* (Paris: Toussainct du Bray, 1620).

Aristotle. *The Basic Works of Aristotle*, ed. Richard McKeon, intro. C. D. C. Reeve (New York: Modern Library, 1941/2001).

Generation of Animals, trans. A. L. Peck (Cambridge, MA: Harvard University Press, 2000).

Meteorologica, trans. H. D. P. Lee (Cambridge, MA: Harvard University Press, 1952).

Arnulf of Orléans. *Allegoriae*, in *Arnolfo d'Orléans, un cultore di Ovidio nel secolo XII*, ed. Fausto Ghisalberti, *Memorie del Reale Istituto lombardo di scienze e lettere* 24 (Milan: Libraio del R. Istituto Lombardo di scienze e lettere, 1932).

Aubery, Jean. *L'Antidote d'amour* (Paris: Claude Chappelet, 1599).

Joannis Auberii . . . restituenda et vindicanda Medicinae Dignitate (Paris: Cottereau, 1608).

Aubigné, Agrippa d'. *Les Tragiques*, in *Œuvres*, ed. Henri Weber (Paris: Gallimard, 1969).

Auton, Jean d'. *Chroniques de Louis XII*, ed. R. de Maulde La Clavière for the Société de l'histoire de France, 4 vols. (Paris: H. Laurens, 1889–1895).

Baïf, Jean-Antoine de. *Euvres en rime de Ian Antoine de Baïf, Secretaire de la Chambre du Roy*, 4 vols. (Paris: Pour Lucas Breyer, 1572).

Poésies choises de J.A. de Baïf suivies de poésies inédites, ed. L. Becq de Fouquières (Paris: Charpentier et Cie., 1874).

[Barnaud, Nicolas?]. *Le Cabinet du Roy de France, dans lequel il y a trois Perles precieuses d'inestimable valeur* (n. p.: no pub., 1581).

Le Reveille-matin des François: et de leurs voisins, compose par Eusebe Philadelphe, cosmopolite, en forme de dialogues (Paris: Editions d'histoire sociale, 1977).

Beaujoyeulx, Balthazar de. *Le Balet Comique, 1581. A Facsimile with an Introduction*, ed. Margaret M. McGowan (Binghamton: Center for Medieval and Renaissance Studies, 1982).

Belleau, Rémy. *Œuvres poétiques de Rémy Belleau*, ed. Charles Marty-Laveaux, 2 vols. (Geneva: Slatkine, 1878).

Bembo, Pietro. *Gli Asolani di messer Pietro Bembo* (Venice: Aldo Romano, 1505).

Les Azolains de Monseigneur Bembo (Paris: M. de Vascosan, pour luy et G. Corrozet, 1545).

Berni, Francesco. *Tutti le Opere di Berni* (Venice: B. Zanetti, 1542).

Bersuire, Pierre. *Metamorphosis Ovidiana, moraliter explanata* (Paris: Ascensianis et sub Pelicano, 1509).

Bianchini, Giovanni. *Tabulae astronomicae et canones in eas Joannis Blanchini* (Venice: Simon Bivilaqua, 1495).

Boccaccio, Giovanni. *The Decameron*, trans. and intro. G. H. McWilliam, 2nd edn. (London and New York: Penguin, 1995).

Bodier, Thomas. *De ratione et usu dierum criticorum opus recens natum* (Paris: Audoënus Parvus, 1555).

Boethius, Anicius Manlius Severinus. *The Consolation of Philosophy*, trans., ed., and intro. William Anderson (Carbondale: Southern Illinois University Press, 1963).

Bouchel, Laurens. *La Bibliothèque ou thresor du droict françois*, 3 vols. (Paris: Jean Girin et Barthelemy Riviere, 1671).

Boucher, Jean. *Histoire tragique et memorable de Pierre de Gaverston* (n. p.: no pub., 1588).

Bouquet, Simon. *Bref et sommaire recueil de ce qui a esté faict, de l'ordre tenüe à la ioyeuse & triumphante Entree de tres-puissant, tres-magnanime & tres-chrestien Prince Charles IX . . . Avec le couronnement de tres-haute, tres-illustre & tres-excellente Princesse Madame Elizabeth d'Austrice son espouse, le Dimanche vingtcinquiesme* (Paris: Denis du Pré, 1572).

Bowen, Barbara C., ed. *One Hundred Renaissance Jokes: An Anthology* (Birmingham, AL: Summa Publications, 1988).

Brantôme, Pierre de Bourdeille, seigneur de. *Les Dames galantes* (Paris: Garnier, 1955).

Budé, Guillaume. *De Asse et partibus eius libri quinque* (Paris: Venundantur in edibus Ascensianis, 1516).

   De l'Institution du Prince: Livre contenant plusieurs histoires, enseignements & saiges dicts des anciens tant grecs que latins (Ivry: N. Paris, 1547).

   De Studio litterarum recte et commode instivendo, ad inuictissimum, & potentissimum principem Franciscum regem Franciae (Basle: Apud I. Walderum, 1533).

Bury, Jacques. *Le Propagatif de l'Homme et secours des femmes en travail d'enfant* (Paris: Chez Melchior Mondiere 1623).

Calendar of State Papers, Foreign Series, of the Reign of Elizabeth, 1575–1577, ed. Allan James Crosby (London: Longman, 1880).

Calvin, John. *Advertissement contre l'astrologie judiciaire*, ed. Olivier Millet (Geneva: Droz, 1985).

Carbone, Ludovico. *Facezie e Dialogo de la partita soa*, ed. Gino Ruozzi (Bologna: Commissione per i Testi di Lingua, 1989).

Castiglione, Baldassare. *The Courtier, The Book of the Courtier*, trans. and intro. George Bull (Harmondsworth: Penguin, 1983).

   Le Courtisan, nouvellement traduict de ytalicque en françoys par Jacques Colin d'Auxerre (Paris: Jehan Longis et Vincent Sertenas, 1537).

Champier, Symphorien. *Contenta in hoc volumine Pimander Mercurii Trismegisti liber de sapientia & potestate dei* (Paris: H. Stephani, 1505).

   De quadruplici vita (Lyon: Stephani Gueynardi & Jacobi Huguentanni, 1507).

   De Triplica Disciplina (Lyon: no pub., 1508).

   Le Livre de vraye amour, intro. and ed. James B. Wadsworth (The Hague: Mouton, 1962).

   La Nef des dames vertueuses, ed. Judy Kem (Paris: Champion, 2007).

   Nef des dames vertueuses composees par maistre Simphorien Champier Docteur en medicine (Paris: Jehan de La Garde, 1515).

   Nef des Princes (Lyon: G. Balsarin, 1502).

   Symphonia Platonis cum Aristotele: & Galeni cum Hippocrate D. Symphorani Champerii (Paris: I. Badio, 1516).

Theologie orphice, in *De Triplica Disciplina* (Lyon: no pub., 1508).

Theologie trismegistice in *De Triplica Disciplina* (Lyon: no pub., 1508).

Chapoton, François de. *La Descente d'Orphée aux enfers. Tragédie (1640)*, ed. Hélène Visentin (Presses universitaires de Rennes, 2004).

Chavigny, *Commentaires de Sr de Chavigny Beaunois sur les centuries et prognostications de feu M. Michel de Nostradamus* (Paris: Anthoine du Breuil, 1596).

Clement of Alexandria. *Exhortation to the Greeks*, trans. G. W. Butterworth (Cambridge, MA: Harvard University Press, 2003).

Stromata, in *Ante-Nicene Fathers. Fathers of the Second Century: Hermes, Tatian, Athenagoras, Theophilis and Clement of Alexandria*, ed. A. Cleveland Coxe (Grand Rapids: Eerdmans, 1986).

Collerye, Roger de. *Oeuvres de Roger de Collerye*, ed. Charles d'Héricault (Paris: J. Jannet, 1855).

Corrozet, Gilles. *L'Hecatongraphie (1544) & Les Emblemes du Tableau de Cebes (1543)*, ed. and intro. Alison Adams (Geneva: Droz, 1997).

[Corrozet, Gilles?] *La Diffinition et Perfection d'Amour. Le Sophologe d'Amour. Traictez plaisantz & delectables oultre l'utilité en iceulx contenue* (Paris: Gilles Corrozet, 1542).

Dariot, Claude. *A Breef and most easie Introduction to the Astrologicall iudgement of the Starres* (London: Thomas Purfoote, 1583[?]).

L'Introduction au iugement des astres, Avec un Traité des elections propres pour le commencement des choses (Lyon: Maurice Roy et Loys Pesnot, 1558).

Desjardins, Abel, ed., *Négociations diplomatiques de la France avec la Toscane. Documents recueillis par Giuseppi Canestrini et publiées par Abel Desjardins*, 6 vols. (Paris: Imprimerie nationale, 1876).

Des Masures, Louis. *Oeuvres poëtiques de Louis des Masures, Tournisien* (Lyon: Jean de Tournes, 1557).

Desportes, Philippe. *Les Amours de Diane. Second Livre*, ed. Victor E. Graham (Geneva: Droz, 1959).

Cléonice, dernières amours, ed. Victor E. Graham (Geneva: Droz, 1961).

Diverses Amours et autres oeuvres meslées, ed. Victor E. Graham (Geneva: Droz, 1963).

Elégies, ed. Victor E. Graham (Geneva: Droz, 1961).

Œuvres de Philippe Desportes, ed. Alfred Michiels (Paris: Adolphe Delahays, 1858).

Dolce, Lodovico. *Dialogo della pittura intitolato l'Aretino* [1557], in *Scritti d'arte del Cinquecento*, ed. Paola Barocchi, 3 vols. (Milan and Naples: Riccardo Ricciardi, 1973).

Dolet, Etienne. *La manière de bien traduire d'une langue en aultre. D'advantage, de la punctuation de la langue francoyse. Plus, des accents d'ycelle* (Lyon: E. Dolet, 1540).

Donatus, *Donati grammatici peritissimi fabularum breviatio Ovidii nasonis elegans et luccinta* (n. p.: no pub., n. d. [1480?]).

Du Bellay, Joachim. *La Defense et illustration de la langue francoyse* (Paris: Arnoul L'Angelier, 1549).

La Deffence, et illustration de la langue francoyse pour l'instruction des jeunes studieus et encor peu avancez en la poésie françoise (Geneva: Droz, 2001).

Divers jeux rustiques, ed. Verdun L. Saulnier (Geneva: Droz, 1947).

Œuvres poétiques, ed. Henri Chamard, 9 vols., 3rd edn. (Paris: Nizet, 1961–1982).

Du Mont, Nicolas. *Advertissement venu de Rheims du sacre, couronnement et mariage de Henry III, très chrestien roy de France et de Pologne* (Paris: D. Du Pré, 1575).

Du Peyrat, Gabriel. *Stances au Roy faictes avant son mariage* (n. p.: no pub., 1601[?]).

Du Pont, Gratien. *Art et science de rhetoricque metriffiee* (Toulouse: Nicolas Vieillard, 1539).

Equicola, Mario. *Libro di natura d'amore di M. Equicola* (Venice: Pietro di Nicolini da Sabbio, 1536).

Les Six livres de Mario Equicola d'Alveto, trans. Gabriel Chappuys Tourangeay (Paris: Jean Housé, 1584).

Euripides. *Bacchae, Iphigenia at Aulus*, Rhesus, ed. and trans. David Kovacs (Cambridge, MA: Harvard University Press, 2002).

Cyclops, Alcestis, Medea, ed. and trans. David Kovacs (Cambridge, MA: Harvard University Press, 1994).

Eusebius of Caesarea. *Eusebium Pamphili De evangelica praep[ar]atione Latiunu[m] ex Graeco beatissime pater iussu tuo effeci* (Venice: Leonhardus Aurl, 1473).

Nicene and Post-Nicene Fathers of the Christian Church, ed. Philip Schaff and Henry Wace (Grand Rapids: Eerdmans, 1952).

Fabri, Pierre. *Le grant et vray art de pleine rhetoricque* [1521], ed. A. Héron, 3 vols. (Rouen: Lestringent, 1889–1890). Reprint: 1 vol. (Geneva: Slatkine, 1969).

Ferrand, Jacques. *Traicté de l'essence et guerison de l'amour ou de la melancolie erotique* (Toulouse: Veuve J. et R. Colomiez, 1610).

Ferrerio, Giovanni. *De vera cometae significatione contra astrologorum omnium vanitatem* (Paris: M. de Vascosan, 1540).

Ferrier, Oger. *Des jugemens astronomiques sur les nativités* (Lyon: Jean de Tournes, 1550).

Ficino, Marsilio. *Commentaire de Marsile Ficin, Florentin: sur le Banquet d'Amour de Platon* (Poitiers: A l'enseigne du Pelican, 1546).

Commentaire sur le banquet de Platon, ed. and trans. Raymond Marcel (Paris: Société d'édition "Les belles lettres," 1956). [Referred to in text as *De amore.*]

Commentary on Plato's Symposium, trans. Sears Jayne (Dallas: Spring Publications, 1978).

Della religione christiana (Florence: Giunti, 1563).

De religione christiana et fidei pietate opusculim (Paris: Bertholdi Rembolt et Joannis Waterloes, 1510).

De triplici vita (Paris: Georges Wolf, c.1496).

Discours de l'honneste amour sur le Banquet de Platon (Paris: Chez Jean Macé, 1578).

Discours de l'honneste amour, sur le Banquet de Platon: Par Marsile Ficin, trans. Guy le Fevre de la Boderie (Paris: Abel L'Angelier, 1588).

Epistolae Marsilii Ficini Florentini (Nuremberg: Antonio Koberger, 1497).

The Letters of Marsilio Ficino, trans. London School of Economics and Political Science, 6 vols. (New York: Schocken Books, 1981, 1985).

Marsilio Ficino interprete . . . De vita coelitus comparanda (Paris: Apud Thomam Richardum, 1547).

Marsilio Ficino's Commentary on Plato's Symposium, trans. and intro. Sears Reynolds Jayne (Columbia, MO: University of Missouri, 1944).

Mercurii Trismegisti Liber de Potestate et Sapienta Dei per Marsillium Ficinum traductus: ad Cosmum Medicem (Paris: Wolffgango Hopyl, 1494).

Platonic Theology, trans. Michael J. B. Allen and ed. James Hankins and William Bowen, 6 vols. (Cambridge, MA: Harvard University Press, 2001–2006).

Platonis opera a Marsilio Ficino traducta (Paris: Impressa in aedibus Ascensianis, 1518).

Supplementum Ficinianum, ed. Paul O. Kristeller, 2 vols. (Florence: Leonis S. Olschki, 1937).

Theologica Platonica de immortalitate animorum duo de viginti libris (Paris: Apud Aegidium Gorbinum, 1559).

Théologie platonicienne, ed. and trans. Raymond Marcel, 3 vols. (Paris: Les Belles Lettres, 1964–1970).

Three Books on Life, ed. and trans. Carol V. Kaske and John R. Clark (Binghamton: Renaissance Society of America, 1989).

Timaeus: vel De natura. Marsilio Ficino interprete (Paris: P. Calvarin, 1536).

Finarensis, David. *L'Epitome de David Finarensis, medicin, de la vraye astrologie* (Paris: Estienne Groulleau, 1547).

Finé, Oronce. *Les canons & documens très amples, touchant l'usage et pratique des communs Almanachz, que lon nomme Ephemerides* (Paris: Guillaume Cavellat, 1556).

Florence, Cardinal de. *Lettres du Cardinal de Florence sur Henry IV et sur la France, 1596–1598*, ed. Raymond Ritter (Paris: Bernard Grasset, 1955).

Fontaine, Charles. *La Contr'amye de court par Maistre Charles Fontaine Parisien* (Lyon: Sulpice Sabon pour Antoine Constantin, 1543).

Le Quintil Horatian sur le premier livre de La Defense, et illustration de la langue françoise, et la suycte (Lyon: Jean Temporal 1551).

Le Quintil Horatian sur le premier livre de La Defense, et illustration de la langue françoyse, et la suycte (Paris: veufve Françoys Regnault, 1555).

Fontaine, Jacques. *Discours de la puissance du ciel, sur les corps inférieurs, & principalement de l'influence contre les Astrologues judiciaries* (Paris: Gilles Gorbin, 1581).

Fregosa, Battista da Campo. *Baptistae C. Fulgosi Anteros* (Milan: Pachel, 1493).

Fulgentius, Fabius Planciades, *C. Iulii Hygini Augusti Liberti Fabularum Liber, Ad Ominium poëtarum lectionem mire necessarius & ante hac nunquam excusas* (Basle: Joan Hervagium, 1535).

Garland, John of. *Integumenta Ovidii: poemetto inedito del secolo XIII*, ed. Fausto Ghisalberti (Milan: Principato, 1933).

Gaurico, Luca. *Tractatus astrologicae judiciariae de nativitatibus virorum et mulierum* (Nuremberg: Johannes Petreium, 1540).

Tractatus astrologicus in quo agitur de praeteritis multorum hominum accidentibus per proprias eorum genituras ad unguem examinatis (Venice: Curtium Troianum Navò, 1552).

Génin, François, ed. *Nouvelles lettres de la Reine de Navarre addressées au Roi François Ier son frère* (Paris: Jules Renouard et Cie., 1842).

Godefroy, Theodore and Denys. *Le Ceremonial François*, 2 vols. (Paris: Sébastien Cramoisy, 1649).

Habert, François. *Déploration poétique de feu M. Antoine du Prat* (Lyon: Jean de Tournes, 1545).

Les Epistres héroïdes, pour servir d'exemple aux chrestiens (Paris: M. Fezandat, 1560).

La Nouvelle Vénus (Lyon: Jean de Tournes, 1547).

Les quinze livres de la Metamorphose d'Ovide interpretez en rime françoise, selon la phrase latine (Rouen: Thomas Mallard, 1590).

Hamellius, Paschasius. *Divi Alphonsi romanorum et Hispaniarum regis, astronomicae tabulae in propriam integritatem restitutae* (Paris: Chrestien Wechel, 1545).

Hebreo, Leone [Léon Hébreu; Judah Abrabanel]. *Dialoghi di amore* (Venice: Aldo, 1545).

Dialogues d'Amour, trans. Pontus de Tyard (Lyon: Jean de Tournes, 1551).

Dialogues d'amour [par] Leon Hebreu. The French translation attributed to Pontus de Tyard and Published in Lyon, 1551, by Jean de Tournes, trans. T. Anthony Perry (Chapel Hill: University of North Carolina Press, 1974).

Philosophie d'amour de M. Leon Hebreu (Lyon: Guillaume Roville et Thibauld Payen, 1551).

Henri III. *Lettres de Henri III, Roi de France*, ed. Michel François, 8 vols. (Paris: Klincksieck, 1959–2006).

Henri IV. *Lettres d'amour et écrits politiques*, ed. Jean-Pierre Babelon (Paris: Fayard, 1988).

Recueil des Lettres Missives, ed. Berger de Xivrey and J. Gaudet, 9 vols. (Paris: Imprimerie nationale, 1843–1876).

Herodotus. *The History*, trans. David Grene (University of Chicago Press, 1987).

Héroët, Antoine. *Compleincte d'une dame surprinse nouvellement damour*, in *La Parfaicte Amye* (Troyes: Maistre Nicole Paris, 1542).

Œuvres poétiques, ed. Ferdinand Gohin (Paris: Cornély, 1909).

La Parfaicte Amye, ed. Christine M. Hill (University of Exeter, 1981).

Hotman, François. *Le Tigre de 1560 reproduit pour la première fois en fac-similé d'après l'unique exemplaire connu (qui a échappé à l'incendie de l'Hôtel de Ville en 1871) et publié avec des notes historiques, littéraires et bibliographiques par M. Charles Read*, ed. Charles Read (Geneva: Slatkine, 1970).

Hurault, Philippe, comte de Chiverny. *Mémoires de Mre. Philippe Hurault, comte de Chiverny, Chancelier de France sous les rois Henri III & Henri IV*, 2 vols. (The Hague: Chez T. Johnson, 1720).

Ibn Ezra, Abraham Ben Meir. *Abrahe Auenaris Judei Astrologi pertissimi in re iudicali opera* (Venice: Petrus Liechtenstein, 1507).

Livre d'Arcandam docteur et astrologue, Traictant de Predictions d'Astrologie (Lyon: Benoist Rigaud, 1587).

Indagine, Johannes de. *Chiromance & Physiognomie par le regard des membres de Lhomme faite par Jan de Indagine*, trans. Antoine du Moulin (Lyon: Jan de Tournes, 1556).

Isambert, François André, Athanase-Jean-Léger Jourdan, Decrusy, and Alphonse-Honoré Taillandier, eds. *Recueil général des anciennes lois françaises*, 29 vols. (Paris: Librairie Belin-Leprieur, 1822–1829).

Jeake, Samuel. *An Astrological Diary of the Seventeenth Century. Samuel Jeake of Rye 1652–1699*, ed. and intro. Michael Hunter and Annabel Gregory (Oxford: Clarendon, 1988).

Jesuits. *Ratio studiorum: Plan raisonné et institution des études dans la Companie de Jesus*, ed. Adrien Demoustier trans. Léone Albrieux and Dolorès Pralon-Julia (Paris: Belin, 1997).

Jodelle, Etienne. *Œuvres complètes: I – Le Poète chez les hommes*, ed. Enea Balmas, 2 vols. (Paris: Gallimard, 1965).

    Les Oeuvres et meslanges poetiques d'Estienne Jodelle, sieur du Lymodin, ed. Charles Marty-Laveaux, 2 vols. (Geneva: Slatkin, 1966).

    Le Recueil des inscriptions, figures, devises, et masquarades, ordonnees en l'hostel de ville à Paris, le Ieudi 17 de Fevrier, 1558 (Paris: André Wechel, 1558).

Junctin, François. *Discours sur ce qui menace devoir advenir la comete apparue a Lyon le 12 de ce mois de Novembre 1577 laquelle se voit encore a present par Maistre Francois Junctin* (Paris: Gervais Mallot, 1577).

La Boderie, Guy Le Fèvre de. *La Galliade* (1582), ed. François Roudout; preface Robert Aulotte (Paris: Klincksieck, 1993).

La Borderie, Bertrand de. *L'Amie de court. Nouvellement inventée par le Seigneur de la Borderie* (Lyon: Estienne Dolet, 1543).

Lactantius. *Lucii Coelii Lactantii Firmiani, Opera quae extant, Ad fidem MSS. Recognita et Commentariis illustrata* (Oxford: Theatro Sheldoniano, 1684).

    The Works of Lactantius, trans. William Fletcher, 2 vols. (Edinburgh: T. & T. Clark, 1871).

La Perrière, Guillaume de. *Les Cents considerations d'amour, composées par Guillaume de la Perriere Tholosain. Avec une Satire contre fol Amour* (Lyon: Jaques [*sic*] Berion, 1536).

    Les considerations des quatre mondes, à savoir est: divin, angelique, celeste, & sensible (Lyon: Macé Bonhomme, 1552).

Leowitz, Cyprian von. *Brevis et perspicua ratio judicandi genituras, ex physicis causis & vera experientia extructu* (London: H. Suttonus, 1558).

    De coniunctionibus magnis insignioribus superiorum planetarum, solis defectionibus, et cometis, in quarta monarchia, cum eorundem effectuum historica expositione (London: Langingae ad Danubium, 1564).

Le Riche, Guillaume. *Journal de Guillaume et de Michel le Riche, avocats du roi à Saint-Maixent (de 1534 à 1586)* (1846; Geneva: Slatkine, 1971).

Le Roy, Louys. *Le Phédon de Platon, traittant de l'immortalité de l'âme* (Paris: S. Nyvelle, 1553).

    Le Sympose de Platon, ou de l'amour et de beauté, tradit de Grec en François (Paris: Jehan Longis & Robert le Mangnyer, 1558).

L'Estoile, Pierre de. *Journal pour le règne de Henri III*, ed. Louis-Raymond Lefèvre (Paris: Gallimard, 1943).

    Mémoires-Journaux de Pierre de L'Estoile, ed. G. Brunet, A. Champollion, E. Halphen, P. Lacroix, C. Read, T. de Larroque, 12 vols. (Paris: Alphonse Lemerre, 1875–1896).

Lomazzo, Gian Paolo. *Trattato dell'arte della pittura, scoltura et architettura* [1584] and *Idea del Tempio della Pittura* [1590] in *Scritti sulle arti*, ed. Roberto Paolo Ciardi, 2 vols. (Florence: Marchi and Bertolli, 1974).

Lorris, Guillaume de and Jean de Meun. *The Romance of the Rose*, trans. Charles Dahlberg, 3rd edn. (Princeton University Press, 1995).

Lucinge, René de. *Lettres de 1587. L'année des reîtres*, ed. James J. Supple (Geneva: Droz, 1994).

Lettres sur la cour d'Henri III en 1586, ed. Alain Dufour (Geneva: Droz, 1966).

Lettres sur les débuts de la Ligue (1585), ed. Alain Dufour (Geneva: Droz, 1964).

Magny, Olivier de. *Œuvres complètes*, ed. François Rouget (Paris: Champion, 1999).

Malherbe, Théophile de Viau, and Marc-Antoine Gérard, sieur de Saint-Amant. *Malherbe, Théophile, and Saint-Amant: A Selection*, ed. R. G. Maber (Durham, UK: University of Durham, 1983).

Marchant, Clément. *Remonstrance aux francoys, sur les vices qui de ce temps regnent en tous estats avec le remede à iceux* (Paris: Chez Nicolas Chesneau & Jean Poupy, 1576).

Marconville, Jean de. *De l'heur et malheur de mariage* (Paris: J. Dallier, 1564).

Marot, Clément. *Œuvres poétiques complètes*, ed. Gérard Defaux, 2 vols. (Paris: Bordas, 1990).

Six sonnets de Pétrarque (Paris: Corrozet, n. d. [1539]).

Marot, Clément and Barthélemy Aneau. *Les Trois Premiers Livres de la "Métamorphose" d'Ovide*, ed. Jean-Claude Moisan with Marie-Claude Malenfant (Paris: Champion, 1997).

Marstellarus, Gervasius, ed. *Artis divinatricis* (Paris: Christianus Wechelus, 1549).

McFarlane, I. D., ed. *The Entry of Henri II into Paris 16 June 1549* (Binghamton: Medieval and Renaissance Texts and Studies, 1982).

Medici, Catherine de'. *Lettres de Catherine de Médicis*, ed. Hector de La Ferrière, II vols. (Paris: CDI, 1880–1943).

Mizauld, Antoine. *Advertissement sur les Jugemens d'Astrologie à une studieuse damoyselle* (Lyon: Jean de Tournes, 1546), in *Le Trésor des pièces Angoumoisines inédites ou rares publié sous les auspices et par les soins de la Société archélogique et historique de la Charente*, vol. II (Angoulême: F. Goumard, 1867).

L'Explication, usage et practique de l'Ephemeride celeste d'Antoine Mizauld (Paris: Jacques Keruer, 1556).

Harmonia superioris naturae mundi et inferioris (Paris: Federici Morelli, 1577).

Paradoxa rerum coeli, ad Epiponum Philuranum, & socios (Paris: Federici Morelli, 1577).

Secrets de la lune (Paris: Federic Morel, 1571).

Montaigne, Michel de. *The Complete Essays of Montaigne*, trans. Donald Frame (Stanford University Press, 1965).

Montreux, Nicolas de. *L'Arimène, ou Berger desespere, pastorale. Par Ollenix de Mont-Sacre Gentil-homme du Maine* (Paris: Abraham Saugrain, 1597).

Münster, Sébastien. *Cosmographie Universelle de Tout le Monde*, trans. François Belleforest, 3 vols. (Paris: Michel Sonnius, 1575).

Navarre, Marguerite de. *The Heptameron*, trans. P. A. Chilton (London and New York: Penguin, 1984).

La Navire ou Consolation du Roi François Ier à sa sœur Marguerite, ed. Robert Marichal (Paris: Champion, 1956).

Nevers, Louis de Gonzague, duc de. *Les Memoirs de Monsieur le Duc de Nevers, Prince de Mantouë* (Paris: Jolly, 1665).

Nostradame, Michel de. *Nostradamus: lettres inédites*, ed. Jean Dupède (Geneva: Droz, 1983).

Ovid [P. Ovidius Naso]. *Accipe Studiose Lector P. Ovidii Metamorphosin cum luculentissimis Raphaelis Regii ennarionibus: quibus plurima ascripta sunt: que in exemplaribus antea impressis non inveniuntur. Que sunt rogas. Inter legendum facile tibi occurrent* (London: Per claudiu Davost al's de troys, 1510).

Ars Amatoria/The Art of Love and Other Poems, trans. J. H. Mozley, rev. G. P. Goold, 2nd edn. (Cambridge, MA: Harvard University Press, 1979).

La Bible des poëtes, Métamorphoses d'Ovide moralisé par Thomas Walleys et traduite par Colard Mansion (Paris: A. Venard, 1484).

Cy commence Ovide de Salmonen son livre intitule Methamorphose. Contenant xv livres particuliers moralisie par maistre Thomas Whaleys docteur en theologie de Tolose sainct dominique Translate & Compile par Colard mansion en la noble ville de Bruges (Paris: Anthoine Verard, 1484).

Ex P. Ovidii Nasonis Metamorphoseon Libris XV. Electorum Libri Totidem, Ultimo Integro. Ad eosdem novi Commentarii, sum Sectionibus & Argumentis: Studio & opera Iacobi Pontani de Societate Iesu (Antwerp: Heredes Martini Nutii, 1618).

Fabularum Ovidii Interpretatio, Tradita in Academia Regiomonta, a Georgio Sabino (Wittenberg: Clemens Schleich & Antonius Schöne, 1572).

[Metamorphoses], ed. Johannes Andreae (Leuven: Joannes de Westphalia, 1471).

[Metamorphoses], ed. Bonus Accursius (Milan: Philip de Lavagnia, 1475).

Metamorphoses, trans. Frank Justus Miller, rev. G. P. Goold (Cambridge, MA and London: Harvard University Press, 1977, 1984).

Metamorphoseos libri cum commento, Raph. Regii (Venice: B. Locatellus for Oct. Scotus, 1493).

P. Ovidii Nasonis Metamorphoseaon Libri XV. Raphaelis Regii Volterrano luculentissa explanatio, cum novis Iacobi Micylli, viri eruditissimi, additionibus. Lactantii Placiti in singulas fabulas argumenta. Eruditissimorum virorum coelii rhodigini, Ioan. Baptistae Egnatii, Henrici Glareani, Giberti Longolii, & Iacobi Fanensis, in pleraque omnia loca difficiliora annotationes (Venice: apud Ioan Gryphium, 1565).

P. Ovidii Nasonis metamorphoseos libri moralizati: cum pulcherrimis fabularum principalium figuris (Lyon: Jacob Maillet, 1511).

P. Ovidii Nasonis Metamorphosin castigissimam, cum Raphaelis Regii commentariis emendatissimis, & capitulis figuratis decenter appositis (Parma: Francisci Mazalis, 1505).

P. Ovidii Nasonis Poetae Sulmonensis Opera Quae Vocantur Amatoria, cum Doctorum Virorum Commentariis partim huscusque etiam alibi editis, partim iam primum adiectis: quorum omnium Catalogum versa pagina reperies. His accesserunt Iacobi Micylli Annotationes (Basle: Ioannem Hervagium, 1549).

Pub. Ovidii Nasonis Metamorphoseon, hoc est, Transformationum Libri quindecim. Com Donati clariss. Grammatici in potiores metamorphoseos Ovidii fabulas argumentis compendiarii, suis locis interiectis. His adiectae sunt ad dilucidam clamque lectionem adnotationes marginalis D. Gyberti Longolii. Henrici quoque Glareani adnotationes non vulgares res ad finem libri additae (Cologne: Joannes Gymnicus, 1542).

Pub. Ovid Nasonis Metamorphoseon Libri XV. In singulas quasque Fabulas Argumenta. Ex postrema Iacobi Micylli Recognitione (Frankfurt: Moenum, 1582; Paris: Hieronymum de Marnef & Viduam Gulielmi Cavellat, 1587).

Pub. Ovidii Nasonis Metamorphoseon Lib. XV. Ex accuratiss. Andreae Naugerii castigatione. Reliqua proximè sequens pagella indicabit (Antwerp: Christophe Plantin, 1566).

Pasquier, Etienne. *Le Monophile par Estienne Pasquier* (Paris: Estienne Groulleau, Charles l'Angelier, Jean Longis, and Vincent Sertenas, 1555).

Les Recherches de la France, Reveuës & augmentees de quart Livres (Paris: Jamet Mettayer & Pierre L'huillier, 1596).

Passerat, Jean. *In nuptias Henrici IIII Gallicae Navarraeque regis et Mariae Medicieae* (n. p.: no pub., 1600).

Pausanias. *Description of Greece*, trans. W. H. S. Jones (Cambridge, MA: Harvard University Press, 1918–1935).

Peletier du Mans, Jacques. *L'Amour des amours*, ed. A. van Bever (Paris: Société des Médicins bibliophiles, 1926).

L'Art poëtique de Iaques Peletier du Mans. Departi en deus Livres (Lyon: Jean de Tournes, 1555).

L'Art Poëtique, departi an deus livres (Lyon: J. de Tournes et G. Gazeau, 1555).

L'Art poétique d'Horace (Paris: Vascosan, 1541).

Commentarium de constitutione horoscopi in Iacopi Peletarii Cenomani Commentarii tres (Basle: Joannem Oporinum, 1563).

Dialogue de l'orthographe e prononciation Françoise, departi en deus livres par Jacques Peletier du Mans (Poitiers: Jan e Enguilbert de Marnes, 1550).

Les Oeuvres poétiques (Paris: Vascosan, 1547).

Petrarch, Francesco. *Canzoniere*, ed. Gianfranco Contini (Turin: Einaudi [1964], 1992).

Canzoniere, Trionfo, Rime varie, eds. C. Muscetta and D. Ponchiroli (Turin: Einaudi, 1958).

[Vaisquin Philieul]. *Laure d'Avignon, au nom et adveu de la royne Catherine de Médicis, royne de France* (Paris: Jacques Gazeau, 1548).

Messire François Petrarcque, des Remèdes de l'une et l'autre fortune prospère et adverse, trans. Nicole Oresme (Paris: Galliot du Pré, 1524).

Les Parolles joyeuses et dictz mémorables des nobles et saiges homes anciens rédigez par le gracieulx et honneste poète messier Francoys Petrarcque (Lyon: Par Denys de Harsy, pour Romain Morin, 1531).

Singulier et proufitable exemple pour toutes femmes mariées qui veullent faire leur devoir en marriage envers Dieu et leurs marys et avoir louenge du monde (n. p. [Lyon?]: no pub., n. d. [c. 1500]).

Les triomphes messire Françoys Petrarcque translatez de langaige tuscan en francois, trans. Georges de La Forge (Paris: B. Vérard, 1514).

Peucer, Kaspar. *Le Devins, ou Commentaire des principales sortes de devinations* (Antwerp: Henrick Connix, 1584).

Peurbach, Georg von. *Theorice nove planetarum cum commento* (n. p.: Vespuccius, 1508).

Pico della Mirandola, Giovanni. *Le Commentaire du tres-illustre seigneur Comte Jean Picus Mirandulanus, sur une Chanson d'Amour, composé par Hierosme Benivieni* (Paris: Abel L'Angelier, 1588).

De hominis dignitate, Heptaplus, De ente et uno, ed. Eugenio Garin (Florence: Vallecchi, 1942).

Disputationes adversus astrologium divinatricem, ed. and intro. Eugenio Garin, 2 vols. (Florence: Vallecchi: 1946–1952).

Pighius, Albertus. *Adversus prognosticatorum vulgus, qui annuas predictions edunt et se astrologos mentiuntur, astrologiae defensio* (Paris: Henri Estienne, 1518).

Pinselet, Charles. *Le martyre des deux freres*, in *Archives curieuses de l'histoire de la France, depuis Louis XI jusqu'à Louis XVIII, ou Collection de pièces rares et intéressantes, telles que chroniques, mémoires, pamphlets, lettres, et vies*, ed. L. Cimber and F. Danjou (Paris: Beauvais, 1834–1837).

Pitatis, Petrus. *Almanach Novum Petri Pitati Veronensis mathematici* (Tübingen: Morhardum, 1544).

Compendium Petri Pitati veronensis in academia philarmonica mathesim profitentis (Verona: Apud Paulum Ravagnanum, 1560).

Pithoys, Claude. *Traitté curieux de l'Astrologie Judiciaire, ou préservatif contre l'astronmantie des généthaliques* (Montbelliard: Jacques Foylet, 1641).

Plato. *Deux dialogues de Platon. Scavoir est: l'ung intitulé Axiochu*, in *Le Second enfer d'Estienne Dolet* (Paris: I. Tastu, n. d.).

Dialogue de Platon intitulé Criton, trans. Pierre du Val (Paris: Michel Vascozan, 1547).

Le dialogue de Plato intitulé Io (Paris: Chrestien Wechel, 1546).

Le discours de la Queste d'amytie dict Lysis de Platon, in *Recueil des oeuvres de feu Bonaventure des Periers* (Lyon: Iean de Tournes, 1544).

Opera quae extant omnia. Ex nova Ioannis Serrani interpretatione, 3 vols. (Paris: Henr. Stephanus, 1578).

Phaedrus, trans. John H. Nichols, Jr. (Ithaca, NY: Cornell University Press, 1998).

The Republic, ed. G. R. Ferrari, trans. Tom Griffith (Cambridge University Press, 2000).

Symposium, trans. Christopher Gill (London: Penguin, 1999).

Plato [Michael J. B. Allen]. *The Platonism of Marsilio Ficino: A Study of the Phaedrus Commentary, Its Sources and Genesis* (Berkeley: University of California Press, 1984).

Plutarch [Jacques Amyot]. *Les Oeuvres morales et meslees de Plutarque, Translatees de Grec en François*, 3 vols. (Paris: Vasconsan, 1574).

Poliziano, Angelo. *La Favola di Orfeo composta da M. Angelo Poliziano, e ridotta ora la prima volta all sua vera e sincera lezione* (Padua: G. Comino, 1749).

Ptolemy. *The Almagest*, trans. R. Catesby Taliaferro, in *Great Books of the Western World 15: Ptolemy, Copernicus, Kepler*, ed. Mortimer J. Adler, 2nd edn. (University of Chicago Press, 1990), 1–478.

Liber Ptholomei quattuor tractatuum (Venice: Bonetus Locatellus apud Octavianus Scotus, 1493).

Tetrabiblos, trans. F. E. Robbins (Cambridge, MA: Harvard University Press, 1940/1998).

Rabelais, François. *The Histories of Gargantua and Pantagruel*, ed. and trans. J. M. Cohen (New York: Penguin, 1955).

Pantagruel, in *Œuvres complètes*, ed. Mirelle Huchon (Paris: Gallimard, 1955).

La Pantagrueline prognostication, ed. François Bon and Louis Dubost (Charente: Le Dé bleu, 1994).

La Pantagrueline prognostication. Certaine, veritable & infaillable pour l'an perpetuel. Nouvellement composée au prouffit & advisement de gens estourdis & musars de nature, Par maistre Alcofribas, architriclin dudict Pantagruel (Lyon: François Juste, 1542).

Le Quart Livre, ed. Gérard Defaux (Paris: Livre de poche, 1994).

Rapine, Claude. *Des choses merveilleuses en la nature, où est traicté des erreurs des sens, des puissances de l'ame, et des influences des cieux*, trans. Jacques Girard de Tournus (Lyon: Macé Bonhomme, 1557).

Reinhold, Erasmus. *Prutenicae Tabulae Coelestium Motuum* (Tübingen: Morhardus, 1551).

Ronsard, Pierre de. *Abbregé de l'art poëtique françois. À Alphonse Delbene, abbé de Hautecombe en Savoye* (Paris: chez Gabriel Buon, 1565).

Œuvres complètes, ed. Jean Céard, Daniel Ménager, and Michel Simonin, 2 vols. (Paris: Gallimard, 1993).

Œuvres complètes, ed. Paul Laumonier, Isidore Silver, and René Lebègue, 20 vols. (Paris: Marcel Didier, 1914–1967).

Les Quatre premiers livres des odes de Pierre de Ronsard, Vaudomois; Ensemble son Bocage (Paris: G. Cavellat, 1550).

Ronsard, Pierre de and Marc-Antoine de Muret. *Commentaires au Premier Livre des Amours de Ronsard*, ed. Jacques Chomart, Marie-Madeleine Fragonard, and Gisèle Mathieu-Castellani (Geneva: Droz, 1985).

Rossant, André de. *Les Meurs humeurs et comportemens de Henry de Valois representezx au vray depuis sa naissance* (Paris: Anthoine le Riche, 1589).

Rotier, Esprit. *In praefatores Prognostiquósque futurorum eventuum, divinatricémque Astrologiam Libro duo* (Toulouse: Iacobi Colomerii, 1555).

Roussat, Richard. *Des elements et principes d'Astronomie, avec les universelz iugements d'icelle* (Paris: Nicolas Crestien, 1552).

Sacrobosco, John of. *La sphere de Jean de Sacrobosco, augmentee de nouveaux Commentaires, & figures servant grandement pour l'intelligence d'icelle* (Paris: Chez Hierosme de Marnef, & la veufve Guillaume Cavellet, 1584).

Sainte-Marthe, Charles de. *La poésie françoise de Charles de Saincte-Marthe . . . Plus un Livre de ses Amys* (Lyon: chez le Prince, 1540).

Sainte-Marthe, Scévole de. *Les oeuvres de Scevole de Sainte-Marthe. Derniere Edition* (Paris: Jacques Villery, 1619).

Saint-Gelais, Mellin de. *Advertissement sur les Jugemens d'Astrologie à une studieuse damoyselle* (Lyon: Jean de Tournes, 1546).

Œuvres poétiques françaises, ed. Donald Stone, Jr., 2 vols. (Paris: Société des textes français modernes, 1993).

Sonnets, ed. L. Zilli (Geneva: Droz, 1990).

Saint-Gelais, Octavien de. *Le Séjour d'honneur*, ed. Frédéric Duval (Geneva: Droz, 2002).

Saint-Yon, Louis de. *Histoire tres-veritable de ce qui est advenu en ceste ville de Paris, depuis le septiesme de May 1588, jusques au dernier jour de Juin ensuyvant audit an* (Paris: Michel Joüin, 1588).

Salutati, Colucio. *Colucii Salutati de laboribus Herculis*, ed. B. L. Ullman, 2 vols. (Zurich: Thesauri Mundi, 1951).

Salviati, Antonio Maria. *Correspondance du nonce en France Antonio Maria Salviati, (1572–1578)*, ed. Pierre Hurtubise and Robert Toupin, 2 vols. (Rome: Université pontificale grégorienne, 1975).

Saulnier, Jean. *Cosmologie du Monde, tant celeste que terrestre* (Paris: Michel Daniel, 1618).

Savonarola, Girolamo. *Opus eximium adversus divinatricem astronomiam, in confirmationem confutationis eiusdem astronomicae praedictionis, Ioan. Pici Mirandulae Comitis, ex Italico in Latinum translatum. Interprete F. Thoma Boninsignio* (Florence: Apud Georgium Marescotum, 1581).

Scève, Maurice. *Délie, object de plus haulte vertu*, ed. Gérard Defaux, 2 vols. (Geneva: Droz, 2004).

Sébillet, Thomas. *Art poétique françoys*, ed. Félix Gaiffe (Paris: Droz, 1932).

   Art poétique françoys. Pour l'instruction dés jeunes studieus, & encor peu avancéz en la pöesie françoise (Paris: Gilles Corrozet, 1548).

   "Paradoxe contre l'Amour," in *Contramours . . . Paradoxe, contre l'Amour* (Paris: Gillez Beys, 1581), 2–222.

Serres, Jean de. *Voeu pour la prosperité du Roy & du royaume* (Paris: J. Mettayer, 1597).

Speroni, Sperone. *Dialogi di M. S. Speroni. Nouvamente ristampati, & con molta diligenza riveduti, & corretti* (Venice: Aldine, 1543).

Stadius, Johann. *Ephemerides novae et auctae Ioannis Stadii Leonnovthesii* (Cologne: Haeredes Arnoldi Birckmanni, 1560).

Sully, Maximilien de Béthune, duc de. *Mémoires des sages et royales oeconomies d'estat, Nouvelle collection des mémoires pour servir à l'histoire de France*, ed. Michaud and Poujoulat, 32 vols. (Paris: Imprimerie d'Edouard Proux, 1836–1839).

Taxil, Jean. *L'Astrologie et physiognomie en leur splendeur* (Tournon: R. Reynaud, 1614).

Thou, Jacques-Auguste de. *Histoire universelle de Jacques-Auguste de Thou, depuis 1543, jusqu'en 1607*, 15 vols. (London [Paris]: no pub., 1734).

Tommaseo, Niccolò, ed. *Les relations des ambassadeurs vénitiens sur les affaires de France au XVIᵉ siècle*, 2 vols. (Paris: Imprimerie royale, 1838).

Tyard, Pontus de. *Continuation des Erreurs amoureuses* (Lyon: Jean de Tournes, 1551).

   Ephemerides Octavae Sphaerae seu Tabullae diariae ortus (Lyon: Jean de Tournes, 1562).

   Les Erreurs amoureuses, ed. John A. McClelland (Geneva: Droz, 1967).

   Mantice: Discours de la verité de Divination par Astrologie, ed. Sylviane Bokdam (Geneva: Droz, 1990).

   Œuvres poétiques complètes, ed. John C. Lapp (Paris: Librairie Marcel Didier, 1966).

   Le solitaire premier, ed. Silvio F. Baridon (Lille: Giard, 1950).

   Solitaire premier, ou Dialogue de la fureur poétique (Paris: Galiot du Pré, 1575).

Vallambert, Simon de. *Cinq Livres, de la maniere de nourrir et gouverner les enfans de leur naissance* (Poitiers: de Marnefs & Bouchetz, Freres, 1565).

Valois, Marguerite de. *Mémoires de Marguerite de Valois*, ed. Ludovic Lalanne (Paris: P. Jannet, 1858).

Vias, Antoine de. *Le Sophologe d'Amour. Traictez plaisantz & delectables oultre l'utilité en iceulx contenue* (Paris: Gilles Corrozet, 1542).
Virgil. *Eclogues, Georgics, Aeneid I–VI*, trans. H. Rushton Fairclough and G. P. Goold, rev. edn. (Cambridge, MA: Harvard University Press, 2006).

SECONDARY SOURCES

Abbreviations for the titles of periodicals may be found on p. xvi.

Adhémar, Jean. "Aretino: Artistic Advisor to Francis I," *Journal of the Warburg and Courtauld Institutes* 17 (1954): 311–18.
"Thomas de Leu et les portraits gravés d'Henri IV," *Maso Finiguerra* 2 (1937): 219–26.
Albertini, Tamara. "Intellect and Will in Marsilio Ficino: Two Correlatives of a Renaissance Concept of Mind," in *Marsilio Ficino: His Theology, His Philosophy, His Legacy*, ed. Michael J. B. Allen and Valery Rees (Leiden: Brill, 2002), 203–25.
Allen, Don Cameron. *The Star-Crossed Renaissance: The Quarrel about Astrology and Its Influence in England* (Durham, NC: Duke University Press, 1941).
Allen, Michael J. B. "Cosmogony and Love: The Role of Phaedrus in Ficino's *Symposium* Commentary," *JMRS* 10 (1980): 131–53.
"Ficino's Theory of the Five Substances and the Neoplatonists' *Parmenides*," *JMRS* 12 (1982): 19–44.
Marsilio Ficino and the Phaedran Charioteer (Berkeley: University of California Press, 1981).
The Platonism of Marsilio Ficino: A Study of the Phaedrus Commentary, Its Sources and Genesis (Berkeley: University of California Press, 1984).
Allen, Michael, J. B., trans., ed. James Hankins and William Bowen. *Platonic Theology*, 6 vols. (Cambridge, MA: Harvard University Press, 2001–2006).
Allen, Michael J. B. and Valery Rees with Martin Davies, eds. *Marsilio Ficino: His Theology, His Philosophy, His Legacy* (Leiden: Brill, 2002).
Althusser, Louis. *Lenin and Philosophy and Other Essays*, trans. Ben Brewster (London: New Left Books, 1971).
Ames-Lewis, Francis. "Neoplatonism and the Visual Arts at the Time of Marsilio Ficino," in *Marsilio Ficino: His Theology, His Philosophy, His Legacy*, ed. Michael J. B. Allen and Valery Rees (Leiden: Brill, 2002), 327–38.
Anderson, William S. "The Orpheus of Virgil and Ovid: *flebile nescio quid*," in *Orpheus: The Metamorphoses of a Myth*, ed. John Warden (University of Toronto Press, 1982), 25–50.
Arnoux, Jules. *Un précurseur de Ronsard: Antoine Héroët, néo-platonicien et poète* (Digne: Imprimerie Chaspoul, 1912).
Arnoux, Pascal. *Favorites et "Dames de cœur" d'Agnès Sorel à Mme de Pompadour* (Paris: Rocher, 2005).
Bachinger, Katrina. *Male Pretense: A Gender Study of Sir Philip Sydney's Life and Texts* (Lewiston: Mellen, 1994).
Badel, Pierre-Yves. *"Le Roman de la Rose" au XVIᵉ siècle: étude de la réception de l'œuvre* (Geneva: Droz, 1980).

Balmas, M.-E. "De la Brigade de la Pléiade," in *Lumières de la Pléiade*, ed. Pierre Mesnard (Paris: Vrin, 1966), 13–20.

Balsamo, Jean. "Marot et les origines du pétrarquisme français (1530–1540)," in *Clément Marot, "Prince de poëtes françois," 1496–1996. Actes du Colloque international de Cahors en Quercy, 1996*, ed. Gérard Defaux (Paris: Champion, 1997), 323–37.

  "Pétrarque en France à la Renaissance: un livre, un modèle, un mythe," in *Les Poètes français de la Renaissance et Pétrarque*, ed. Jean Balsamo (Geneva: Droz, 2004), 13–32.

  Les Rencontres des Muses: italianisme et anti-italianisme dans les lettres françaises de la fin du XVIe siècle (Geneva: Slatkine, Bibliothèque Franco Simone, 1992).

Bamforth, Stephen. 'Clément Marot, François I et les muses," in *Clémont Marot, "Prince de poëtes François", 1496–1996: actes du colloque international de Cahors en Quercy 21–25 mai 1996*, ed. Gérard Defaux and Michel Simonin (Paris: Champion, 1997), 225–35.

Bardon, Françoise. *Diane de Poitiers et le mythe de Diane* (Paris: Presses universitaires de France, 1963).

Bardon, Henri. "Sur l'influence d'Ovide en France au 17ème siècle," in *Atti del Convegno Internationale Ovidiano di Sulmona del 1958*, 2 vols. (Rome: Istituto di Studi Romani, 1959), vol. II, 69–83.

Barstow, Anne. *Married Priests and the Reforming Papacy* (New York and Toronto: Mellen, 1982).

Baudrier, Henri. *Bibliographie lyonnaise* (Lyon: Société des amis de la Bibliothèque municipale de Lyon, 1895).

Beam, Sara. *Laughing Matters: Farce and the Making of Absolutism in France* (Ithaca, NY and London: Cornell University Press, 2007).

Beecher, D. A. "Erotic Love and the Inquisition: Jacques Ferrand and the Tribunal of Toulouse, 1620," *SCJ* 20:1 (1989): 41–53.

Béguin, Sylvie. "Contribution à l'iconographie d'Henri IV," *Avènement d'Henri IV quatrième centenaire, V: Les arts au temps d'Henri IV* (Pau: J. & D., 1992), 41–61.

  L'Ecole de Fontainebleau: le maniérisme à la cour de France (Paris: Gonthier-Seghers, 1960).

Beik, William. *Absolutism and Society in Seventeenth-Century France: State Power and Provincial Aristocracy in Languedoc* (Cambridge University Press, 1985).

Bell, David A. "Unmasking a King: The Political uses of Popular Literature under the French Catholic League, 1588–89," *SCJ* 20 (1989): 371–86.

Bellati. Giovanni. "Il primo traduttore dal *Canzoniere* petrarchescho nel Rinascimento francese: Vasquin Philieul," *Aevum* (1985): 371–98.

  "La traduction du *Canzoniere* de Vasquin Philieul," in *Les Poètes français de la Renaissance et Pétrarque*, ed. Jean Balsamo (Geneva: Droz, 2004), 203–28.

Benedict, Philip. "Of Marmites and Martyrs: Images and Polemics in the Wars of Religion," in *The French Renaissance in Prints from the Bibliothèque nationale de France*, ed. Karen Jacobson (Los Angeles: Grunwald Center for the Graphic Arts, 1994), 108–37.

Betteridge, Tom, ed. *Sodomy in Early Modern Europe* (Manchester University Press, 2002).

Bird, Phyllis A. "'Male and Female He Created Them': Gen. 1:27b in the Context of the Priestly Account of Creation," *Harvard Theological Review* 74:2 (1981): 129–59.

Blanc, Pierre, ed. *Dynamique d'une expansion culturelle: Pétrarque en Europe, XIVe– XXe siècle: actes du XXVIe congrès international du CEFI, Turin et Chambéry, 11–15 décembre 1995: à la mémoire de Franco Simone* (Paris: Champion, 2001).

Bloch, R. Howard. *Medieval Misogyny and the Invention of Western Romantic Love* (University of Chicago Press, 1991).

Blumenfeld-Kosinki, Renate. *Reading Myth: Classical Mythology and Its Interpretations in Medieval French Literature* (Palo Alto: Stanford University Press, 1997).

Boes, Maria R. "On Trial for Sodomy in Early Modern Germany," in *Sodomy in Early Modern Europe*, ed. Tom Betteridge (Manchester University Press, 2002).

Bollème, Geneviève. *Les Almanachs populaires aux XVIIe et XVIIIe siècles: essai d'histoire sociale* (Paris: Mouton, 1969).

Boswell, John. *Christianity, Social Tolerance, and Homosexuality: Gay People in Western Europe from the Beginning of the Christian Era to the Fourteenth Century* (University of Chicago Press, 1980).

"Revolutions, Universals and Sexual Categories," in *Hidden from History: Reclaiming the Gay and Lesbian Past*, ed. Martin Duberman, Martha Vicinus, and George Chauncey (New York: NAL Books, 1989), 17–36.

Boucher, Jacqueline. *La Cour de Henri III* (Rennes: Ouest France, 1986).

"Culture des notables et mentalité populaire dans la propagande qui entraîna la chute de Henri III," in *Mouvements populaires et conscience sociale, XVIe–XIXe siècles*, ed. Jean Nicolas (Paris: CNRS, 1985), 339–49.

Deux épouses et reines à la fin du XVIe siècle: Louise de Lorraine et Marguerite de France (Université de Saint-Etienne, 1995).

Société et mentalités autour de Henri III, 4 vols. (Paris: Champion, 1981).

Bourgeon, Jean-Louis. *L'Assassinat de Coligny* (Geneva: Droz, 1992).

Charles IX devant la Saint-Barthélemy (Geneva: Droz, 1995).

Bowen, William R. "Love, the Master of all the Arts: Marsilio Ficino on Love and Music," in *Love and Death in the Renaissance*, ed. Kenneth R. Bartlett, Konrad Eisenbichler, and Janice Liedl (Ottawa: Dovehouse, 1991), 51–60.

Braden, Gordon. "Shakespeare's Petrarchism," in *Shakespeare's Sonnets: Critical Essays*, ed. James Schiffer (New York and London: Garland, 1999), 164–83.

Bray, Alan. *The Friend* (University of Chicago Press, 2003).

"Homosexuality and the Signs of Male Friendship in Elizabethan England," in *Queering the Renaissance*, ed. Jonathan Goldberg (Durham, NC: Duke University Press, 1994), 40–61.

Homosexuality in Renaissance England (London: Gay Men's Press, 1982).

Breitenberg, Mark. *Anxious Masculinity in Early Modern England* (Cambridge University Press, 1996).

Brind'Amour, Pierre. *Nostradamus astrophile: les astres et l'astrologie dans la vie et l'œuvre de Nostradamus* (Ottawa and Paris: Presses de l'Université d'Ottawa and Klincksieck, 1993).

Brooten, Bernadette J. *Love between Women: Early Christian Responses to Female Homoeroticism* (University of Chicago Press, 1996).

Brown, Peter. *Augustine of Hippo: A Biography*, 2nd edn. (Berkeley: University of California Press, 2000).

The Body and Society: Men, Women and Sexual Renunciation in Early Christianity (New York: Columbia University Press, 1988).

Brownlee, Kevin and Sylvia Huot, eds. *Rethinking the Romance of the Rose: Text, Image, Reception* (Philadelphia: University of Pennsylvania, 1992).

Brugnoli, Giorgio. "Ovidio e gli esiliati carolingi," in *Atti del Convegno Internationale Ovidiano, Sulmona, maggio* 1958, 2 vols. (Rome: Istituto di Studi romani, 1959), vol. II, 209–16.

Brundage, James A. *Law, Sex, and Christian Society* (University of Chicago Press, 1987).

"Sex and Canon Law," in *Handbook of Medieval Sexuality*, ed. Vern L. Bullough and James A. Brundage (New York: Garland, 1996), 33–50.

Sex, Law and Marriage in the Middle Ages (Brookfield, VT: Variorum, 1993).

Bryant, Lawrence M. *The King and the City in the Parisian Royal Entry Ceremony: Politics, Ritual and Art in the Renaissance* (Geneva: Droz, 1986).

Buisseret, David. *Henry IV* (London and New York: Routledge, 1984).

Bullough, Vern L. and James A. Brundage, eds. *Handbook of Medieval Sexuality* (New York: Garland, 1996).

Sexual Practices and the Medieval Church (Buffalo, NY: Prometheus, 1982).

Burckhardt, Jacob. *The Civilization of the Renaissance in Italy* trans. S. G. C. Middlemore (New York: Modern Library, 2002).

Burger, Glenn and Steven F. Kruger, eds., *Queering the Middle Ages* (Minneapolis: University of Minnesota Press, 2001).

Burgess, Robert M. *Platonism in Desportes* (Chapel Hill: University of North Carolina Press, 1954).

Burke, Peter. *The Fortunes of "The Courtier": The European Reception of Castiglione's "Cortegiano"* (Cambridge: Polity, 1995).

Burlingham, Cynthia. "Portraiture as Propaganda: Printing during the Reign of Henri IV," in *The French Renaissance in Prints from the Bibliothèque nationale de France*, ed. Karen Jacobson (Los Angeles: Grunwald Center for the Graphic Arts), 139–51.

Bushnell, Rebecca. "Tyranny and Effeminacy in Early Modern England," in *Reconsidering the Renaissance*, ed. Mario A. Di Cesare (Binghamton: Medieval and Renaissance Texts and Studies, 1992), 339–54.

Cadden, Joan. *Meanings of Sexual Difference in the Middle Ages: Medicine, Science, and Culture* (Cambridge University Press, 1993).

"Sciences/Silences: The Natures and Languages of 'Sodomy' in Peter of Albano's *Problemata* Commentary," in *Constructing Medieval Sexuality*, ed. Karma Lochrie, Peggy McCracken, and James A. Schultz (Minneapolis: University of Minnesota Press, 1997), 40–57.

Cady, Joseph. "The 'Masculine Love' of the 'Princes of Sodom' 'Practising the Art of Ganymede' at Henri III's Court: The Homosexuality of Henri III and His Mignons in Pierre de L'Estoile's *Mémoires-Journaux*," in *Desire and Discipline: Sex and Sexuality in the Premodern West*, ed. Jacqueline Murray and Konrad Eisenbichler (University of Toronto Press, 1996), 123–54.

Cameron, Keith. *Henri III: Maligned or Malignant King?* (University of Exeter Press, 1978).

Carmona, Michel. *Marie de Médicis* (Paris: Fayard, 1981).

Caroll, Eugene. "Rosso in France," in *Actes du colloque international sur l'art de Fontainebleau*, ed. André Chastel (Paris: CNRS, 1975), 17–28.

Carrasco, Rafael. *Inquisición y represión sexual en Valencia: historia de los sodomitas (1565–1785)* (Barcelona: Laertes, 1985).

Cassirer, Ernst. *The Individual and the Cosmos in Renaissance Philosophy*, trans. and intro. Mario Domandi (New York and Evanston: Harper & Row, 1963).

Castarède, Jean. *Les Femmes galantes du XVIe siècle* (Paris: France-Empire, 2000).

Cave, Terence. *The Cornucopian Text: Problems of Writing in the French Renaissance* (Oxford University Press, 1979).

"Scève's *Délie*: Correcting Petrarch's Errors," in *Pre-Pléiade Poetry*, ed. Jerry C. Nash (Lexington: French Forum, 1985), 112–24.

Céard, Jean. *La Nature et les prodiges: l'insolite au XVIe siècle, en France* (Geneva: Droz, 1977).

Chamard, Henri. *Histoire de la Pléiade*, 4 vols. (Paris: Didier, 1939–1963).

Chance, Jane. *Medieval Mythography from Roman North Africa to the School of Chartres, AD 433–1177* (Gainesville: University Press of Florida, 1994).

Chartier, Roger, Marie-Madeleine Compère, and Dominique Julia. *L'Education en France du XVIe au XVIIIe siècle* (Paris: Société d'édition d'enseignement supérieur, 1976).

Chastel, André. *French Art: The Renaissance, 1430–1620* (Paris and New York: Flammarion, 1995).

Marsile Ficin et l'art (Geneva: Droz, 1975).

Chevalier, C. *Histoire de Chenonceau, ses artistes, ses fêtes, ses vicissitudes* (Lyon: Imprimerie Louis Perrin, 1868).

Chevalier, Pierre. *Henri III: roi shakespearean* (Paris: Fayard, 1985).

Clark, Charles W. "The Zodiac Man in Medieval Medical Astrology", Ph.D. diss. (University of Colorado, 1979).

Clark, Danielle. "'The Sovereign's Vice Begets the Subject's Error': The Duke of Buckingham, 'Sodomy,' and Narratives of Edward II, 1622–28," in *Sodomy in Early Modern Europe*, ed. Tom Betteridge (Manchester University Press, 2002).

Clements, Robert J. "Anti-Petrarchism of the Pléiade," *Modern Philology* 39 (1941): 15–21.

Critical Theory and Practice of the Pléiade (Cambridge, MA: Harvard University Press, 1942).

Cohen, Jeffrey Jerome and Bonnie Wheeler, eds. *Becoming Male in the Middle Ages* (New York and London: Garland, 1997).

Cohen, Thomas V. and Elizabeth S. Cohen. *Words and Deeds in Renaissance Rome: Trials before the Papal Magistrates* (University of Toronto Press, 1993).

Colliard, Lucienne. "Tableaux représentant des bals à la cour des Valois," *Gazette des Beaux-Arts* 105 (1963): 147–56.

Collins, James B. *From Tribes to Nation: The Making of France 500–1780* (Toronto: Nelson Thomson Learning, 2002).

Cornell, Drucilla, ed. *Feminism and Pornography* (Oxford University Press, 2000).

Cosandey, Fanny. *La Reine de France: symbole et pouvoir, XVe–XVIIIe siècle* (Paris: Gallimard, 2000).

Coulson, Frank T. "A Checklist of Newly Discovered Manuscripts of Pierre Bersuire's *Ovidius moralizatus*," *Scriptorium* 51 (1997): 164–86.

"Hitherto Unedited Medieval and Renaissance Lives of Ovid (I)," *Mediaeval Studies* 49 (1987): 152–207.

The "Vulgate" Commentary on Ovid's "Metamorphoses": The Creation Myth and the Story of Orpheus (Toronto: Centre for Medieval Studies, 1991).

Coulson, Frank T. and Bruno Roy, *Incipitarium Ovidianum: A Finding Guide for Texts in Latin Related to the Study of Ovid in the Middle Ages and Renaissance* (Turnhout: Brepols, 2000).

Courcelle, Pierre, Paul. *La Consolation de Philosophie dans la tradition littéraire: antécédents et postérité de Boèce* (Paris: Etudes augustiniennes, 1967).

"Etude critique sur les commentaires de la 'Consolation' de Boèce (IX–XVe siècles)," *Archives d'histoire doctrinale et littéraire du Moyen Age* 12 (1939): 5–140.

Cox-Rearick, Janet. *Dynasty and Destiny in Medici Art: Pontormo, Leo X and the two Cosimos* (Princeton University Press, 1984).

"Imagining the Renaissance: The Nineteenth-Century Cult of François I as Patron of Art," *RQ* 50:1 (1997): 207–50.

Crawford, Katherine. "Constructing Evil Foreign Queens," *JMEMS* 37:2 (2007): 393–418.

"The Impossibility of Indeterminacy: The Androgyne in Renaissance France." (In preparation.)

"Love, Sodomy, and Scandal: Controlling the Sexual Reputation of Henry III." *JHS* 12:4 (2003): 513–42.

"Marsilio Ficino, Neoplatonism, and the Problem of Sex," *Renaissance and Reformation; Renaissance et réforme* 28:2 (2004): 3–35.

"The Politics of Promiscuity: Masculinity and Heroic Representation at the Court of Henry IV," *FHS* 26:2 (2003): 225–52.

Crompton, Louis. *Homosexuality and Civilization* (Cambridge, MA and London: Belknap Press, 2003).

Crouzet, Denis. *La Genèse de la Réforme française, 1520–1562* (Paris: SEDES, 1996).

Les Guerriers de Dieu: la violence au temps des troubles de religion, vers 1525–vers 1610, 2 vols. (Seyssel: Champ Vallon, 1990).

La Nuit de la Saint-Barthélemy: un rêve perdu de la Renaissance (Paris: Fayard, 1994).

Daston, Lorraine and Katharine Park. "The Hermaphrodite and the Orders of Nature: Sexual Ambiguity in Early Modern France," *Gay and Lesbian Quarterly* 1 (1995): 419–73.

Davidson, Nicolas. "Theology, Nature and the Law: Sexual Sin and Sexual Crime in Italy from the Fourteenth to the Seventeenth Century," in *Crime, Society and the Law in Renaissance Italy*, ed. Trevor Dean and K. J. P. Lowe (Cambridge University Press, 1994), 74–98.

Davis, Natalie Zemon. *Society and Culture in Early Modern France* (Stanford University Press, 1975).

De Grazia, Margreta. "The Scandal of Shakespeare's Sonnets," in *Shakespeare's Sonnets: Critical Essays*, ed. James Schiffer (New York and London: Garland, 1999), 89–112.

Dédéyan, Charles. "Ronsard et Bembo," in *Ronsard e l'Italia / Ronsard in Italia* (Fasaon di Puglia: Schena, 1988).

Dejob, Charles. *Marc-Antoine Muret: un professeur français en Italie dans la seconde moitié du XVIe siècle* (Geneva: Slatkine, 1970 [1881]).

Dellaneva, Joann. *Song and Counter-song: Scève's "Délie" and Petrarch's "Rime"* (Lexington: French Forum, 1983).

Denis, Auguste. *Recherches bibliographiques et historiques sur les almanachs de la Champagne et de la Brie précédées d'un essai sur l'histoire de l'almanach en général* (Chalons-sur-Marne: Chez l'Auteur, 1880).

Desclouzeaux. "Gabrielle d'Estrées et Sully," *Revue historique* 33 (1887): 241–95.

    "Le mariage et le divorce de Gabrielle d'Estrées d'après des documents nouveaux," *Revue historique* 30 (1886): 49–106.

Diefendorf, Barbara B. *Beneath the Cross: Catholics and Huguenots in Sixteenth-Century Paris* (New York: Oxford University Press, 1991).

    From Penitence to Charity: Pious Women and the Catholic Reformation in Paris (Oxford University Press, 2004).

Dimier, Louis. *Histoire de la peinture de portrait en France au XVIe siècle*, 3 vols. (Paris and Brussels: G. Van Oest et Cie., 1924).

    Le Primatice: peintre, sculpteur et architecte des rois de France (Paris: Leroux, 1900).

Dinshaw, Carolyn. *Getting Medieval: Sexualities and Communities, Pre- and Postmodern* (Durham, NC and London: Duke University Press, 1999).

Di Stephano, Giuseppe. "L'Hellenisme en France à l'orée de la Renaissance," in *Humanism in France at the End of the Middle Ages and in the Early Renaissance*, ed. A. H. T. Levi (Manchester University Press, 1970), 29–42.

Divination et controverse religieuse en France au XVIe siècle (Paris: Ecole normale supérieure de jeunes filles, 1987).

Dover, Kenneth J. *Greek Homosexuality* (New York: MJF Books, 1978).

Dubost, Jean-François. *La France italienne: XVIe–XVIIe siècle*, preface Daniel Roche (Paris: Aubier Montaigne, 1997).

Dubrow, Heather. *Captive Victors: Shakespeare's Narrative Poems and Sonnets* (Ithaca, NY and London: Cornell University Press, 1987).

    Echoes of Desire: English Petrarchism and Its Counterdiscourses (Ithaca, NY: Cornell University Press, 1995).

Duhem, Pierre Maurice Marie. *Le Système du monde*, 10 vols. (Paris: A. Hermann et fils, 1913–1959).

Dülmen, Richard von. *Theatre of Horror: Crime and Punishment in Early Modern Germany*, trans. Elisabeth Neu (Cambridge, MA: Polity, 1990).

Eade, J. C. *The Forgotten Sky: A Guide to Astrology in English Literature* (Oxford: Clarendon, 1984).

Elliott, Dyan. *Spiritual Marriage: Sexual Abstinence in Medieval Wedlock* (Princeton University Press, 1993).

Engels, Joseph. *Etudes sur l'Ovide moralisé* (Groningen: Wolters, 1945).

Enterline, Lynn. *The Rhetoric of the Body from Ovid to Shakespeare* (Cambridge University Press, 2000).

Evans, Richard J. *Rituals of Retribution: Capital Punishment in Germany, 1600–1987* (Oxford University Press, 1996).

Farr, James R. *Authority and Sexuality in Early Modern Burgundy (1550–1730)* (Oxford University Press, 1995).

Febvre, Lucien Paul Victor. *Le Problème de l'incroyance au XVIe siècle: la religion de Rabelais* (Paris: Michel, 1968).

Fedi, Roberto. *La memoria della poesia: canzonieri, lirici e libri di Rime nel Rinascimento* (Rome: Salerno, 1990).

Ferguson, Gary. *Mirroring Belief: Marguerite de Navarre's Devotional Poetry* (Edinburgh University Press, 1992).

Festugière, Jean. *La Philosophie de l'amour de Marsile Ficin et son influence sur la littérature française au XVIe siècle* (Paris: Vrin, 1941).

ffolliott, Sheila. "Catherine de' Medici as Artemisia: Figuring the Powerful Widow," in *Rewriting the Renaissance: The Discourses of Sexual Difference in Early Modern Europe*, ed. Margaret W. Ferguson, Maureen Quilligan, and Nancy J. Vickers (University of Chicago Press, 1986), 227–41.

Findlen, Paula. "Humanism, Politics and Pornography in Renaissance Italy," in *The Invention of Pornography: Obscenity and the Origins of Modernity*, ed. Lynn Hunt (New York: Zone, 1996), 48–108.

Fineman, Joel. *Shakespeare's Perjured Eye: The Invention of Poetic Subjectivity in the Sonnets* (Berkeley: University of California Press, 1986).

Finucci, Valeria. *The Manly Masquerade: Masculinity, Paternity, and Castration in the Italian Renaissance* (Durham, NC and London: Duke University Press, 2003).

Fisher, Will. "The Renaissance Beard: Masculinity in Early Modern England," *RQ* 54 (2001): 155–87.

Fontaine, Marie Madeleine. "Débats à la cour de France autour du *canzoniere* et de ses imitateurs dans les années 1533–1548," in *Les Poètes français de la Renaissance et Pétrarque*, ed. Jean Balsamo (Geneva: Droz, 2004), 104–35.

Ford, Philip. "Classical Myth and its Interpretation," in *The Classical Heritage in France*, ed. Gerald Sandy (Leiden and Boston: Brill, 2002), 331–49.

Foucault, Michel. *The History of Sexuality: An Introduction*, trans. Robert Hurley (New York: Pantheon, 1976).

Frantz, David O. *Festum Voluptatis: A Study of Renaissance Erotica* (Columbus: Ohio State University Press, 1989).

Frantzen, Allen J. "Between the Lines: Queer Theory, the History of Homosexuality, and Anglo-Saxon Penitentials," *JMEMS* 26 (1996): 245–96.

Frazee, Charles A. "The Origins of Clerical Celibacy in the Western Church," *Church History* 41 (1972): 149–67.

Freccero, Carla. *Queer/Early/Modern* (Durham, NC and London: Duke University Press, 2006).

Freedberg, Sydney. "Rosso's Style in France and its Italian Context," in *Actes du colloque international sur l'art de Fontainebleau*, ed. André Chastel (Paris: CNRS, 1975), 13–16.

French, Roger. "Astrology in Practical Medicine," in *Practical Medicine from Salerno to the Black Death*, ed. Luis Garcia-Ballester, Roger French, Jon Arrizabalaga, and Andrew Cunningham (Cambridge University Press, 1994), 30–59.

 "Foretelling the Future: Arabic Astrology and English Medicine in the Late Twelfth Century," *Isis* 87 (1996): 453–80.

Freudenthal, Gad. "Maimonides' Stance on Astrology in Context: Cosmology, Physics, Medicine, and Providence," in *Moses Maimonides: Physician, Scientist, and*

Philosopher, ed. Fred Rosner and Samuel S. Kottek (Northvale, NJ and London: Jason Aronson, 1993), 77–90.

Freyburger, Pierre. "Le problème du fatalisme astral dans la pensée protestante en pays Germaniques," in *Divination et controverse religieuse en France au XVIe siècle* (Paris: Ecole normale supérieure de jeunes filles, 1987), 35–55.

Friedman, John Block. *Orpheus in the Middle Ages* (Cambridge, MA: Harvard University Press, 1970).

Funke, Anne. "Marguerite de Navarre et son influence spirituelle sur les vitraux de la cathédrale Sainte-Marie d'Auch," in *Patronnes et mécènes en France à la Renaissance*, ed. Kathleen Wilson-Chevalier (Université de Saint-Etienne, 2007), 321–40.

Gaisser, Julia Haig, *Catullus and His Renaissance Readers* (Oxford: Clarendon, 1993).

Garin, Eugenio. *Astrology in the Renaissance: The Zodiac of Life*, trans. Carolyn Jackson, June Allen, and Clare Robertson (London: Routledge & Kegan Paul, 1983).

Garrison, Daniel H. *Sexual Culture in Ancient Greece* (Norman: University of Oklahoma Press, 2000).

Garrisson, Estèbe Janine. *Tocsin pour un massacre: la saison de Saint-Barthélemy* (Paris: Centurion, 1968).

Gendre, André. "Pierre de Ronsard," in *Les Poètes français de la Renaissance et Petrarque*, ed. Jean Balsamo (Geneva: Droz, 2004), 229–51.

Ghisalberti, Fausto. *L'"Ovidius Moralizatus" di Pierre Bersuire* (Rome: Ditta Topografia Cuggiani, 1933).

Girard, René. *La Violence et le sacré* (Paris: Grousset, 1972).

Goldberg, Jonathan. *Sodometries: Renaissance Texts, Modern Sexualities* (Stanford University Press, 1992).

Goldberg, Jonathan and Madhavi Menon. "Queering History," *PMLA* (2005): 1608–17.

Grafton, Anthony. *Cardano's Cosmos: The World and Works of a Renaissance Astrologer* (Cambridge, MA and London: Harvard University Press, 1999).

"Geniture Collections, Origins and Uses of a Genre," in *Books and the Sciences in History*, ed. Marina Frasca-Spada and Nick Jardine (Cambridge University Press, 2000).

Joseph Scaliger: A Study in the History of Classical Scholarship, 2 vols. (Oxford: Clarendon, 1983–1993).

Grafton, Anthony and Nancy Siraisi. "Between Election and My Hopes: Girolamo Gardano and Medical Astrology," in *Secrets of Nature: Astrology and Alchemy in Early Modern Europe*, ed. William R. Newman and Anthony Grafton (Cambridge, MA and London: MIT Press, 2001), 69–131.

Gray, Floyd. *Gender, Rhetoric and Print Culture in French Renaissance Writing* (Cambridge University Press, 2000).

Greene, Roland. *Unrequited Conquests: Love and Empire in the Colonial Americas* (University of Chicago Press, 1999).

Grell, Ole Peter and Bob Scribner, eds. *Tolerance and Intolerance in the European Reformation* (New York: Cambridge University Press, 1996).

Guidici, Enzo. "Bilancio di un 'annosa questione': Maurice Scève e la 'scoperta' della 'tomba' di Laura," in *Quaderni di filologia e lingue romanze* (Rome: Ed. dell'Ateneo, 1980), vol. II, 7–70.

Guthrie, W. K. C. *The Greeks and Their Gods* (Boston, MA: Beacon Press, 1966).

Orpheus and the Greek Religion: A Study of the Orphic Movement (London: Methuen, 1952).

Halberstam, Judith. *Female Masculinity* (Durham, NC: Duke University Press, 1998).

In a Queer Time & Place: Transgender Bodies, Subcultural Lives (New York University Press, 2005).

Halperin, David M. "Forgetting Foucault: Acts, Identities, and the History of Sexuality," *Representations* 63 (1998): 93–120.

Hankins, James. *Plato in the Italian Renaissance*, 2 vols. (Leiden and New York: Brill, 1990).

Hankins, James, ed. *Renaissance Civic Humanism: Reappraisals and Reflections* (Cambridge University Press, 2000).

Heller, Henry. *Anti-Italianism in Sixteenth-Century France* (University of Toronto Press, 2003).

Hendy, Andrew von. *The Modern Construction of Myth* (Bloomington: Indiana University Press, 2002).

Herrup, Cynthia B. *A House in Gross Disorder: Sex, Law, and the 2nd Earl of Castlehaven* (New York: Oxford University Press, 1999).

Hillman, David and Carla Mazzio, eds. *The Body in Parts: Fantasies of Corporeality in Early Modern Europe* (New York and London: Routledge, 1997).

Hirai, Hiroshi. "Concepts of Seeds and Nature in the Work of Marsilio Ficino," in *Marsilio Ficino: His Thought, His Philosophy, His Legacy*, ed. Michael J. B. Allen and Valery Rees (Leiden: Brill, 2002), 257–84.

Hoffman, Philip T. *Church and Community in the Diocese of Lyon, 1500–1750* (New Haven: Yale University Press, 1984).

Holt, Mack P. *The Wars of Religion* (Cambridge University Press, 1995).

Hopkinson, Neil, ed. *A Hellenistic Anthology* (Cambridge University Press, 1988).

Hunkeler, Thomas. *Le Vif du sens: corps et poésie selon Maurice Scève* (Geneva: Droz, 2003).

Huppert, George. *Public Schools in Renaissance France* (Urbana and Chicago: University of Illinois Press, 1984).

The Style of Paris: Renaissance Origins of the French Enlightenment (Bloomington and Indianapolis: Indiana University Press, 1999).

Hutton, James. *The Greek Anthology in France and the Latin Writers of the Netherlands to the Year 1800* (Ithaca, NY: Cornell University Press, 1946).

Irwin, Eleanor. "The Songs of Orpheus and the New Song of Christ," in *Orpheus: The Metamorphosis of a Myth*, ed. John Warden (University of Toronto Press, 1982), 51–62.

Jackson, Richard A. *Vive le Roi! A History of the French Coronation from Charles V to Charles X* (Chapel Hill: University of North Carolina Press, 1984).

Jacobson, Karen, ed. *The French Renaissance in Prints from the Bibliothèque nationale de France* (Los Angeles: Grunwald Center for the Graphic Arts, 1994).

Jesnick, Ilona J. *The Image of Orpheus in Roman Mosaic* (Oxford: Archaeopress, 1997).

Jodogne, Pierre. *Lemaire de Belges, écrivain franco-bourguignon* (Brussels: Palais des Académies, 1972).

Johnson, Patricia J. *Ovid before Exile: Art and Punishment in the "Metamorphoses"* (Madison: University of Wisconsin Press, 2008).

Jordan, Mark D. *The Invention of Sodomy in Christian Theology* (University of Chicago Press, 1997).

Jouanna, Arlette. "Faveur et favoris: l'exemple des *mignons* de Henri III," in *Henri III et son temps: actes du colloque international du Centre de la Renaissance de Tours, octobre 1989*, ed. Robert Sauzet (Paris: Vrin, 1992), 155–65.

"Un programme politique nobiliare: les Mécontents et l'Etat (1574–1576)," in *L'Etat et les aristocraties (France, Angleterre, Ecosse) XIIe–XVIIe siècle*, ed. Philippe Contamine (Paris: Presses de l'Ecole normale supérieure, 1989), 247–77.

Joukovsky, Françoise. *Orphée et ses disciples dans la poésie française et néo-latine du XVIe siècle* (Geneva: Droz, 1970).

Jourda, Pierre. *Marguerite d'Angoulême, duchesse d'Alençon, reine de Navarre (1492–1549) étude biographique et littéraire*, 2 vols. (Paris: Champion, 1930).

Judson, Lindsay. "Heavenly Motion and the Unmoved Mover," in *Self-Motion: From Aristotle to Newton*, ed. Mary Louise Gill and James G. Lennox (Princeton University Press, 1994), 155–71.

Jung, Marc-René. *Hercule dans la littérature français du XVIe siècle: de l'Hercule courtois à l'Hercule baroque* (Geneva: Droz, 1966).

Kaschuba, Wolfgang. "The Emergence and Transformation of Foundation Myths," in *Myths, Memory and History in the Construction of Community: Historical Patterns in Europe and Beyond*, ed. Bo Strath (Brussels: Peter Lang, 2000).

Keach, William. "Ovid and 'Ovidian' Poetry," in *Ovid: The Classical Heritage*, ed. William S. Anderson (New York and London: Garland, 1995), 179–217.

Kelley, Donald R. "France," in *The Renaissance in National Context*, eds. Roy Porter and Mikulás Teich (Cambridge University Press, 1992), 123–45.

Kelly, Kathleen Coyne. *Performing Virginity and Testing Chastity in the Middle Ages* (London and New York: Routledge, 2000).

Kelly, Kathleen Coyne and Marina Leslie, eds. *Menacing Virgins: Representing Virginity in the Middle Ages and Renaissance* (Newark, DE and London: Associated University Presses, 1999).

Kerr, W. A. R. "Antoine Héroët's *Parfaite Amye*," *PMLA* 20:3 (1905): 567–83.

Knecht, R. J. *Francis I* (Cambridge University Press, 1982).

The French Renaissance Court (New Haven and London: Yale University Press, 2008).

Renaissance Warrior and Patron: The Reign of Francis I (Cambridge University Press, 1994).

Kristeller, Paul O. "The European Significance of Florentine Platonism," in *Medieval and Renaissance Studies: Proceedings of the Southeastern Institute of Medieval and Renaissance Studies, Summer, 1967* (Chapel Hill: University of North Carolina Press, 1968), 206–29.

Il pensiero filosofico di Marsilio Ficino (Florence: Sansoni, 1953).

The Philosophy of Marsilio Ficino, trans. Virginia Conant (New York: Columbia University Press, 1943).

"The Scholastic Background of Marsilio Ficino: With an Edition of Unpublished Texts," in *Studies in Renaissance Thought and Letters* (Rome: Edizioni di storia e letteratura, 1956; reprint 1969), 35–97.

Kritzman, Lawrence D. *The Rhetoric of Sexuality and the Literature of the French Renaissance* (Cambridge University Press, 1991).

Kuchta, David. *The Three-Piece Suit and Modern Masculinity: England, 1550–1850* (Berkeley: University of California Press, 2002).

Kuefler, Mathew. "Male Friendship and the Suspicion of Sodomy in Twelfth-Century France," in *The Boswell Thesis: Essays on Christianity, Social Tolerance and Homosexuality*, ed. Mathew Kuefler (University of Chicago Press, 2006), 179–212.

Kurze, Dietrich. "Popular Astrology and Prophecy in the Fifteenth and Sixteenth Centuries: Johannes Lichtenberger," in *"Astrologi Hallucinati": Stars and the End of the World in Luther's Time*, ed. Paola Zambelli (Berlin and New York: Walter de Gruyter, 1986), 176–93.

Labalme, Patricia H. "Sodomy and Venetian Justice in the Renaissance," *Tijdscrift voor Rechtsgeschiedenis* 52 (1984): 217–54.

Lachèvre, Frédéric. *Le Libertinage au XVIIᵉ siècle*, 11 vols. (Paris: Champion, 1914).
    Le Procès du poète Théophile de Viau, 2 vols. (Paris: Champion, 1909–1924).
    Les Recueils collectives de poésies libres et satiriques publiés depuis 1600 jusqu'à la mort de Théophile (1626) (Geneva: Slatkine, 1968 [1909–1928]).

Lamarque, Henri. "L'édition des œuvres d'Ovide dans la Renaissance française," in *Ovide en France dans la Renaissance* (Toulouse: Service des publications de l'Université de Toulouse–Le Mirail, 1981), 13–40.

Landry, Hilton. *Interpretations in Shakespeare's Sonnets* (Berkeley and Los Angeles: University of California Press, 1963).

Langermann, Y. Tzvi. "Some Astrological Themes in the Thought of Abraham ibn Ezra," in *The Jews and the Sciences in the Middle Ages* (Aldershot and Brookfield, VT: Ashgate, 1999), 28–85.

Langlois, Ernest, ed. *Recueil d'arts de seconde rhétorique* (1902; reprint Geneva: Slatkine, 1974).

Laqueur, Thomas. *Making Sex: Body and Gender from the Greeks to Freud* (Cambridge, MA: Harvard University Press, 1992).
    "Orgasm, Generation, and the Politics of Reproductive Biology," *Representations* 14 (1986): 1–41.

Larsen, Anne R. "Paradox and the Praise of Women: From Ortensio Lando and Charles Estienne to Marie de Romieu," *SCJ* 28:3 (1997): 759–74.

Lauster, Jörg. "Marsilio Ficino as a Christian Thinker: Theological Aspects of his Platonism," in *Marsilio Ficino: His Theology, His Philosophy, His Legacy*, ed. Michael J. B. Allen and Valery Rees (Leiden: Brill, 2002), 45–69.

Lavaud, Jacques. "Les noces de Joyeuse," *Humanisme et Renaissance* 2 (1935): 44–52.

Lecercle, François. *La Chimère de Zeuxis: Portrait poétique et portrait peint en France et en Italie à la Renaissance* (Tübingen: Narr, 1987).

Lecoq, Anne-Marie. "Une fête italienne à la Bastille en 1518," in *"Il se rendit en Italie": études offertes à André Chastel* (Rome and Paris: Edizioni dell'Elefante and Flammarion, 1987), 149–68.
    François Iᵉʳ imaginaire: symbolique et politique à l'aube de la Renaissance française (Cahors: Tardy Quercy, 1987).

Lee, M. Owen. *Virgil as Orpheus: A Study of the Georgics* (Albany: State University of New York, 1996).

Lees, Claire A., ed. *Medieval Masculinities: Regarding Men in the Middle Ages* (Minneapolis: University of Minnesota Press, 1994).

Lemay, Richard. "The True Place of Astrology in Medieval Science and Philosophy: Towards a Definition," in *Astrology, Science, and Society: Historical Essays*, ed. Patrick Curry (Woodbridge, Suffolk: Boydell, 1987), 57–73.

Le Person, Xavier. *"Practiques" et "practiqueurs": la vie politique à la fin du règne de Henri III, 1584–1589*, preface Denis Crouzet (Geneva: Droz, 2002).

Le Roux, Nicolas. *La Faveur du Roi: mignons et courtisans au temps des derniers Valois (vers 1547–vers 1589)* (Seyssel: Champ Vallon, 2000).

Lever, Maurice. *Les Bûchers de Sodome* (Paris: Fayard, 1985).

Levi, A. H. T., ed. *Humanism in France at the end of the Middle Ages and in the Early Renaissance* (Manchester University Press, 1970).

Levine, Laura. *Men in Women's Clothing: Anti-Theatricality and Effeminization, 1579–1642* (Cambridge University Press, 1994).

Lewis, John. "Les prognostications et la propagande évangelique," in *Divination et controverse religieuse en France au XVIᵉ siècle* (Paris: Ecole normale supérieure de jeunes filles, 1987).

L'Hoest, Benoît. *L'Amour enfermé: amour et sexualité dans la France du XVIᵉ siècle* (Paris: Olivier Orban, 1990).

Lindemann, Mary. *Medicine and Society in Early Modern Europe* (Cambridge University Press, 1999).

Linforth, Ivan M. *The Arts of Orpheus* (Berkeley and Los Angeles: University of California Press, 1941).

Long, Kathleen P., ed. *High Anxiety: Masculinity in Crisis in Early Modern France* (Kirksville, MO: Truman State University Press, 2002).

Loughlin, Marie H. *Hymeneutics: Interpreting Virginity on the Early Modern Stage* (Lewisburg: Bucknell University Press, 1997).

Luria, Keith P. *Sacred Boundaries: Religious Coexistence and Conflict in Early Modern France* (Washington, DC: Catholic University Press of America, 2005).

Lynch, Joseph H. *Godparents and Kinship in Early Medieval Europe* (Princeton University Press, 1986).

Maclean, Ian. *The Renaissance Notion of Woman: A Study in the Fortunes of Scholasticism and Medical Science in European Intellectual Life* (Cambridge University Press, 1980).

Maggi, Armando. "On Kissing and Sighing: Renaissance Homoerotic Love from Ficino's *De Amore* and *Sopre Lo Amore* to Cesare Trevisani's *L'impresa* (1569)," *Journal of Homosexuality* 49:3/4 (2005): 315–39.

Makowski, John F. "Bisexual Orpheus: Pederasty and Parody in Ovid," *The Classical Journal* 92:1 (1996): 25–38.

Margolin, Jean-Claude. "Du *De amore* de Ficin à la *Délie* de Maurice Scève: lumière, regard, amour et beauté," in *Ficino e il ritorno di Platone*, ed. Gian Carlo Garfagnini, 2 vols. (Florence: Olschki, 1986), vol. II, 587–614.

"Le Roy, traducteur de Platon et la Pléiade," in *Lumières de la Pléiade*, ed. Pierre Mesnard (Paris: Vrin, 1966), 49–62.

Matthews Greico, Sara. *Ange ou diablesse: le représentation de la femme au XVIᵉ siècle* (Paris: Flammarion, 1991).

McCartney, Elizabeth. "The King's Mother and Royal Prerogative in Early Sixteenth-Century France," in *Medieval Queenship*, ed. John Carmi Parsons (New York: St. Martin's, 1993), 117–41.

McGlynn, Margaret and Richard J. Moll, "Chaste Marriage in the Middle Ages: 'It Were to Hire a Greet Merite,'" in *Handbook of Medieval Sexuality*, ed. Vern L. Bullough and James A. Brundage (New York: Garland, 1996), 103–22.

McGowan, Margaret. "1581: The Spectacle of Power," in *A New History of French Literature*, ed. Denis Hollier (Cambridge, MA: Harvard University Press, 1989), 243–8.

McKinley, Kathryn L. *Reading the Ovidian Heroine: "Metamorphoses" Commentaries 1100–1618* (Leiden: Brill, 2001).

McLaren, Margaret A. *Feminism, Foucault and Embodied Subjectivity* (Albany: State University of New York Press, 2004).

Meeks, Wayne. *The Origins of Christian Morality* (New Haven: Yale University Press, 1993).

Melzer, Sara E. and Kathryn Norberg, eds. *From the Royal to the Republican Body: Incorporating the Political in Seventeenth- and Eighteenth-Century France* (Berkeley: University of California Press, 1998).

Merrick, Jeffrey. "Commissioner Foucault, Inspector Noël, and the 'Pederasts' of Paris, 1780–3," *Journal of Social History* 32 (1998): 287–307.

Merrick, Jeffrey and Bryant T. Ragan, Jr., eds. *Homosexuality in Early Modern France: A Documentary Collection* (New York: Oxford University Press, 2001).

Merrill, Robert V. "Eros and Anteros," *Speculum* 19:3 (1944): 265–84.

"The Pléiade and the Androgyne," *Comparative Literature* 1:2 (1949): 97–112.

Merrill, Robert V. and Robert J. Clements. *Platonism in French Renaissance Poetry* (New York University Press, 1957).

Mesnard, Pierre, ed. *Lumières de la Pléiade* (Paris: Vrin, 1966).

Meylan, Edouard F. "L'Evolution de la notion de l'amour platonique," *Humanisme et Renaissance* 5 (1938): 418–42.

Middlebrook, Leah. "'Tout Mon Office': Body Politics and Family Dynamics in the *verse epîtres* of Marguerite de Navarre," *RQ* 54:4 (2001): 1108–41.

Minnis, A. J. *Medieval Theory of Authorship: Scholastic Literary Attitudes in the Later Middle Ages* (London: Scholar Press, 1984).

Minnis, A. J. and A. B. Scott, eds. (with the assistance of David Wallace). *Medieval Literary Theory and Criticism, c. 1100–1375: The Commentary Tradition* (Oxford and New York: Clarendon, 1988).

Minta, Stephen. *Love Poetry in Sixteenth-Century France: A Study in Themes and Traditions* (Manchester University Press, 1977).

Monter, E. William. *Frontiers of Heresy: The Spanish Inquisition from the Basque Lands to Sicily* (Cambridge University Press, 1990).

"Sodomy and Heresy in Early Modern Switzerland," *Journal of Homosexuality* 6 (1980/1981): 41–53.

Moore, R. I. *The Formation of a Persecuting Society: Power and Deviance in Western Europe, 950–1250* (Oxford: Blackwell, 1987).

Morelli, Gabriele. *Hernando de Acuna: un petrarchista dell'epoca imperiale* (Parma: Studium Parmense, 1977).

Moss, Ann. *Ovid in Renaissance France: A Survey of the Latin Editions of Ovid and Commentaries in France before 1600* (London: Warburg Institute / University of London, 1982).

Moulton, Ian Frederick. *Before Pornography: Erotic Writing in Early Modern England* (Oxford University Press, 2000).

Muir, Edward and Guido Ruggiero, eds., *History from Crime*, trans. Corrada Biazzo Curry, Margaret A. Gallucci, and Mary M. Gallucci (Baltimore: Johns Hopkins University Press, 1994).

Munari, Franco. *Ovid im Mittelalter* (Zurich and Stuttgart: Artemis, 1960).

Murat, Inès. *Gabrielle d'Estrées* (Paris: Fayard, 1992).

Naphy, William. *Sex Crimes from Renaissance to Enlightenment* (Stroud: Tempus, 2002).

Neugebauer, Otto. "The Study of Wretched Subjects," *Isis* 42:2 (1951): 111.

Nolhac, Pierre de. *Ronsard et l'humanisme: avec un portrait de Jean Dorat et d'un autographe de Ronsard* (Paris: Champion, 1921).

North, J. D. *Horoscopes and History* (London: Warburg Institute, 1986).

North, John. *The Norton History of Astronomy and Cosmology* (New York and London: W. W. Norton, 1995).

Norton, Rictor. *The Myth of the Modern Homosexual: Queer History and the Search for Cultural Unity* (London: Cassell, 1997).

Nye, Robert A. *Masculinity and Male Codes of Honor in Modern France* (New York: Oxford University Press, 1993).

Nye, Robert A., ed. *Sexuality* (Oxford University Press, 1999).

O'Donnell, Katherine and Michael O'Rourke, eds. *Love, Sex, Intimacy and Friendship between Men, 1500–1800* (London: Palgrave, 2003).

Oestmann, Günther, H. Darrel Rutkin, and Kocku von Stuckrad, eds. *Horoscopes and Public Spheres: Essays on the History of Astrology* (Berlin and New York: Walter de Gruyter, 2005).

O'Meara, John. "St. Augustine's Attitude to Love," *Arethusa* 2 (1969): 46–60.

Orth, Myra Dickman. "Francis Du Moulin and the *Journal* of Louise of Savoy," in *SCJ* 13:1 (1982): 55–66.

Otis, Brooks. *Ovid as an Epic Poet*, 2nd edn. (Cambridge University Press, 1970).

Paetow, Louis John. "*Morale Scolarium* of John of Garland (Johannes de Garlandia), A Professor in the Universities of Paris and Toulouse in the Thirteenth Century," in *Memoirs of the University of California* 4.2 (1927): 65–258.

Pallier, Denis. *Recherches sur l'imprimerie à Paris pendant la Ligue* (1585–1594) (Geneva: Droz, 1976).

Panofsky, Erwin. *Studies in Iconology: Humanistic Themes In the Art of the Renaissance* (New York: Icon, 1972).

Paris, Paulin. *Etudes sur François Premier, roi de France, sur sa vie privée et son règne*, 2 vols. (Paris, 1885; reprint Geneva: Slatkine, 1970).

Park, Katharine and Robert A. Nye. "Destiny Is Anatomy," Review of *Making Sex: Body and Gender from the Greeks to Freud* by Thomas Laqueur, *New Republic* (February 18, 1991): 53–7.

Payer, Pierre J. *The Bridling of Desire: Views of Sex in the Later Middle Ages* (University of Toronto Press, 1993).

"Confession and the Study of Sex in the Middle Ages," in *Handbook of Medieval Sexuality*, ed. Vern L. Bullough and James A. Brundage (New York: Garland, 1996), 3–31.

Sex and the Penitentials: The Development of a Sexual Code, 550–1150 (University of Toronto Press, 1984).

Percy, William Armstrong. *Pederasty and Pedagogy in Archaic Greece* (Urbana: University of Illinois Press, 1996).

Pigman, G. W. "Versions of Imitation in the Renaissance," *RQ* 33:1 (1980): 1–32.

Poirier, Guy. *L'Homosexualité dans l'imaginaire de la Renaissance* (Paris: Champion, 1996).

Porter, Roy and Lesley Hall. "Medical Folklore in High and Low Culture: Aristotle's Master-Piece," in *The Facts of Life: The Creation of Sexual Knowledge in Britain, 1650–1950*, ed. Roy Porter and Lesley Hall (New Haven: Yale University Press, 1995), 33–64.

Potter, David. "Kingship in the Wars of Religion: The Reputation of Henri III of France," *European History Quarterly* 25 (1995): 485–528.

Prescott, Anne Lake. *French Poets and the English Renaissance: Studies in Fame and Transformation* (New Haven: Yale University Press, 1978).

Puff, Helmut. *Sodomy in Reformation Germany and Switzerland, 1400–1600* (University of Chicago Press, 2003).

Purcell, William M. *Ars Poetriae: Rhetorical and Grammatical Invention at the Margin of Literacy* (Columbia: University of South Carolina Press, 1996).

Quaife, G. R. *Wanton Wenches and Wayward Wives: Peasants and Illicit Sex in Early Seventeenth-Century England* (London: Croom Helm, 1979).

Quainton, Malcolm. *Ronsard's Ordered Chaos: Visions of Flux and Stability in the Poetry of Pierre de Ronsard* (Manchester University Press, 1980).

Rackin, Phyllis. "Historical Difference / Sexual Difference," in *Privileging Gender in Early Modern England*, ed. Jean R. Brink (Kirksville, MO: Sixteenth-Century Essays and Studies, 1993), 37–63.

Ranke-Heinemann, Uta. *Eunuchs for the Kingdom of Heaven: Women, Sexuality and the Catholic Church*, trans. Peter Heinegg (New York: Doubleday, 1990).

Reeser, Todd W. *Moderating Masculinity in Early Modern Culture* (Chapel Hill: University of North Carolina Press, 2006).

Rey, Michael. "Parisian Homosexuals Create a Lifestyle, 1700–1750: The Police Archives," *Eighteenth-Century Life* 9 (1985): 179–91.

Richards, Jeffrey. *Sex, Dissidence and Damnation: Minority Groups in the Middle Ages* (London and New York: Routledge, 1994).

Rickard, Peter. *A History of the French Language* (London: Hutchinson, 1974).

Rigolot, François. *Poésie et Renaissance* (Paris: Seuil, 2002).

   Le Texte de la Renaissance: des rhétoriqueurs à Montaigne (Geneva: Droz, 1992).

Risset, Jacqueline. *L'Anagramme du désir* (Rome: Bulzoni, 1971).

Riviere, Joan. "Womanliness as Masquerade," in *Female Sexuality: Contemporary Engagements*, ed. Donna Bassin (London and Northvale, NJ: Jason Aronson, 1999), 127–37.

Robathan, Dorothy M. "Ovid in the Middle Ages," in *Ovid*, ed. J. W. Binns (London: Routledge & Kegan Paul, 1973), 191–209.

Rocke, Michael. *Forbidden Friendships: Homosexuality and Male Culture in Renaissance Florence* (Oxford University Press, 1996).

Roelker, Nancy Lyman. *One King, One Faith: The Parlement of Paris and the Religious Reformations of the Sixteenth Century* (Berkeley: University of California Press, 1996).

Rogers, John. "The Enclosure of Virginity: The Poetics of Sexual Abstinence in the English Revolution," in *Enclosure Acts: Sexuality, Property, and Culture in Early Modern England*, ed. Richard Burt and John Michael Archer (Ithaca, NY and London: Cornell University Press, 1994).

Romier, Lucien. *Les Origines politiques des Guerres de Religion*, 2 vols. (Paris: Perrin, 1913–1914).

Rosenmeyer, Patricia. "The Greek Anacreontics," in *The Classical Heritage in France*, ed. Gerald Sandy (London: Brill, 2002), 393–424.

Rouget, François. "Philippe Desportes, médiateur du Pétrarquisme français," in *Les Poètes français de la Renaissance et Pétrarque*, ed. Jean Balsamo (Geneva: Droz, 2004), 331–51.

Ruby, Sigrid. "Diane de Poitiers: veuve et favorite," in *Patronnes et mécènes en France à la Renaissance*, ed. Kathleen Wilson-Chevalier with Eugénie Pascal (Université de Saint-Etienne, 2007), 381–99.

Ruggiero, Guido. *The Boundaries of Eros: Sex, Crime and Sexuality in Renaissance Venice* (Oxford University Press, 1985).

Russell Major, J. *From Renaissance Monarchy to Absolute Monarchy: French Kings, Nobles, & Estates* (Baltimore: Johns Hopkins University Press, 1994).

Saitta, Giuseppe. *Il pensiero italiano nell'umanismo e nel Rinascimento*, vol. I, *L'Umanismo* (Bologna: Cesare Zuffi, 1949).

Salaman, Clement. "Echoes of Egypt in Hermes and Ficino," in *Marsilio Ficino: His Theology, His Philosophy, His Legacy*, ed. Michael J. B. Allen and Valery Rees (Leiden: Brill, 2002), 115–35.

Salisbury, Joyce E. *Sex in the Middle Ages: A Book of Essays* (New York: Garland, 1991).

Samaran, Charles and Jacques Monfrin. "Pierre Bersuire, prieur de St-Eloi de Paris," *Histoire littéraire de la France* 39 (1962): 259–450.

Sandy, Gerald, ed. *The Classical Heritage in France* (London: Brill, 2002).

Saslow, James M. *Ganymede in the Renaissance: Homosexuality in Art and Society* (New Haven and London: Yale University Press, 1986).

Sawday, Jonathan. *The Body Emblazoned: Dissection and the Human Body in the Renaissance* (London and New York: Routledge, 1995).

Schachter, Marc. "Louis le Roy's *Sympose de Platon* and Three Other Renaissance Adaptations of Platonic Eros," *RQ* 59 (2006): 406–39.

   "'That Friendship Which Possesses the Soul': Montaigne Loves La Boétie," in *Homosexuality in French History and Culture*, ed. Jeffrey Merrick and Michael Sibalis (New York and London: Haworth, 2001), 5–21.

Schibanoff, Susan. "Sodom's Mark: Alan of Lille, Jean de Meun, and the Medieval Theory of Authorship," in *Queering the Middle Ages*, ed. Glen Burger and Steven F. Kruger (Minneapolis and London: University of Minnesota Press, 2001), 28–56.

Schiffer, James. "Reading New Life into Shakespeare's Sonnets: A Survey of Criticism," in *Shakespeare's Sonnets: Critical Essays*, ed. James Schiffer (New York and London: Garland, 1999), 3–71.

Schiffman, Zachary Sayre. *On the Threshold of Modernity: Relativism in the French Renaissance* (Baltimore and London: Johns Hopkins University Press, 1991).

Schilling, H. "History of Crime or History of Sin? Some Reflections on the Social History of Early Modern Church Discipline," in *Politics and Society in Reformation Europe*, ed. E. I. Kouri and Tom Scott (London: St. Martin's, 1987).

Schoenfeldt, Michael. *Companion to Shakespeare's Sonnets* (Malden, MA: Blackwell, 2007).

Schutz, Alexander H. *Vernacular Books in Parisian Private Libraries of the Sixteenth Century According to the Notarial Inventories* (Chapel Hill: University of North Carolina Press, 1955).

Schwarz, Kathryn. *Tough Love: Amazon Encounters in the English Renaissance* (Durham, NC and London: Duke University Press, 2000).

"The Wrong Question: Thinking through Virginity," *differences* 13:2 (2002): 1–34.

Screech, M. A. "An Interpretation of the *Querelle des Amyes*: A Study of the Exchange of Poems between B. de La Borderie, G. des Autelz, Charles Fontaine, Paul Angier, Héröet, A. du Moulin, Sébillet, Papillon and François Habert, together with Certain Attitudes of Rabelais's," *Bibliothèque d'humanism et Renaissance* 21 (1959): 103–30.

Scrivano, Riccardo. "Platonic and Cabalistic Elements in the Hebrew Culture of Renaissance Italy: Leone Ebreo and his *Dialoghi d'amore*," in *Ficino and Renaissance Neoplatonism*, ed. Konrad Eisenbichler and Olga Zorzi Pugliese (Ottawa: Dovehouse, 1986), 123–39.

Segal, Robert A. *Myth: A Very Short Introduction* (Oxford University Press, 2004).

Sieburth, Richard. "Introduction," *Emblems of Desire: Selections from the "Délie" of Maurice Scève* (Philadelphia: University of Pennsylvania Press, 2003).

Silver, Isidore. *Three Ronsard Studies* (Geneva: Droz, 1978).

Silverman, Kaja. *Male Subjectivity at the Margins* (London: Routledge, 1992).

Simone, Franco. *Il Rinascimento francese: studi e ricerche* (Turin: Società editrice internazionale, 1961).

Siraisi, Nancy G. *The Clock and the Mirror* (Princeton University Press, 1997).

Medieval and Early Renaissance Medicine: An Introduction to Knowledge and Practice (University of Chicago Press, 1990).

Smith, Bruce R. *Shakespeare and Masculinity* (Oxford University Press, 2000).

Smoller, Laura Ackerman. *History, Prophecy, and the Stars: The Christian Astrology of Pierre d'Ailly, 1350–1420* (Princeton University Press, 1994).

Sozzi, Lionello. *Rome n'est plus Rome: la polémique anti-italienne et autres essais sur la Renaissance* (Paris: Champion, 2002).

Steinberg, Sylvie. *La Confusion des sexes: le travestissement de la Renaissance à la Révolution* (Paris: Fayard, 2001).

Steiner, Grundy. "Source-Editions of Ovid's *Metamorphoses* (1471–1500)," *Transactions of the American Philological Association* 82 (1951): 219–31.

Stephenson, Barbara. *The Power and Patronage of Marguerite de Navarre* (London: Ashgate, 2004).

Stone, Donald, Jr. *Ronsard's Sonnet Cycles: A Study in Tone and Vision* (New Haven and London: Yale University Press, 1966).

Strath, Bo, ed. *Myth, Memory and History in the Construction of Community: Historical Patterns in Europe and Beyond* (Brussels: Peter Lang, 2000).

Strier, Richard. "The Refusal to Be Judged in Petrarch and Shakespeare," in *A Companion to Shakespeare's Sonnets*, ed. Michael Schoenfeldt (Oxford: Blackwell, 2007), 73–89.

Stuckrad, Kocku von. "The Function of Horoscopes in Biographical Narrative: Cardano and After," in *Horoscopes and Public Spheres: Essays on the History of Astrology*, ed. Gunther Oestmann, H. Darrel Rutkin, and Kocku von Stuckrad (Berlin and New York: de Gruyter, 2005).

Geschicte der Astrologie. Von den Anfängen bis zur Genenwart (Munich: Beck, 2003).

Sturm-Maddox, Sara. *Ronsard, Petrarch, and the Amours* (Gainesville: University of Florida Press, 1999).

Talvacchia, Bette. *Taking Positions: On the Erotic in Renaissance Culture* (Princeton University Press, 1999).

Tardiff, Guillaume. *Les Facecies de Poge: traduction du "Liber facetiarum" de Poggio Bracciolini*, ed. Frédéric Duval and Sandrine Hériché-Pradeau (Geneva: Droz, 2003).

Taylor, Dianna and Karen Vintges, eds. *Feminism and the Final Foucault* (Urbana: University of Illinois Press, 2004).

Tenenti, Alberto. *Il senso della morte e l'amore della vita nel Rinascimento: (Francia e Italia)* (Turin: Einaudi, 1989).

Theibault, John. *German Villages in Crisis: Rural Life in Hesse-Kassel and the Thirty Years' War, 1580–1720* (Atlantic Highlands, NJ: Humanities Press, 1995).

Thomas, Keith. *Religion and the Decline of Magic* (New York: Scribner, 1971).

Thompson, Roger. *Unfit for Modest Ears* (London: Macmillan, 1979).

Thorndike, Lynn. *A History of Magic and Experimental Science*, 8 vols. (New York: Columbia University Press, 1923–1958).

Science and Thought in the Fifteenth Century: Studies in the History of Medicine and Science, Philosophy and Politics (New York: Columbia University Press, 1929).

Traub, Valerie. "The Perversion of 'Lesbian' Desire," *History Workshop Journal* 41 (1996): 19–51.

The Renaissance of Lesbianism in Early Modern England (Cambridge University Press, 2002).

Trinkaus, Charles. *In Our Image and Likeness: Humanity and Divinity in Italian Humanist Thought*, 2 vols. (University of Chicago Press, 1970).

Trinkaus, Charles and Heiko Oberman. eds., *The Pursuit of Holiness in Late Medieval and Renaissance Religion. Papers from the University of Michigan Conference* (Leiden: Brill, 1974).

Trumbach, Randolph. *Sex and the Gender Revolution*, vol. I, *Heterosexuality and the Third Gender in Enlightenment London* (University of Chicago Press, 1998).

Ure Peter. "The 'Deformed Mistress' Theme and Platonic Convention," *Notes and Queries* 193/13 (1948): 280–70.

Vaissière, Pierre de. *Messieurs de Joyeuses (1560–1615)* (Paris: Albin Michel, 1926).

Val, Santina C. "Equicola and the School of Lyons," *Comparative Literature* 12:1(1960): 19–32.

Van der Meer, Theo. "Sodom's Seed in the Netherlands: The Emergence of Homosexuality in the Early Modern Period," *Journal of Homosexuality* 24 (1997): 1–16.

Van Dyke, Paul. *Catherine de Médicis*, 2 vols. (New York: Charles Scribner's Sons, 1923).

Vasoli, C. "Le débat sur l'astrologie à Florence: Ficin, Pic de la Mirandole, Savonarole," in *Divination et controverse religieuse en France au XVIe siècle* (Paris: Ecole normale supérieure de jeunes filles, 1987), 19–33.

Venard, Marc. "Arrêtez le massacre," *Revue d'histoire moderne et contemporaine*, 39 (1992): 645–61.

Vickers, Nancy J. "Diana Described: Scattered Woman and Scattered Rhyme," in *Writing and Sexual Difference*, ed. Elizabeth Able (University of Chicago Press, 1982), 95–109.

"Members Only: Marot's Anatomical Blazons," in *The Body in Parts: Fantasies of Corporeality in Early Modern Europe*, ed. David Hillman and Carla Mazzio (London and New York: Routledge, 1997), 3–21.

Viennot, Eliane. *Marguerite de Valois: histoire d'une femme, histoire d'un mythe* (Paris: Editions Payot, 1993).

Vray, Nicole. *La Guerre des religions dans la France de l'ouest. Poitou–Aunis–Saintonge, 1534–1610* (La Crèche: Geste, 1997).

Waddington, Raymond B. "The Bisexual Portrait of Francis I: Fontainebleau, Castiglione, and the Tone of Courtly Mythology," in *Playing with Gender: A Renaissance Pursuit*, ed. Jean R. Brink, Maryanne C. Horowitz, and Allison P. Coudert (Urbana: University of Illinois, 1991), 99–132.

Waele, Michel de. "Pour la sauvegarde du roi et du royaume: l'expulsion des Jésuites à la fin des guerres de religion," *Canadian Journal of History* 29 (1994): 267–80.

Wakefield, Walter and Austin P. Evans. *Heresies of the High Middle Ages* (New York: Columbia University Press, 1969).

Walker Anita M. and Edmund H. Dickerman. "The King Who Would Be a Man: Henry III, Gender Identity and the Murders at Blois, 1588," *Historical Reflexions / Réflections historiques* 24 (1998): 252–81.

Walker, D. P. "Orpheus the Theologian and the Renaissance Platonists," *Journal of the Warburg and Courtauld Institutes* 16 (1953): 100–20.

"The *Prisca Theologica* in France," *Journal of the Warburg and Courtauld Institutes* 17 (1954): 204–59.

Spiritual and Demonic Magic from Ficino to Campanella (London: University of London and Warburg Institute, 1958).

Wanegffelen, Thierry. *Ni Rome ni Genève: des fidèles entre deux chaires en France au XVIe siècle* (Paris: Champion, 1997).

Warden, John. "Orpheus and Ficino," in *Orpheus: The Metamorphosis of a Myth*, ed. John Warden (University of Toronto Press, 1982), 85–110.

Weber, Henri. "Platonisme et sensualité dans la poésie amoureuse de la Pléiade," in *Lumières de la Pléiade*, ed. R. Antoniolli, R. Aulotte, M.-E. Balmas, A. Cioranescu (Paris: Vrin, 1966), 157–94.

Weeks, Jeffrey. *Sexuality*, 2nd edn. (London and New York: Routledge, 2003).

Weil, Rachel. "Sometimes a Scepter is Only a Scepter: Pornography and Politics in Restoration England," in *The Invention of Pornography: Obscenity and the Origins of Modernity, 1500–1800*, ed. Lynn Hunt (New York: Zone Books, 1993), 124–53.

Westra, Laura. "Love and Beauty in Ficino and Plotinus," in *Ficino and Renaissance Neoplatonism*, ed. Konrad Eisenbichler and Olga Zorzi Pugliese (Toronto: Dovehouse, 1986), 175–87.

Wiesner, Merry E. "Disembodied Theory? Discourses of Sex in Early Modern Germany," in *Gender in Early Modern German History*, ed. Ulinka Rublack (Cambridge University Press, 2002), 152–77.

Williams, Craig A. *Roman Homosexuality: Ideologies of Masculinity in Classical Antiquity* (New York: Oxford University Press, 1999).

Willis, Roy and Patrick Curry. *Astrology, Science and Culture: Pulling Down the Moon* (Oxford: Berg, 2004).

Wilson-Chevalier, Kathleen. "Women on Top at Fontainebleau," *Oxford Art Journal* 16:1 (1993): 34–48.

"Femmes, cour et pouvoir: la chambre de la duchesse d'Etampes à Fontainebleau," in *Royaume de fémynie: pouvoirs, contraintes, espaces de libertés des femmes, de la Renaissance à la Fronde*, ed. Kathleen Wilson-Chevalier and Eliane Viennot (Paris: Champion, 1999).

Wind, Edgar. *Pagan Mysteries in the Renaissance* (London: Faber & Faber, 1958).

"Platonic Justice, Designed by Raphael," *Journal of the Warburg Institute* 1 (1937): 69–70.

Wolfe, Martin. *The Fiscal System of Renaissance France* (New Haven: Yale University Press, 1972).

Wood, James B. *The King's Army: Warfare, Soldiers, and Society during the Wars of Religion in France, 1562–1576* (Cambridge University Press, 1996).

Woods-Marsden, Joanna. "Portrait of a Lady, 1430–1520," in *Virtue and Beauty: Leonardo's Ginevra de' Benci and Renaissance Portraits of Women*, ed. David Alan Brown (Princeton University Press, 2001), 62–87.

Wright, Neil. "Creation and Recreation: Medieval Responses to *Metamorphoses* 1.5–88," in *Ovidian Transformations: Essays of the "Metamorphoses" and Its Reception*, ed. Philip Hardie, Alessandro Barchiesi, and Stephen Hinds (Cambridge Philological Society, 1999), 68–84.

Yates, Frances A. *The French Academies of the Sixteenth Century* (London: The Warburg Institute / University of London, 1947).

"Poésie et musique dans les 'Magnificences' au mariage du duc de Joyeuse," in *Musique et poésie au XVIe siècle* (Paris: CNRS, 1954): 241–60.

Zambelli, Paola, ed. *"Astrologi Hallucinati": Stars and the End of the World in Luther's Time* (Berlin and New York: Walter de Gruyter, 1986).

Zerner, Henri. *Renaissance Art in France: The Invention of Classicism*, trans. Deke Dusinberre et al. (Paris: Flammarion, 2003).

Žižek, Slavoj. *The Sublime Object of Ideology* (London: Verso, 1989).

Zorach, Rebecca. *Blood, Milk, Ink, Gold: Abundance and Excess in the French Renaissance* (University of Chicago Press, 2005).

Index